Map 1-1 China

REDISCOVERIN

REDISCOVERING CHINA

Dynamics and Dilemmas of Reform

Cheng Li

ROWMAN & LITTLEFIELD PUBLISHERS, INC.
Lanham • New York • Boulder • Oxford

ROWMAN & LITTLEFIELD PUBLISHERS, INC.

Published in the United States of America
by Rowman & Littlefield Publishers, Inc.
4720 Boston Way, Lanham, Maryland 20706

12 Hid's Copse Road
Cummor Hill, Oxford OX2 9JJ, England

British Library Cataloguing in Publication Information Available

Library of Congress Cataloging-in-Publication Data

Li, Cheng, 1956–
    Rediscovering China : dynamics and dilemmas of reform / Cheng Li.
        p.   cm.
    Includes bibliographical references.
    ISBN 0-8476-8337-0 (cloth : alk. paper). — ISBN 0-8476-8338-9
(paper : alk. paper)
    1. China—Economic conditions—1976– 2. China—Social
conditions—1976– I. Title.
HC427.92.L464   1997
338.951—dc21   96-45616
                                                                     CIP

ISBN 0–8476–8337–0 (cloth : alk. paper)
ISBN 0–8476–8338–9 (pbk. : alk. paper)

Printed in the United States of America

∞ ™ The paper used in this publication meets the minimum requirements of
American National Standard for Information Sciences—Permanence of Paper for
Printed Library Materials, ANSI Z39.48–1984.

Dedicated to
Peter Bird Martin

Contents

Tables

Figures

xi

Maps

Foreword

A. Doak Barnett

This is an extraordinary—and in many respects unique—book by a remarkable Chinese scholar. Cheng Li (or, in Chinese, Li Cheng—Li is his surname) has written a revealing and compelling profile of a rapidly changing China during 1993–95, two years of China's reform era—a watershed period during which China has been undergoing a far-reaching economic, social, and political transformation.

The book is based on the author's intensive, on-the-spot travel, observation, interviewing, and research in China, made possible by a fellowship from the United States–based Institute of Current World Affairs. This institute has, over many years, given a small group of carefully chosen fellows unparalleled opportunities to study and write about selected foreign countries, offering them unusual freedom to decide what is important to study but also requiring them to demonstrate discipline and responsibility by effectively analyzing and writing about what they have learned. Several institute fellows have been given the opportunity to study and write about China in the past. (As an institute fellow, I myself wrote about China during another watershed period, 1947–49). However, Cheng Li was the first Chinese citizen chosen for an institute fellowship that enabled him to return to study his home country.

Cheng Li was remarkably well qualified to make good use of this opportunity. Both his early experiences in China—always challenging and sometimes traumatic—and his exceptional educational experiences in the United States provided him with an unusual variety of perspectives from which to understand, compare, judge, and attempt to bridge differences between two countries, eras, cultures, and societies.

Born in Shanghai in the late 1950s, he grew up in the era of Mao Zedong and still has vivid memories of the chaotic tumult of the Cultural Revolution, when both his father, a one-time industrialist, and his elder brother, a student at Shanghai's leading university, Fudan, were sent to remote areas—where his brother met a violent death. Cheng Li's early education was truncated and disrupted, but when opportunities for higher education opened up in the post-Mao period, he grasped them. He first enrolled in a three-year medical training program at the Jing An Medical School in Shanghai, and after receiving a medical degree in 1979, he spent several years practicing medicine. But finding this unsatisfying, he decided to change his field and career, and he enrolled in the East China Normal University, also in Shanghai, where in 1985 he received a B.A. degree. His major in English language and literature (he wrote an honors thesis on two well-known women writers, one Chinese, one British) greatly broadened his view of the world and honed his knowledge of the English language. When in 1985 he was offered an opportunity to take graduate work in the United States at the University of California at Berkeley, he seized it. This proved to be an important turning point in his life and career, leading him to study political science, with a special focus on China, and to acquire the skills and credentials necessary for an academic career, which started in the United States.

Since 1985, Cheng Li has been based in the United States, working as a student and scholar. In 1987, after receving an M.A. in Asian studies from Berkeley, he moved to Princeton University, where he spent the next four years in advanced graduate study in the field of political science, receiving a second M.A. in 1987 and his Ph.D. in 1992. (His Princeton dissertation was on the rise of technocracy in post-Mao China.) Since 1991 he has been a member of the faculty of Hamilton College.

Since starting his scholarly career in the United States, he has authored or coauthored more than a dozen book chapters and journal articles, which have been published in journals such as the *China Quarterly, Asian Survey,* and *World Politics.* While the main focus of this scholarly work has been on Chinese government and politics, his study of China's political situation and economy has been broad, and he has developed wide-ranging intellectual interests in Western thought and society through a voracious reading of Western social science writings. Along the way, he has achieved an impressive mastery of the English language, including an ability to write felicitously as well as clearly.

During his two years in China as a fellow of the Institute of Current World Affairs, Cheng Li wrote 30 fascinating *ICWA Letters,* each of which dealt with an important aspect of the historic transformation now taking place in China. These reports skillfully combine scholarly analysis and journalistic reportage. When I read them, as they were being written, I judged them to be far more perceptive, revealing, and illuminating about the important trends than most other writings about contemporary China, either by scholars or journalists.

Cheng Li's book is based on these *ICWA Letters.* Each chapter focuses on particular developments that he believes—rightly, in my view—to be of crucial importance to an understanding of both the dynamics driving the changes that are now rapidly remaking China and the problems resulting from rapid change that have created great challenges, and dilemmas, for the future.

The author's descriptions of places and his profiles of people bring to life China in the mid-1990s, and he was able to give a human face to the facts and figures in the book. His scholarship and his ability through interviewing and observation to gather large amounts of up-to-date and relevant data provided him with a strong basis for understanding and evaluating situations and trends. His past experiences, wide personal contacts, and linguistic skills permitted him to probe below the surface appearance of things and to learn about changes in thinking, values, and human relationships. In virtually every chapter, he provides both useful historical background and comparisons between China and other countries that add meaning to his discussions of contemporary developments in China.

Cheng Li traveled widely, but he devoted special attention to the lower Yangtze River valley—the dragon that winds through central China—and its dragon head, Shanghai—the most important economic center in the country and Cheng Li's hometown. In most of the past decade and a half of rapid development in China, a large percentage of Western writing on China's reform, opening to the outside world, and rapid economic growth has focused on coastal China, especially Guangdong Province, adjacent to Hong Kong. The picture that this book presents of the extraordinary boom that has been modernizing the Yangtze Valley and coastal areas linked to Shanghai will be an eye-opening one for most Westerners. Cheng Li is well aware of the differences between this region and more remote interior areas of China. But much of what he says in the book is relevant, in varying degrees—as the author intended it to be—to trends and problems in the country as a whole.

After spending eight years in the United States, a Chinese scholar such as Cheng Li, still a citizen of the People's Republic of China, obviously faced special challenges when he returned to his homeland, to try to understand, analyze, and write about the great changes that had taken place since the early 1980s and the complex and sensitive issues that by the 1990s posed difficult conundrums for both Chinese and foreigners. Cheng Li's assignment required him to demonstrate great intellectual integrity and honesty and unusual sensibility, perceptivity, and diplomacy. One of the many things that impresses me about his book is the remarkable balance and objectivity he shows in dealing with and writing about extremely complicated situations and issues.

As the title of his book indicates, Cheng Li set out to "rediscover China." In the early 1980s, when he left China, it had just begun, under Deng Xiaoping's leadership, to emerge from the deadening totalitarian rigidity, isolationism, and economic dead end of the late Maoist era. By the early 1990s, China had become the most dynamic, rapidly growing country in the world, undergoing a far-reaching transformation through reform rather than revolution, and it was moving rapidly toward unprecedented engagement with the world community. The challenge facing Cheng Li was to understand and analyze both the powerful new forces responsible for the mind-boggling changes that he observed in China and the huge new problems that these changes created—which he encapsulated in his subtitle as the "dynamics and dilemmas of reform." In this book, he is eminently successful in doing this.

The book is a delight to read. Overall, it presents a very personal yet objective and coherent picture of the profound economic, social, and political—yes, political, too—metamorphosis of China that is now in progress. The author skillfully weaves into his narrative memorable profiles of unforgettable individuals, interviews that are extremely revealing about people's attitudes and values, and startlingly vivid word pictures of places that have totally changed in a single generation. The book also contains essential statistics that support his generalizations without overburdening his discussion. Each chapter has a central focus on particular trends, issues, or problems, and can be read on its own merits, but I believe most readers will choose to read the entire book from start to finish, following Cheng Li's personal odyssey, and sharing the learning experiences that expanded his understanding and led to his basic judgments and conclusions.

The book provides an illuminating picture of the details of China's recent economic reform and growth and of the achievements that have propelled it to the forefront of developing economic powers. It has much to say about the dynamism of the growing market economy in China, the expansion of private enterprises, the rise of technocrats in China's leadership, the emergence of rich and influential new entrepreneurs (including rags-to-riches peasant entrepreneurs), the unprecedented construction boom in China's cities, the extraordinary rural industrialization that in many regions has fundamentally altered the countryside, the dramatic rise in living standards not just among urban residents but among the majority of Chinese, the progress (without parallel elsewhere) in rapidly raising millions of Chinese out of poverty, and the increasing links between China and the world economy.

The book also has much to say about the undesired side effects of rapid reform and development, the dark side of economic and social change, the growing problems that pose dilemmas that cannot be easily resolved, and a pervasive sense of uncertainty about the future. When Cheng Li returned to China, one of the things that immediately disturbed him deeply was the general preoccupation with materialistic values, the obsessive search for wealth, the glorification of consumerism, the pervasiveness of corrosive corruption, and the rise in crime. The book discusses at length the great increase in geographical as well as social mobility, which has been both a result of reform and a driving force for rapid change and has resulted in the migration of tens of millions of "surplus" rural peasants and workers, many of whom have left farming to work in new rural industries, but millions of whom have joined the "floating population" in cities, searching for whatever jobs can be found. The result has been an internal migration of unprecedented scale, which has created huge new problems that leaders are now attempting to deal with but that cause deep concerns about the potential for social unrest. Cheng Li also discusses his own concerns about growing economic inequities separating regions and groups in China.

In many Chinese cities, despite rising living standards, the building boom has led to the displacement of many inhabitants, who have been forced to move to distant suburbs, and thus has exacerbated the problems of daily life and created widespread dissatisfaction. The book discusses these growing urban problems. It also discusses the large structural economic problems that remain unsolved in China's still only partially reformed economy, problems for which there is no easy solution in sight; high on the list is the difficulty of reforming China's largest state-owned industries, most of which are still highly inefficient, lose money, and impose a huge burden on the government and the entire economy.

Cheng Li provides revealing details about the rise to power of China's technocrats, who have played key roles in the country's recent economic successes, but he also discusses his concerns about the kinds of mistakes that such technocrats could make (after studying and visiting the great Three Gorges Yangtze dam project, he fears that it may prove to be such a mistake), and he articulates his worries about the possibility that technocratic attitudes might complicate rather than facilitate eventual democratic change. While the growth of new entrepreneurs—as well as other new social and economic class groups—clearly is leading to a more pluralistic society, Cheng Li discusses one of China's richest and most economically successful villages, which he visited, where, he felt, the entrepreneurs who have become political leaders are promoting Confucianist values that seem to be leading toward a Singapore-style authoritarianism rather than toward the kind of gradual democratization that he believes would best serve China's interests. Cheng Li also discusses his concerns about the impact of reforms on China's intellectuals, they have felt left behind by other groups economically, are disturbed by rapid changes in many values, and, while recognizing the successes of reforms in the Deng era, are uncertain about their own—and China's—future. One of his profiles, however, is about a well-known Chinese intellectual who has refused to become an emigrant dissident, but instead, still living in China, has shown courage in publicly articulating her individual, independent views in a way that Cheng Li found admirable. In a thought-provoking dialogue between the two on the Tiananmen tragedy of 1989, they agreed that both China's leaders and the student leaders bore responsibility for serious mistakes that led to the tragic outcome.

In his final chapter, the author discusses what he believes to be major Western misconceptions about China. One is the widely held view that, despite all the economic changes, the political regime in post-Mao China is still essentially a Communist system resistant to any significant political change. Cheng Li argues that political change is inseparable from economic and social change, and that to understand China in the 1990s it is necessary to grasp the importance of the evolution from totalitarianism to a much looser authoritarianism, the decentralization of power, the growing privatization of the economy and pluralization of society, the rise of technocrats, the decline of ideological and political controls, the impact of foreign ideas and influences of many sorts, and numerous other trends. In his years in the United States, Cheng Li was profoundly influenced by Western values, and now he is not only critical of the slow pace of political reform in China, but also convinced that the Chinese political system must and will undergo major change. But he also is critical of Westerners who underestimate the problems of change and do not understand what process and pace of change are likely to be possible.

A second Western misperception—or misjudgment—in Cheng Li's opinion is the view that "the continuation of China's economic reform is inevitable because this reform has brought about one of the greatest development[s] in human welfare in Chinese history." When he returned to China in 1993 he held this view, he says, but by the time he finished his fellowship in 1995, what he had learned about the immense problems facing China in the period ahead made him less confident about China's future. (Whether his doubts are justified remains to be seen. My own view is that while I agree that no one can be sure exactly how, and how well, China will be able to meet the challenges it now faces, many of the major changes that already have fundamentally altered China in numerous respects will be irreversible in the foreseeable future. Each reader can make his or her own judgment about this.)

Cheng Li also discusses his concern about what he believes to be another misconception gaining currency in the West: the idea that because China is becoming an economic power, it is therefore becoming a threat to the West, which, in the opinion of some, may justify a policy of containment. He argues that, even though coastal China has already become an economic powerhouse, much of the country will remain relatively poor for decades. He disagrees with those who predict a coming culture-based clash of civilizations in which Western values will confront East Asian Confucian values. This view, he argues, fails to take account of the fact that, while there are important differences between Chinese and Western values, those that will shape China are not monolithic; they are being strongly influenced by Western values, and China, like many other countries, is finding it increasingly necessary to respond to and adapt to international trends and shared global problems. Chinese nationalism, in Cheng Li's opinion, is not uniquely Chinese, but instead is similar to nationalism in many other countries, and, as in other major nations, there are both doves and hawks in China. He argues that Americans should avoid exaggerating China's military strength, which will lag far behind that of the United States for a long time. What is needed in United States–China relations, he maintains, is a greater recognition of shared interests and a more effective dialogue to address the serious problems that have troubled and strained relations in recent years. Nothing could be more counterproductive, he says, than a policy of containment directed against China.

This is a book that is full of stimulating ideas and insights as well as useful facts. Anyone desiring to increase their understanding of the historic changes now taking place in the largest and most rapidly developing nation in the world—whether they already know a great deal or only very little about China—will be richly rewarded by reading it.

Acknowledgments

Any large-scale look at China always involves a great deal of intellectual collaboration. Over the three years that I have worked on this book, I have received help from scores of people on both sides of the Pacific. These individuals have contributed interviews, information, and inspiration to this effort. It simply could not have been done without them. I regret that I cannot thank each of them here. My gratitude to all of them, however, is profound.

Some of my teachers, colleagues, and friends have had a direct hand in contributing to the content of this effort; I would like to acknowledge their help. I am deeply indebted to the Institute of Current World Affairs (ICWA), which offered me a fellowship to study and write in China during 1993–1995, and which has granted me permission to revise my ICWA reports into this book. I am particularly indebted to Peter Bird Martin, executive director of the ICWA, who always gave detailed comments from which I greatly benefited. His own writings set a high standard for thoroughness of research, depth of thinking, clarity of expression, and grace of style. His brilliance as a generalist in international affairs has had a profound impact upon all those who have been privileged to be institute fellows under him. I am honored to dedicate this book to him.

My greatest gratitude is to Professor A. Doak Barnett, whose intellectual guidance influenced all the major stages of my effort to "rediscover China." As I started my fellowship in China, Professor Barnett's earlier work helped me to realize that the world of academic study of China should not be separated from the world of journalistic reporting on the country. Through his letters and visits to Shanghai, Professor Barnett not only encouraged me to grasp broad issues and trends in today's China, but also reminded me that we should never lose a historical perspective in exploring contemporary issues; we should consider Chinese history and politics as a succession of related events, not just as a series of incidents, isolated in space and time. As I finished my work in China, Professor Barnett suggested that I revise my reports from the field and publish them in book form. Finally, despite his busy schedule, he kindly wrote the illuminating foreword for this book. The impact of his mind and his example have been the most significant factors in shaping this work as well the intellectual endeavors of many generations of students of Chinese politics whom he taught.

I would also like to express my appreciation for other members and trustees of the ICWA who gave me advice and encouragement during my fellowship. Peter Geithner, director of the Asian program of the Ford Foundation, Phillips Talbot, former president of the Asian Society, and Stephen Bosworth, president of the U.S.-Japan Foundation, visited me in Shanghai and helped me identify new topics for my reports and important issues for further scholarly investigation. Gary Hansen, Program Administrator of the ICWA, provided me with all the logistic help for my travel and research as well as the circulation of my reports.

Mrs. Sally Carman, my colleague and friend at Hamilton College, has been my constant critic during the years I have been working on the project. She commented on almost all of my ICWA reports through fax and air mail across the Pacific. Many of the improvements to the writing of the manuscript must be attributed to her careful reading and insightful critiques. At countless points when ideas and data turned from inspiration to confusion, it was Sally Carman who helped me back on the road to clarity. It is difficult to convey in words my appreciation to her for the time and effort she has given in the preparation of this manuscript.

I am deeply grateful to Eugene Tobin, former dean of faculty and now president of Hamilton College, for encouraging me to take a two-year leave of absence to bridge the gap between classroom teaching and "real world" exploration. At Hamilton I also received generous and considerate advice on both my fellowship in China and the revision of the manuscript from Frank Anechiarico, Alan Cafruny, David Paris, Douglas Raybeck, Hermine Williams, and Thomas Wilson. I also want to thank the reference librarian, Lynn Mayo; the graphic artist, Christine Ingersoll; and the college photographer, Marianita J. Amodio for their excellent technical assistance with the manuscript. I am grateful to Bobby Fong, the dean of faculty of the college, for generously approving financial support for the revision of this manuscript.

Distinguished China experts Anita Chan, Thomas B. Gold, Carol Lee Hamrin, Harry Harding, Joyce Kallgren, Andrew Nathan, Michel Oksenberg, Orville Schell, Richard Peter Suttmeier, and especially my mentors, Robert Scalapino and Lynn White, kindly commented on my ICWA reports and urged me to put them in book form. Drawing on their own wide familiarity with Chinese politics during the reform era, Maiyue Cheng, Bai Gao, Solomon Karmel, Thomas Moore, Hongying Wang, Daniel B. Wright, and Dali L. Yang made many helpful suggestions for the earlier version of the manuscript. I also want to thank Weijie Xu, Naeem Sheikh, Arraaf A. Mochny, and Fenghua Wang for their research assistance and the students who made helpful comments on my ICWA reports during my course on "Politics in China."

When I was in China writing ICWA reports, several foreign correspondents in Shanghai, my "comrades-in-arms"—Andrew Browne from Reuters, Seth Faison from the *New York Times*, Joseph Kahn from the *Wall Street Journal*, and others—shared with me their knowledge and judgments, views and ideas, anecdotes and jokes. Some shared with me the trips and adventures upon which some of my reports were based. We did not know each other until we converged on Shanghai at the same time as foreign correspondents. During those two years we became close friends as we all struggled to understand this rapidly changing country and its people.

During my stay in China, both the Shanghai Institute of International Affairs and the Center for American Studies at Fudan University hosted me as a visiting research associate. They provided me with much-needed research facilities. I owe a profound intellectual debt to Professors Ni Shixiong and Ji Guoxing, among many others.

I wish to express my appreciation to those at Rowman & Littlefield who helped to bring this book into being. Julie Kuzneski, production editor, and Susan Walton, copy editor, were invaluable in providing critical and constructive editorial help on the manuscript. I particularly wish to thank Susan L. McEachern, acquisitions editor, for her expert insights and comments about many of the topics analyzed in this study, and for initially encouraging me to turn my ICWA reports into a book.

Finally, I would like to express deep thanks to my parents and my family, who have shared with me the years of effort and now, I hope, the satisfaction.

Parts of chapter 2 were first published in my article "Rediscovering Urban Subcultures: Contrast between Shanghai and Beijing," *China Journal* 36 (July 1996): 139–153. Parts of chapters 7 and 8 were also printed in my article "Surplus Rural Laborers and Internal Migration in China: Current Status and Future Prospects," *Asian Survey* 36 (November 1996): 1122–1144.

I am very grateful to all these individuals and institutions for their interest in my work, for the financial support they provided, and for the contribution they made to improving the quality of my effort. As for any errors of fact, argument, interpretation, or conceptualization, I naturally accept full responsibility.

The values that I nurtured during those two years in China—a fondness for writing, an awareness of China's contradictions and complexities, and an inclination to learn new things—are treasures that will benefit me throughout my life. Probably no other words can better describe the conclusion I reached during my fellowship in China than John Cotton Dana's remark: "Who dares to teach must never cease to learn."

Part I

Impressions

My family. This photo was taken in 1960 when I was four years old. This is probably the earliest memory of my childhood. As I remember, I was criticized by the photographer for dressing in a light-color jacket, which differed from other members of the family. Uniformity was the norm at that time. All of my family members went through great hardship during the years that followed.

Our family reunion at home in Shanghai in the New Year of 1996. So much change has taken place in our family over the past three decades. Now two of my brothers, including my half brother, work as managers in state-owned firms. The other two brothers earn large salaries by working in the private sector—one is a stock speculator and the other is a representative for Pierre Cardin. One of my sisters is a medical doctor in a hospital in Wujiang. The other sister and I have immigrated to the United States.

1

Searching for an Old Home, Searching for a New China

China's ongoing economic reform is undoubtedly one of the most intriguing events in human history. Western scholars are grappling with how to explain the causes, inner workings, and sociopolitical effects of the reform. Numerous academic studies analyze aspects of the post-Mao era. In recent years, a growing number of journalistic books have been written on China's economic boom and social changes in the 1990s. Yet, ironically, the result of more information or even more knowledge is greater ignorance about the true nature of China's reform and more uncertainty about the future of this most populous country in the world.

To most Americans, China remains obscure and paradoxical. Our media (and some members of the academic community as well) have often sought to exaggerate one fact or the other or to replace facts with a surfeit of oversimplified approaches to events in China. Only a few years ago, the Western media, especially on television, reported virtually nothing but the "Tiananmen incident" when they covered China. A great number of books on the Tiananmen crisis also left the reader with the impression that China was an intractably Communist regime that had hardly changed during the reform era and would probably remain the same in the foreseeable future.

However, American studies of China are now dominated by a new theme: the strongest remaining Communist regime in the world is now rushing towards capitalism! All of a sudden, this stagnant Communist country has turned into a dynamic "economic giant," one that will, according to the American media, surpass Japan and the United States and become the greatest economic power in the world in a couple of decades. This more positive image of China, however, soon turns into a new round

3

of American China-bashing. The mass media seem to be more interested in portraying the Chinese who eat dog meat, kill baby girls, and abuse handicapped orphans than in providing a more comprehensive perspective on China and the Chinese.

Obstacles in the Western Studies of China

The reasons for misunderstanding and misperceptions vary. Cultural barriers between China and the West, China's domestic events, the international environment, the role of interest groups in both the United States and China, as well as China's misrepresentations and Western illusions, are all important factors affecting our understanding of China. As China continues to open itself to the outside world, a great number of foreigners visit the country. While this provides foreign visitors with a firsthand look at China, it also creates many instant China experts who give distorted—either favorable or derogatory—images and perceptions of China.

Some misperceptions and misinterpretations of China are due to the political interests of Western politicians and ideologues. For some Americans, China is now taking over the role of the former Soviet Union as the main enemy of the United States. The evil Russian bear is being replaced by the dangerous Chinese dragon. As a Hong Kong newspaper editor commented: "Some American politicians have felt uncomfortable ever since the Cold War ended. They desperately need a new enemy. China is an ideal target, partially because it still claims to be a Communist regime, and partially because its recent economic surge has made many American politicians nervous." Narrow-minded strategic interests lead some policy makers in the West to hold a distorted view of China.

Probably the main reason for this misunderstanding is that China has been undergoing such drastic and complicated socioeconomic changes that Western studies of the country simply cannot keep abreast of China's reality. The field of Western studies of Chinese politics, as some American scholars have observed, is rapidly approaching the time when all the accepted clichés about China's political-economic structure will become outdated. We need to search for new concepts, novel approaches, and fresh perspectives as we look at a new China. Most importantly, we need to have a better understanding and a more objective view of the dynamics and dilemmas of China's reform.

From September 1993 to August 1995 I had an extraordinary opportunity, as a fellow of the Institute of Current World Affairs, to live in Shanghai and travel across China. The Institute of Current World Affairs, based in Hanover, New Hampshire, is not a research institute focusing on China, but has a long-standing interest in Chinese society. It was founded in 1925 by Charles Crane, who served as American ambassador to China under President Wilson. During the seven intervening decades, the institute sent several fellows to China. The best known is Professor A. Doak Barnett, who kindly wrote a foreword for this book. His fellowship took place during the late 1940s, on the eve of the Communist takeover.

The principal assignment for a China fellow was *not* to pursue conventional academic research, but to be absorbed into the society and gain an in-depth understanding of various aspects of life. While there, I had the opportunity to interview people from all walks of life, including local officials, technocrats, entrepreneurs, intellectuals, workers, peasants, military officers, and migrant laborers. During these two years, in addition to serving as a research associate at both Fudan University and the Shanghai Institute of International Affairs, I wrote 30 reports dealing with a wide range of issues. The Institute of Current World Affairs distributed these reports to a limited number of interested people in academia, public administration, business, and journalism in the United States and abroad. Subsequently, it was suggested that they might form a book for both scholars and general readers interested in China's reform, especially college students who study Chinese politics and society. This is the result.

Three unique characteristics distinguish this volume from most other books on China's economic reform. First, the book is distinctly personal—it provides the reader with my own thoughts and stories. My journey in China was indeed a personal one. By that I do not mean that I write about myself instead of about the country. Rather, my own background gives me some idiosyncratic viewpoints on my subject. I feel it is important to acknowledge this up front. My microanalysis of changes in China is from the perspective of a Chinese native who, after an eight-year absence, returned to the country, perceived these differences in daily life, and struggled to understand them. In addition, my own recollections about prereform China, as well as the experiences of my family, provide the historical perspective essential for an understanding of what is taking place in today's China.

Second, the book is not written in the form of a conventional scholarly work in the social sciences. It does not have a monolithic format, but instead includes interviews, travelogues, case studies, data analysis, and personal reminiscence. By using this form, I intend to guide the reader on a journey that shows the transformation of China not only through the eyes of a Western-educated political scientist but also from the vantage point of a local resident who lived through many changes in daily life. The book presents theoretical concerns; for example, the discussion of the rise of technocrats and entrepreneurs is an essential part of scholarly debates in political science. But the main goal is to provide the reader with the sounds and smells, tastes and textures, of this rapidly changing country. By doing so, I hope to give a human expression to China's hard face.

Third, the book covers a wide variety of topics rather than a single subject. Many of these, such as land lease and relocation of urban residents, surplus rural laborers and internal migration, often are neglected in the Western political science studies of China. But these topics are crucial to understanding political stability, economic growth, and social stratification in the country. What relates some seemingly disparate topics is the overarching theme that one cannot assess China's present and China's future without a solid understanding of the dynamics and dilemmas of reform. The following pages elaborate further on the three distinctive features of the book.

Searching for an Old Home: Long Night's Journey into Day

Living in China for two years represented a great deal more to me than just a sabbatical abroad. It meant going home—back to the country in which I was born and which I knew well in a different time. It was a journey to search for my old home, my own identity.

Every immigrant, suspended between an old home and a new one, has a double identity. For the Chinese, the old home (*laojia*) usually means one's birthplace. No matter how long ago they settled in their adoptive countries, the overseas Chinese often continue to feel cultural, linguistic, and psychological ties to their motherland. At least in part, their attachments play a role in their economic investments in mainland China. A report published by the *Economist* argued that direct investment from overseas Chinese in mainland China has been a driving force in China's economic boom. Hong Kong and Taiwan together accounted for two-thirds of the direct investment flow.[1] The Chinese of Southeast Asia added another 10–15 percent, while the percentages contributed by the Chinese of America, Europe, Oceania, and other places are as yet unknown. This is a development resource that Russia and other Eastern European countries, according to the report, "can only dream about."

An old home is often kept alive by memory, especially childhood memory. For the generation of Chinese who grew up during the Cultural Revolution, like myself, remembering childhood is hardly enjoyable.

I spent most of my boyhood fleeing the "Red Terror" of the Cultural Revolution. My father, the former owner of two textile factories in Shanghai and thus a "class enemy," suffered immediate attack in 1966, as the Cultural Revolution began, when I was only nine years old. That summer, Shanghai was unusually hot and extremely humid. Virtually every night, a group of Red Guards banged on the door of our house and forced us out of our beds. Every Red Guard had a belt in his hand and beat my parents and brothers whenever he liked.

At the end of the summer, my father was forced to leave the family and was sent to a remote and isolated place. I was not able to go to school for three years because if I stepped out of the house, I would be beaten by my neighbors, not only by my peers but by adults as well. They would spit in my face and on my body. Afterwards, causing me more pain than the physical attacks, my mother would cry as she washed my spittle-stained clothes.

Yet in my family, I was the lucky one. At least I was spared the fate of my eldest brother, Li Yifu. He was a student at Fudan University when he was caught listening to the Voice of America, the "foreign enemy's anti-China broadcasting." Maoists charged him as a "counterrevolutionary" and tortured him numerous times in "denunciation meetings." In 1968, when Yifu was rusticated to a small town in Hunan province, the persecution presumably continued. My family never heard from him again. Several months later, two men came to see my mother and gave her Yifu's belongings, including a smashed watch. They told us Yifu had committed suicide by lying on a railway track. Not until many years later did we learn that Maoists had actually beaten Yifu to death and then moved his body to the railway track.

My brother listened to the Voice of America not to hear the news programs but to practice his English comprehension. Because of this, my mother did not allow me to learn English for many years after the Cultural Revolution. Poor mother! She had become so confused under the Red Terror; so many innocent activities had been deemed "counterrevolutionary" that who could know what to expect next?

My childhood memories were thus filled with scenes of men's inhumanity towards other human beings. The political climate, however, changed significantly when China's reform began in 1978. My father returned to our old house. My brother was posthumously cleared of the false charge. I went to the university, and it seemed as if the dream that I had never dared to have during the Cultural Revolution had come true. The nightmare of the past, however, still recurred in my thoughts.

My eldest brother, Li Yifu, a college student at Fudan University, was killed by the Red Guards during the Cultural Revolution.

One can imagine how thrilled I was in 1985 when the University of California at Berkeley offered me a scholarship for its master's degree program in Asian studies. But when I said good-bye to my parents in front of our house, all our eyes were filled with tears. We thought it might be a final farewell.

"Don't come back. You should settle down in America." Those were my father's only words to me, and they were uncharacteristic because he usually liked to give me long lectures. Those words, however, reflected his lifelong experience. As a "patriotic capitalist" (the term by which the Chinese Communists referred to entrepreneurs like him), he had decided to remain in Shanghai after the 1949 revolution. What later happened to my father and his family made him feel that his love of his country had been betrayed. He was trying to tell me, I believed, that we had not abandoned our country but that our country had abandoned us.

Since then, I have made the United States my home. During those years, whether working in a downtown Oakland restaurant as a dishwasher or studying at Princeton University as a Ph.D. candidate, I enjoyed things once foreign to me: freedom, independence, and tranquility. I always remember an episode that happened a few weeks after I arrived in America. A staff member at the Institute of East Asian Studies at Berkeley kindly offered me a tour of the Bay area. She was in her early forties. Born and raised in Taiwan, she had come to the United States in the early 1970s for her postgraduate education and later settled down in California. For many years now, whenever Chinese students, visiting scholars, or government officials have come to Berkeley, she has always voluntarily helped to familiarize them with the area. People all like her, partly because she can speak many Chinese dialects, but mainly because of her boundless enthusiasm for bridging the cultural gap for newcomers, for helping Chinese understand America and Americans.

I asked her to take me to her favorite spot in the Bay area. "That's easy," she said. I thought she would show me famous places such as the Golden Gate Bridge, Fisherman's Wharf, Chinatown, or the Stanford University campus. Instead, she guided me to an ice cream shop on Telegraph Avenue in Berkeley. The shop was nothing special; you can find one like it in any city across America. But as a person who had just arrived from China, I was absolutely amazed by so many varieties of ice cream.

"It's hard to choose among them," I said to her. "Could you give some advice?"

"I'm afraid I couldn't," she said. "I haven't eaten ice cream for many years."

"But this is your favorite place?"

"Yes, and what I really enjoy is the freedom of choice and availability of options," she said in a half-serious, half-humorous tone. "Eating too much ice cream, however, is not healthy."

She was not talking only about the choice of ice cream. Her metaphor told me much more about the American way of life than any book on the subject could. More than ten years have passed, but our conversation in the ice cream shop remains vividly imprinted on my mind. Freedom does have its cost. For freedom, or rather, an excess of freedom, can be dangerous. Yet, as Henry Grunwald, former editor-in-chief of *Time* magazine, has forcefully argued, "freedom also holds within it the means to correct its defects, for it allows, indeed encourages, people to criticize their society, to tinker with it, to improve it."[2]

Emphasis on individuality, respect for diversity, and a constant search for new opportunities have constituted some of the basic American values. The longer I have stayed in the United States, the more I have appreciated those values. Meanwhile, I have also become aware of some of the serious political and socioeconomic problems in the country. I no longer conceive of America as a unified entity, as I did prior to my arrival in the United States. Instead, I relish the subtlety, the ambiguity, and the complexity that I encounter when I try to understand my new home country.

One question I frequently ponder is this: How could the country that strongly emphasizes the principle of equality have one of the most unequal records of income distribution in the world? Americans like to criticize Japan, with great validity, for its hierarchical social structure. But ironically, the income gap between business executives and employees in Japan is far smaller than that found in American firms.

In the same way, the country whose defining symbol is the Statue of Liberty has yet to solve its racial and ethnic problems. The verdict in the 1992 Rodney King case and the consequent violence in southern California shocked the entire world, and showed America the potential for nationwide violence and chaos. While watching the Los Angeles riots on television, I suddenly realized that the evil, suffering, and cruelty embodied in China's Cultural Revolution were not unique.

Fernand Braudel, a French-born historian, remarked of his learning experiences in a new place:[3]

> Live in London for a year and you will *not* get to know much about England. But through comparison, in the light of your surprise, you will suddenly come to understand some of the more profound and individual characteristics of France, which you did not previously understand.

What I have learned in America—for example, about how a democratic political system deals with political conflicts and social crises—has shed light on my understanding of China, my old home.

When I returned to China in 1993, it had changed very quickly and become altogether different from the place I left. China's economic performance in the late 1980s and early 1990s has brought about one of the greatest developments in human welfare anywhere at any time. In the 1980s, more that 100 million Chinese peasants were lifted out of "absolute poverty" (i.e., not enough food). This figure equals the population of two Britains, one Japan, or one-half of America. China's real gross national product (GNP) has grown by an average of 9 percent each year since economic reforms started in 1978. According to the British journal, *Economist*, China's economy by 2002 will be eight times larger than it was in 1978.[4]

China's rush to a market economy is also a rush towards individual liberty. With sufficient financial means, people not only have the chance to choose nice restaurants or select fancy clothes, but can decide where to work and how to live. Before I left China, every Chinese citizen was assigned to a *danwei*—a unit, whether a factory, a school, a shop, or a neighborhood committee. *Danwei* distributed industrial coupons; for example, one could buy a watch with five coupons, a bicycle with twenty coupons, or a television set for forty coupons. One had to receive approval from *danwei* if one wanted to get married or to have a child. *Danwei* decided who should be recruited into the Communist Party, who should be promoted, and who should be punished in political campaigns. *Danwei* served as an institutional means for Communist elites to determine both the political and economic life of an individual. But now *danwei* are losing importance, because people are able to freely choose *danwei* or start their own private "*danwei*." Economic reform is passing power "from repressive institutions to individual enterprises," as a Western journalist observed; "the further this empowerment goes, the harder it is to reverse, and the more the role of the Communist Party fades."[5]

No one will be persecuted or criticized for merely listening to the Voice of America, even though some foreign radio stations did help incite the Chinese political protest against the government during the 1989 Tiananmen turmoil. Today, communication and exchange with the outside world have become part of daily life in China. For my family and myself, nothing illustrates this change more dramatically than the fact that I returned to Shanghai as a visiting professor at the Department of International Politics of Fudan University. There, my eldest brother had been falsely charged and later killed when he was 23. Now, a quarter of a century later, I was in the same place as "a Chinese-American scholar," lecturing on politics and doing research on Sino-American relations. The place, which had abandoned its native sons and daughters, now warmly welcomes them back. Ten years ago, I could not have imagined that happening.

My personal experience may be too dramatic to be representative, but it does reflect some fundamental changes in Chinese society. Unfortunately, American policy makers and the general public often lack a historical perspective when they assess political conditions in China. Issues concerning human rights are in the spotlight in United States–China relations today. But ironically, when President Nixon visited China in 1972, human rights issues were never even raised by the American government. Then, the Cultural Revolution was still going on. Millions of Chinese were under totalitarian repression, and the entire country was like a prison. But those American guests who came back from China often talked about the country's greatness.

In 1972, for example, John King Fairbank, a historian at Harvard and the dean of American sinology, wrote that "the Maoist revolution is on the whole the best thing that has happened to the Chinese people in many centuries."[6]

At that time, it was a great oversight, if not entirely misleading, for some people in the United States to portray Mao's China as a great place. It is equally inappropriate now to conceive of post-Mao China as a repressive country without acknowledging that it has been transformed from a totalitarian regime to an authoritarian one.

Dual Perspectives from the Grassroots: The View of a Western-Trained Scholar and a Local Resident

One of the common problems in Western studies of contemporary China is that scholars see the country only through the lens of Westerners. The comments on and analysis of China and the Chinese are often based on the moral values and political interests of the West.

I do not mean that we should emphasize only progress and overlook problems in today's China; neither do I have an unreserved optimism about recent changes in the country. As I stayed in China longer, I learned about some of the serious problems and constraints that it faces. I came to realize how complicated the country is and how easy it would be for some foreign visitors to travel there for a few weeks and write the sort of "insightful" view that gets it all hopelessly wrong. A long-term Western sinologist showed true insight about his experience in China when he said, "if you visit China for two weeks, you want to write a book; if you stay in China for two months, you want to write an article; if you live in China for two years, you don't want to write anything."

My two years of work in China seems to me not long enough. It was only long enough to make me realize how much I do not know about this rapidly changing country and how deeply attached I am to its people. The length of stay not only gave me the opportunity to travel to various places and meet thousands of people in various walks of life, but also expanded my perspective from that of a foreign visitor, a Western-educated political scientist, to that of a local resident. Mark Twain was absolutely right when he said that until a visitor becomes a resident, it is impossible to have an accurate understanding of a place and its people.[7] Some of the important issues explored in this book are not conventional topics in Western studies of Chinese politics. I probably would never have become aware of these problems had I remained in an "ivory tower."

To live in China today means to live with complexity and contradictions. While that has always been true to some degree, the heightened tempo and broad scale of social changes, as well as their paradoxical consequences in today's China, are truly unique. Privatization in economic structure and liberalization in the political system are the broad directions in which China is moving, but the priority, timing, leadership, public consensus, social safety net, consolidation of the legal system, role of the military, and international environment are all important factors in determining the future of the country. The rise of a market economy has not only brought about rapid economic development, but has also led to serious problems such as corruption, inflation, and polarization. The Chinese Communist Party has undoubtedly been losing its authority and power. But if these processes of privatization and liberalization happen too fast, the country will be in chaos. I am not sure that the American media has yet adequately emphasized the complexity of China's reform and the moral dilemmas involved.

Now, many of the foreign visitors to China are business people. The business community of the United States has become very influential in the public perception of the country and the government's policy toward China. I sometimes wonder how much a foreign business executive can know about real life in China after one or two brief trips to the country.

I remember that an American friend told me about his experience as a consul in a city of East Asia.

"Many tourists apply for visas to the United States from East Asia every year," said my friend. "I routinely asked applicants: 'Why do you want to come to the United States?' Nine out of ten times, you could anticipate their answer: 'I want to visit Los Angeles [what they really meant was Disneyland, my friend added], and I want to see America.' Most of them have actually visited only Los Angeles and Las Vegas, but they feel they have seen America."

Similarly, in Shanghai, for example, if a foreign businessman lives in a five-star luxury hotel, walks along the beautiful Bund, shops along nice commercial streets such as Nanjing Road, takes a taxicab instead of a crowded bus to a distant place, dines at fancy restaurants, and drinks real X.O. Cognac, his view of the city must be wonderful.

In the fall of 1993 Morgan Stanley hosted a tour of China for leading American and European fund management groups, representing combined funds valued at about $400 billion. The tour participants visited four major Chinese cities and met top Chinese government and financial officials as well as Chinese entrepreneurs. The key conclusion of the tour was that investing in China's future would be the world's most profitable opportunity for the next ten years.[8]

Although the report provided a variety of important data and sound analysis, some of the statements it contained were astonishing. The head of the group, the economist Barton M. Biggs, for example, expressed his impression of Chinese political elites in the following remark: "the Chinese politicians we met all looked terrific. Lean, vigorous, worked the crowds. . . . These people are interested in power, not wealth."[9] I suspect that Deng Xiaoping would not endorse his junior colleagues as favorably. Ironically, two months after the release of this report, Morgan Stanley withdrew its huge investment in Hong Kong due to some political problems in China.

I certainly do not argue that only Chinese living in China today can fully understand the country, and that foreigners, including students of China, are inherently unable to comprehend Chinese politics. As some critics have noted, if this were true, it would mean "the end of all social sciences." On the contrary, as some prominent social scientists in China have noted, "in many respects, China research in the PRC lags behind foreign scholarship."[10] A scholar's knowledge of various cultures and political systems and a sort of detachment about the object of the research often greatly enhance understanding. For instance, a classical study of American society, *Democracy in America*, was written by a Frenchman, Alexis de Tocqueville.

Whether one can have a solid understanding of China largely depends on one's intellectual sensitivity and seriousness about the subject. However, distortions about today's China are prevalent in the United States, whether the euphoria about China's economic boom or the neglect of China's political progress in the reform era. There is a danger that people, such as economist Barton M. Biggs and other American experts on China, who are now celebrating the great opportunity the Chinese market provides and the triumph of capitalism there, may understand today's China as poorly as some famous sinologists understood the China of Mao's regime.

This book tries to provide a more comprehensive view of China's reform by combining quantitative data with stories about the lives of the Chinese people. On each major issue explored, I generally discuss history, explore theoretical controversies, and include some statistics. But the real highlights are usually the conversations with local people whom I interviewed. For example, the stories of migrant workers—their happiness and bitterness, their motivation and frustration, their hardships and dreams—probably can tell the Western reader more effectively about the ongoing rural-urban migration and China's social mobility than can any statistics.

The structural change of the Chinese economy has generated much discussion among Western scholars. One of the central concerns is how this change affects the Chinese people. In urban areas, state-owned enterprises in many industries now have heavy deficits. Many workers are ordered to stay at home waiting for a job. The government uses a new term, "off-post" (*xiagang*), to refer to those "job-waiting" workers. Off-post workers receive only part of their regular salaries. The number of off-post workers is, of course, not shown in China's book of statistics on unemployment. In Shanghai, over three-quarters of the textile factories—the city's largest industry—had to shut down operations in the early 1990s and, as a result, thousands of workers have become unemployed or off-post.

In December 1994 I attended my high-school class reunion. Twenty-four former classmates showed up, and among them, four were off-post. Like me, they are in their late thirties or early forties. It is difficult for them to learn new skills quickly and start new jobs. Many jobs in the city, especially in the entertainment and service sector, are open only to those in their early twenties. Our reunion party became a "meeting of complaints." One former classmate said that he missed the old days under Mao—poorer but simpler and certainly more equal. My former classmate earns 400 yuan ($47) a month. But a tour guide who takes a bus full of Japanese and American tourists for a day's outing in Shanghai can make some $40 in tips.[11] Compare their incomes, then one will have an idea of the existing disparities.

My former classmate is certainly right; life was much simpler in the old days. China's reform programs have been targeted at solving the old problems of socialism, but many of these solutions are becoming new problems. One of the major challenges for China is to figure out how to progress economically while still dealing with social problems.

Dynamics and Dilemmas of Reform: The Focus and Organization of the Book

This book is primarily based on the 1993–95 reports from China that I wrote for the Institute of Current World Affairs. I have reorganized these reports into five major categories, rather than simply presenting them in chronological sequence as they were originally written. Some substantial cuts have been made and some information updated, but I have tried carefully not to do anything that might change the original character of the reports or to rewrite their contents using the benefit of hindsight.

The five major categories of this volume reflect five words that describe China's reform: "impressions," "impetus," "impact," "incongruities," and "implications." This arrangement is intended to better represent the dynamic changes and major constraints and dilemmas of reform—the main focus of this book. Each chapter illustrates both the moral and policy dilemmas.

My two-year stay in China was a fascinating intellectual journey—a time to laugh, a time to cry, a time to reminisce, and a time to wonder. The very best journey, as someone said, is all in the mind. To share my thoughts is therefore also to share my journey. The greatest challenge for me has always been to find out how the uniqueness of my experience and concerns links me with other people instead of separating me from them. This journey is a testimony to our shared simple human qualities and aspirations, and thus dispels the cultural differences between Chinese and Americans.

2

"The Color of Money"

Shanghai Surprises

In 1988, an American journalist named James Fallows visited Shanghai and wrote an article entitled "Shanghai Surprise." What surprised him was not something new in the city, but the buildings and streets that had remained unchanged over half a century. In his words, visiting Shanghai was "like rolling time back fifty years."[1]

He was absolutely right. The appearance of Shanghai changed little in the first four decades since the founding of the People's Republic of China. Only since the beginning of the 1990s did Shanghai begin its serious effort to become a born-again giant city.

Today's Shanghai is truly a city filled with surprises. It was a marvelous experience for me, after living in the United States for eight years, to return to Shanghai and to observe the fascinating changes in the city where I was born and raised. If life means responding to surprises, witnessing the unfolding of human dramas, or seeing familiar things from a new perspective, then Shanghai is surely a "fountainhead of life" for me.[2]

A Born-Again Giant City

People in the West have heard stories about the economic boom in the largest city in China. But hearing about it simply is not the same as seeing it. Living in Shanghai, I saw the earth move as developers ripped up the city, street after street. Over 1,000 skyscrapers have risen from the ground due to the property boom during the past few years. For almost half a century, the 13-story, 78-meter Park Hotel on Nanjing Road was the highest building in Shanghai. It was exceeded only in 1983 when the 92-meter Shanghai Hotel was built. Now Shanghai's skyline is catching up with Manhattan. The newly built Oriental Pearl TV Tower is 468 meters high.

Shanghai has regained its past glory as a pacesetter for China's socio-economic development and a world-class metropolis. For about 100 years (from the 1840s to the 1940s), foreign presence turned Shanghai into a commercial center and cosmopolitan city—the "Paris of Asia" or "New York of the East." Then, during the past several decades, Shanghai lagged far behind many other cosmopolitan cities in East Asia such as Tokyo and Taipei. To a certain extent, modern Hong Kong was built on the ruins of Shanghai as a large number of Shanghai-based capitalists moved there prior to the Communist victory.[3]

It has been widely noted that the Communist government fished too much out of Shanghai. In 1980, for example, Shanghai was listed as first in the nation in terms of total industrial output (accounting for one-eighth of the total), total output for export (one-quarter of the total), revenue

The newly built Oriental Pearl TV Tower in Shanghai. This gigantic 468-meter-high TV tower makes a 40-floor building nearby look like a tiny toy.

sent to the central government (one-sixth), and the transfer of technical personnel to other regions (1 million). But meanwhile, Shanghai had the lowest percentage, on average, in the nation in terms of housing, roads, and transportation, and the highest rate of cancers caused by industrial pollution.[4]

In the early years of post-Mao reform, the Chinese government had a policy favorable to other cities such as Beijing, Guangzhou, and the newly built Shenzhen. During his tour of Shanghai in early 1992, the paramount leader Deng Xiaoping finally realized the great potential of Shanghai and therefore urged the municipal government to achieve a "change in the appearance of the city every year and a great change every three years." The municipal government has signed a contract with the central government that allows the city to take more initiative in developing the local economy and attracting foreign investment.

Municipal officials now claim that Shanghai should become an economic, financial, and trade center in the Far East by the beginning of the next century. They like to use the image "head of the dragon" to describe the leading role of Shanghai in China's economic development. The dragon symbolizes power and prosperity. But a better symbol for Shanghai, at least a more appropriate one, is the crane, which represents the huge construction machine. The entire Shanghai city is like a construction site where hundreds of skyscrapers are being built at the same time.

Not only Shanghai but also virtually all its neighboring cities are engaged in what people call "construction fever." Similarly, vast rural areas around Shanghai have been transformed into new towns and cities. A reporter for the *Wall Street Journal* was not entirely exaggerating when he wrote: "What's going on in Shanghai, and up and down the China coast, might be the biggest construction project the planet has ever seen since the coral polyps built the Great Barrier reef after the last Ice Age."[5]

The city completed more municipal works during the past four years than in the previous four decades. In 1993, for instance, the city attracted more foreign investment than during the preceding 10 years.[6] Among the 500 largest transnational corporations in the world, 121 now operate in Shanghai; they have invested $2.35 billion and initiated 195 projects.[7] In 1995, the city completed its first subway line and the first highway overpass circling the city. Two bridges and a new tunnel now span the Huangpu River and link the west side of the city to the east side (Pudong), where China's largest economic zone is emerging. Asia's highest television tower (the Oriental Pearl TV Tower) and largest department store (Yaohan, a 21-story, 144,000-square-meter joint-venture complex with Japan) stand on the east side of the Huangpu River. When I left in 1985, this was merely empty land or vegetable plots, but now it is a new metropolitan district with many elegant residential and office buildings.

Greater Shanghai has been undergoing such a drastic and dramatic physical change that no maps of the city are accurate, and every guidebook about Shanghai becomes outdated as soon as it is printed. People have to visit China to find out what is happening.[8] On his trip to China in 1993, the former president of Colombia asked his tour guide the name of the city that they were passing in coastal China. He was told that the city was new, and it was not identified even on the 1992 map.[9] I had a similar experience in Shanghai. In the fall of 1993, I went to see a friend living on Huanghe Road, an ordinary residential street in downtown Shanghai. But when I visited him again on Christmas Eve of the same year, Huanghe Road was unrecognizable—dozens of nice restaurants had opened there, and it had become one of three "gourmet streets" (*meishi jie*) in the city.

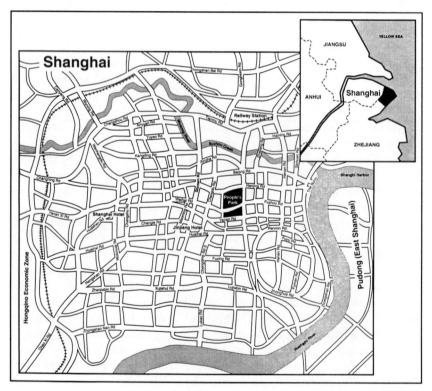

Map 2-1   Shanghai (City Streets)

The New Shanghai

What impressed me the most, however, was not the physical appearance of the city—mushrooming skyscrapers—but the appearance and apparel of Shanghai residents. I was struck by their elegant style, sophisticated taste, and various colors.

When I grew up in Shanghai during the Mao era, my fellow Shanghainese, male and female, dressed the same way—all wore the Sun Yat-sen jacket (Westerners call it the Mao jacket) in grey or dark blue. Conformity in clothes, in color, and in behavior was one way that totalitarian regimes, such as Mao's China, destroyed individuality and plurality within society. The fruit of conformity is uniformity. As Václav Havel observed, "standardized life creates standardized citizens with no wills of their own."[10]

Indeed, my childhood memories of life in Shanghai were all in shades of grey. The famous poem "Feeling" by the young Chinese poet Gu Cheng vividly reflects the collective memory of my generation, growing up during the Cultural Revolution:

> The sky is grey
> The road is grey
> The building is grey
> The rain is grey

But now hardly anyone in the streets of Shanghai wears the Sun Yat-sen jacket. I thought I should buy some as gifts for my American friends, or to wear myself when I teach Chinese politics at Hamilton College. Unfortunately, no department stores in Shanghai sell the Sun Yat-sen jacket.

"You want to buy a Sun Yat-sen jacket?" a former college classmate wanted to make sure he understood me correctly. "People will think you are a Chinese Rip Van Winkle if you wear a Sun Yat-sen jacket now."

"Among Chinese leaders, only Deng Xiaoping still wears the Sun Yat-sen jacket," his wife added. "You may borrow one from Mr. Deng, but you need to hurry." Both her husband and I laughed.

Although the Sun Yat-sen jacket is not available in the stores of Shanghai, a wide variety of clothing is for sale, even garments that Michael Jackson or Cher might wear. When I left Shanghai in 1985, the city had only a handful of department stores and a couple of supermarkets. But starting in 1993, luxurious joint-venture department stores began to sprout along the main streets of Shanghai. Now you can find many of these stores in every district of the city. For example, fourteen large, elegant department stores were built on Huaihai Road in 1994 and 1995. Across the street from my parents' house is a fabulous, six-story shopping center that has a French name, *Printemps*. A year earlier, this area had nothing but a number of shabby grocery stores.

In 1982, an arrogant American, James Kenneson, wrote an article in *Harper's* magazine entitled "China Stinks," expressing his disdain of China and the Chinese: "When Americans are bored, they tend to go out and buy something. There is very little to buy [in China] . . . Locally made clothing is very shoddy and years out of fashion, even by Chinese standards."[11]

He could never have imagined that only a decade later there would be so much to buy in China. The irony of Kenneson's article is obvious. I don't know what the author would say today as Chinese "locally made clothing" floods American department stores.

Kenneson's 1982 remark was not entirely inaccurate; in the early 1980s, just a decade ago, some necessities in China, such as clothes, sugar, oil, rice, eggs, and meat, required government coupons. In today's Shanghai, even in most of the "Mom and Pop" shops, you can find products such as Nescafé, Heineken beer, California pistachios, and even Switzerland Sea Shell chocolate. Some of the goods are produced by joint ventures in China. I am astounded by the abundance of market items in the city.

"Shanghai has whatever New York has," a manager in the newly built, six-floor shopping mall, the Shanghai Orient Shopping Center, said to me. He had been in the United States and visited several dozen shopping malls in New York and New Jersey.

"Could you tell me anything that New York City has, but Shanghai does not?" he challenged me.

I thought for a while and then remembered what I missed so much after I left the United States: a fresh bagel. An American student later told me that several hotels in downtown Shanghai do have well-baked, fresh bagels.

The elegant department stores sell imported brand-name products such as Gucci bags, Ralph Lauren ties, and Calvin Klein bikinis. These goods are even more expensive than the same products sold in Rockefeller Center in Manhattan or Sogo in Yokohama.

One may ask how people in Shanghai can afford these luxuries. Who are the consumers of luxury goods? This is precisely the question that I asked when I first arrived in Shanghai. I was born into a rich family in the late 1950s. Until the beginning of the Cultural Revolution, my family maintained a high standard of living. But a high standard of living in those days meant no more than three dishes per meal for a family.

I still remember my first day of kindergarten. I brought a lunch box and an orange. But I found that I was the only child among 50 children in the class that had brought a lunch box. Others had only steamed bread or crackers. Some did not bring anything. I never opened my lunch box because I could not stand to have everyone looking at me. Later that day, I tearfully told my mother that I would never again bring a lunch box to school. All the children in this kindergarten came from a relatively wealthy neighborhood, but still their parents could not afford to give them enough food.

Now even the poorest families in Shanghai can afford meat and fruit every day. Never in history have so many people made so much economic progress in a single generation as residents of coastal China. Some have become incredibly rich. In Shanghai these rich people are called *dahu*, a new term that may be translated as the "big money-bugs." The property of *dahu* varies, but no one is considered a *dahu* unless he or she has over 1 million yuan ($172,400). It is unknown how many millionaires China has at present, although some scholars place the figure at 1 million. Altogether 340,000 luxury apartments or houses (each unit costs over 1 million yuan) were sold in the country by 1993, and approximately half of the purchasers were Chinese citizens. Shenzhen city alone has 1,000 millionaires. One in 10 has more than 10 million yuan ($1,724,000). China's rapid growth rate and new economic structures have produced, for the first time in the PRC's history, an entrepreneurial class, the embryonic form of middle class.

The Emergence of a Middle Class

At present, this new middle class includes mainly the following groups (some overlapping): (1) urban private entrepreneurs; (2) rural industrialists; (3) speculators in the stock market; (4) real estate agents or agents of other businesses; (5) managers in collective firms who earn profits through contracts; (6) CEOs of large, state-owned enterprises; (7) government officials who have made fortunes through corruption; (8) Chinese representatives for foreign firms; (9) Chinese executives in large joint ventures; (10) sport stars and famous artists; (11) Chinese who used to work abroad, especially in Japan and Australia, where they saved a great deal of money; and (12) smugglers. Even professional call girls, whom people in China call "Oriental Hollywood Heidis," have also moved into the middle class.

"Compared with the prereform years, when everything required coupons and families didn't have enough food, our life is luxurious now," a childhood friend said to me. He opened a small restaurant in Shanghai in 1992 and made 120,000 yuan ($21,000) profit in the following year.

"When you've got 100 times as much money as you used to, you feel rich," he said. He plans to open a bigger restaurant with 80 tables within a year. In Shanghai, approximately 100 new private restaurants open every day.

Unlike the middle class in advanced industrial countries, which usually accounts for a larger portion of the population, the middle class in China is still a marginal part of the whole. Most people cannot afford a middle-class lifestyle.

"Can ordinary Chinese afford these expensive goods?" I asked a couple who were window-shopping in a fancy department store on Huaihai Road.

"Of course not," both of them said at the same time.

They called themselves *"gongxin jieceng"* (salary earners), a term that has been widely used in the past few years to distinguish those who earn salaries through the state from those who are private entrepreneurs. They showed me the price of a Gucci belt in the window—it sells for 11,000 yuan ($1,930)!

"This is almost equal to five years of my salary," the man said.

"We are always hesitant to come to places like this," his wife said. "There is so much that we would like to buy, but we can afford nothing."

Some market analysts believe that the current consumption level of Chinese city dwellers does not match the target market of the luxurious department stores. Hongkongcheng, a deluxe department store in Nanjing, for example, was closed because it had only window shoppers but no real buyers. Some other market analysts, however, hold a different view. If 1 percent of Chinese people become members of the middle class, that would be 12 million people! China's middle class is disproportionally distributed along the southeast coastal region. Many international retail companies, therefore, have continued to open expensive department stores, often in the form of joint ventures, in China's coastal cities.

More importantly, the standard of living of the population as a whole has improved significantly. Private savings of Shanghai residents increased from 3 billion yuan in 1980 to 25.2 billion yuan in 1990 and to 97.6 billion yuan in 1994, a 32-fold growth in about 14 years (see Figure 2–1).[12] Chinese citizens nationwide had more than 2,000 billion yuan ($244 billion) in financial assets by 1993.

This 2,000 billion yuan is twice the value of all state assets in the mid-1990s. As recently as 1978, the ratio of reported nonstate assets to state

FIGURE 2-1

Year-end Private Savings of Urban and Rural Residents in Shanghai

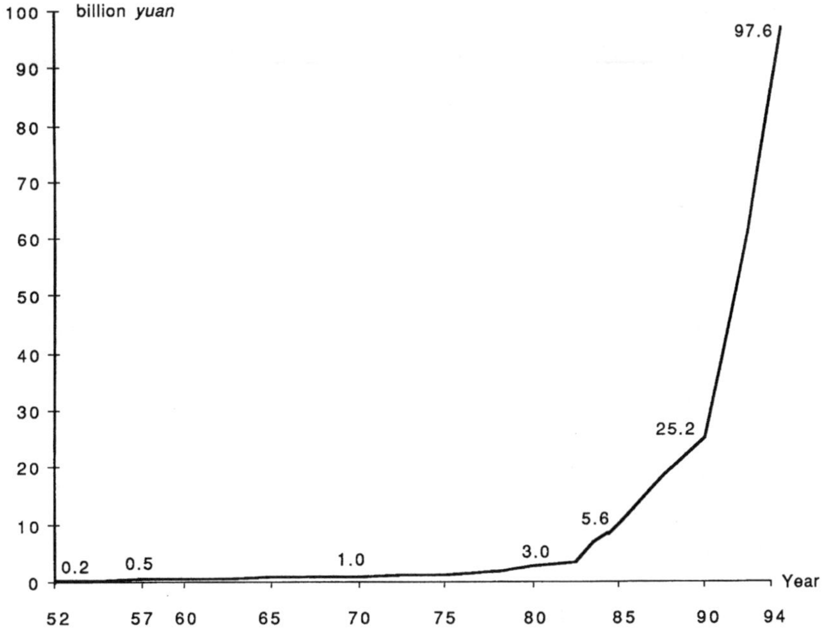

Sources: Cai Laixing, *Maixiang xiandaihua de juizhe* (Choices in the road towards modern-ization) (Shanghai: Far East Press, 1993), 312; *Shanghai tongji nianjian* (Statistical yearbook of Shanghai) (Beijing: Zhongguo Tongji Press, 1995), 123.

assets was 1:200—but 15 years later, in 1993, it was 2:1.[13] This rapid change from 1:200 to 2:1 tells us a great deal about the fundamental change in the relationship between the state and its citizens. The govern-ment has lost the material resources to control the lives of its citizens.

Changing Social and Political Life in Shanghai

Westerners, including many China experts, have assumed that post-Mao China has made tremendous progress in economic reform, but less in political reform. They assume that Chinese people now have economic freedom, but not much political freedom. This assumption is too simplis-tic, if not entirely wrong. China is, of course, not a democratic country. But I found, surprisingly, that ordinary Chinese enjoy a great degree of individual freedom. For myself, to be honest, except for a few occasions, I hardly noticed that I was in an oppressive, Communist country during my stay in Shanghai.

People in China now can more openly criticize government policies, though their criticism may not get published. Actually, cynicism about authorities has already become routine in conversations among Shanghai residents. A local saying in Shanghai reflects this newly won "civil right." The saying goes like this: "The powerful people can do whatever they want to do; rich people can buy whatever they like to buy; and ordinary people can condemn whatever they need to condemn." A friend of mine calls this phenomenon "a tripartite balance of forces" (*sanquan fenli*).

If one takes a taxi in Shanghai and chats with the taxi driver, nine out of ten times he will make fun of the Communist Party and its leaders. Once, a taxi driver and I discussed current top leaders. For him, none was good enough to succeed Deng.

He said "Li Peng does not have a brain, and Jiang Zemin does not have a heart."

I told him that if he made this kind of remark about Chinese leaders a couple of decades ago, he would be in jail.

"Yes," he replied jokingly, "that information was a state secret then, but not now."

The Chinese government still firmly controls the mass media and has rejected any societal demand for "freedom of the press." Yet quite often I came across articles in newspapers and programs on television voicing public reservations about government policies. Channel 8 on Shanghai TV, for example, has a special program called *Editorial Office of Documentary*. This program reminds me of CBS's *Sixty Minutes* in the United States because it tells some outrageous stories about Chinese society. In 1995, it broadcast a series on the ongoing construction of the Three Gorges Dam on the Yangtze River. A friend of mine, after seeing the series, called me and said that this film made him realize how stupid and irresponsible the Chinese government was to start this dam project.

Live talk radio has also found its way into Chinese cities and has attracted millions of young listeners. Sex and sexuality were considered taboo during the Mao era, but now can be openly discussed. Shops selling sexually explicit items have started to appear in large and medium-sized cities. These sex shops are allowed to exist because they all have euphemistic names: "Adam and Eve" shops; more accurate names would compel authorities to act against them.

I remember that when I was a college student in Shanghai in the early 1980s, a few fellow students were expelled because they were caught having sex with their girlfriends in the college dormitory. Today, no student would be expelled for this reason. A former classmate told me that in some colleges in Shanghai the penalty for this kind of "inappropriate conduct" is simply a fine of 20 yuan. Some students now readily throw 20 yuan underneath the door of their room and do not even bother to open the door. College officials are happy to collect the money quietly.

When I left for the United States in 1985, Shanghai was a city without night life. All stores were closed at 7 P.M. But now one cannot fail to be impressed by the glaring and glamorous neon lights in miles and miles of hotels, theaters, restaurants, karaoke bars, and nightclubs that have made the city so vibrant and colorful. I have never seen a city with as many neon lights and nightclubs as Shanghai (yes, I have been to Las Vegas). Shanghai has over 5,000 nightclubs and karaoke bars, and most of them opened in 1992 and 1993.[14] I was particularly amazed that a nightclub called "French Red Mill" has been built on the site of the primary school that I attended as a young boy.

Residents of Shanghai have much more leisure time today than they did a decade ago. Wang Shaoguang, a political scientist at Yale University,

A night scene along Nanjing Road: there are numerous 24-hour restaurants, karaoke bars, nightclubs, movie theaters, and joint-venture department stores. Shanghai now has over 5,000 nightclubs, most of them opened during the past two years.

observed that urban Chinese now enjoy a relatively larger private sphere than at any time since 1949.[15] According to some studies, the average leisure time of urban Chinese increased from 2 hours and 21 minutes in 1980 to 4 hours and 48 minutes in 1991.[16] Official work days in the country decreased from five and one-half days in 1993 to five days in 1995.

In the Mao era, especially during the Cultural Revolution, people's leisure time was strictly restrained by the authorities. People were told to expect no more than four basic routines in daily life: "work, study, eat, and sleep." The Chinese Communist Party even issued an order determining that "people should have eight hours of sleep a night so that they could energetically participate in work and study the following day."[17] Personal hobbies such as hunting, fishing, and keeping pet birds were all considered "unhealthy bourgeois conduct." Today, fads in *qigong*, martial arts, fashion design, chess, body building, and philately have drawn in hundreds of people. Now over 30 nongovernmental organizations that promote entertainment and personal hobbies exist in Shanghai. Some of these organizations have a quarter of a million members.

The Return of Shanghai Culture

All these dynamic changes reflect the resurgence of some distinctive cultural characteristics of Shanghainese, such as tolerance and respect for diversity and individualism. During the Mao era, just as individuals were supposed to wear the same style and color of dress, China's major cities, such as Shanghai, were expected to suppress their own distinctive characteristics. The authorities emphasized Chinese national identity and characteristics rather than regional ones.[18] Consequently, people in different regions followed the cultural standards of Beijing—the "authentic socialist culture."[19] Someone used the term "collective lack of consciousness" to refer to the residents who lost their regional identities. Following the founding of the PRC, Shanghai did not even have a book of its own city history until 1989.[20] A scholar in the Chinese Academy of Social Sciences observed that both popular and cosmopolitan culture had been slighted, even forbidden, in prereform China.[21]

One of the fascinating developments during the early 1990s was what a *Beijing Review* article called the "Shanghai Boom in Cultural Studies."[22] Publications such as *A Shanghai Dictionary, An Encyclopedia of Shanghai, A Shanghai Lexicon, Shanghai and Its People* (a 10-volume series), *Studies in the Cultural History of Shanghai, A Chronicle of Modern Shanghai, Modern Architecture in Shanghai,* and *A Dictionary of the Fa-*

mous People, Events, and Objects in Shanghai, flooded city bookstores during 1990 alone.

Some intellectuals have searched for a distinctive cultural identity for Shanghai and Shanghainese. Yu Tianbai's *Shanghai: Her Character Is Her Destiny*, Yu Qiuyu's *The Bitter Travel of Culture*, and Yang Dongping's *City Monsoon* reflected this new wave of subcultural consciousness in the city.[23] For example, Yu Qiuyu, professor and president of the Shanghai Drama Institute, argued that the Shanghai culture—tolerant, diverse, and individual—contrasts sharply with the "capital mentality" of Beijing that reflects feudal hierarchy and cultural arrogance.[24] According to Yu Qiuyu, one of the most important social norms in Shanghai is demonstrated by the Shanghai idiom *guannong shashiti* ("It's none of your business")—everyone should take care of their own affairs and not interfere in others' lives.[25] In a way, this phrase reflects the values of social pluralism and diversity. In contrast, people in Beijing like to comment on what other people do and show off their own "political correctness."

A recent article in an English newspaper in Shanghai noted, "Shrewd, wily, open-minded, sly, glamorous, greedy, curious, sophisticated, vulgar, money-oriented, business-minded, ambitious, cosmopolitan—these adjectives have all been used" to describe Shanghainese.[26]

These collective characteristics reflect the location and history of the city. As an immigrant city, Shanghai is the meeting place of not only many subcultures but also Chinese and Western civilization. From 1852 to 1949, the population of the city increased from 540,000 to 5,450,000. Over 80 percent of the residents of Shanghai during the middle of this century came from other areas, such as Jiangsu and Zhejiang provinces, while only 20 percent were born in the city.[27] This mobility is unparalleled and unprecedented in contemporary China. Moreover, approximately 120,000 foreigners, representing over 50 nationalities, lived in Shanghai in the early decades of this century.[28] Jews who escaped from Nazi Germany were rejected in many places in the world, including some Western democratic countries, but they were allowed to settle in Shanghai, a city that "required neither a visa nor a police certificate for entrance."[29] From 1939 to 1941, about 18,000 Jews found homes in Shanghai.[30]

Some foreigners called Shanghai a "city of odd juxtaposition." A bestselling travel book described pre-1949 Shanghai as a city of bums, adventurers, pimps, child prostitutes, swindlers, gamblers, sailors, socialists, dandies, drug runners, coolies, rickshaw drivers, student activists, strikers, intellectuals, rebels, and more.[31] This was true 50 years ago, and for the most part it is true today. Shanghai has been both a cradle of industrialists and a breeding ground for writers and artists in modern China. In addition, many prominent political figures in contemporary China, such as Sun Yat-sen, Huang Xin, and Chiang Kai-shek, started their political careers in Shanghai. Seemingly coincidental, these facts actually suggest a high degree of tolerance for diverse views and lifestyles. As a Shanghainese writer said, "we can perceive Shanghai in a hundred different ways" and "there are a hundred kinds of Shanghainese."[32]

The cultural identity of Shanghai was restrained in the Mao era, but now the distinctive identity of the Shanghainese has been revived. Some of the Shanghainese characteristics, for example, gentleness and tolerance, concern for the quality of life, interest in accepting new things, displaying an open mind, have been blended with the values of the emerging entrepreneurial class. This is a main reason why it is easier for the Shanghainese to adapt to a new environment and succeed abroad. More importantly, this also explains why and how Shanghai has rapidly risen to prominence in the 1990s.

Money Worship and the "Other Side" of Shanghai

Shanghai, however, was not always a pleasant surprise for me. The longer I stayed in Shanghai, especially living like a Chinese resident rather than a foreign visitor, the more I began to see the "other side" of the city and come to know some of the serious problems and constraints that it faces.

Transportation is one major problem. Foreign visitors to Shanghai can easily notice the traffic jams. Taxi drivers in the city are always proud of their driving skills. "If one can drive in Shanghai, he will have no problem driving in hell," a taxi driver said to me as he suddenly made a U-turn in the middle of the street when he saw the traffic jam ahead. Foreigners are often frustrated and angry as their taxis are stuck on the narrow streets of the city. But probably very few of them can really imagine the far worse hardship and frustration of residents who are bus riders. In the hot, humid summer, they are packed in overcrowded buses, and every passenger is wet with sweat. In the cold Shanghai winter, many bus riders wait in the rain or wind and still cannot manage to get on the already overcrowded buses. The number of bus passengers in the city reached 4.6 billion annually in the late 1980s, 18 times that of 1949, but the city had only four times the number of buses and twice the road space.[33]

The situation will get much worse. Thousands of downtown residents have moved to distant suburbs because the local government has leased the downtown area to foreign investors. But the displaced people usually work downtown. Street protests occurred a number of times during the past few years, and the government used force to crack down on these demonstrators. Protesters resented the authorities' ruthlessness in this postrevolutionary urban land reform.

People also complain that the local government is more interested in building fancy hotels and offices than in helping those low-income families with insufficient housing. According to an official report, about 900,000 families in Shanghai lacked adequate housing (meaning they had less than four square meters per person); and among them, 70,000 families had no room at all to live.[34] A great number of people still live in slums.

I had a wet nurse (*naima*) when I was a baby. She lived in a tiny room eight meters square in a shabby house with her husband and three children. She is a wonderful woman and has a happy family. Working as a wet nurse or a maid, she brought up her three children. Two of them later went to college. Now all are married, and each has a child. She no longer worries about food and clothing for the family. But what makes her anxious is that after 38 years, five people still live in this same tiny room—my wet nurse, her husband, her son, her daughter-in-law, and her granddaughter—with no bathroom, no kitchen, no privacy. She and her family have saved some money over the past decade, planning to buy an apartment. But money is devalued because of inflation, so their savings are never enough. Also, because of real estate speculation, the cost of purchasing an apartment in Shanghai is too high for an ordinary family.

Another major problem for the city is environmental deterioration. Shanghai has become even more polluted because of large-scale construction. Furthermore, according to a recent investigation, of a total of 89 public parks in the city, 27 are going to be leased, either partially or entirely, to foreign companies.[35] They will no longer be either public or parks.

While Shanghai residents seem to earn more and eat and dress much better today than a decade ago, they do not necessarily feel happier. "We have a sense of unfairness and injustice as we see *dahu*, especially those corrupt government officials, having their money snowball, and spending money like water." A middle-aged writer whom I interviewed made his point using a literary expression.

"You must have read Scott Fitzgerald's novel *The Great Gatsby*?" He asked.

"Yes," I said. I have admired Fitzgerald's talent for making the reader see the hypocrisy and decadence underlying the superficial splendor of a mysterious New Yorker, Gatsby.

"Probably Gatsby would have felt dwarfed if he had seen the way that the Chinese *dahu* spend money," the Chinese writer said.

He gave me an example. Nine people went to a fancy restaurant for dinner. The restaurant had famous-brand bottles of X.O. Cognac. Each cost 18,000 yuan ($3,150), and they ordered three bottles.

"They must have drunk them like drinking Qingdao beer," the writer said. "The difference between the American Gatsby and the Chinese *dahu* is that the former spent his own money, while the latter more often than not spend the money of the public or of foreign companies."

A local newspaper in Shanghai had a story about a newly rich *dahu*. He went to an elegant department store to buy a sport coat. But the shop assistant in the store didn't allow him to try on the coat because she doubted whether he could afford it. The *dahu* was so angry that he bought this 10,000 yuan sport coat immediately and then used a pair of scissors to cut it into dozens of pieces in front of the shop assistant. "The cult of money," as the newspaper editor commented, "has become prevalent in the city."

Not surprisingly, a recent issue of the *New York Times Magazine* described Shanghai as a "metropolis where money and only money rules."[36] Many city residents, especially intellectuals, are critical of the tendency toward money worship, though they themselves sometimes have to keep abreast of this new social norm. Wang Ning (not his real name) was a classmate in the Department of Foreign Languages at the East China Normal University in Shanghai. He loved literature, especially the works of William Faulkner and John Steinbeck, and continued his postgraduate study in American literature. After receiving his master's degree, he became a lecturer in the department. I was very happy to talk with him since we hadn't seen each other for eight years. After an exchange of pleasantries, I asked him to tell me about his professional activities.

"How is your research going?" I asked.

"My research?" He seemed entirely unprepared for the question.

"What's your current research project?" I repeated my question.

"Are you kidding? This is China, not the United States. I don't have any research project. A university teacher should be first concerned about earning enough money to support himself or his family."

He continued, "Today is pay day, but I call it 'pain day.' Look at how much I earned for the month: 300 yuan [$53], including both salary and bonus. Nowadays, a chicken costs 30 yuan. My monthly salary can buy only ten chickens."

"How much does an associate professor or a full professor earn?" I asked.

"Probably 450 yuan for an associate professor and 600 yuan for a full professor. So they can eat five or ten more chickens than I do."

We laughed, with a sense of bitterness.

"Everyone in the university is moonlighting." He told me that nowadays very few scholars, especially in the arts, humanities, and pure sciences, are really interested in doing academic research. Students are far less serious about academic learning than we were a decade ago. Some Ph.D. and M.A. candidates left their academic programs to work as clerks in joint ventures. According to a recent survey of China's major cities, 32 percent of the average income of employees, in both the state and private sectors, is from sources other than regular salaries.[37] People make money through moonlighting, investment in the stock market, and other means. Making money has become the foremost aim in life.

A philosophy professor at the Shanghai Normal University told me that his colleagues at the Shanghai Academy of Social Sciences earned much more money than he did. This is not because the government subsidizes the academy or because the researchers at the academy have made fortunes through their research projects. The reason that scholars there earn more, ironically, is that the academy has made a fortune by renting part of its large building to some joint ventures. The feeling of being mistreated has spread widely among the scholars with whom I talked. They felt that the government should pay more than lip-service to the importance of intellectuals in China's modernization.

Intellectuals are, of course, not the only social group that complains about the increasing polarization of society. Many workers are unemployed because of the structural changes in the Chinese economy. Chinese peasants, who benefited from the rural economic reform in the early years of the Deng era, now feel that they have lagged far behind those who live in urban areas.

"These complaints are both wrongheaded and nearsighted," said a *dahu* I interviewed, expressing a different view. He said, "What's the alternative? If one really wants to be equal, go back to the Mao era." He spoke straightforwardly, though he did not give me his business card.

"Privatization is the only solution for China. It is not we, the owners of private firms, who have caused unemployment. We have actually created jobs. I pay my workers a total of 60,000 yuan every month. I have contributed to society." He told me that he owns three factories and one restaurant in Shanghai.

"Do you think it is appropriate that scientists and professors earn less than vendors in streets?" I asked.

"If they're so smart, why ain't they rich?" he answered. I was impressed by his quick and concise response. "What law says that schoolteachers should earn more than street vendors?" he said.

"You are right. There is no such law in the world. Yet," I continued to ask, "can a society really develop if everyone is doing business and no one is concerned about the advance of knowledge in science and humanities?"

"Well . . . ," he fell silent.

I asked him to comment on people's complaints about the corruption of government officials.

"Corruption is a universal problem. Look at Japan, where so many top members in the previous cabinet were involved in corruption," he said.

"But the Japanese mass media reported the scandals, and the cabinet was replaced. Does China at present have any institutional means to solve these problems?"

"I'm not interested in politics. I am only concerned about making money."

"Can anyone in China make a lot of money without knowing Chinese politics?" I asked.

He smiled and did not say a word. After a couple of minutes, he told me that he had to go to a banquet in his own restaurant, but he would like to let his chauffeur give me a ride back to the apartment where I was staying.

"Why not?" I accepted his offer. I told him that I hoped to have a more comprehensive interview with him soon.

The chauffeur who drove the black Mercedes did not mind taking me back along Nanjing Road, one of the most spectacular streets in Shanghai. It was a beautiful autumn night. The neon lights in fancy department stores, five-star hotels, the gigantic TV tower and hundreds of restaurants and nightclubs made the city colorful. Gone are the days when everything was gray and some foreigners complained that life in Chinese cities was nothing but boring. This is the Shanghai that differs profoundly from the Shanghai I left eight years ago. Shanghai has changed in all important ways—its physical appearance, its economic condition, the lifestyles of residents, its political structure, its cultural identity, and its social and moral values.

I like the new Shanghai, especially its vivid colors. One color, however, seems to be much more glaring and glamorous than others. I call it "the color of money," borrowing the title of an American movie. That color worries me constantly.

3

Daxing

Shanghai Panorama

Few people outside Shanghai know the term *"daxing"* (pronounced *da-hsing*). This is probably now the most frequently used idiom among the Shanghainese. Whether a newcomer to the China market, especially to the Shanghai market, or an old China hand, you had better know what *daxing* means.

Daxing has two meanings. First, it refers to all kinds of falsities—for example, a bad check or an empty promise in business deals, counterfeit money, phony goods, forged identifications, and official big talkers. Second, it means poor quality of products, lousy service, and mediocre work performance.

Although Shanghai-born and raised, I had never heard this idiom until my return to Shanghai. I was told that the term became popular in the Shanghai dialect in the early 1990s. Virtually every day during my stay in the city, I heard this idiom many times.

Daxing: **Shanghai's Favorite Idiom**

The origin of the term *daxing* is not absolutely clear. Many Shanghainese, however, told me that it originated from the name of a street in Shang-hai—Daxing Street. The street, located in Nanshi District, had two well-known gold and silver stores in the 1940s. But the goods they sold were not real gold or silver, but imitations. After 1949, especially in the 1980s, the street was famous for its market where cheap and counterfeit goods were sold. Electronic devices, clothes, and shoes with the labels of world-famous brands are sold at extremely low prices here. For example, an oxford-cloth shirt is usually sold for about 400 yuan ($70) in department stores on other streets, but salesmen here ask for only 20 yuan ($3.50). Buyers, of course, know that these are poor quality fakes, but they are still attracted by the label and low price.

Daxing Street is certainly not the only street in Shanghai where counterfeits are sold. Just as the term *daxing* has become very common in the Shanghai dialect, *daxing* goods have flooded all corners of the Shanghai market. Some state-owned large department stores have also sold fake products, including goods with foreign brand names. Shanghai residents have become very suspicious of expensive goods with foreign labels, because more often than not these goods are phony.

When I arrived in Shanghai in the fall of 1993, I gave my nine-year-old nephew a nice tee shirt that I had bought in the United States. My nephew did not accept the gift at first. I thought that he was just being polite. But when I insisted he take it, he asked his mother, "Mom, is it *daxing*?"

"No, it's real. Your uncle did not buy it in China," his mother said. "It's safe."

"Thanks," the boy finally said to me. He relaxed and was satisfied.

I also thanked the boy for teaching me so vividly this very important new Shanghainese idiom.

According to a recent survey of consumers in Shanghai, 98 percent claimed that they had been victimized by purchasing fake or poor quality goods in 1993.[1] Almost every day, China's Consumers' Association receives thousands of letters complaining about the misconduct of some manufacturers and their salesmen. For example, a 2,000 yuan ($350) sofa lasted for only a week; an 800 yuan ($140) pair of lady's shoes lost one heel the first day they were worn, and after it was fixed, the other heel broke off.

It is also common for private restaurants to serve their customers fake foreign brandy and wine. A Western businessman told me that he ordered a small glass of X.O. Cognac in a fancy private restaurant in Shanghai.

"I was shocked when I got the bill—I was charged 400 yuan [$70] for that glass of shit!" He was still angry. "Only a person who had never drunk brandy would believe it was good Cognac," he said. The same thing happened again when his French friends tried "X.O. Cognac" in another Shanghai restaurant.

This phenomenon does not seem to bother some local entrepreneurs, who see "good reasons" to order X.O. Cognac other than to really enjoy the taste. Some rich entrepreneurs in Shanghai perceive this as a way to show one's high socioeconomic status.

"It doesn't really matter much whether the X.O. Cognac is real or phony, so long as it serves the need of our customers," a restaurant owner said to me.

"Oh, really?" I responded, "What about a customer who pays you counterfeit money? Does it matter to you?" The restaurant owner laughed.

A humorous cartoon that I recently saw in *People's Daily*, the official newspaper of the Chinese Communist Party, told exactly the same story: a restaurant owner served a customer a glass of phony foreign wine while the customer paid the owner with counterfeit money. Each side played a trick on the other, neither realized that he was fooled, and both were happy. The cartoonist gave a thoughtful title to the cartoon: "Equal Trade."[2]

Counterfeit money has been found in circulation in shops, restaurants, banks, post offices, and other places in Shanghai as well as in many other areas in the country. If you buy something with a 50 yuan ($9) or a 100 yuan ($18) bill, the cashier will routinely check to see whether the bill is counterfeit. The Shanghai police recently arrested a group of counterfeiters and ferreted out counterfeit money equal to 163,000 yuan ($28,600) and $5,000.[3]

"Equal Trade"   Source: *People's Daily* (9 January 1994, p. 8).

Both the Chinese government and consumers are uneasy about the current situation. Fake and poor quality products are ruining the reputation of China's commerce and infringing upon the interests of millions of Chinese consumers. The explosion of poor quality beer bottles has been widely publicized in the country. In 1994 alone, over 6,000 serious accidents were due to exploding bottles.[4] According to an official investigation, only 28.1 percent of the bottles were up to standard in 1993.[5] The construction sector in China is another area that lacks quality control. Because of the 1990s construction fever, China now has 31.88 million construction workers. Among them, 12 million have come from the countryside and often, as a Chinese newspaper reported, "have received no training whatsoever."[6] Construction accidents occur frequently. In 1995, for example, because of the collapse of a bridge project in Shanghai, the municipal government ordered all construction teams working in the city to halt their projects for a day to review regulations for work safety.

The damaging effects of fake and poor quality products are even more acute in items such as unsafe agricultural and health-related products. In 1995, for example, because they planted bogus hybrid rice seeds acquired from a Hunan company, 30,000 peasants in a poor region of Anhui gathered in nothing from their valuable farmland.[7]

Some towns and cities have become manufacturing and distribution centers for phony and poor quality products, and these manufacturers are often "under the umbrella of local protectionism." Fuyang, Anhui Province, for example, has become a center of fake medicines. Tianjin, China's third-largest city, has some 200 workshops that produce counterfeit "Flying Pigeon" (*feige*) bicycles, one of the most famous brands of bicycles in the country.[8]

The penetration of fake and pirated products has also caused great concern about intellectual property rights in the international community. According to the International Federation of Phonographic Industries, in 1995 alone approximately 220 million cassette tapes and 45 million CDs, worth a total of $250 million, were copied illegally in Chinese factories.[9] For the same year, the Business Software Alliance reported that an estimated $525 million worth of software was duplicated illegally.[10] Some Western reporters found it hard to walk a block in fake-flooded downtown Beijing without being solicited by pirates.[11]

Prevalence of *Daxing* in Daily Life

Earlier in 1993, representatives of major mass media groups in the country, including China's Central Television (CCTV) and *People's Daily*, jointly formed a team to conduct a nationwide investigation of fake and poor quality products. The team was named the "10,000 Miles Investigation of the Quality of Chinese Products" (*zhongguo zhiliang wanli xing*).

The most interesting story resulting from the investigation, as reported in the Chinese media, was the team's visit to Huangshan, a resort mountain city in Anhui Province. When the team arrived in Huangshan, the mayor of the city held a reception. During the middle of the reception, the mayor was informed by his secretary that another team, under the same name, "10,000 Miles Investigation of the Quality of Chinese Products," would arrive in Huangshan in a few hours, and he was asked to prepare for a reception.

The mayor was totally confused. The fact was that one of the two teams was phony. The mayor decided to let the two teams meet each other. The result was quite simple: the fake team had to "withdraw."

Only the genuine team could enjoy the mayor's reception banquet!

A team that claimed to investigate fake products was itself a fake! This incredible but real incident suggests the prevalence and penetration of counterfeits in Chinese society. *People's Daily* recently reported that an organization in Chongqing, Sichuan Province, hosted a nonprofit fundraising concert. The organization invited a Hong Kong popular singer to perform and sold out the available 11,000 tickets. The price of some tickets was as high as 750 yuan ($131) apiece. Many enterprises donated a large amount of money to the concert because the organization claimed that the income would be entirely used for socially useful causes. But according to the *People's Daily*'s investigation, the profit from the concert all went to some agents and the organization.[12]

During the first few months of my stay in Shanghai, I had many bad experiences and became "*daxingphobic.*" You may think that I am a yuppie who loves to follow the latest fashions. No! I have never been fooled into purchasing fake products marked with a famous foreign brand name. This is simply because whether I am in China or in the United States, I usually do not buy any famous name-brand clothes, shoes, or other things. I studied and taught in some of the "elite schools" in the United States. It is fair to say that snobbishness, especially intellectual snobbishness, exists in these places. I cannot conceive, however, that any faculty member would try to show off by wearing famous brand-name clothes. A student who is too much concerned about brand names would likely become a laughingstock among his or her peers.

When a salesperson in Shanghai tried to persuade me to buy a well-known brand of shirt by insisting it was not a fake product, I responded: "I don't want it even if it's real." Counterfeit products, therefore, do not bother me a bit. What really annoyed me were poor quality products, empty promises, lousy service, and mediocre work performance.

I stayed in a hotel for foreign teachers and students when I first arrived in Shanghai in the fall of 1993. The rent was reasonable, and the service was not really bad. I became disappointed and even angry, however, when I requested a wake-up call. A hotel clerk promised to phone me on time, but failed to do so three out of the four times that I made the request.

While expected calls did not come, unexpected calls kept coming. In the middle of the night, the phone rang, and I heard a female voice: "Sir, would you like to have a massage? You would sleep well after my massage."

"I was sleeping well," I almost yelled. "Go to the nightclub! Please don't harass customers in the hotel."

This kind of harassment, I was told by both Chinese and foreigners, actually happens quite often in middle-ranking hotels in China's coastal cities, especially in Guangzhou and Shenzhen. Many hotel customers in these places often unplug the telephone line in their rooms at night.

After experiencing all these incidents, I decided to move out of the hotel and rent an apartment. It was in a newly built apartment complex located in downtown Shanghai. The company that constructed the building claimed that this complex would be a model for urban residences in twenty-first-century Shanghai. Nobody except myself could really know how much pain I have gone through by living in this "model apartment building for twenty-first-century Shanghai."

The apartment did not have a kitchen range when I moved in. I was told that it would be installed very soon. Four months passed. I was still not able to cook because of the absence of a gas range. You may say that I could buy an electric stove. I thought of this too and asked a friend of mine whether I could use an electric cooking stove.

"No way, you should not even think about it," my friend said to me. "The electrical capacity of your apartment is already overloaded."

"Overloaded?" I said. "The apartment only has a refrigerator, a television, an electric heater, a small hot water heater, and two lamps."

"Yes, they are overloaded. You should not use the electric heater and the hot water heater at the same time," he said.

My friend was correct. The fuse in my apartment blew when I used them at the same time. This means that I could not take a hot shower in the apartment because the bathroom would be too cold in winter. Shanghai's winter can be terribly cold.

Foregoing a hot shower did not guarantee a warm temperature in the apartment. Many times, the electricity in the whole building was shut down for the entire day. Residents of the building were not notified in advance. The apartment building has 24 stories. With great difficulty, residents in the upper floors, especially elderly people and parents with a small baby, had to go up and down the stairs.

I talked to a manager of the apartment building and complained that at least they should have informed residents prior to the shutdown.

"This is China. No one is required to give notice in advance for small things such as an electrical shutdown. This is the way it has been and will be," the manager said.

If living in a "model apartment building for twenty-first-century Shanghai" is such a painful experience, one can imagine what kinds of hardship millions of Shanghai residents have gone through as they have lived in houses built many decades or even a century ago.

Compared with many other problems of daily life endured by Shanghai residents, one may say that no electricity for one day or a few days is indeed a small thing. Even during the New Year holiday, local newspapers in Shanghai, for example, received hundreds of letters and phone calls complaining about malfunctioning flush toilets in residences.[13] Construction companies or apartment maintenance firms that are supposed to take care of these matters often refused to take responsibility. In many newly decorated apartments, the flush toilets have overflowed into the living room or bedroom, but no one comes to fix them.

The same thing also happened in my apartment. I went to the construction company and was told that it was not their business after the apartment was sold or rented. I then went to see the person in charge of maintenance, and he told me that it was my fault because I threw toilet tissues into a flush toilet. I found it was a waste of time to talk to people like him. I went to see the manager in charge of sales and rentals.

"How could you say this apartment building is the model for residential living in twenty-first-century Shanghai?" I asked.

He smiled and responded, "If I don't say this, probably very few people will buy or rent an apartment from us."

"Short-term behavior [*duanqi xingwei*]"—a research fellow from the Shanghai Academy of Social Sciences used this term to refer to the attitudes that the sales manager represents.

"The mentality of people here in Shanghai, whether government officials or private business people, is to seize the opportunity to maximize their political and/or economic interests." The research fellow continued, "People are not so much concerned about long-term relationships and cooperation."

Although while in Shanghai I met some political and economic elites who are not shortsighted, I do find that the research fellow's observation above is accurate. The prevalence of *daxing* in today's Shanghai reflects this mentality. Trust and credit are not as important as immediate benefit. My own experience again offers examples. The apartment I moved into did not have a window frame for hanging curtains. I asked a carpenter to make the frame. After he completed the job, I asked him to give me his address. I thought that I might recommend him to my neighbors who probably would also need to have a window frame in their apartments. The carpenter said that he was a migrant worker from Anhui Province, and I could not reach him at his address in Anhui. "Besides," he said, "construction sites are everywhere in Shanghai. I have no lack of jobs."

A few days later, I found there was another reason that he did not give me his address. The heavy wood frame fell down, and it almost damaged my laptop computer, which I had placed on the small table near the window. The lousiness of his work is both inconceivable and conceivable: it is inconceivable because the job he did was not difficult, and I paid him well; it is also conceivable because he has indeed "no lack of jobs." He did not care much about trust, credit, or long-term customers; neither did he need to worry about the legal system, which does not work effectively.

A Chinese scholar of East Asian studies with whom I worked in Shanghai believes that *daxing* as well as "short-term behavior" becomes inevitable when the Chinese government decreases its macro-and microeconomic control, and the country moves to a market economy.

"China is in the stage that we may identify as the 'primitive accumulation of capital,'" the scholar said.

"Many other countries and regions, both in the East and the West," he continued, "experienced a similar stage of capitalist development. Japan, Hong Kong, and Taiwan, for example, were well known for imitations of foreign products, fake famous brands, and poor quality goods in the 1960s or 1970s. Americans were also great imitators of European products and technology in pre-Edison America. As China's economy continues to enjoy rapid development, problems such as poor quality products, lousy service, and mediocre work performance will gradually be solved. A real market economy will not allow these problems to get out of control."

"All these countries and regions have made great efforts to consolidate their legal systems to deal with these problems," I said.

"China is also moving in that direction," he responded.

He gave me an article clipped from a local newspaper, claiming that Shanghai has established 325 legal regulations since 1987, including 182 economic laws and regulations.[14] He admitted, however, that "China's legal system does not keep pace with the rapid economic development in the country."

I also showed him an article clipped from the *New York Times* that reported that the Agricultural Bank of China disclosed the previous June that officers of one of its branches had issued fraudulent letters of credit for $10 billion. The fraud was revealed only because the bank wanted to make clear that it would not honor the documents.[15]

He read the clipping and said in a serious tone, "Now it's time for China to establish a new set of rules and values to regulate economic deals, social relationships, attitudes, and behavior. We, the Chinese people, shouldn't tolerate falsities anymore."

"Mao Fever" and *Daxing* in Politics

This scholar's view, unfortunately, represents that of only a small number of people in China. During my stay, I was often struck by the high tolerance of falsities among the Chinese people, not only for the events in their economic lives but also in their political lives. In December 1993, a few months after I arrived in China, memorial services were held across China to commemorate the centennial of the late Chairman Mao Zedong's birth. In late December, regular programs on Chinese television were postponed. Instead, all channels were filled with commemorative programs such as "The Reddest Thing Is the Sun, the Most Beloved Person Is Mao Zedong," "Mao Zedong and His Son," a 12-part series called, "China Has a Mao Zedong," and others.

The Chinese Communist Party organized a mass rally in Beijing. A top Party leader delivered an hour-long speech praising Mao as "a great patriot and national hero." He said that Mao Zedong's thoughts would remain "a theoretical treasure-house for the Chinese Communists, a spiritual pillar of the Chinese nation, and a guide for building China into a socialist and modernized country."[16] Similar mass rallies were also held in Shanghai and many other places. A 10-meter-high Mao statue was unveiled and now towers above Shaoshan, Mao's hometown. Commemorative essays were published on the front pages of all major newspapers. Bo Yibo, a veteran revolutionary and a former Politburo member, wrote an article claiming that if Mao were still alive, he would have adopted the reform policies that Deng Xiaoping has instituted in the past 18 years.

"That's baloney!" a Chinese historian said when I asked him to comment on Bo Yibo's statement.

"This statement was absolutely *ahistorical*. One might even claim—ridiculously, of course—that if Stalin had been alive in the late 1980s, he would have been very happy to see the disintegration of the Soviet Union and the democratization of Russia," the historian added.

Since Mao died in 1976, virtually all institutions and policies in China—from the communes to the colleges, from intellectual to industrial policy—have undergone fundamental changes. Turning away from the emphasis on revolutionary campaigns, class conflict, socialist planning, and ideological indoctrination that characterized the first three decades of the PRC and especially the Cultural Revolution, post-Mao leaders in China under the new watchword of "reform" have stressed political institutionalization, economic development, market mechanisms, and social stability. Although current Chinese leaders swear that Dengism is simply the logical development of Maoism, as a foreign reporter noted, they know that they owe loyalty either to Deng or to the late chairman. They do not owe loyalty, "unless they are masters of self-deception, to both Mao and Deng."[17]

Why, then, did the current Chinese leadership organize such a grand memorial service to commemorate Mao? Do the Chinese people really owe him a great deal?

Mao certainly deserves credit for his role and vision in ending imperialism and establishing the People's Republic of China. On the eve of the Communist victory in 1949, millions of Chinese thought that they would live in a new state under Chairman Mao—politically strong, socially pure, and internationally respected.

In a way, Mao did profoundly influence more human lives than anyone else in our century, for he ruled a quarter of mankind for a quarter of a century. As the Chinese authorities now acknowledge, for many years prior to his death, Mao was seen as God in Mainland China. This Godlike figure, according to the current Chinese leadership, made mistakes during the so-called Great Leap Forward and the Cultural Revolution.

"Mistakes?" An overseas Chinese man with whom I had a chat in a cafe in Shanghai pointed out the word to me as both of us glanced at commemorative essays in local newspapers. He said with anger, "Twenty million people died during the Great Leap Forward and 100 million suffered in the Cultural Revolution. Couldn't one find a more appropriate term than 'mistakes' to refer to the causes of these catastrophes?"

Twenty million and *100 million* were the numbers provided by the Chinese government after the Cultural Revolution. During the Great Leap Forward, Mao gave undue prominence to heavy industry at the expense of agriculture. The agricultural labor force in the country, for example, was reduced by over 20 percent in 1958. Famine and natural disasters aggravated grain shortages, but the main cause of death was Mao's radical policy, driven by his desire for infinite power. Human suffering was also the most prominent aspect of the Cultural Revolution. Millions of Chinese people were arbitrarily arrested and sent to prisons or labor camps, and many more millions were shipped off to work in the remote areas. Families were broken, careers destroyed, and lives wasted.

Although many other factors led to these events, Mao's personal responsibility for the catastrophes was undeniable. Nothing could justify the loss of 20 million people or rationalize the suffering of 100 million (this is just under half of the total population of the United States). But strangely, China has continued to pay tribute to Mao. As a British social scientist noted, "of this century's dead tyrants, Mao is almost alone in still being honored in his own country."

A small number of people in Mainland China did voice their concerns and resentment about the memorial activities. Well-known writers such as Ba Jin, Bing Xin, and Zhou Gucheng wrote a joint letter to the Central Committee of the Chinese Communist Party. They claimed that any commemorative activities dedicated to Mao would "turn back the wheel of history."[18] A young Shanghai writer reminded readers that "a nation that has lost its memories is doomed to be a tragic nation."[19]

Most people in Shanghai, however, seemed indifferent to the government's attempt to celebrate Mao's 100th birthday. They were more interested in things that could help them make money. Mao occurred to them only if he had a market value. A Shanghai watch factory produced 10,000 commemorative gold watches of Mao and sold each for over 2,000 yuan ($350). The cost of the watch was only about 200 yuan.

"Who now cares about *Mao* or *Marx*? We're only concerned about *market* and *money*," a manager of the watch factory said to me in English. "The year of 1996 will be the Year of the *Mouse* in the Chinese lunar calendar. We're going to produce a lot of goods with the image of a mouse." He asked, "Does this mean that we like mice?"

I was amazed by the way that this factory manager expressed his ideas. He was an absolute master at playing on English words.

Some people were more respectful of the late chairman than was this man. I heard that cab drivers in cities such as Shenzhen often stick Mao's portrait in the corner of the taxi's windshield. In Shanghai, I occasionally took cabs with a Mao picture. Once I asked a cab driver why he kept it there.

"Mao is a patron saint [*shouhushen*] who can bless and protect me from adversity," he answered.

The cab driver was in his middle forties. I was so curious about the seriousness of his tone that I asked him to tell me about his life. He was born in a worker's family in Shanghai. As a teenager with a "red family"

Mao's birthday happens to be one day after Christmas. All fancy restaurants in Shanghai were full at Christmas in 1993. A young couple with
their daughter and nieces stood in front of Christmas decorations at the
Shanghai Sheraton Hotel. I asked the three girls whether they knew anything about Chairman Mao. Two said, "No."

"Yes," the third said, "Mao was the dead Santa Claus."

"Santa Claus can never be dead," the elder girl corrected her younger
cousin. "Only a phony Santa Claus could die."

background, he enthusiastically participated in the Red Guard movement when the Cultural Revolution began in 1966. But three years later, like millions of other Red Guards, he was sent to a remote rural area (in his case to Jiangxi Province) to work as a peasant.

"I experienced all kinds of difficulties in the countryside," he said. "We worked day and night, but still didn't have enough food to eat. I had nightmares of starvation almost every night. Sometimes I dreamed that I was going to eat a piece of fat meat." He told me that he had retained a fondness for fat meat ever since.

He did not move back to Shanghai until 10 years later, when he was allowed to succeed his father in his job in a steel factory. He married a textile worker with similar life experiences when both were in their middle thirties. They now have a 10-year-old son. He told me that he started to drive a taxi two years ago because he wanted to earn more money so that his son would have a better life than he had.

"How do you spend money on your son?" I asked.

"Now I'm able to earn about 1,500 yuan [$260] a month if I work 12 hours a day, seven days a week. I have hired three college students to be tutors for my son. They teach him Chinese, calligraphy, and arithmetic, respectively. I pay each tutor 250 yuan a month."

"That amount is half your monthly salary?" I wanted to make sure that I had heard him correctly.

"Yes."

"Why don't you or your wife teach your son?" I continued. "It shouldn't be very difficult to teach these subjects to a 10-year-old child."

"To be honest, both my wife and I are almost illiterate," he said, somewhat embarrassed. "I guess you are from abroad, you probably haven't heard of the term 'lost generation.' My wife and I belong to that generation," he said in a matter-of-fact way.

I certainly knew the term "lost generation," which refers to the young people who grew up during the Cultural Revolution and lost formal schooling because of it. But what I didn't understand was his favorable attitude towards Mao, the person who had launched this revolution.

"Do you really think that you owe something to Mao and that you need his blessing?" I asked.

"My wife said the same thing to me the other day," he said. "She often made fun of me for sticking Mao's photo on the window of the taxi. She argued that Mao couldn't even protect his wife from adversity." He was referring to the episode when Jiang Qing, Mao's wife, committed suicide in prison a few years ago.

"But anyway, I like Mao. He was a powerful leader when he was alive.

Corruption and inflation were not prevalent under him." The taxi driver's tone seemed conclusive as he made this statement. We didn't say anything in the remaining 15 minutes of the taxi ride.

China's Falsities and China's Future

This kind of conversation, however, happened to me many times during my stay in China. The Cultural Revolution not only had a destructive effect on the generation of the taxi driver and his wife, who have still not recovered from it a quarter of a century later, but also continues to affect the next generation. How could it be possible that people who had lost the opportunity of receiving a basic education and experienced all kinds of hardships in primitive rural areas are still unwilling to be critical of Mao's role?

"Astonishing" is sinologist Lucian Pye's impression of the mentality of the Chinese people during the post–Cultural Revolution era. Pye found that those who had suffered because of the Cultural Revolution were usually apathetic about their experiences in this catastrophic era.

"If people who were unjustly jailed for a decade will not criticize what was done to them," Pye asked forcefully, "why should the Chinese authorities worry about the future?"

The Chinese authorities, however, do worry about the future. The authorities' memorial service for Mao was a way to demonstrate power and authority. It is an important rule in China—probably everywhere—that "who controls the past will control the future." But all the efforts of the Chinese government to commemorate Mao, according to some Chinese intellectuals, only point out the irrelevance of official propaganda.

"No ordinary person in China could be such a fool as to believe that the official applause for Mao is sincere," a scholar at the Shanghai Academy of Social Sciences said. "Many current leaders, including Deng Xiaoping himself, were persecuted by Mao. One of Deng's sons was maimed by Maoists during the Cultural Revolution. A few current Politburo members, for example, Zhu Rongji, were labeled 'rightist'—thus 'enemies of the people'—in the Mao era.

"Let me cite a saying," he continued. " 'History often repeats twice, the first time occurs as a tragedy, the second time a farce.' "

He was quoting Karl Marx.

"Are you saying that the nationwide, month-long memorial service to commemorate Mao is a falsified event?" I asked.

"Absolutely," was his simple answer.

"Isn't it odd?"

"Mr. Li, you forget the way you grew up in China."

"But that was during the Cultural Revolution, the dark age of modern Chinese history."

"Nevertheless, you have been away from China for too long."

He was right. I had been away from my old home country for too long. But being away from China for a while has both advantages and disadvantages. The disadvantage is that I need more time to become familiar with my native land. The advantage is that I look at things from a new perspective.

"Well," I said to him, "maybe you have lived in such an odd situation for so long that you fail to see how absurd it is. As the Chinese saying goes, '*jian guai bu guai.*' "

"Maybe," he responded.

Despite all the *daxing* and other puzzling phenomena, probably because of them, I learned a great deal during my stay in China. Every society has its own oddities or falsities, especially in certain periods of a nation's growth. China is no exception. The *daxing* phenomenon today, including fake and poor quality products, may seem trivial to some people. Yet as a Chinese official noted, "the quality of products represents the image of a country, the spirit of a nation."[20] Whether China will overcome *daxing* and related phenomena in its socioeconomic development will largely depend on whether its political system transforms itself into a more responsive and more creditable one in the near future. Someone said that "a society cannot develop normally without knowing where it came from, what it is, and what it should overcome."

I would add: a country's "coming of age" cannot be truly realized until its people start calling things by their real names.

Part II

Impetus

A street poster in Shenzhen presents Deng's instruction: "China should stick to the basic line of the Communist Party for one hundred years."

"What is the basic line of the Communist Party?" I asked a local official in Shenzhen. "Moving away from socialism to capitalism," the official answered.

You probably think that this big building must be located in the United States because of its Western style and the American flags around it. But you are wrong! This is one of the many surprises that I encountered during my ride from Shanghai to Sunan. This is a yacht club for rich people, which has an unusual English name, "Fooke."

4

Dynamism of Market Economy

Stock Market, Private Enterprises, and Foreign Investment

One of the most memorable events during my fellowship in China was my reunion in our native city with A. Doak Barnett, a Shanghai-born former fellow of the Institute of Current World Affairs and a distinguished sinologist. From 1947 through 1949, Professor Barnett, then a young American journalist, journeyed to virtually every part of China and wrote about political and socioeconomic changes in the country. His two-year fellowship, as he described it, took place during "a watershed in modern Chinese history—a period in which the Nationalist regime collapsed and the Communist Party assumed power." The reports that he wrote later became the basis of *China on the Eve of Communist Takeover*, now a classic in Chinese studies.[1]

During my stay in Shanghai, Professor Barnett visited me twice. Each time we both were overwhelmed by historical ironies as we discussed the events of half a century ago and those taking place today. Witnessing the remarkable changes around us, we had no doubt that this is another watershed in modern Chinese history. When I told him that I planned to publish my reports from the field as a book, Professor Barnett asked me, with a twinkle in his eyes, "Are you going to write a book entitled *China on the Eve of the Capitalist Takeover*?"

We, of course, are not sure whether the capitalist takeover is the most likely scenario for China's future. However, the rapid rise of the capitalist and entrepreneurial class, accompanied by large-scale privatization and foreign investment in urban China, is undoubtedly one of the nation's most important politicoeconomic developments today. After almost 50 years of Communist revolution and socialist transformation, China is going "back to the past"—to embrace capitalism.

Make no mistake, pre-Communist China was not completely a capitalist society. Rather, it was a mixture of feudalism and capitalism. This same combination can also be arguably used to refer to today's China. Two important differences, however, distinguish the late 1940s from today. First, the ruling party of today's China is the self-proclaimed Communist Party. Second and even more ironically, this Communist ruling party has, in the past few years, been enthusiastic about the ongoing transformation of the country from socialism to capitalism.

"China is no longer a Communist country in any meaningful sense," the *New York Times*' Beijing bureau chief, Nicholas Kristof, argued in a fall 1993 article. He noted that no Communist country "has ever so fully embraced stock markets . . . In the 1990s the business of the party is business."[2]

People in the West have often seen a sharp contrast when comparing the former Soviet Union and China: the collapse of communism in the former and its prolongation in the latter. But it can also be argued that the rejection of communism occurred in China a decade before the collapse of the former Soviet Union. The stock market, a notably capitalist phenomenon, has played a remarkably important role in the Chinese economy during the reform era. Meanwhile, China has been the largest recipient of foreign direct investment in the world during the past few years.[3] An immense foreign presence has turned some Chinese cities, such as Shanghai and Guangzhou, into cosmopolitan places.

Although the state-owned sector has remained a cornerstone of the Chinese economy, private enterprises have made enormous strides during the 1990s. Their number increased from 91,000 in 1989 to 420,000 in 1994.[4] In 1992, for the first time in PRC history, non-state-owned enterprises, including collective, private, and foreign-owned firms, accounted for a larger share (52 percent) of the gross value of industrial output than did state-owned enterprises (48 percent). The dynamism of the market economy, including the rapid development of the stock market, private enterprises, and foreign investment, has been one of the most notable features of China in the 1990s.

Shanghai's Stock Market Revived

During the early twentieth century, Shanghai was called the "paradise of speculators." In the 1940s, the volume of buying and selling stocks in

Shanghai was greater than it was in Hong Kong and about the same as in the Tokyo market.[5] The stock market was closed after Communists came to power. During the first three decades of the PRC, Chinese Communists often used the phrase "a paradise for foreign speculators and Chinese bureaucratic capitalists" to describe how the "evil of capitalism had haunted the city."

Stock markets did not reappear until August 1986 when Shanghai opened the first stock exchange in the PRC—the "first exchange in the world to be approved by a self-proclaimed Communist government."[6] Both the number of listed stocks and the volume of trade grew dramatically during the decade. The number of stock agencies from other provinces based in Shanghai increased from 10 in 1992 to 111 in 1993, a 10-fold rise.[7] These 111 companies with capital stock of 3 billion yuan and a total market value of 230 billion yuan were listed on the Shanghai Stock Exchange. The daily turnover in 1995 was 4.1 billion yuan ($500 million).[8]

According to a comprehensive study of the securities market in China, the volume of Shanghai's stock market sometimes rivaled the volume of stock market trade in Hong Kong.[9] The author found that many companies in China issued stocks without government approval. In 1994, over 10,000 enterprises "conducted shareholding experiments, with some 25 million shareholders and capital stock of at least 200 billion yuan."[10]

At present, China has three kinds of share listings: (1) "A" share listings are for Chinese investors; (2) "B" shares are listed by joint ventures and for purchase in foreign currencies (U.S. dollars in Shanghai and Hong Kong dollars in Shenzhen); and (3) "H" shares are Mainland company listings in Hong Kong and foreign markets.

The Chinese authorities seem unconcerned about this resurgence of capitalism. When reform began in the late 1970s and early 1980s, Chinese leaders defined whatever they wanted to do as "socialism," although some of the economic measures that they took were clearly capitalistic. But now, Chinese leaders do not even bother to justify their policies in the name of socialism. In 1992, *People's Daily* published an editorial in which China was identified as in a primary stage of socialism, and thus "capitalism cannot be completely eradicated."[11]

The publication of this article was significant. It echoed Deng's remarks about economic reform during his tour to southern China in the spring of 1992. During the trip, Deng told his junior colleagues that they "should be bolder and dare to try things out instead of acting like a woman with bound feet."[12] After hearing Deng's instruction, Chinese officials called for "adequately developing the capitalist economy inside China."[13] The most salient aspect of the market economy is, of course, the reemergence of the private sector in the Chinese economy.

A scene outside Shanghai Wanguo Securities Company. There is always a crowd both inside and outside any branch office of the stock exchange (brokerage house) in Shanghai every weekday. The number of registered stockholders in Shanghai increased from 45,000 in 1990 to 4,600,000 in 1993.

The Reemergence of the Private Sector

Before 1949, the private sector accounted for a significant portion of China's economy. Private industries contributed 48.7 percent of gross national industrial output while state-owned businesses accounted for only 26.2 percent. For the first three decades of the PRC, the government strictly restrained the existence of private enterprises. The 4 million private firms and stores that had existed prior to the 1949 revolution had all disappeared by the mid-1950s.[14] During the Cultural Revolution, even petty bourgeoisie such as the owners of "family-run stores" were considered "the tails of the bourgeoisie" and thus were subject to being "cut off."

Private enterprises began to reappear in the mid-1980s, but at that time each private firm was allowed to hire no more than eight workers. The legal status of these small businesses was ambiguous. In 1988, the Seventh National People's Congress passed a constitutional amendment that authorized the legitimate status of the private economy.[15] At present there are five principal participants in the Chinese economy:

1. State-owned enterprises—enterprises wholly owned by the government
2. Collective enterprises—enterprises owned by local groups, where the government is not responsible for wages or similar obligations
3. Private enterprises—businesses operated by private individuals
4. Stock-share enterprises—companies owned partially or wholly by shareholders, including companies partially owned by the state
5. Foreign-invested enterprises or joint ventures—enterprises owned at least 25 percent by foreign individuals or companies.

Private enterprises have grown rapidly in the early 1990s. In 1992, approximately 7.7 million—89 percent—of the retail sales outlets in China belonged to private firms or individually owned businesses. Nowadays, signs of the private economy are visible everywhere. About 80 percent of the 140,000 shops in Beijing, for example, are either owned or run by private entrepreneurs.[16] Nationwide, the number of self-employed business people expanded to more than 15 million in urban areas. Before 1992, the official dividing line between a *getihu* (individual business firm) and a *shiren qiye* (private enterprise) was determined by the number of full-time personnel it employed: when a business reached eight or more it became a private enterprise. But more recently, a capital value of 500,000 yuan or more has become the criterion. In 1994 alone, more than 182,000 private enterprises were established (see Table 4–1). In addition, thousands of private stores have spread throughout the country.

The private sector has developed fastest along the southeast coast of China, where 70 percent of the country's private businesses are located. Another 19 percent are in central China and only 1 percent are in the western part of the country.[17] By 1994, Shanghai, for example, had about 14,000 private industrial firms and 117,000 private stores. More than 2,000 private enterprises held a registered capital of 500,000 yuan ($58,140) each. The one with the highest capital was worth 15 million yuan ($1.7 million).[18]

Make no mistake, the role of the private sector in the Chinese national economy is still small. But what is truly remarkable is the heightened tempo of change.

"When we discuss privatization in socialist countries," a scholar from the Shanghai Academy of Social Sciences told me, "we are talking about creating a private sector where there has not been one for decades or generations. Keeping this historical fact in mind, everyone will be impressed by the remarkable growth of the private economy in China."

The State Administration for Industry and Commerce, which oversees economic activities of private enterprises, reported that the registered capital of private enterprises increased from 45.2 billion yuan in 1992 to 68.03 billion yuan in 1993 and to 138.90 billion yuan in 1994 (see Table 4–1). The number of private enterprises whose registered capital exceeded 1 million yuan increased from 662 in 1991 to 8,784 in 1993 and to over

TABLE 4-1
Growth of Private Enterprises (1989–1994)

Year	Number	Employed	Registered Assets (billion yuan)
1989	91,000	1,850,000	na
1990	98,000	1,700,000	na
1991	108,000	1,830,000	na
1992	140,000	2,310,000	45.2
1993	238,000	3,720,000	68.03
1994	420,000	6,350,000	138.9

Sources: Economic Information Daily, 31 May 1994, 4; *People's Daily,* 11 January 1995, 2; *China News Analysis,* 15 February 1995, 2.

12,000 in 1994.[19] Over 2,000 private firms extended their businesses abroad in 1993, earning about 1.58 billion yuan ($181.6 million) in foreign exchange.[20]

In 1994, private enterprises nationwide had 104 billion yuan ($12 billion) in registered funds, an increase of 53 percent from 1993. These firms turned in 29 billion yuan ($3.4 billion) to state coffers, up 44 percent from 1993.[21] According to a survey of 134 large private enterprises, 7 claimed that their capital exceeded 100 million yuan.[22] In Shanghai, the average registered capital of private enterprises was 275,200 yuan ($31,600) in 1994, a five-fold increase over that of 1991.[23] The total number of private enterprises in the city increased by 223 percent compared to 1993.[24]

With a mandate to redraw the country's economic landscape, the private sector has now been encouraged to buy into or take over failing state-owned enterprises and commercial networks. In 1994, 65 percent of China's GDP came from nonstate enterprises. About 80 percent of newly added value came from non-state-owned enterprises.[25] Private and collective firms, joint stock companies, and foreign-funded ventures accounted for 84.8 percent of the growth in industrial output value in 1994, according to a report by the State Statistics Bureau.[26] The private sector's share of total investment in China increased from 16 percent in the late 1970s to 37 percent in the late 1980s and the early 1990s. By 1993, private enterprises and self-employed small businesses had created 33.1 million jobs.[27] This number exceeded the total number of newly employed workers in state firms during the past decade.

Table 4–2 shows that in 1992 non-state-owned enterprises, including collective, private, and foreign-owned firms, for the first time in the PRC history, accounted for a larger share of the gross value of industrial output (52 percent) than did state-owned enterprises (48 percent). In the coastal provinces, the nonstate sectors account for an even larger portion. In Guangdong Province, for example, the registered capital of the state-owned, collective, and private (including foreign-owned) enterprises in 1993 was, respectively, 30.2 percent, 16.4 percent, and 53.4 percent.[28] According to an estimate by China's State Information Center, the private sector will constitute 25 percent of the output of the country's economy by the turn of the century (see Table 4–3).[29]

A large number of collective enterprises are actually private firms that operate under the facade of collectives (*jiajiti* or *guakaoqiye*). Many township and village enterprises (TVEs), among the factors contributing the most to the economic miracle in post-Mao China, are private firms by nature, though not by name, as will be discussed in the following chapter.

Private enterprises not only increase quickly in number, but also ex-

TABLE 4-2
Ownership Structure of Industrial Production

Ownership	Percentage		
	1978	1985	1992
State	78	65	48
Collectives	22	32	38
Urban	(13)	(16)	(11)
Rural	(9)	(16)	(27)
Private	neg*	2	7
Foreign-invested	neg*	neg*	4

Sources and Notes: China's Statistical Yearbook, various years; *Statistics Abstracts,* various years.
*Negligible percentages.

TABLE 4-3
Output of State-owned, Collective, and Privately Run Enterprises as a
Percentage of China's Total GNP

	1988	1991	2000 (Projected)
State-owned enterprises	76.0	51.3	27.2
Collective enterprises	23.5	36.9	47.7
Private enterprises	0.5	11.8	25.1

Source: Figures from the State Information Center, Beijing, reported in *Zhongguo shibao* (China times), Taipei, 16 July 1992, 10. Quoted from Chang Chen-pang, "The Resurgence of the Bourgeoisie in Mainland China," *Issues and Studies* 30 (May 1994): 42.

pand in size and kind. Private schools, private hospitals, private churches, private banks, private airline companies, and private satellites have all developed in China in the past few years. At a recent auction of bankrupt state-owned department stores in Shanghai, Chen Jingyi, an entrepreneur from Zhejiang, purchased all the stores. The managers from state-owned or collective firms in Shanghai were dumbfounded. Chen owns three factories, two trade companies, and two stock-share companies. His registered capital in 1993 was 15 million yuan, and 2,300 employees worked for him.[30]

The rapid development of rural industries, urban private enterprises, and joint ventures has produced Chinese entrepreneurs, a new social stratum in the PRC. In the Chinese context, an entrepreneur is defined as a manager-owner of private property—a person who has managed to possess property either through capitalization of personal income or through the private operation of a collective, public, or joint-venture enterprise.[31] This entrepreneur class consists mainly of the following five groups: (1) owners of private firms in both rural and urban areas; (2) managers in collective firms who make a fortune through contracts; (3) real estate agents or agents of other businesses; (4) Chinese representatives of foreign firms; and (5) Chinese executives in big joint ventures.

It is difficult to estimate the number of entrepreneurs and private enterprises in China at present. This is partially because the rise of both is a recent phenomenon. Chinese entrepreneurs are a diverse lot. Some can be identified as what is known in the West as members of the "middle class." Unlike the middle class in advanced industrial countries, which usually accounts for a larger portion of the population, the middle class in China is a marginal part of the whole. But if 1 percent of the Chinese become members of the middle class, that would be 12 million people. China's middle class is disproportionally distributed along the southeast coastal area.

Some entrepreneurs have become incredibly rich and are called *dahu* or *dakuan* in China—new terms that may be translated as "big money-bugs." They usually own three-story houses with Jacuzzis, drive Lincoln Town Cars, wear Rolex watches, and have body guards and personal secretaries. It is appropriate to identify them as bourgeois instead of middle class. They are usually the owners of big private enterprises with "assets running into scores of millions, hundreds of millions or even billions of yuan."[32] A recent issue of *China Rich* reports the success stories of 15 entrepreneurs in China, and each has private assets exceeding 100 million yuan.[33] The richest among them, Rong Zhijian, son of Rong Yiren, vice president of China, is reported to have private assets of 3.5 billion yuan.[34]

Most of the entrepreneurs, of course, do not have as prominent a family background as Rong. Han Wei, a celebrated peasant-turned-entrepreneur, for example, was born into a poor family with nine children in Lushun, Liaoning Province. In 1984, this junior-high-school graduate started his entrepreneurial career with only 3,000 yuan by running a chicken farm. Ten years later, his enterprise employs over one thousand workers and owns 11 livestock husbandry companies. The enterprise group has a total registered capital of 239 million yuan. His personal property is estimated at 300 million yuan.

Mu Qizhong, president of the Land Economic Group, is one of the largest and best-known private entrepreneurs in China.[35] Mu was sentenced to death about 20 years ago for denouncing socialism and advocating a market economy. He was pardoned when the Cultural Revolution ended. Now his private company has assets of 1.5 billion yuan ($260 million). The Land Economic Group now owns colleges, launches satellites, and has purchased state-run enterprises in both China and Russia. Mu also plans to run his own TV station and to establish a joint-venture airline.[36]

Rong, Han, and Mu are, of course, at the top of the country's entrepreneur class. Most private entrepreneurs in China own small businesses or are self-employed in industrial and commercial ventures (*getihu*). They may not be really wealthy, but their standard of living has greatly improved since becoming entrepreneurs. They are usually from the less privileged and less respected part of Chinese society. They are self-made men with little formal schooling or other privileges, as illustrated in chapter 6. Many of them were jobless youths who had just returned to the urban area after being sent to the countryside during the Cultural Revolution or landless peasants who sought opportunities in rural enterprises.[37]

Table 4–4 presents two large surveys of *getihu* in Shanghai conducted in 1985 and 1993; in both, more than half of them were migrants from rural areas. A significant number were previously unemployed, and some were released prisoners. A study of *getihu* in Beijing also shows that *getihu* had very low social status before they became well-off.[38] They became entrepreneurs not out of convenience or choice, but because this was the only way for them to make a living.

Former poor peasants with little education constitute a significant portion of China's emerging entrepreneur class.[39] A number of factors—the pressure to pursue a nonagricultural career, market opportunities, the availability of cheap laborers in rural areas, structural changes in the Chinese economy and entrepreneurship—all contribute to the success of peasants-turned-industrialists. The emergence of this social stratum reflects the dynamism of the country's social mobility.

The upward social mobility of entrepreneurs also represents a historical change in Chinese society. Traditional Chinese society, which was dominated by the gentry-scholar class, tended to look down upon peasants and to devalue the role of merchants. The rapid emergence and increasingly important role of peasants-turned-entrepreneurs in the past decade has challenged this tradition and profoundly changed the social structure of the country.

TABLE 4-4
Formation of Self-Employed Industrial/Commercial
Entrepreneurs in Shanghai

Origin	1985 Survey		1993 Survey	
	Number	%	Number	%
Urban Residents	53,864	48.12	79,022	43.16
Unemployed	26,283	23.48	23,161	12.65
Job-waiting youths	8,765	7.83	11,555	6.31
Retired workers	7,858	7.02	17,980	9.82
Resigned workers	5,932	5.30	19,037	10.40
Released prisoners	5,026	4.49	7,289	3.98
Rural-Urban Migrants	58,073	51.88	104,074	56.84
Total	111,937	100	183,096	100

Source: Chen Baorong, *Jiushi niandai Shanghai geti siying jingji fazhan yanjiu* (Study of the development of private economy in Shanghai in the 90s), working paper, Shanghai Academy of Social Sciences, 1994, 14.

As a result of the rapid growth of the market economy, citizens' bank savings have also dramatically increased. By the end of 1993, total savings by Chinese citizens amounted to 1,400 billion yuan ($162 billion). Six months later, private bank savings had increased to 1,772 billion yuan ($203.8 billion), despite double-digit inflation and massive purchases of state treasury bonds.[40] In Shanghai, for example, private savings of residents increased from 3 billion yuan in 1980 to 25.2 billion yuan in 1990 and to 97.6 billion yuan in 1994 (see Figure 2–1).[41] Individual savings have become the major source of bank funds.

In addition, in 1994 citizens nationwide had 500 billion yuan of cash in hand, 400 billion yuan invested in stocks and securities, and 4.5 million charged to credit cards. Citizens' savings accounts in foreign currency surpassed $20 billion, one-fourth of the foreign reserves of the country. Half of that sum belongs to residents of three cities: Shanghai ($4 billion), Beijing ($3.4 billion) and Guangzhou ($2 billion).[42] The latest official statistics indicate that Chinese citizens possess more than 2,000 billion yuan ($230 billion) in financial assets.[43] All these data suggest the great impact of the rapid development of nonstate sectors.

Foreign Investment in Shanghai

The development of the stock market and private enterprises in Shanghai has been accompanied by the rapid growth of foreign investment. Foreign investment in China mainly takes three forms: equity joint ventures, cooperative joint ventures, and wholly foreign-owned enterprises. Equity joint ventures are "limited liability companies," incorporated and registered in China. The legal owners of equity joint ventures are usually Chinese enterprises, which have the right to own, use, and dispose of the property. In contrast, in a cooperative joint venture, each Chinese and foreign party is responsible for paying its own taxes on profits derived from the venture and bears its own liability for risks and losses. A wholly foreign-owned enterprise is owned completely by one or more foreign investors and does not involve any Chinese joint-venture parties.

At the 1994 National Conference on Management and Registration of Foreign Firms in China, the Chinese government claimed that in 1993 the country had about 167,300 foreign enterprises, including 107,800 equity joint ventures, 25,500 cooperative joint ventures and 34,000 wholly foreign-owned enterprises.[44]

According to a report published by the World Bank, the influx of total capital into China increased from $11 billion in 1991, to $24 billion in 1992, to $27 billion in 1993, which includes $15 billion in direct investment, $5 billion in bonds, $3.5 billion in private capital, $2.5 billion in governmental aid and loans, and $1 billion in commercial bank loans. China has received the largest foreign capital input in the past few years.[45] In the 1993–94 fiscal year, China remained the World Bank's biggest borrower, with a total of $3.07 billion in loans for 14 major projects.[46]

A 1992 comparison of Shanghai and four other major cities showed that Shanghai was far ahead in the main indexes of foreign business (see Table 4–5). In 1994, Shanghai had 9,719 foreign-funded enterprises, which had invested a total of $35.635 billion.[47] Foreign-funded enterprises accounted for 30 percent of the city's gross industrial sales in the same year.[48] A large portion of foreign investment in Shanghai came from Hong Kong (see Table 4–6).

An official newspaper in Shanghai reported that by early 1995, Pudong (East Shanghai) had registered 2,897 foreign-funded projects involving a total investment of $11.3 billion, up from only 53 projects and $1.1 billion in 1990.[49] A total of 44 renowned multinational companies have invested $1.8 billion in Pudong in the past five years. One of the prime attractions for foreign firms in Pudong is the reduced corporate tax rate. The standard corporate tax for foreign companies in the country is 33 percent of

TABLE 4-5
A Comparison of Foreign Investment and Foreign Trade in
China's Four Major Cities (1992)
($100 Million)

	Shanghai	Beijing	Tianjin	Guangzhou
Total Foreign Trade	98	22	24	42
Export	66	15	18	NA
Actual Use of Foreign Investment	71	31	31	27
Direct Foreign Investment	24	22	7	17

Source: Chengshi jingji yanjiu (Research on urban economy), no. 6 (1994): 7.

profits, while in Pudong the rate is 15 percent. In addition, the companies are exempt from taxes for the first two years of profitability and pay only half (7.5 percent) the following three.[50]

Meanwhile, foreign investment and trade have become a major new source of state revenue. Tax collected from foreign-funded businesses in Shanghai hit a record high of 3.8 billion yuan ($436 million) in 1993. This figure represented a 92 percent surge from the previous year and pushed Shanghai a step up to rank second in the country. The proportion of city taxes from foreign-funded businesses also rose from 10 percent in 1992 to nearly 16 percent in 1993.[51]

Foreign investors, however, have often been frustrated by many problems in the investment environment in Shanghai—indeed, in the whole country. Hu Faguang, a well-known Hong Kong businessman, told the Chinese media that six factors worry foreign investors. They are (1) the ambiguities in Chinese law; (2) poor infrastructure conditions, such as transportation and communication; (3) the redundancy of investment projects; (4) numerous and heavy taxes; (5) inflation; and (6) poor accounting systems.

Political uncertainty and the political attitudes of local people also concerned the businessman. "Some Shanghai people feel that foreign companies come to Shanghai to grasp the wealth of Shanghai which is otherwise owned by Shanghainese," he said. "This is wrong. We come to create wealth, not seize wealth, to create jobs, not eliminate jobs."[52]

To a certain extent, Mr. Hu is right. China has greatly benefited from foreign investment since its opening in 1978. In 1994, more than 10 mil-

TABLE 4-6
Foreign Investment in Shanghai (1993)

	Project Contracts Assigned (Number)	Intended Investment ($10,000)	Investment at Work ($10,000)
Total	6,939	1,370,529	513,244
By Investment Form			
Joint Venture (Capital)	5,072	820,729	275,699
Joint Venture (Management)	1,080	283,085	97,363
Solely Foreign	774	224,372	61,088
By Sector			
Agriculture/Animal Husbandry	39	1,951	1,749
Industry	5,081	564,845	277,593
Construction	266	14,525	3,916
Communication/Transportation	51	11,021	32,827
Restaurants	298	55,472	23,034
Real Estate	283	505,175	153,823
Social Service	294	135,900	2,356
By Country (Region)			
Hong Kong	3,375	700,196	205,074
United States	865	166,552	93,613
Japan	637	119,006	55,661
Germany	43	23,599	23,599
Taiwan	1,002	91,689	12,475
Singapore	182	37,143	11,096
Great Britain	76	33,100	9,632
Thailand	56	18,904	7,084
Italy	19	6,477	5,506
Canada	134	27,059	5,000
France	34	5,437	3,099
Macao	85	23,719	4,947
Australia	82	5,284	1,336
South Korea	18	2,448	482

Source: Shanghai fangdichan shichang 1994 (Shanghai real estate market) (Shanghai: Zhong-guo Tongji Chubanshe, 1995), 9.

lion domestic laborers were employed in over 70,000 of the 174,000 for-eign-funded enterprises in the country.[53] However, business owners prob-ably are not aware of the increasing dissatisfaction and resentment among Chinese workers toward foreign managers, especially managers from Hong Kong, Taiwan, and Singapore.

According to the Shanghai Bureau of Labor, the number of labor dis-putes in the city's overseas-funded joint ventures has been increasing rap-idly. A study found that in 1991, 73 labor disputes in overseas-funded firms were tried, and a year later the figure rose to 181. In 1993, 290 cases were submitted. During the first half of 1994, local courts heard more than 200 such cases.[54]

Foreign investment in the property development of Chinese cities has caused strong resentment among local residents who have to move from downtown to bleak suburban areas. Chapter 11 provides a detailed discussion of the problems associated with the relocation of urban residents in Shanghai.

Many Chinese industries have been in jeopardy or have even gone into complete bankruptcy under the impact of foreign investment. For example, foreign brands control 85 percent, 72 percent, and 81 percent of the shampoo, chocolate, and carbonated soft drink markets, respectively, in Shanghai, Beijing, Guangzhou, and Chengdu.[55] Out of the eight leading Chinese beverage companies, six have now been enlisted under the "flags of Pepsi-Cola and Coca-Cola." In the words of a high-school teacher in Hangzhou, China's soft drink industry has been "cocacolonized."

Foreign investors have been engaged in all kinds of industries and businesses in the city, including large electrical power plants and insurance. This raises a question: How flexible can, and should, the government be in allowing them to run risky businesses or to own crucial industries in the city? At present, however, Chinese officials seem more interested in attracting foreign capital and promoting foreign trade, than in dealing with political issues, such as the exploitation in foreign-owned firms. Foreign investment and foreign trade have been increasing at an unprecedented rate in Shanghai during the past few years. In the view of some Shanghai leaders, without land leasing and the growth of foreign investment, the ongoing large-scale urban construction of Shanghai would be absolutely impossible.[56]

Undoubtedly, economic dynamism released by the market forces—the rapid development of the stock market, private enterprises, and foreign investment—has greatly contributed to the economic boom of the country. To say the least, the Chinese economy before 1978 was stagnant. In the Mao era, monolithic state ownership, rigid central planning, and the "iron-bowl" distribution system deprived Chinese workers of incentives. Today, the nonstate sector has revitalized the economy and improved the standard of living of millions of people. But this does not mean that market forces can solve all the problems that China confronts. To a certain extent, the solutions that the post-Mao authorities have found to deal with old problems have now become new problems. Progress is real; so are the problems. The dilemmas of China's economic reform were illustrated vividly during my visit to Wenzhou, a medium-sized city located in Zhejiang Province on the southeast coast of China.

Wenzhou—the Breeding Ground of Chinese Capitalism

Wenzhou has long been known for its dynamic private economy. People in China often call Wenzhou the "breeding ground of China's capitalist development."[57] The Wenzhou region, with a population of 6,200,000, includes 2 urban districts, 9 counties, and 87 towns. While private enterprises were strictly banned during the Cultural Revolution, some petty entrepreneurs actually survived in Wenzhou and developed their small businesses underground. Wang Hongwen, former vice chairman of the Chinese Communist Party and a member of the "Gang of Four," said during the Cultural Revolution that "if one wants to see the lingering presence of capitalism under socialist China, go to Wenzhou."

When economic reform began in 1978, Wenzhou immediately emerged as a pilot region for China's capitalist development. In 1986, the Office of the Central Committee of the Chinese Communist Party circulated a notice that Wenzhou would serve as an experimental city for the development of the private sector.[58] By 1990, state-owned enterprises' percentage in the total industrial output value in the city was only 11.7 percent, while collectives and private firms accounted for 52.3 percent and 32.5 percent, respectively (see Table 4–7). The average annual growth rate of the total industrial output values of private firms was much faster than those of state-owned enterprises and collectives.

Several geopolitical factors have contributed to the rapid development of the private economy in Wenzhou. First, Wenzhou has long been recognized as a region with too many people and too little arable land. The arable land per person in the region is 0.46 *mu* (one *mu* is about 670 square meters).[59] According to the current condition of agricultural mechanization and electrification in China, a rural laborer is able to cultivate about five *mu* of land on average. Thus, the region has an overwhelmingly large number of surplus rural laborers. These workers either must migrate to other regions or change their primary economic activities from the agricultural sector to industrial and commercial sectors. Thus, the geographical disadvantage actually contributed to the economic boom in the region.

Secondly, Wenzhou is located on the southeast coast of China, just opposite Taiwan across the Taiwan Strait. Because of this proximity, the Chinese government was unwilling to invest in the region. For the first three decades, the government invested only 760 million yuan in state-owned enterprises in the region. As a result, the industrial base in Wenzhou was very weak. The lack of government support and the pressure of unemployment, however, have provided the opportunity for the development of the private sector.

Third, the geopolitical disadvantages of Wenzhou have also nurtured a strong and distinctive sense of entrepreneurship in its people. During the past few decades, a large number of residents have migrated to other areas

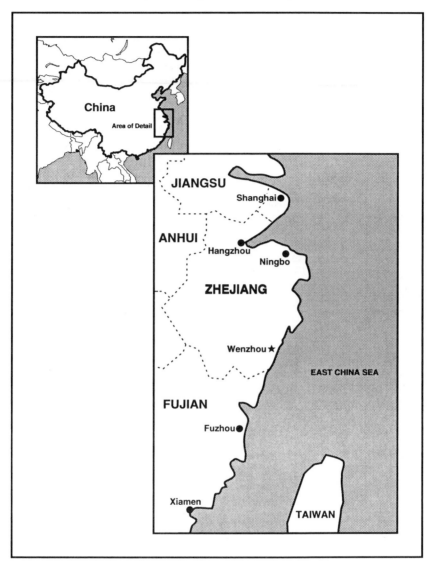

Map 4-1 Wenzhou (Zhejiang Province)

TABLE 4-7

Changes of Total Industrial Output Values and the Economic
Structure in Wenzhou
(unit: 1 million yuan)

Year	Total Industrial Output Value	State Firms		Collective Firms		Private Firms	
		Total	%	Total	%	Total	%
1978	1,103	393	35.6	603	55.1	101	9.3
1980	1,647	532	32.9	878	54.3	165	10.2
1986	4,821	822	17.1	2,712	56.3	1,228	25.5
1988	8,565	999	11.7	4,477	52.3	2,787	32.5
1992	18,299	2,515	13.7	10,184	55.7	5,600	30.6
Average Annual Growth Rate (%) from 1978 to 1988		18.6	7.5		18.5		31.7

Sources: Yuan Enzhen, *Zhongguo siying jingji xianzhuang fazhan yu pinggu* (China's private economy: conditions, development, and evaluation) (Shanghai: Renmin Press, 1993), 120; Hiroshi Sato, "Market Conversion in Wenzhou, Zhejiang Province," *JETRO China Newsletter,* no. 112 (1994): 7.

or other countries where they have formed Wenzhou communities, for example, in Beijing, Hangzhou, Paris, and Rome. They have been engaged in various kinds of businesses in new places while maintaining close ties with Wenzhou. The money they made elsewhere provided capital for them and their relatives to establish private firms in Wenzhou. In 1983 and 1984, for example, the overseas remittance to Wenzhou was $12,680,000, which accounted for 30 percent of the total overseas remittance of the entire Zhejiang Province.[60]

Currently, Wenzhou has over 3,000 private enterprises and about 200,000 private stores. The annual output value of many private enterprises is as high as 10 million yuan. It is widely believed that Wenzhou is one of the richest areas in China, and the city has thousands of millionaires.

I went to Wenzhou in May 1995 with my friend Joseph Kahn, the *Wall Street Journal*'s bureau chief in Shanghai. This was the first visit to Wenzhou for both of us. We had anticipated seeing a burgeoning city like other coastal cities in the country.

What I saw, however, was an old and shabby city. Some buildings were under construction, but I did not see any skyscrapers or any sign of an emerging commercial center in southeast China. We stayed at the Huaqiao

Hotel, the best hotel in the city, where my father had stayed over 30 years ago. Some old hotels could be distinguished by architectural styles or other unique characteristics, but there was nothing special about the Hua-qiao Hotel. I was surprised that Wenzhou had not built good hotels and other modern urban facilities during the past decade, while other coastal cities seemed to build too many elegant hotels. Wenzhou seemed to pay little attention to urban reconstruction.

I was even more disappointed by the inconvenience of the local trans-portation and the poor quality of the roads. I have never seen a city with as many bumpy streets as Wenzhou. The city actually does not license small automobiles because they cannot survive the city's poor road condi-tions.

"I have heard some stories of how rich entrepreneurs have contributed to the public welfare," Joe Kahn said, "but this is certainly not what I see here in Wenzhou."

I absolutely agreed with Joe. The municipal government of Wenzhou often boasted that the city used local capital, including money raised from the private sector, for urban development projects. But we did not see any major projects except the construction of the new Wenzhou Airport.

"You could not expect China to become a 'welfare capitalist country' overnight," said Mr. Zhu, a 27-year-old rich entrepreneur with whom we chatted in a restaurant.

"But it has already been 20 years since the reemergence of private en-terprises in Wenzhou," Joe commented.

"Yes," Mr. Zhu replied, "but we still need to accumulate capital."

Mr. Zhu was born into a poor peasant family in a small town near the city. In the early 1970s, Zhu's parents started a small business selling fruit and seafood in the black market. The family moved to Wenzhou in the early 1980s. With the initial capital of 20,000 yuan that Zhu's parents provided, Zhu and his two brothers and three sisters established garment factories, first in Wenzhou, then in Qingdao and Tianjin. The registered capital of their family business increased from 560,000 yuan in 1988 to 3,280,000 in 1995. Zhu told us that each of his brothers and sisters has several million yuan in capital.

"But we still have a long way to go to become a big entrepreneurial family in Wenzhou," Mr. Zhu explained.

At this point, private entrepreneurs like Mr. Zhu seem to be only inter-ested in making their fortunes. No one is really concerned about the so-cioeconomic well-being of the community. The disparity between rich and poor is a serious problem in the region. A survey of 84 private enter-prises showed that the average annual income reported by owners was

35.6 times that of their employees. The real income gap was believed to be even greater. Another study of 50 private enterprises found that 46 percent of workers were not satisfied with their incomes or benefits.[61]

During our trip, we visited a number of shoe factories in downtown Wenzhou. Shoemaking has become one of the core industries, along with the garment and electronic industries, during the reform era. A manager of a shoe factory told us that the city had about 6,000 shoe factories and workshops.

We were struck not only by the large number of shoe factories, but also by their terrible working conditions. Shuixin, a small industrial complex located a few minutes away from the Huaqiao Hotel, has hundreds of shoe workshops and stores. A typical shoe workshop in the complex was actually no more than an old, shabby house where several hundred laborers crowded along the assembly line. These worn-down factory houses used to be one-story houses, but owners or managers of the factories added a second story. Tall workers had difficulty walking through the factory house. Usually, they did not have enough lights, not only because they had few windows, but also because the owners wanted to reduce electricity costs.

What struck me the most, however, was the awful smell caused by chemical glues and other materials. Not surprisingly, the workshops we visited had no ventilation installed. Every visitor would feel nauseated, but these workers had to work for long hours in such a heavily polluted work environment.

"How many hours do you work every day?" I asked a teenage girl.

"It depends on whether I can complete my quota in a day," she replied. "But usually I work from 8 in the morning to 2 at night."

"Do you have a work contract with the owner of the factory?" I asked.

"No."

"Do you have any social welfare benefits?" Joe asked.

"Social welfare benefits?" the girl seemed puzzled by the term. "Yes, I get pay every day."

"Do you have any medical insurance?" Joe asked, more specifically.

"I don't understand," the girl replied. She had never heard of the term "medical insurance."

I shared concerns about such benefits. China's safety net has become increasingly inadequate in the reform era. Like many other countries that have gone through a transformation in economic structure, the Chinese government hasn't given high priority to welfare issues and is unable to allocate more resources to social programs in employment, income equalization, pricing control, social security, occupational benefits, health services, housing, and so on. In fact, the past few years witnessed a large-scale retreat of the state in service provision at the very time when problems such as unemployment, inflation, polarization, and the fast-rising costs of medical treatment became acute.[62] Meanwhile, the private sector is unable to take over social programs.

"Don't talk to foreigners!" a middle-aged woman who looked like a manager appeared and interrupted our conversation. "Please go away!" she said to Joe and me bluntly.

"We want to know whether your workers have any concerns or problems with the working conditions here," I said to her straightforwardly.

"If they have any problems, they can quit their jobs here any time," the woman replied. "My workers should be grateful to be able to work here. Go see the jobless people in the 'labor markets' [*laodongli shichang*], and you will understand what I mean."

I certainly didn't need her to remind me of the "labor markets." This was one of the most memorable, and indeed most miserable, scenes I observed during my journey in China. In virtually every large and medium-sized city that I visited, there were places in which hundreds of young adults, both men and women (most in their twenties) waited for hours and days, hoping to be picked up by anyone who could offer them jobs, including temporary or hourly work.

These "labor markets" were usually located on busy streets, in the plazas of ports, bus terminals, and railway stations, near construction sites, and in front of the factories that hire temporary workers. Each time I saw this scene, my mind would be filled with words such as "exploitation," "oppression," and "dehumanization."

On my taxi ride from downtown to Wenzhou Airport, I saw a labor market in which about 300 jobless migrants gathered. It was already afternoon, and most of them must have been waiting there since the early morning. Their frustration was visible in their facial expressions.

As the taxi passed these people, I suddenly realized—not what the middle-aged manager in the shoe factory meant about the justification for capitalist exploitation—but ironically, why the Chinese people enthusiastically embraced socialism half a century ago.

Here I do not intend to make an ideological judgment, nor do I want to give any simplistic comparison of the pre-1949 regime, Mao's China, and the reform era solely in the light of socialism and capitalism. The above discussion, I hope, not only shows the dynamic changes and great achievements of the market economy, but also reveals the dilemmas—both moral and policy—that the country faces in the process of privatization.

The main issue for China at present is not about the choice between returning to a previous socialist-planning economy or transforming to a conventional capitalist market. The central concern is the problem of transition—transition to whatever kind of a mixed economy and form of political system and social safety net will correspond to the rapid economic changes. The following chapter on Sunan will discuss the cooperative development of rural industries there and its implication for the ongoing transformation of China.

5

Sunan's Miracle

Rural Industrial Revolution Changes China's Landscape

What strikes me first, and shocks me, is the prosperity of the rural area. As we travel by car through southern Jiangsu, we notice rows upon rows of newly built peasant villas in elegant colors and a variety of shapes. These homes line both sides of spacious boulevards. Woven into this rich countryside is a concentration of towns with modern factories and commercial centers. We pass by a town roughly every 15 minutes. Most of these towns are new or rebuilt. They are clean and charming, and there seem to be no noise and no traffic jams—the things that have driven me crazy in Shanghai.

Southern Jiangsu, or Sunan, as it is known in China, lies in the middle of the Yangtze River Delta, neighboring Shanghai to the south and Nanjing to the north. The Sunan region, with a population of 13 million, covers 432 towns and 12 counties under the jurisdiction of three prefecture-level cities: Wuxi, Suzhou, and Changzhou. The enormous area within these three cities is now often called "the Golden Triangle" (*jin-sanjiao*), a booming economic zone in the country.

Seeing Is Believing

Sunan has long been known as the land of "fish and rice," which is symbolic of agricultural abundance. As a student of China, I know that Sunan is one of the fastest-growing areas in post-Mao China. In 1992, for example, Jiangsu Province's gross national product (GNP) increased 27 per-

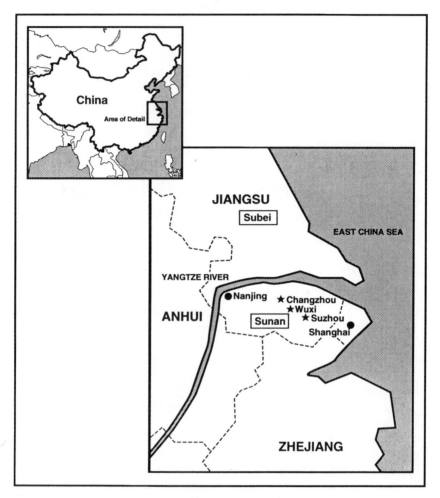

Map 5-1 Sunan (Wuxi, Suzhou, and Changzhou)

cent over the previous year, far ahead of other booming provinces such as Guangdong (18.7 percent), Zhejiang (17 percent), Shandong (16.9 percent), Fujian (16.3 percent), and Shanghai (14.4 percent).[1] Yet I find it difficult to imagine that the region has made such tremendous progress in reshaping its landscape within only a few years.

This was not my first trip to Sunan. I lived in a nearby town for a month over 10 years ago when, as a medical student, I was assigned to work temporarily in a rural clinic. The economic condition of the town was terrible. The clinic, for example, was located in the building that used to be a Buddhist temple. The building needed repair, but the local government could not afford it. The doctors in the clinic would cancel surgical operations whenever it rained, because the roof of the operating room leaked in heavy rain. During my stay in this so-called land of "fish and rice," I actually never had the chance to taste fish. In addition, rice was limited to one bowl a day per person.

During my last trip to China in 1990, I visited Sunan briefly. The economic boom had already begun in the region. The living standard of the people had improved significantly. Most of the families in Sunan had built new houses and owned color television sets, refrigerators, and motorized bicycles. But then I wouldn't call these peasants or rural entrepreneurs wealthy, because the things that they possessed were quite common by American standards. They were considered necessities of life in many places of the world.

But now the situation is quite different. When I see BMWs and Mercedes-Benzes parked at a karaoke bar in a small town—and when a Hong Kong Jacuzzi dealer tells me that his company has sold dozens of Jacuzzi tubs to peasants' households in Sunan at a cost of $10,000 each—I realize a profound historic change is really taking place in the region.

"Seeing is believing!" I tell other people in the car. "I'm so glad that I took this trip."

Two other passengers travel with me, Stanley Harris, import director of Roytex, Inc. a New York–based dealer for Pierre Cardin, and my elder brother Li Zifu, chief representative in Shanghai for a Hong Kong trading company. Both Mr. Harris and my brother know the region very well, because their companies have had business dealings with six garment factories in Sunan for almost a decade. They take this trip to the factories in Sunan, as they have done monthly for the past decade, to inspect the quality of the garments before shipment to the United States.

"Every time I travel to Sunan," my brother says, "I always see a lot of new peasant villas under construction, or completed. You see hardly any shabby houses in the vast rural land of Sunan. The houses that were built in rural Sunan in the mid-1980s already look old and outdated, and many have been torn down and replaced."

A study conducted in 1993 confirmed my brother's observation—almost every family in rural Sunan has moved into a new house at least once since 1978.[2] In cities and towns of Jiangsu Province, 8 million people, half of the urban population, have moved into new residences. The living space per capita has also doubled.[3]

"These luxury villas sometimes make me wonder if I am in southern Jiangsu or in the suburbs of New York City," Mr. Harris says.

A rural entrepreneur's mansion in Changzhou is built right in the middle of his farmland.

"Yes," I respond. "Some of the nice towns in Sunan remind me of towns or cities in the United States, such as Lawrenceville in New Jersey or Mountain View in California." I lived in these two American towns while I studied in the nearby universities. The Sunan region, however, has more factories and commercial districts.

"It is more like the suburbs of Osaka in Japan," I add.

"I don't think that people in the United States, including some China experts, really know the fascinating changes happening in Sunan," Mr. Harris continues. "There are many reports in Western media about the economic development in Shenzhen or in Shanghai. It seems to me that Western business people or China watchers seldom bother to take a two-hour car ride from Shanghai to visit the rural area of Sunan. For me, the changes in Sunan are even more impressive and profound, although Sunan has neither a World Trade Center like the one in Shenzhen nor a gigantic TV tower like the one recently built in Shanghai."

I felt embarrassed because this was my first trip to Sunan after living in China for over eight months, although this area was always at the top of my travel list. (Since this trip with Mr. Harris and my brother in May 1994, however, I returned to Sunan seven times and I have traveled to many villages and towns in the area. All these visits have been great eye-openers for me.)

I agree with Mr. Harris that what has taken place in Sunan deserves to receive more international attention. The changes are impressive, not just because a few former peasants own BMWs and fancy villas with Jacuzzis—not even because the living standard of the majority of people in the area has significantly improved. These changes are important because they reflect three broad trends in today's China: the rapid development of the market economy (*shichanghua*), rural industrialization (*gongyehua*), and urbanization (*chengshihua*).

China's New Frontier of Economic Development

Since 1978, the gross domestic production in Sunan has increased by 19.6 percent yearly. This growth rate has not only exceeded that of other regions in China, but has also surpassed that of Japan, Taiwan, and South Korea during peak periods of their economic development.

In 1993, China's State Statistics Bureau ranked "100 supercounties [*baiqiangxian*]," in terms of social and economic strength, out of 2,100 counties in the entire country. This was the second time that the Chinese government conducted a comprehensive evaluation of the level of development in rural areas. The statistical norms included a 12-point index focusing on social, economic, educational, scientific, and technological achievements, including factors such as the increase of output value, living space per capita, medical care, expenditures on clothes, recreation, and other cultural activities. All 12 counties in Sunan were on the list of the 100 supercounties.

These 100 supercounties accounted for less than 7.4 percent of the population, but contributed 24 percent of China's rural output and 27 percent of rural taxes. Their production rate was 1.9 times higher than the national average.[4] Among the top ten counties, Sunan had seven. They were Wuxi (first), Jiangyin (second), Zhangjiagang (fourth), Changshu (sixth), Wuxian (seventh), Wujin (eighth), and Taicang (ninth). Wuxi's agricultural and industrial output value was 34.4 billion yuan ($3.95 billion) in 1992, four times that of 12 years ago. This output value has even exceeded that of an inland province such as Gansu or Qinghai.

Major economic indices comparing Sunan with Jiangsu Province and the national average in 1991 showed that Sunan was far ahead of other areas (see Table 5–1). The GNP per capita in Sunan was 3,978 yuan, while the Jiangsu average was 2,124 yuan and the national average was 1,706

TABLE 5-1

A Comparison of Major Economic Indexes of Sunan, the Whole Jiangsu Province, and the Nation (1991)

	GNP		National income		Industrial output value		Agricultural output value		Revenue	
	¥10000/ Sq km	¥/ Person	¥10000/ Sq km	¥/ Person	¥10000/ Sq km	¥/ Person	¥10000/ Sq km	¥/ Person	¥10000/ Sq km	¥/ Person
Suzhou	277	4178	246	3717	777	11694	69	1040	24	351
Wuxi	397	4406	340	3774	1165	12866	63	693	43	468
Changzhou	234	3136	204	2745	692	9258	64	850	28	360
Suzhou/Wuxi/Changzhou	298	3978	261	3481	859	11464	66	881	30	400
Average in Jiangsu	142	2124	122	1825	308	4618	57	849	–	–
Average in the Country	21	1706	17	1392	29	2437	9	704	4	309

Source: Wu Liangyong, "Jingji fada diqu chengshihua jingchengzhong jianzhu huanjing de baofu yu fazhan" (Environmental protection and urbanization in economically developed regions), *Chengshi guihua* (City planning), no. 5 (1994): 4.

yuan. If it is calculated by 10,000 yuan per square kilometer, the differ- ence between Sunan and the national average is even more striking.

In 1993, the GNP of Suzhou, Wuxi, and Changzhou grew 35 percent over the previous year, reaching 112 billion yuan, ahead of better-known Chinese success stories such as Guangzhou, Shanghai, and Beijing. The industrial and agricultural output value in Sunan was 400 billion yuan. The revenue was 9 billion yuan. Foreign trade was 122 billion yuan and export was $2.4 billion. Foreign investment in the region reached $6 bil- lion.[5]

"What has contributed to the economic miracle in Sunan? How has Sunan, a region with only 0.88 percent of China's population, in less than 16 years become an economic powerhouse that produces 16.8 percent of the output value of rural industries in the country?" I always asked these two questions when I interviewed people in Sunan.

Some people attribute Sunan's rapid economic development to its natu- ral resources, while others emphasize strong entrepreneurship and other human resources in the region. Some argue that Sunan's geographical proximity to Shanghai is the main reason for its success, and others be- lieve that local governments play a crucial role in the growth of Sunan. Although I think these explanations miss the most important explanation for the economic miracle of Sunan, they do provide some background on Sunan's development. A brief review of some of Sunan's characteristics is needed before we discuss the role of township and village enterprises (TVEs)—the driving force of the area's economic success.

Sunan: "Venice of the East"

With its fertile soil, mild climate, and abundant rainfall, Sunan is richly endowed by nature. Lake Taihu, the fourth-largest freshwater lake in the country, with a total area of 2,200 square kilometers and an average depth of two meters, is just outside Wuxi and Suzhou. The Yangtze River, the longest river in China, passes through Jiangsu and divides the province into Sunan and Subei (northern Jiangsu). Part of the south side of the Yangtze River in the territory of Jiangsu Province, including its capital, Nanjing, is called Suzhong (central Jiangsu). The Grand Canal, the long- est artificial waterway in the world, runs through each and every one of the three main cities in Sunan—Changzhou, Wuxi, and Suzhou.

Because of the advantages of water transportation and other natural resources, the towns in the Sunan area flourished as centers of rice mar- keting and ancient silk production over a thousand years ago. Suzhou, for example, with the completion of the Grand Canal in the Sui Dynasty (581–618), emerged as a center of shipping, silk production and trade, and grain storage.

Geographical features and natural resources also molded the characteristics of the people in the region—a diligent work ethic, a fondness for the arts and entertainment, a strong sense of entrepreneurship, and an inclination toward peace and tranquility.

The name of Wuxi means *tinless* in Chinese. The area used to have a tin mine, which was exhausted during the Han Dynasty (106 B.C.–A.D. 220). It was said that the locals were actually glad that no more tin could be found. A stone tablet dug out of the region was engraved, *"Where there is tin, there is fighting; where there is no tin, there is tranquility."* Indeed there was tranquility in the region for a long period after the Han Dynasty.[6]

Sunan was home to scholars, painters, poets, calligraphers, storytellers, musicians, architects, cloth designers, artisans, and, of course, merchants. When Marco Polo came to Suzhou along the Grand Canal in 1276, he was amazed by the beauty of the "Garden City, Venice of the East"— whitewashed housing, decorated roofs, cobbled roads, tree-lined avenues, stone bridges, and winding rivers. What impressed him most, however, were the people—talented and civilized.

Marco Polo mused that "if the inhabitants had turned their talents to the military arts, they would easily have overrun the whole province," if not the whole country. But they hadn't, because they were totally preoccupied with raising silkworms, manufacturing silk products, selling them in local markets, and exporting them to other regions.[7]

But in this century, as some China experts observed, Sunan, especially its main cities, "experienced the long sleep" and was often under the shadow of its neighbors. In the early decades of this century, foreign capitalists rushed to Shanghai and turned it into a booming port and industrial city. Meanwhile, Chinese Nationalists made Nanjing the capital— the center of China's political power. The Sunan region lagged behind.

During the Mao era, both light industry and agricultural production, on which the strength of Sunan lay, were restricted, as was the market economy. Although Sunan was always a relatively prosperous region of China, it didn't differ much from the rest of the country. Under the repressive political environment and restricted economic structure, the advantages of Sunan were lost, and the talents of its people were wasted.

Only after 1978, when China started its rural reform featuring the "household contract responsibility system," did Sunan begin to take the lead in agricultural modernization and the structural change in the Chinese economy. Under the household contract responsibility system, plots of collectively owned land were made available to peasants' households for a fixed period. Peasants were required to supply a share of production according to contracts, to pay agricultural taxes, and to contribute to collective service. At the same time, the household could dispose of the remaining output on the free market or sell it to the state at negotiated prices.

It seems as if history is dramatically accelerating in this small land, as if a geographical endowment such as oil had recently been found in Sunan, as if God's invisible hand were pushing only this land forward, or as if Confucius were suddenly waking from a long sleep.

"The reason behind Sunan's miracle is simple," Chen Xiwen, an expert on rural economy and the author of *China's Rural Reform*, said. "The rapid development of township and village enterprises [*xiangzhen qiye*] in Sunan has brought about all these achievements." Many people I interviewed shared his view.

"TVEs," a peasant-turned entrepreneur in Jiangyin said to me, "have remade Sunan."

TVEs: "A New Force Suddenly Coming to the Fore"

If one reads Chinese writings on township and village enterprises, one will often come cross the term *yijun tuqi*, which literally means "a new force suddenly coming to the fore." Deng Xiaoping, China's paramount leader, used this term to refer to TVEs when he was interviewed by foreign guests in the mid-1980s.

Chinese officials are not famous for their modesty. They are never willing to pass up a chance to give credit to themselves when they talk about China's economic growth. Nevertheless, they have to admit that the rapid development of TVEs has been as much of a surprise to them as it has been to the rest of the world. As an article in the *Economist* noted, Deng expected the creation of the household contract responsibility system to drive up farm incomes and output, but "had no inkling of the rural industrial revolution that would follow."[8]

TVEs emerged in the process of the structural transformation of the Chinese economy, from traditional to modern agriculture, from a subsistence into a market economy. The birth and growth of TVEs are spontaneous indeed. Rural industries are also called "grassroots industries" (*caogen gongye*). As some Chinese scholars have described them, TVEs are born in "the narrow space between traditional agriculture and modern industry."[9]

TVEs have several organizational forms based on different levels of ownership and management. They include township-run enterprises, village-run enterprises, team enterprises, and private enterprises. Most TVEs are rural collectives at the township and village level. Although the first two forms are collective and are supposed to be run by officials of local governments, many are actually private companies. It has been common for private enterprises to be registered under the name of a collective, or using a Chinese expression, to have a "red hat." This type of enterprise is called *guakao qiye*, a private firm under the name of a collective or cooperative.

A sample study of TVEs shows that a large number of private enterprises (over 50 percent) are registered as collective. In 1992, Dalian, for example, had registered 2,938 private enterprises, but over 5,000 additional businesses were believed to have a "red hat."[10] According to Kristen Parris, a researcher who did a case study of Wenzhou, a coastal city in Zhejiang province, "a collective name not only allowed these firms to avoid political risk and the stigma long associated with private business in China, it also gave them greater access to credit and resources and certain tax benefits."[11]

TVEs are engaged in various forms of business—industry, construction, transportation, commerce, agriculture, catering, service industries, and others. Most TVEs, however, are involved in manufacturing. In 1991, for example, rural manufacturing accounted for three-fourths of the total output value of all the nation's TVEs.[12]

TVEs mushroomed in China during the mid-1980s. Four main factors contributed to the arrival of the rural industrial revolution. First, peasants began to have surplus capital as a result of rural reform, especially the household contract responsibility system. Prior to the 1978 economic reform, personal savings in both urban and rural areas totaled 21 billion yuan. The savings per person in rural areas was only seven yuan. Only after the economic growth in the late 1970s and early 1980s did Chinese peasants have the means to invest money in nonagricultural production.

Second, the abolition of the People's Commune system in the early 1980s led to the end of the "iron bowl" in rural China. Millions of surplus rural laborers were liberated from agricultural jobs and allowed to work in the industrial and service sectors. They provided the great human capital for the rural industrial revolution.

Third, although the government did not establish any favorable policies to help TVEs, as it did for state-owned firms in the form of providing loans and subsidies, it did let TVEs flourish on their own. Private enterprises were also allowed to exist in the late 1980s.

Finally, commodity markets between urban and rural areas became extremely dynamic as economic reform accelerated in the 1980s. They provided great economic opportunities for the growth of TVEs.

China's rural industries, however, did not start with the Deng era. The origin of TVEs can be traced back to the late 1950s, when a great number of commune-run enterprises (*sheban qiye*) were established under the impact of the Great Leap Forward. But TVEs differ from the previous rural enterprises in three respects. First, the previous rural enterprises were under the control of the government; TVEs have more autonomy and many are privately owned. Second, before the reform, rural enterprises were largely autarkic because of the segregation between rural and urban economies; by contrast TVEs have close links with urban industries, and they cooperate with each other in capital, technology, labor, and management. The third and most important difference between TVEs and their predecessors is that TVEs get rid of the bondage of the planned economy; they are the product of the market economy.

TVEs also differ greatly from state-owned enterprises. In a recent issue of *Social Sciences in China*, Wang Haijun, a Chinese scholar, made a five-point summary and comparison of the salient features of TVEs and state-owned enterprises:

1. TVEs are market-oriented and seek to maximize profits. State-owned enterprises produce according to mandatory quotas or government guidelines.
2. TVEs have more autonomy than state-owned enterprises in decision making, development strategy, pricing, marketing, and personnel administration.
3. TVEs are responsible for their own losses, whereas many state enterprises receive subsidies to cover loss.
4. In TVEs, workers' incomes depend more heavily on the performance of the enterprises than is the case with state enterprises. The disparity in earnings between workers is also greater, which can lead to more efficient management and improved professional skills.
5. TVEs can hire and fire staff, and conditions of employment are flexible—this is not the case in state enterprises, where employment is strictly controlled.[13]

The most salient feature of TVEs, however, is their increasingly important role in the Chinese economy. In 1978, a total of 1.5 million nonstate industrial firms in the countryside employed 28 million people (9.3 percent of the total rural labor force). By 1992 over 21 million TVEs employed 112 million people (24.2 percent of the total rural labor).[14] This means that each town had about 150 TVEs. The output of these firms has been growing an average of nearly 30 percent per year for more than a decade.[15]

Although the state has done little to help TVEs, revenue contributed to the state by TVEs quickly increased, from 2.2 billion yuan in 1978 to 45.86 billion yuan in 1992. The tax paid by TVEs as a percentage of total state revenue increased from 2 percent in the late 1970s to 13 percent in the late 1980s.

In 1987, the output value of TVEs accounted for 52.4 percent of the total output value of national agriculture. This was a historic point in China's agriculture; for the first time more than half of the economic output of rural China came from nonagricultural production. In 1992, the output of TVEs accounted for 66.4 percent of total agricultural output.

Meanwhile, the percentage that rural industrial output contributed to the total industrial output also significantly increased, from 9.1 percent in 1978 to 36.8 percent in 1992. According to a Chinese official, industrial output value of TVEs was expected to exceed 50 percent of the national total by the mid-1990s. This means that half of China's industrial output would come from the rural areas.[16]

China's GNP has grown by an average of 9 percent since economic reforms started in 1978. The larger portion of the growth has been the result of the TVEs' contribution. A study conducted by the State Statistics Bureau showed that the industrial output of state-owned firms increased only 3.2 percent in 1989, compared to 22.8 percent for TVEs. Although the fixed assets per person of rural industries are far lower than those of the state-owned firms, the former have a much higher growth rate in total labor productivity than the latter (see Table 5–2).

Two recent books emphasize this dramatic shift. In *Dragon Wakes*, the authors observe that it took 31 years for China's total output to increase from 100 billion yuan in 1952 to 1 trillion yuan in 1983, but only 7, from 1984 to 1991, for the TVEs to achieve the same rate of growth.[17] Similarly, in *China Wakes*, Nicholas Kristof and Sheryl Wudunn (the *New York Times*' correspondents in Beijing from 1988 to 1993) also make some illuminating calculations based on an international comparison.[18] In a related article, they write:

> Britain was the first country to enjoy an industrial revolution, beginning in the late eighteenth century, and it took 58 years for per capita British gross

TABLE 5-2
A Comparison of the Total Labor Productivity between Rural Industrial
Enterprises and State-owned Industrial Enterprises (1987)

	Fixed Assets per Person (10,000 yuan)	Growth of Total Labor Productivity (%)	
		Total Growth	Annual Growth
State-owned Industrial Enterprises	1.88	49.5 %	5.15 %
Rural Industrial Enterprises	0.38	161.3 %	17.92 %

Source: Zhou Dongtao and Cui Quanhong, *Shizi lukou shangde zhongguo* (China at the crossroads) (Lanzhou: Lanzhou University Press, 1992), 367.

domestic product to double. The American industrial revolution was a bit faster, with per capita output doubling in *47* years from 1839. Beginning in 1885, Japan doubled its per capita gross domestic product in *34* years. . . . China is roaring along with its own industrial revolution, doubling its per capita output every *10* years.[19]

As a result of the household contract responsibility system and the development of TVEs, a total of 170 million Chinese peasants have risen from absolute poverty since 1978.

"China's rural industrial revolution," noted a World Bank official in Beijing, "has brought about the greatest improvement in human welfare anywhere at any time."

Sunan: "Kingdom of Township and Village Enterprises"

The rural industrial revolution is reshaping China's landscape, making a strong impact on all aspects of the Chinese society. Nowhere, however, is this revolution having a greater effect than in Sunan.

Sunan is widely recognized in China as the "Kingdom of Township and Village Enterprises" (*xiangzhen qiye de wangguo*), and it well deserves the title. Within 12 years the output of TVEs there increased twenty-five-fold, from 3.77 billion yuan in 1978 to 98.55 billion yuan in 1991. By the end of 1993, Jiangsu Province had 386 rural industrial enterprises that each produced over 100 million yuan in output value. Among them, 346 are located in Sunan. Their combined profits last year were 66.6

billion yuan. On average, each enterprise exported 31.3 million yuan worth of products.[20]

Although Sunan has only 0.88 percent of China's population, it produces 16.8 percent of the output value of rural industries in the country.[21] The output of rural industries in Sunan has recently accounted for over 70 percent of the region's total. In Zhangjiagang county, for example, the percentage of TVEs in the total output value was as high as 81.8 percent in 1991. In 1992, the county's GNP increased 87 percent over the previous year.[22]

The huge rural area of the Sunan region has rapidly been industrialized since the early 1980s. At present agriculture accounts for only 8 percent of the region's total combined industrial and agricultural output, and industry accounts for 92 percent.[23] Many industrial towns have emerged in the area, blurring the distinction between rural and urban areas.

One of Sunan's great achievements over the past decade is that it has absorbed a large number of surplus rural laborers, from both Sunan and elsewhere, into its rural industries. In 1986 alone, TVEs in Sunan successfully transformed 3,360,000 agricultural workers, 65 percent of the total

The living standard of people in Sunan has greatly improved since the economic reform started in 1978. A fruit peddler in Bacheng, a small town in Kunshan, wears a Western suit. He does not look like the conventional image of a street peddler in rural China at all.

labor force in the region, to nonagricultural employees.[24] According to local officials, there are no surplus rural laborers in Sunan. On the contrary, Sunan has absorbed over 2 million surplus rural laborers from other areas.[25] This number does not even include the temporary workers hired without work permits or the "floating population."[26]

As *China Daily* reported, in some economically advanced market towns in Sunan, the number of nonlocal laborers has surpassed the number of local residents employed.[27] In Shengze, a town famous for silk production in Wujiang county, two-thirds of the workers in the silk and cotton mills are from other regions. According to a study, the "floating population" of Luoshe, a town in Wuxi County, is 6,000. About 88 percent of these migrants are engaged in industrial and construction work.[28] In the whole of Wuxi County, migrant laborers account for 38 percent of the total labor force.[29]

The rapid development of TVEs has reduced the pressure of surplus rural laborers—one of the most perplexing problems in the country. The experience of Sunan in absorbing these workers from other areas is particularly remarkable, because Sunan itself is one of the most populous regions in China. Some scholars call Sunan's TVEs the "sponges of surplus rural labor."

The growth of rural industries in Sunan has actually helped agricultural development in the region. In the late 1980s, for example, TVEs in Sunan provided over 4 billion yuan to support local agriculture, five times the amount of money received from the state.[30] Most of the farmers in the region are equipped with advanced machinery. Because of the support from rural industries, grain production has increased during recent years, although the number of laborers who work on farms has greatly decreased. It was reported that one-half of the farming output has resulted from the use of more advanced machinery, application of chemical fertilizer, more efficient use of land, and the introduction of scientific techniques.[31]

Problems and Prospects of TVEs in Sunan

Make no mistake, the rapid development of TVEs in Sunan is not happening without costs and problems. One of the most serious problems, both in Sunan and the entire country, is that TVEs are scattered randomly here and there in the countryside. As a result, not only have their construction and production costs increased, but also precious arable land and other resources are wasted. According to the survey of the total 21 million

TVEs in the country during 1992, only 1 percent were located in county seats (*xiancheng*), 7 percent were in towns, and an overwhelming majority (92 percent) were scattered throughout the countryside.[32]

There were, for example, 15,000 TVEs in the rural area of Shanghai, but they were spread over 4,000 sites. This dispersion has made the infrastructure (e.g., water and electric supply, transportation and road construction, and disposal of waste) more difficult to install and less efficient.[33] In Wuxi County, the groundwater has not only been used excessively, but has also become polluted because of the lack of planning in the development of TVEs.[34]

The overall productivity of TVEs is comparatively low at present; their technology is old and outdated, their equipment crude and backward. Some of the advantages that TVEs used to have may become disadvantages in the future. The factors that influenced the rapid development of TVEs in the 1980s have now changed, and TVEs face some new challenges. In the early 1980s, for instance, the small scale of TVEs helped these firms to respond quickly to the demands of the market and compete better with overburdened large enterprises. But now, as some Chinese scholars observe, their small scale often leads to "excessively high production cost and lack of specialization and competitiveness."[35]

Furthermore, rural industries in most areas duplicate one another's efforts, which has led to two problems. One is a shortage of raw materials, and the other is an increasing economic imbalance. In the late 1980s, for example, a large number of TVEs in Sunan were cotton mills, but cotton production in the region could meet only two-thirds of their needs.[36] The duplication of industries has also caused excessive competition for local markets.

Another common problem of TVEs in Sunan is the lack of capital. Almost all the TVE officials that I met in Sunan told me that their firms faced shortages of capital as they pursued further economic development. In Changzhou, for example, 40 percent of construction projects could not continue because of the unavailability of capital.[37]

These problems are significant. The solutions, however, rely on how TVEs themselves adjust to the new socioeconomic environment. Yang Xiaotang, Party secretary of Suzhou, told journalists that Sunan will have a "new historical take-off by adopting three strategies: incorporation (*jituanhua*), specialization (*zhuanyehua*), and internationalization (*guojihua*)."[38] The problems arose, he said, because Sunan's previous development was largely limited to its own area, the scale of TVEs was usually too small, and their profits were seldom used to invest in other regions or countries. According to Yang, Sunan's new strategies will change all these conditions.

Sunan seems ready for these new strategies. In recent years, it has become common for smaller TVEs to form corporate groups through mergers, leasing arrangements, sales, or other means. TVEs in the region have lately paid more attention to the development of new products and specialization. In Wuxi, for instance, factories now produce two new products every day, on average. From 1991 to 1993, the city invested 12.7 billion yuan in research and development and introduced 1,381 technology-intensive projects. About 80 percent of county-level enterprises have completed their technological renovation. Technological innovation now accounts for 42 percent of the economic growth.[39]

Meanwhile, about 50,000 TVEs in Sunan have established cooperative relationships of various kinds with over 1,000 research institutions, universities, and colleges in the country. More than 10,000 scientists and technicians have settled in the Sunan region to help with economic expansion. So far, Sunan has set up over 800 scientific research institutions employing 200,000 scientists and technicians.[40]

In recent years, the rural industry of Sunan has continued to expand and more foreign capital has flowed in.[41] In 1992 alone, Suzhou approved 2,162 firms with foreign investment and joint ventures, four times the total number in previous years. In 1993, TVEs in Jiangsu Province established 140 firms overseas, twice the previous years' total.[42] In the first 10 months of 1994, 400 more TVEs placed branches overseas.[43]

All these efforts to promote TVEs in the new economic environment suggest that the rapid growth of Sunan will likely continue. Many Sunan rural entrepreneurs told me that the achievements there in the past decade are just the beginning.

"The prosperity in Sunan may mean little to some foreign visitors from advanced countries," noted Mr. Guo Jilie, a middle-aged rural entrepreneur, "because there is still a big gap between the economic condition of Sunan and that of advanced countries like the United States and Japan. But the achievements that TVEs have made are very important for us, I mean, peasants-turned-industrialists. As you know, true prosperity is the result of well-placed confidence in ourselves.

"We, the people in Sunan, know that our rural enterprises are faced with some problems and new challenges for further development," Mr. Guo said. "Sunan's TVEs, like those elsewhere, were born in hardship. Neither God nor the government gave us much help. In 1991 Sunan experienced the largest flood in this century, but we survived. We never had enough capital resources for the development of our enterprises, but we managed and even flourished. We will accept these new challenges and will promote TVEs' development on a larger scale."

"You have confidence that if you have done a little thing well, you can do a bigger thing well, too," I commented, quoting a sentiment expressed in the West.

"Yes, precisely," Mr. Guo replied.

6

Who Created China's
Economic Miracle?

Meet Chen Jinhai, Peasant-Turned-Industrialist

In his study of the American industrial revolution, sociologist Daniel Bell raised one of the most interesting questions in contemporary American history: "Who created America's economic miracle?" His answer, which surprised and even disappointed many, was that people who contributed to the socioeconomic development of the United States in the nineteenth and early twentieth centuries were usually from the poor, less educated, and "relatively uncivilized" part of the American society.

Like the United States in the nineteenth century, China now has been undergoing its own industrial revolution. Does the conclusion that Daniel Bell made in his study of the American industrial revolution also apply to today's China? Who has created the economic miracle in post-Mao China? Who are the real contributors to the ongoing Chinese industrial revolution? These are certainly not easy questions. They are no less controversial than the long-standing questions in international affairs such as "who ended the Cold War?" Different people can reach completely different conclusions.

If one asks Deng Xiaoping's children (and, unfortunately, many Western China experts as well), it is their father who created socioeconomic development in China since 1978, the year in which Deng came to power. Their cliché is "Without Deng, without China's economic reform"—that's why they use the term "Deng's Revolution" to refer to the reform era. While no one would deny that Deng has courageously changed Mao's course for the country, I often wonder whether Deng may have received more credit than he deserves. A few fundamental changes in China's economic structure are unintentional. Rapid development of township and village enterprises, as discussed in the previous chapter, was neither initiated nor anticipated by Deng.

If one asks the technocrats who now dominate China's central and provincial leadership, it was their scientific and technical expertise and managerial skills that brought about all the progress in the reform era. They argue that it is not accidental that the emergence of technocratic elites in China's leadership parallels the rapid technological development and economic boom in the country. Correlation, however, is not causation. Technocrats' technical expertise does not necessarily lead to the economic well-being of the population, but instead, may even tire the people and drain the treasury of the country. The ongoing Three Gorges Dam project, which will be discussed in chapter 10, is a case in point. Because of their elitist mentality, technocrats tend to be out of touch with China's reality.

Who, then, really created China's economic miracle? While acknowledging that there can be more than one contributing social group, I believe that peasants-turned-industrialists have played a vital role in China's economic boom. Analogous to Bell's findings in the United States, these Chinese peasants-turned-industrialists were usually from the poor, less educated, and unprivileged part of society. They have contributed to China's rural industrial revolution—one of the greatest industrial revolutions in human history.

Never in history have so many families made so much money in a single generation as have peasants-turned-industrialists on the coast of China. Some entrepreneurs have made a fortune for themselves while simultaneously contributing to the economic growth of the country. During my two-year stay in China, I met several dozen rich rural industrialists, visited their homes, and listened to their life stories. Often, I felt I was hearing the story of a Chinese Carnegie or Rockefeller—I was always impressed by both the hardship that they had experienced and the successes they achieved. Chen Jinhai, a peasant-turned-industrialist in Wujiang County, Suzhou, is one of the remarkable people I met.

The very first time I met Chen Jinhai was in 1984. I saw him in Wujiang where both my sister and her husband were doctors in the county hospital. Chen, who was already a factory director then, happened to be visiting my sister's apartment. He brought several crabs, the most treasured food in the area, to my brother-in-law as a token of appreciation for the successful surgery that he had performed on Chen's mother.

Because my brother-in-law refused to accept the crabs, Chen explained that he did not buy them, but caught the crabs himself in the river nearby. I remembered that Chen said that when he was a boy, his family used to make a living by catching crabs. By the age of six, he had already started helping his parents beginning at four o'clock every morning during the fishing season. He of course was no longer associated with the fishing business since he had become a factory director. But occasionally, as he had that day, Chen still got up very early to catch crabs for enjoyment. I forget what else he said during that meeting, but the picture of a six-year-old who got up at four o'clock every morning to go fishing moved me then, and I have remembered it ever since.

The second time I saw him was in 1990, when I made my first return trip to China after studying in the United States for five years. I revisited my sister and her husband in Wujiang. They hosted a dinner party for me at the Songlin Restaurant, the best in the county town. Chen Jinhai was among the guests they invited. He was dressed in an expensive Western suit.

My sister told me that Chen was doing very well in his business and had become one of the richest entrepreneurs in the town. At that time, I had a stereotypical view of rural entrepreneurs. These industrialists, I thought, usually had a couple of workshops, hiring six to seven employees in each. They were considered rich because they could smoke foreign brands of cigarettes, wear Hong Kong–made tee shirts, and ride red motorcycles.

Chen and other guests at the dinner did not speak much. They seemed to be more interested in hearing me talk about America—about elegant department stores in Manhattan and homeless people in New York subways; the freedom of the American press, and the notoriously endless soap operas; the increasing resale value of Japanese cars in the American market, and declining "family values" in American society. Chen invited me to visit his house, but I stayed in Wujiang for only a day during that trip. I told him that I would visit him next time.

"Next time," however, came five years later, in 1995. As a fellow of the Institute of Current World Affairs writing about the rise of the entrepreneurial class on the coast of China, I was really eager to revisit Wujiang and to see Chen again. Chen's house is located in Songlin town, Wujiang County, 16 miles from Suzhou City. Wujiang County, with 23 towns in its jurisdiction and a total population of 772,000, is situated in the middle of the Yangtze Delta, neighboring Shanghai to the east, Hangzhou to the south, Lake Taihu to the west, and Suzhou to the north. The ancient Grand Canal runs through its territory from north to south.

As a minibus took me around the town, I found Songlin town had changed remarkably during the previous five years and was completely unrecognizable. The Songlin Restaurant, at which my sister and her husband had hosted dinner for me and that was then considered the best in town, had become a canteen-like place for casual meals. Many newer, elegant restaurants had been established. The newly built Wujiang Hotel, with its combination of modern architecture and traditional gardens, was one of the most glamorous hotels that I have ever seen, both in China and elsewhere.

In the lobby of the Wujiang Hotel was a special map that showed the location of Wujiang County. A statement on the top of the map attracted people's attention: "In heaven there is paradise, down below there are Suzhou and Hangzhou, between is Wujiang."

"Exaggeration?! Of course," said Xu Jinrong, head of the public administration department in Wujiang. "Many people in the world also call the United States paradise, but the United States has poor and homeless people. Our county can proudly claim that it doesn't have any homeless people.

"The living standard of people in the county," Xu continued, "has indeed improved dramatically in the past few years. In 1993, for example, the GNP in the county surpassed 6 billion yuan, total industrial and agricultural output was 26.7 billion yuan, the revenue was 310 million yuan—an increase of 48 percent, 52 percent, and 43 percent, respectively, compared to the previous year."

Mr. Wang, head of the economic development division in Wujiang, explained that the silk industry was the key traditional industry in the county. The output of silk accounts for one-sixth of all silk produced in the nation and has been the main base for export production. Along with the silk industry, other textiles, light industry, the chemical industry, medical and health services, building materials, machinery, and electronics industries also developed rapidly. In 1993, Wujiang had 900 foreign-owned enterprises and joint ventures. The total foreign investment was $1.3 billion.

"As a result of the economic boom in the county," Mr. Xu added, "some entrepreneurs have become incredibly rich by any standard."

Not until I visited Chen Jinhai's house did I realize what Xu meant by "incredibly rich by any standard." I had lived in the United States for eight years and traveled to many developed countries—Australia, Japan, Singapore, and Denmark. I had visited a few wealthy families in these countries, but I had never been in a house with so many rooms and so many features for entertainment as Chen's mansion, with the exception of the White House in Washington, D.C.

Chen's mansion was built in 1987. It had cost 3 million yuan, about $1 million at the exchange rate then. Chen told me that he recently spent another million yuan for renovations. The main part of the house has a total of 1,300 square meters. The entrance that leads to Chen's mansion is nothing extraordinary. Actually, one passes along a small lane with two houses on each side, including a house belonging to Chen's brother. The outside wall of this three-story mansion is decorated with light-blue glazed tile. The front yard of the mansion is small, but thoughtfully designed with small plants and flowers in every corner.

The first floor has three parts. In the middle are a living room, a tea room, a study, and a few guest rooms. On the east side is a huge meeting room with a seven-meter table that can seat 22 people.

"The Chinese Communist Party can have its Politburo meeting here," my brother-in-law said. China's Politburo happened to have 22 members at that time.

"They can also bring their personal secretaries with them if I add another circle of seats in the meeting room," Chen responded.

On the west side are three dining rooms. Xiao Wang, Chen's wife, explained to me that one is for banquets, one for Chinese meals, and one for Western meals. I noticed that the round dining table in the banquet room could accommodate over 20 people. I had never before seen such a gigantic round table.

The Western dining room is not very Western, except that it has a long table and some Middle Eastern–style lights.

"Do you often have Western-style meals in this Western-style dining room?" I asked Xiao Wang.

"Never," she smiled, "but my husband says that we might have American business partners in the future. We want to impress them by offering them Western food."

"Can you or your husband cook Western dishes?" I asked.

"Yes," Xiao Wang answered. "I know how to cook Kentucky Fried Chicken."

I tried not to burst out laughing but failed. The idea that American business people who traveled all the way to China would be impressed by having KFC with a Chinese family made me laugh.

"We can hire chefs from Suzhou or Shanghai to cook Western food if necessary," Chen explained.

"They have money, and they certainly can do that," my brother-in-law said to me.

Chen in the meeting room of his mansion. I visited many wealthy families in Western countries, but I have never been in a house with so many rooms and so many entertainment features as Chen's mansion. For instance, there are so many bedrooms in Chen's mansion that Mrs. Chen has put a number on every door—201, 202, 203, 204, and so on. "The house also has 30 televisions. Some of them are in the bathrooms." Chen told me proudly.

"Sure, they can even hire chefs from Western countries," I replied.

The second floor mainly consists of bedrooms, although a large television room that can accommodate over 60 people and a small mahjong room are also located on this floor. There are so many bedrooms that there are numbers on every door—201, 202, 203, 204, and so on.

I asked Chen how many rooms the house had. He said that he did not know. "I only know that I bought a total of 14 large, vertical Japanese air-conditioners for the house," Chen told me proudly. "The house also has 30 televisions. Some of them are in the bathrooms."

"A bathroom with a television, what a postmodern idea!" I said to my brother-in-law.

The master bedroom is decorated in a traditional style with a huge redwood bed. The top of the bed is carved with images of dragons and phoenixes, symbolizing the everlasting harmony between husband and wife. Mrs. Chen told me that they seldom sleep in this bed, because her husband is often away on business trips, and she does not like to sleep by herself in this gigantic bed.

Not surprisingly, the bathroom of the master suite has a Jacuzzi.

"It cost $10,000," Chen told me.

"Do you take a bath in this Jacuzzi every day?" I was just curious.

"To tell you the truth," Chen replied, " I have never taken a bath in this peculiar tub. But many of my guests have bathed here, and they seem to enjoy it."

I visited Chen's house a total of four times, the first time by myself, the second with Peter Martin, the executive director of the Institute of Current World Affairs, the third time with a few British friends, and the fourth time with a group of American sinologists. Visitors are always amazed that the house has so many guest rooms.

Andrew Browne, Reuters's chief correspondent in Shanghai, asked Chen why he needed so many guest rooms in the house.

"Too many guest rooms? No, actually, I feel that this house does not have enough rooms to accommodate my guests. I am going to build another bigger house in town."

"An even bigger house?" both Browne and I asked.

"Yes," Chen answered. "I have already leased the land for building. It will be completed in a year. You are welcome to visit when it is done."

"Are these guests your friends, or your business customers?" I asked.

"My business customers are also my friends," Chen replied. "My business customers are usually from Shanghai, Nanjing, Beijing, Tianjin, and Guangzhou. They travel all the way to Wujiang to make a deal with me. I should treat them as friends, shouldn't I?"

"You are a shrewd businessman," Browne commented semiseriously. "You first let them get completely relaxed in the Jacuzzi and then you ask them to sign a contract with you."

Chen smiled, but did not say anything.

The most glamorous part of the mansion is on the third floor. It consists of a large ballroom with a complete set of up-to-date stereo equipment. The ballroom has a huge screen with seven television monitors, which can show eight karaoke CDs simultaneously. A total of 80 seats are available around the dance floor. The bar serves cocktails, X.O. Cognac, and foreign wines. Mrs. Chen told me that everything in the ballroom is foreign-made—audio equipment, television sets, lights, wine glasses, even the napkins.

Chen told me that he often entertains local officials here. I tried to imagine how Chen, local officials, and his business customers enjoy "Western culture with Chinese characteristics." Like many other private entrepreneurs in the country, Chen obviously seeks to emulate the lifestyles of the rich and famous in Taiwan and Hong Kong, if not the West.

I had lunch in Chen's house twice (both meals were served in his Chinese-style dining room). Both times Chen also invited several other guests, including Shi Songsheng, a retired engineer, and Mr. Xia, an official in charge of bank loans at a local bank. Shi, in his mid-seventies, could speak very good English. He had been chief engineer in China's Ministry of Material Industry and a professor in an engineering school before his retirement. Shi visited many Western countries, including two trips to the United States. He started to work for Chen after he retired from his post in the ministry.

"Because of Engineer Shi's expertise," Chen told me, "our factory's products are superior to our competitors'."

"Because of your friendship with Banker Xia," I teased Chen, "you are able to obtain many loans from the local bank?"

"How do you know that?" Chen said. Undoubtedly, Chen has a lot of friends who are very helpful to him.

"Mr. Chen is a very kind and generous man," Banker Xia said to the people at the table. Everyone agreed with him.

How could one not agree with him, I wondered, as the hosts served the guests river crab, eel, turtle, snake, shark's fin, and many other dishes? Any one of these dishes costs the equivalent of the monthly salary of an ordinary worker in China. A river crab costs about 200 yuan in a restaurant in Shanghai, but there were at least 30 crabs served at Chen's lunch party.

"When I came to Wujiang last time, you brought my brother-in-law a few crabs that you caught. Did you catch all these crabs yourself at dawn today?" I asked jokingly.

"Are you teasing me, Dr. Li?" Chen responded. "It would be considered extremely lucky nowadays if one person could catch one or two adult crabs each day. I no longer go catching crabs. I ordered these crabs from the local market."

During the lunch, I noticed that Chen himself did not eat crab at all. When I asked him to have one, he said that he never eats crabs.

"You have a marvelous redwood bed, but you have seldom slept in it; you have a Jacuzzi, but you have never taken a bath in it; now you are telling me that you don't eat crabs though you helped your parents catch crabs at the age of six. Can you tell me why?" I asked.

"I am not accustomed to these nice things, Dr. Li." Chen seemed somewhat embarrassed. "But I am happy to entertain my guests in this way."

Seeing I was still puzzled, Chen said, "You probably don't know my family background."

"No, will you tell me more about your life?" I told Chen that I would like to write a story about him and introduce a self-made Chinese entrepreneur to Western readers.

After lunch, Chen and I retreated to one of his guest rooms. He started to tell me his family background, his previous experience, and indeed, his struggle for success.

Chen was born to a poor peasant family in Pengdong village, one of the poorest villages in Wujiang, in 1949. When he was a young boy, his father was a landless farmer. Therefore, his father built dykes to "make" land from marshes. His mother, a migrant from northern Jiangsu, planted rice on the land, which had a very low yield. So the family had to make a living by fishing and catching crabs. His parents had five children, three sons and two daughters. Chen Jinhai was the eldest child in the family.

The family lived in a straw shed (*caopeng*) for over twenty years after 1949. They planted rice, but could not afford to eat rice themselves; they caught crabs and fish, but always sold all of their catch to the state or in the market. For many years, the family ate rice chaff (*daokang*) mixed with grasses.

For the Spring Festival, the most important holiday in China, they would have a meal of pork and rice, though the whole family could afford only two pounds of pork. Chen Jinhai would have a new jacket and pants made by his mother, because he was the eldest. His brothers and sisters, however, did not have this privilege. Instead they would "inherit" the clothing that was too small for Jinhai or his or her immediate elder brother or sister.

One of the most memorable occasions for Chen, as he told me, was the annual village banquet for the Spring Festival. On that occasion the village administration would order a couple of pigs killed in the People's Commune to celebrate the Chinese lunar new year. But the village government could not invite all the villagers to come to the banquet, because it would be too costly. Instead, they asked each household in the village to send one representative to this event. Each family usually selected the strongest adult with the "biggest stomach" to fully enjoy the pig banquet.

At sixteen, Chen Jinhai was selected by his family to attend the "pig banquet." Although his father told him not to eat beyond his capacity, Chen still overate.

"I was so hungry," Chen said to me, "I ate almost an entire pig leg at the banquet and then was sick for several weeks."

I have heard similar stories in China's rural areas. Some farmers even died from overeating at the Spring Festival banquet. What struck me, as

Chen told me the story, was that poverty and hunger were a part of life for Chen and his family as recently as a few decades ago. Their living standard has changed dramatically within one generation.

Chen started to work full-time on the farm at the age of 15. He quit school after attending junior high for two years. At 20, Chen married a peasant in the same village who was a year older than he. Both worked on the farm, but they earned only a total of 100 yuan annually.

After working on the farm for about 10 years, Chen realized that farming could not improve his life. Only industrial work, he thought, would rid him of poverty. He wanted to be a factory worker in a town or city. The head of the agricultural team in the village, however, was not supportive. In the view of the village leader, it was outrageous that a farmer did not want to do farm work. The leader told Chen that if he left farm work, he would no longer receive any money or the grain ration from the village.

To raise money to live in a city, Chen decided to sell all the pigs that he and his wife privately raised and all their furniture, including a bed, a table, and a few chairs. In 1973, at the age of 24, Chen left the farmland and went to Suzhou to be an apprentice in a fiberglass factory. He was told that fiberglass was greatly needed for construction in both urban and rural areas. During the two years that he was in Suzhou, Chen stayed in a public bathhouse at night because he could not afford to live in a hotel or to rent a room. He usually spent 0.2 yuan (six cents) for food per day.

During these two years in Suzhou, Chen learned the technical skills and procedures for making fiber-reinforced plastics (FRP, or fiberglass, the term commonly used). In 1975, Chen heard that Hujiang Chemical Factory in Shanghai wanted to hire contract workers in fiberglass production. A contract worker could earn 36 yuan ($12) a month. When he went to the factory for an interview, the interviewers were impressed by his knowledge of fiberglass production. But Chen was not hired. They told Chen the reason: he had not graduated from junior high school. Every young worker in this Shanghai factory needed to have a junior high school diploma.

Chen was disappointed. But he thought that if he could not work in a fiberglass factory in the city, he could try to help the village or town government establish a small factory in the countryside. Chen believed that the living standard of peasants could not be greatly improved unless rural industries were developed. Most local officials, however, did not agree with him at that time.

Eventually, Chen persuaded officials in a village located far from his home village to establish a fiberglass workshop. Chen was appointed director of the workshop. In the first year, the workshop had profits of

20,000 yuan. But someone in the village wrote to the administration of the People's Commune, reporting that Chen was a man who "ignored his proper occupation" and was engaged in dishonest work. The People's Commune sent an investigative team to the workshop, and Chen was held in custody for weeks.

The investigative team did not find any improper activities on Chen's part. Instead, they found that Chen was indeed a capable man who created jobs and brought wealth to the village. When Chen was released from custody, officials of his home village asked Chen to come back to establish a fiberglass workshop. The officials gave him 2,000 yuan capital for start-up costs. An official told Chen that the village government did not have high expectations; they hoped only that Chen could make 3,000 yuan every year. Village officials could use these 3,000 yuan for their salaries, instead of depending on the income from the agricultural work of the farmers in the village.[1]

When the workshop was first established in 1976, there were only four workers, including Chen himself. Their capital was no more than the above-mentioned 2,000 yuan, their workplace two small rooms. Chen, however, believed that the workshop had a bright future because fiberglass, as a new construction material, had great potential in China's market. Chen traveled to Shanghai, Suzhou, and Nanjing to borrow money and seek customers. At that time, his monthly salary was 50 yuan. He always had a box of foreign-made cigarettes in his pocket, not for himself, but for his business contacts. He himself smoked cheap domestic cigarettes.

Because of his efforts, business at the workshop grew very well. A year later Chen expanded the workshop into a factory, Wujiang Air-Conditioning Equipment and Materials Factory, and several dozen workers were hired. Meanwhile, the factory became a firm in the contract-system (*chengbao qiye*), which meant that Chen needed to give the village government only about 20,000 yuan annually, and he could keep the rest for the enterprise's future development or for himself.

As a director of a small village-run enterprise, Chen realized that this factory needed to produce first-rate products to survive and compete in the market. Beginning in the early 1980s, he established business relations with many institutions in Shanghai and Nanjing doing research on building industries. He invited scientists and engineers to be consultants of the factory and paid them well.

The main products of the factory, fiberglass-reinforced inorganic composites, were widely used in air-conditioning systems. Chen signed a number of major contracts, including the establishment of an air-conditioning system in the Shanghai subway, the Nanjing International Airport, and the factory buildings under the administration of the Bureau of the Shanghai Textile Industry. Each of these projects brought Chen several million yuan in profits.

Chen's Wujiang Air-Conditioning Equipment and Materials Factory has now become Wujiang Fiberglass Group, Inc., in which Chen serves as both general manager and chair of the board of trustees. The group has seven factories, employing over 350 employees. Chen's brothers, sister-in-law, and brother-in-law have been appointed directors of these factories. The group has continued to be a firm in the contract-system—Chen gives the local government a fixed amount of money every year according to the contract, and he can keep the rest for his firm or for himself.

Chen's Wujiang Fiberglass Group, Inc., has a total of 15 million yuan in registered capital. The annual output value of the group is 40 million yuan. A new 6,000-square-meter workshop with modern equipment and a 2,000-square-meter office building are under construction. Meanwhile, Chen has established joint ventures with Shanghai and Nanjing companies. The products made in his factories are now exported to Japan and Southeast Asian countries.

All these developments have had a strong impact on his personal life. A former poor peasant has now become a rich industrial entrepreneur. Chen and his family have left the village and settled permanently in the county town. A few years ago Chen divorced his first wife (a friend of his told me that Chen gave his ex-wife 50,000 yuan as her compensation). He married Xiao Wang, who is from northern Jiangsu and 16 years younger than Chen.

"Twenty years ago, I was looked down upon by village officials," Chen said to me when I asked him how he felt about changes in his economic condition and social status.

"Village officials used to consider me a man with no occupation, no socialist consciousness, no concern with collective development in the village," Chen explained. "But look at me now. I have contributed more to local collective development than anyone else in the village. I have not only created several hundred jobs in the town and brought several million yuan revenue to the local government, but have also built four bridges and four miles of flood-free road around the village. Several years ago, local Communist officials wanted to recruit me into the Communist Party. But I told them that I have no interest in politics. What Chinese farmers are really interested in is economic prosperity.

"Over 10 years ago," Chen continued, "I gave a total of 40,000 yuan to all of the farmers in our village as an annual bonus. In 1989, my factory gave 550,000 to help neighboring villages get rid of poverty. Recently, I donated 100,000 yuan for commercial development in the town and 30,000 yuan for construction of Number 318 National Expressway. In addition, several times I have donated money to elementary schools and clinics in Wujiang County.

"I don't mean that I have brought all the changes to the village and the town in which my factories are located," Chen said to me. "But I have certainly contributed to the prosperity of my native land."

Seeing I did not comment, Chen asked, "Am I too arrogant? I am not an educated man. I don't know how to say things properly. Do you agree with what I have just said?"

"Yes, I do agree with you," I replied. "Actually, I thought that you have also contributed to the economic development of urban areas such as Shanghai."

Chen's story is by no means unique. Former poor peasants with little education constitute a significant portion of China's emerging entrepreneur class. According to a 1992 comprehensive survey of 1,440 private entrepreneurs conducted by China's Academy of Social Science, 53.5 percent of entrepreneurs in rural areas were former peasants (see Table 6–1).

TABLE 6-1
Previous Occupation and Father's Occupation of
China's Private Entrepreneurs (%)

Occupation	Previous Occupation	Family Background (Father's Occupation)
Peasant	53.5	68.9
Cadre (officials)	17.0	7.9
Industrial Worker	11.6	7.9
Technical Personnel	4.1	3.5
Peddler & Small Business People	6.1	–
Commercial Worker	2.7	6.0
Soldier	0.7	–
Others	4.1	5.8
Total	100	100

Source: Lu Xueyi and others, "Woguo siyou qiye de jingying zhuangkuang yu siyou qi-yezhu de qunti tezheng" (Operational conditions of private enterprises in China and the group characteristics of private entrepreneurs), *Zhongguo shehui kexue* (Social sciences in China), no. 4 (1994): 70.

A majority of entrepreneurs come from peasant-family backgrounds. Entrepreneurs whose father's occupation was that of peasant account for 68.9 percent. Almost half of them (47 percent) received no education beyond junior high school. Approximately 10 percent of the entrepreneurs went only to elementary school (see Table 6–2).

A number of factors—the pressure to pursue a nonagricultural career, market opportunities, the availability of cheap laborers in rural areas, structural changes in the Chinese economy, and entrepreneurship—all contribute to the success of peasants-turned-industrialists like Chen Jinhai. They already form a distinct social stratum in today's China. The emergence of this class reflects the growing social mobility in the country.

One may reasonably argue that the rise of private entrepreneurs has also led to increasing disparity and social tension in Chinese society. Government officials, particularly at the grassroots level, have ambivalent attitudes towards private entrepreneurs. On one hand, they need entrepreneurs to enliven the local economy and bring jobs and prosperity to the region (and to the officials themselves as well). In recent years, about 5,400 private entrepreneurs were selected to be deputies of the People's Congress, and 8,600 were appointed to be members of the political consultant committee, both above the county level.[2] Also, eight deputies and 23 committee members at the national level are entrepreneurs.

TABLE 6-2
Educational Background of China's Private Entrepreneurs

Educational Level	Percentage
Illiterate	1.0
Elementary School	9.9
Junior High School	36.1
Senior High School/Technical School	35.9
Two-Year College	11.7
College	4.7
Post-Graduate	0.6
Total	100

Source: Lu Xueyi and others, "Woguo," 70.

On the other hand, government officials feel their political power and social status are threatened by private entrepreneurs. They cannot accept the reality that some of these businessmen in their villages, towns, or counties earn 10 times or even a hundred times more than they do. Cases of official discrimination against private entrepreneurs are a widespread phenomenon in the country.[3]

While entrepreneurs like Chen Jinhai accumulate their wealth at a rapid pace, the social resentment against them has also become acute. According to a survey recently conducted by the Department of Sociology in People's University, most people perceive that China's private entrepreneurs have a negative, rather than a positive role, in society. Respondents tended to use the Chinese traditional concept "heartless rich" (*weifu buren*) to refer to the newly rich class. In an evaluation of the most important groups contributing to the socioeconomic development of the country, the rich private entrepreneurs were ranked second from the bottom. Only 20 percent of respondents believed that members of the rich entrepreneur class made their fortunes by legal or proper means.[4]

Chinese intellectuals—those who have graduated from college—seem to be particularly resentful of the rapid rise of private entrepreneurs. They often use the term "misplacing the body above the brain" (*naoti daogua*) to express their dissatisfaction. For them, it is "abnormal" and unfair that those "country bumpkins" have become rich. It would be "normal" and "balanced," from their viewpoint, if those who work with their brains had incomes several times higher than those who work with their hands.[5]

Tension between intellectuals and private entrepreneurs is understandable. As David Goodman, an Australian scholar, observed, "compared to the other countries of East and Southeast Asia, China's new rich do not include the professional middle classes: civil servants, academics, public intellectuals, lawyers, doctors, and the like."[6]

In addition, traditional Chinese society, which was dominated by the gentry-scholar class, tended to look down upon peasants and devalue the role of merchants. Education has long been the main ladder for upward social mobility. The rapid emergence and increasingly important role of peasants-turned-entrepreneurs in the past decade have challenged this tradition and changed the social structure of the country.

These tensions and disparities are certainly not unique to China—they exist in virtually all societies. Countries with different political systems, however, have different means to deal with these issues—some depend on legal means and tax systems while some resolve them through violent conflict. It remains to be seen by what means China will deal with the increasing disparity in society and how the tension between private entrepreneurs and the other social strata will be handled.

Entrepreneurs like Chen Jinhai surely have their problems and weaknesses. I do not intend to portray Chen as a flawless hero. A careful reader will not fail to notice my reservation about Chen and his lifestyle. Yet I found that Chen is a man who has great talent, courage, diligence, and vision. The dramatic change in his life reflects the fundamental change in social structure, economic redistribution, and power relationships in Chinese society. The miracle that Chen has created for his life is also part of the economic miracle of China.

"Did you expect all these changes that have occurred to you in the past 20 years?" I once asked Chen.

"No, not at all," Chen replied. "Let me tell you a dramatic but true story, Dr. Li. As I told you before, about 20 years ago I went to a Shanghai factory to look for a job as a contract worker, but I was rejected on the basis that I did not have a junior high school diploma. A few months ago, the general manager of the same Shanghai factory came to my office in Shanghai to discuss potential cooperation between his factory and my firms.

"During the informal chat, the general manager asked me about my 'professional background.' I told him that I did not have any 'professional background,' and actually I did not even graduate from junior high school. The general manager probably wanted to please me so that I would sign the contract with him. He told me that he was amazed that I had been very successful in my business without any professional training.

" 'What would you have been,' the general manager said, 'if you had received a good education?' "

" 'A contract worker in your factory at 36 yuan a month!' I said to the general manager."

Part III

Impact

Migrant workers were jammed in the waiting area of the Changzhou railway station, waiting for the eastbound trains in the spring of 1994.

A view of Zhangjiagang, a newborn modern city in Sunan.

Chinese cities are presently notorious for the lack of green—a few trees and little grass. Also, most Chinese cities have narrow streets, which have made traffic jams a familiar scene for urban dwellers. But Zhangjiagang is exceptional. Trees and grass are planted everywhere in the city. Zhangjiagang has many newly built streets, which are usually over 50 meters wide.

7

"200 Million Mouths Too Many"

China's Surplus Rural Laborers

"What is the Chinese government's most pressing problem at present?" a Spanish journalist asked a Chinese government official at a recent international conference on social effects of economic reforms in China.

"The toughest challenge for China is that it has too many 'mouths'!" the official readily answered.

"Too many mouths?" The journalist was puzzled. "You mean . . . ?"

"The Chinese term for 'population' is *renkou*—it literally means 'people's mouths,' " the official explained. "When a baby is born in China, people usually say that an extra mouth is added to a family."

"How many extra 'adult mouths' does China have now?" asked the Spanish journalist.

"China has 200 million mouths too many!" the Chinese official answered.[1]

"Two hundred million surplus laborers?!" The journalist was shocked. "This is equal to the population of five Spains or two Mexicos."

"Just imagine the population of two Mexicos without jobs!" the Chinese official replied.

The Chinese official was not revealing any secrets when he made these remarks. Anyone who has been observing socioeconomic changes in China should be aware of the problem of overpopulation. Indeed, few issues in the study of the nation's socioeconomic development over the past several years have generated as much public concern and sense of urgency as surplus rural laborers and consequent large-scale internal migration in the country. The so-called surplus rural laborers, as some Chinese scholars stated, are "actually the unemployed rural population."[2]

111

The issue of surplus rural laborers in China is not new. Since at least the nineteenth century, Chinese rulers have been concerned about the lack of arable land and the flow of surplus rural laborers. China accounts for 22 percent of the world's population, but has only 7 percent of the world's arable land. What is new, however, is that those surplus farmers are now free to move and are increasingly choosing to move to urban areas, owing to the rapid economic growth in Chinese cities during the past decade.

As with human migration elsewhere, China's ongoing internal migration is both a cause and consequence of socioeconomic change.[3] While no one seems to doubt the magnitude of the impact of migrants on the country, students of China differ profoundly in their interpretations of its politicoeconomic implications. The sociologist Jack Goldstone argues that China's surplus rural laborers and internal migration pose a major threat to the country's political stability and economic growth. As the agricultural economy becomes virtually incapable of providing more employment, and the industrial growth is not rapid enough to absorb the rural surplus, he expects China to have a "terminal crisis" within the next 10 to 15 years.[4] Masses of unemployed peasants, according to Goldstone, are likely to be the catalysts if China descends into chaos.[5]

In contrast, some other China experts believe that surplus rural laborers provide great human resources for the country to reconstruct the economy, accelerate urbanization, and further rapid economic growth. Gu Shengzu, a Chinese demographer, argues that this flow of surplus laborers is a key step in China's transition from a dual to a modern economy, from a backward agrarian country to an industrialized state.[6] The implication of China's internal migration, as some believe, lies in the impulse not only to reduce the segregation between rural and urban areas that was institutionalized during the Mao era, but also to narrow the widening gap between rich and poor regions during the Deng era. Instead of causing crisis and chaos, the ongoing internal migration will affect China's national integration constructively.[7] Alan Liu, a political scientist, believes that these effects are the most intriguingly significant, especially insofar as they promote the economic interdependence between different regions.[8] Some Western scholars of Chinese politics also argue that the free movement of people will contribute to the formation of a civil society. Dorothy Solinger, for instance, argues that migrant laborers constitute a form of civil society because this social group "stands apart from and against the state."[9]

The contrasting views about surplus rural laborers and internal migration reflect policy dilemmas for the Chinese government. It seems neither possible nor desirable for Chinese authorities to keep millions of surplus rural laborers on farmland, but rapid and large-scale internal migration is seen as politically dangerous to the regime. Not surprisingly, hardliners in the Chinese government advocate controlling and restricting the flow of migrant workers. A best-selling book in China during the early 1990s, *China through the Third Eye*, provides the rationale for these advocates of control.[10] If the government loses control over the flow of migrant laborers, according to the author, it would lose its power to rule because migrants would lead the country to chaos. The author asserts that all Chinese dynasties, without exception, were destroyed by migrants (*liumin*)—those who lost or abandoned farmland.[11]

In the past several years, the Chinese government has tightened its control of migrant laborers. During a recent "clean-up campaign" in a district of Shanghai, policemen caught over 500 migrants in a single day and immediately sent them back to their home areas.[12] The Shanghai government recently issued an order that prohibits any firm in the city from hiring the migrants who do not have three cards—identification, temporary residence, and work permit. In Beijing, the government recently demolished more than 20 migrant enclaves and "vacuumed" the well-known "Zhejiang Village"—a migrant settlement that at one time housed over 100,000 migrants from Zhejiang Province.[13] In late 1995 in Shenzhen, China's first special economic zone, the security force stepped into a dispute between 500 migrant workers from the central provinces and several hundred local residents. The security force opened fire to stop a bloody brawl during which several were killed, and a dozen were seriously injured.[14] These suppressive actions by the government, however, cannot really reduce the pressure of surplus laborers. On the contrary, they have increased the tension and conflict between the government and migrant laborers.

It is, therefore, crucially important to make a broad assessment of the nature, magnitude, dynamics, causal factors, and policy measures of China's surplus rural laborers and internal migration. A number of studies on China's internal migration have recently been published in the West, but most are either highly technical or largely normative.[15] Any possible solution to the problem of surplus rural laborers should start with a better understanding of the reasons that drive people to migrate. One needs to know why, all of a sudden, rural China has so many surplus laborers. Some factors that induce China's internal migration are by now well known, while some others are often overlooked. It is necessary to review briefly all the factors that have contributed to the increasing number of surplus rural laborers and internal migration.

Push Factors

The Lack of Arable Land as a Result of a Geographical Disadvantage.
The phenomenon of surplus agricultural workers in China is a century-
old problem. It is well known that China accounts for 22 percent of the
world's population, but has only 7 percent of the world's arable land and
3 percent of the world's forest. Cultivated land now constitutes only 10.3
percent of China's vast territory.[16] The arable land of China is only one
half of the arable land of the United States, but China has 120 times the
number of rural laborers.[17]

The Decrease of Farmland as a Result of Improper Land Use. Not only
does China have a shortage of arable land in terms of the ratio of land to
laborers, but its cultivated land also has been disappearing at an alarming
speed. From 1952 to 1988, the area under cultivation in China decreased
from 1.5 billion *mu* to 1.4 billion *mu* (one *mu* is about 670 square meters).
According to Chinese official statistics, from 1949 to 1992 the cultivated
land area declined by 2.51 percent.[18] The per capita cultivable land
dropped from 3 *mu* to 1.33 *mu,* which is much less than the world average
of 6 *mu.*[19]

Several factors have caused the loss of arable land. The preference for
high-yielding cash crops over slower organic farming has led farmers to
overuse fertilizers, which have led to soil deterioration. Desertification
and deforestation have also been serious problems in China during recent
decades. In the first three years of the 1990s, for example, China lost 9.37
million *mu* of land (about the size of Qinghai Province) mainly because
of local officials' lack of environmental concern.[20] These factors have rein-
forced each other and resulted in pollution and deteriorating fertility. In
South China's hilly terrain, for example, the organic content of soil has
fallen from 6 percent at initial cultivation to 2 percent now.[21] Environmental pollution in rural areas caused by the spread of township and village enterprises has also aggravated the shortage of farmland. This fast
loss of land is so threatening that both the Central Committee of the
Chinese Communist Party and the People's Congress held special meetings to discuss the problem.[22]

Another major cause for the decrease is the sale of farmland for industrial and commercial use. During the past three decades, China has con-
verted a total of 15,000 hectares of arable land to industrial and other uses.
This number is equivalent to the amount of arable land of France and
Italy combined. The sale of farmland, which the Chinese call "land lease"
or "transfer of the land-use rights" (*tudi pizu*), has become an increas-

ingly common practice in many coastal regions in the past few years, as individuals or institutions are allowed to sell or lease property to foreign joint ventures or domestic companies. In Guangdong Province, for example, 100,000 *mu* of arable land were sold for 9.4 billion yuan in 1992. That represented 44.8 percent of Guangdong's revenue that year.[23] Table 7-1 shows that China's arable land decreased by 0.5 percent during the late 1980s.

The Natural Increase of Agricultural Laborers. Agricultural laborers increased from 180 million in 1950 to over 400 million in 1988.[24] Each year about 10 million new agricultural laborers have joined the rural labor force. China now has 460 million agricultural laborers. It is estimated that the number of agricultural laborers will increase to 540 million by the year 2000.[25]

The Effect of Agricultural Modernization. Because of both the increase in grain yield and the advance of agricultural mechanization, farm work requires far fewer laborers. China's grain yield increased from 163,920,000 tons in 1952 to 442,660,000 tons in 1992. The average annual growth rate from 1949 to 1992 was 3.5 percent.[26] The increasing grain yield is likely to continue in the coming years. According to a recent study completed by Lin Yifu, an economist at Beijing University, the maximum potential of per-unit yield in several decades will be about two to three times more than the present figure.[27] While China has experienced rapid development in agricultural technology, especially the wider use of electricity, agricultural machines, and chemical fertilizers, the number of rural laborers has increased, and arable land has decreased.

The Effect of the Household Contract Responsibility System. The abolition of the People's Commune in the early 1980s "liberated" millions of Chinese peasants. Rural economic reforms, particularly the establishment of the household contract responsibility system, ended the "iron bowl" system in rural China and decentralized farming from the collective to the household level. As a result, efficiency increased, and the number of laborers needed decreased.

Economists usually use the concept "marginal product of labor" (MP_L) to analyze whether a work unit, region, or country has surplus laborers. As more laborers are hired, the marginal product of labor will eventually fall. The work unit or country should stop employing laborers at the point at which any additional labor would cost more than it would produce.

TABLE 7-1
Population and Arable Land Growth Rates (1949–1990)

	1949–1952	1953–1957	1958–1965	1966–1978	1979–1984	1985–1990
Total annual population growth (%)	2.0	2.4	1.5	2.2	1.2	1.3
Annual change of arable land (%)	+3.3	+0.7	+1.0	+0.9	+0.3	-0.5

Source: Qu Geping and Li Jinchang, eds. *Population and Environment in China* (Boulder, Colorado: Lynne Rienner Publishers, 1994), 45.

How many laborers, then, does Chinese agriculture need at present? In other words, how many surplus rural laborers does China have? The exact number of surplus rural laborers in China is difficult to estimate. This is partially because of rapid changes in the Chinese rural economy and partially because of the confusion caused by the way that the Chinese government defines rural population. In China, the category *"nongmin"* (rural laborers or peasants) has been a residential identity rather than an occupational one. When the Chinese government compiles statistics, the "rural population" refers primarily to administrative location and not to occupation.

Mistakenly, people both in China and abroad often describe China as a rural country with 900 million peasants. This number actually refers to the total population of rural areas before the economic reform in the 1980s. According to the State Bureau of Statistics, since China's economic reform 110 million peasants have changed their status by moving to urban areas. The actual rural population at present is 797 million. This number includes 274 million children and aging people who are unable to work. Of the remaining 523 million laborers, 63 million are engaged in nonagricultural work, and 460 million are engaged in agricultural work.[28]

China's agriculture today does not need 460 million peasants. According to the author of *China's Rural Reform: Retrospect and Prospect*, the portion of the GNP devoted to agriculture decreased from 45.4 percent in 1950 to 19.7 percent in 1988, while rural laborers increased from 180 million in 1950 to over 400 million in 1988.[29]

To make the situation even worse, over 10 million young rural residents join the labor force every year as they become adults. But because of the structural change of the Chinese economy, the proportion of rural laborers in the total labor force is supposed to decrease from 57 percent at present to 45 percent in 2000. The burden of surplus rural laborers in China will become even worse in years to come.[30]

One may argue that the notion of "surplus" is ambiguous, because one peasant's job can well be shared by three peasants. This has been the case in rural China for many decades, and this kind of practice may continue without causing any sociopolitical problems. But factors such as geographical disadvantages, improper use of farmland, environmental deterioration, the natural increase of agricultural laborers, and the effects of agricultural modernization are only *push* factors—there are also *pull* factors that cause China's rural to urban migration.

Pull Factors

The Widening Income Disparity between Rural and Urban Areas. The widening gap in income between different areas and trades is one driving force behind this migration. The population living below the poverty line in China has declined significantly as a result of rural economic reform in the past decade. However, Pieter Botteller, head of the World Bank resident mission in China, believes that the opportunities for further reductions in poverty through agricultural growth and rural industries were largely exhausted by the mid-1980s.[31] The rural-urban income disparity grew from 1:1.71 in 1984 to 1:2.55 in 1994. In 1993 the income of urban residents was 12 percent greater than that in 1992, while the income of a peasant increased only 2 percent (see Figure 7–1).[32] Because of the increasing income gap, many peasants move to cities to seek a better life. This is due in part to the soaring prices of fertilizers, insecticides, and machinery needed for agriculture, while farmers can still fetch only relatively low prices for their goods. The government has failed to raise the prices of farm products to keep up with those of manufactured goods. In 1993 the prices of fertilizer, fuel, and other farming necessities rose nearly twice as fast as those of farm commodities.

Not only is the gap between rural and urban areas widening, but also the disparity is increasing between coastal and inland cities. According to a Chinese Academy of Social Sciences survey of 20,000 urban households

FIGURE 7-1
A Comparison of Growth of Personal Income between Rural and Urban Areas

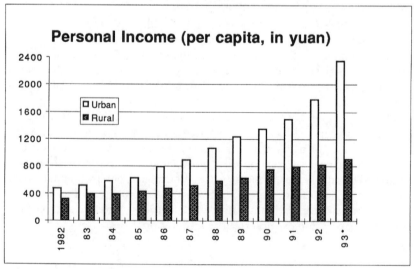

*Chinese government estimate
Source: Wall Street Journal Reports (special report), 10 December 1993.

and a China's Worker Union survey of 50,000 urban households, one-half of China's city and town dwellers live in poverty or *wenbao* (just above the poverty line).[33]

Under these circumstances, the waves of internal migration have swelled rapidly. Statistics from Sichuan, Anhui, Hunan, Hubei, Henan, and Jiangxi Provinces indicate that in 1982, fewer than 1 million peasants "floated" into cities. In 1992, a decade later, the figure became a "tsunami" of at least 24 million. As a Chinese journalist told me, in the first half of 1991 only 200,000 peasants left rural areas in Jiangxi Province, but in 1993, more than 3 million followed the tide.

The Increased Demand of Urban Construction Projects. Construction projects in urban areas need a great number of laborers. Shanghai, for example, completed more municipal works in the past four years than it did in the previous four decades. The city has witnessed over 1,000 new

Young men and women are selling corn in downtown Chongqing. The city is overpopulated and many people cannot find jobs. The increase of migrant workers from the rural area in Sichuan has aggravated the shortage of jobs in the city. These young people make very little money (less than $1 per day) by working as vendors on the street. "This is better than the countryside in which I used to work," a young man said to me. "I could not make a living if I stayed in the countryside."

skyscrapers due to the property boom of the past few years. Two bridges and a new tunnel now link the east and west sides of the city. The Oriental Pearl TV Tower and Yaohan building (two of Asia's highest buildings), pierce the sky on the east bank of the Huangpu River. In 1995, Shanghai opened its first subway line and its first overpass highway ring around the city. Migrants are the main source of the work force for these urban projects. In Pudong, for example, about 4,000 new construction projects were started in 1994, and more than three-fourths of the construction workers were migrants from other provinces. Thousands of migrants have flooded into Pudong since it became a new economic zone a few years ago. Many migrants, however, cannot find jobs there.

The Increased Demand of the Nonstate Sector in Urban Areas. Not only urban construction projects, but also urban private enterprises and foreign joint ventures have sought to hire cheap laborers. For the first three decades of the People's Republic of China, the government strictly restrained the existence of private enterprises. They began to reappear in the mid-1980s, but at that time each private firm was allowed to hire no more than eight workers. In the early 1990s, private enterprises have been growing rapidly. By the end of 1992, approximately 7.7 million—89 percent—of the retail sales outlets in China belonged to private firms or individually owned businesses. About 80 percent of the 140,000 shops and markets in Beijing, for example, are either owned or run by private entrepreneurs.[34] The number of private enterprises in the country increased from 91,000 in 1989 to 420,000 in 1994.

The private sector has developed fastest along the southeast coast of China, where 70 percent of the country's private businesses are located. Another 19 percent are in central China, and only 1 percent are in the western part of the country.[35] It is not clear how the number of workers employed in the private sector is divided between locals or migrants, but some case studies show that in the coastal area, migrants constitute an overwhelming majority of workers in the nonstate firms, including private, collective, and foreign-owned firms. As *China Daily* reported in 1994, in some economically advanced market towns in southern Jiangsu, the number of nonlocal laborers surpassed local residents.[36]

Foreign companies or joint ventures, especially those from Hong Kong and Taiwan, have employed a large number of migrant workers. Dongguan, bordering the Shenzhen Economic Zone, is one of the leading counties in China in terms of foreign investment. The number of migrant workers in 1990 was 4.2 times the number in 1986. In Shenzhen, out of a total population of 1.7 million in 1990, 980,700 were migrants.[37]

The Changing Structure of Labor Markets in Urban Areas. The development of a market economy in urban areas has increased the demand for low-wage labor in service sectors. Permanent city residents, however, have become increasingly unwilling to do "dirty jobs" such as cleaning lavatories or collecting garbage. According to a recent newspaper investigation, migrant laborers have shouldered 80 percent of the "dirty, heavy, and dangerous jobs" in Shanghai.[38] A large number of maids in Shanghai are from Wuwei County, Anhui Province. "Wuwei County," said a girl who works in my friend's house in Shanghai, "exports soldiers in wartime, maids in peacetime." Many of the garbage collectors in Shanghai are from Hunan, and most of them are just teenagers.

All these push and pull factors have contributed to the ongoing rural-to-urban migration. None will disappear in the foreseeable future. There is every reason to expect that the issues related to rural surplus laborers and internal migration will become even more acute, especially as China's urban unemployment rate increases. The crucial question for China is whether its cities are ready to absorb this huge number of laborers. Very few of the social scientists and government officials with whom I spoke seemed optimistic.

China has made rapid progress in urbanization during the past few years. Between 1988 and 1992, the number of population centers designated as cities increased from 223 to 517, with the urban population growing from 135 million to 320 million.[39] Great pressure has already been exerted on the country's urban employment, infrastructure, transportation, health care, and social stability. China's urban areas seem totally unprepared for this large-scale city-bound migration.

"Just about the worst news that China can hear is that the urban unemployment rate is increasing at the same time that millions of rural workers are migrating to the cities. But that's the news we are getting from government reports," a scholar from the Shanghai Academy of Social Sciences said to me.

According to Zhang Xiaojian, director of the Labor Ministry's Employment Department, the urban unemployment rate rose to 2.6 percent in 1993 compared to 2.4 percent in 1992. These government figures underestimate the problem. The number of unemployed during the first three-quarters of 1993 exceeded the total of unemployed in the previous six years. In addition, the reemployment rate decreased from 70 percent to 20 percent. The urban unemployment total hit 4 million in 1993 and 5 million in 1994.[40]

"The real figure of urban unemployment is far more than 5 million," an official in the municipal government of Shanghai who did not want to be identified told me. "The Shanghai municipal government, for example, admits that the city has 200,000 unemployed laborers (not including job-less migrants). But everyone in Shanghai knows that even within the tex-tile industry of Shanghai, at least 250,000 workers actually lost their jobs in the last two years. About 90 percent of textile factories in Shanghai have recently shut down."

I was surprised to hear this. The textile industry is one of the main industrial sectors in Shanghai. "What happened to these textile factories?" I asked.

"These textile factories were faced with all kinds of problems—the shortage of cotton and other resources, insufficient capital, poor manage-ment, and increased competition, among others" the official told me. Ac-cording to China's Association of Textile Industries, over 50 percent of China's textile factories suffered heavy losses in the first three months of 1994.[41]

"We could not compete with our counterparts in rural industries," said the manager of a textile factory in Shanghai. "Although the textile facto-ries in rural areas have also suffered from the increase in cotton prices, they usually have better access to resources and can hire cheap laborers. They are also more flexible in exporting products."

China's textile industry is not the only one that has heavy deficits. Ac-cording to an influential Chinese newspaper, 80 percent of China's state-owned industrial enterprises currently have hidden deficits.[42] The Chinese government has admitted that one-third of state-owned enterprises have overt deficits, and another one-third have hidden deficits.

These enterprises often lay off employees or persuade many middle-aged workers (in their mid-forties) to take early retirement. Many work-ers are ordered to stay at home while waiting for a job. The government uses the term "off-post" (*xiagang*), to refer to those "job-waiting" work-ers. "Off-post" workers receive about 30 to 40 percent of their regular salaries.

The Chinese government does not give any indication on how many "off-post" workers China has now. According to the official Federation of China's Workers, some state-owned enterprises exist only in name. About 7 million workers live in poverty because of China's lack of a social welfare system.[43] A Chinese official magazine estimated that China's state-owned enterprises have 25 million "urban surplus laborers."[44]

I suspect that the real number of "off-post" workers must be an embar-rassment to the authorities. Some of my middle-school classmates in Shanghai are "off-post." In May 1994, I went to a wedding banquet for a relative of mine. Of the 11 people at my table, 3 were "off-post."

Mr. Zhang Xueren is a good friend of mine. He worked in a machine factory in Shanghai for fifteen years before he was recently asked to be "off-post." His factory could not give him even 30 percent of his regular salary. In addition, his nineteen-year-old son also lost his job in a joint-venture restaurant where he had worked for almost a year. Zhang's family, including two aging parents, all depend on Zhang's wife, who works as a janitor in a factory and earns 400 yuan ($48) a month.

In May 1994, I invited Zhang's family to a restaurant for dinner. It was not fancy, but looked nice and clean. I found that my friend was very nervous when we sat down and started to order dishes. He asked his wife and son to go to the rest room and then said to me: "Don't let them see the menu or the bill. They will be upset if they know a meal like this is almost equal to our family's entire monthly income."

I promised him that I would not let them know how much I spent on the dinner. To be honest, I had no appetite for the meal after hearing his words. I was beset by mixed feelings—a sense of guilt, sympathy for my friend, and worry for the family's future. I suddenly realized again why many urban workers I saw in Shanghai and other places were upset with the current situation in the country.

Recently, it has become common for state-owned enterprises to be unable to pay salaries to their employees on time. Zhu Rongji, the Politburo standing committee member who is in charge of China's economy, in 1994 traveled to Heilongjiang, Jilin, Liaoning, Henan, and Hubei Provinces, where a great many state-owned enterprises are located. Many enterprises there were behind in payments. Zhu said during the trip: "It is imperative to make a thorough survey of the enterprises, help them solve their problems, deepen their reform, and transform their operating procedures."[45]

Zhu also dismissed several top provincial officials for their incompetence in dealing with the rise in the unemployment rate and other problems. The disciplinary committee of the Chinese Communist Party issued new regulations in 1994, stating that no county or municipal government could purchase cars if the local government is behind in paying employees' salaries. Those local governments that had purchased cars were required to sell them and use the money to pay salaries. It was reported that in Shandong and other provinces unemployed urban workers and migrants destroyed fancy cars parked on the streets.

Millions of migrant workers have deepened the problems of urban unemployment. The Chinese government seems not to have any effective measures to cope with these two integrated problems. Local governments in major cities have recently adopted some measures to constrain what they called the "reckless flow of job-seeking farmers [*mangliu*]." Earlier in 1994, the Shanghai municipal government issued a year-long and renewable "blue card" (*wugongzheng*) system to permit migrant laborers to work in the city. Some officials in major cities have advocated that local governments should adopt a more restrictive policy to limit the flow of migrant laborers. But no measures seem to be effective in stopping the flow of migrants.

Many scholars who study China's population problems and labor policies believe that the rapid development of township and village enterprises may provide a solution for China's surplus laborers. The authors of *A New Exploration of China's Population Migration*, for example, call rural township enterprises the "reservoirs of surplus rural labor."[46]

In 1978 there were 1,524,000 township and village enterprises, which employed 28,262,000 laborers in the country. By the end of 1992, the total number of China's TVEs had reached 20,779,000. The number of laborers employed in TVEs was 105,810,000, an increase of 274 percent over 1978. In other words, rural township enterprises have absorbed over 77 million peasants into rural industries.[47]

It would be a mistake, however, to assume that rural township enterprises are unlimited labor reservoirs that could employ 200 million surplus laborers. Many recent studies indicate that although TVEs continued to develop rapidly from the end of the 1980s, they did not necessarily create new jobs. From 1988 to 1989, TVEs absorbed an average of 12.6 million rural laborers every year, but from 1989 to 1992, the average decreased to 2.6 million.[48] This situation will not change unless a large amount of capital is poured into rural township enterprises.[49] Many TVEs are being transformed from labor-intensive to technology-intensive firms.

According to a recent report, China will face three "demographic peaks" at the turn of the century or during the early decades of the next century: (1) "population peak"—1.3 billion people by the year 2000; (2) "aging population peak" in 2024—300 million will be over 60 years old; and (3) "labor population peak"—rural laborers (age 15–59) will be 660 million, actual rural laborers will number 590 million, and the total needed rural laborers will be 279 million, leaving a surplus of 311 million.[50]

Furthermore, the massive internal migration has also significantly affected birth control in the country. For over two decades, every family in China has been allowed to have only one child. Local officials have been closely watching the effectiveness of "the one child policy." But birth control is practically impossible to enforce among migrant workers. Some couples come to urban areas in order to avoid enforced birth control in their native villages. They have a female baby, but they still want a son. Many have two children or more. A newlywed couple migrated to Amoy nine years ago and now they have nine children![51] It was reported that Shanghai had 430,000 young female migrant workers (*wailaimei*) in 1993. About 20 percent of them illegally "lived together" with men. Some became concubines. Altogether 12,000 bore children in 1993, accounting for 12.5 percent of the total births in the city.[52]

According to another 1994 survey conducted in Shanghai, over 60 percent of migrant workers wanted to have two children. Unplanned childbirth among the floating population was 30 times higher than among Shanghai residents.[53] Some urban officials are aware of this problem and want to adopt effective methods to control the birth rate of migrant workers. But when they do so, the migrant workers just float to other places.

"My wife and I will move repeatedly until we have a male baby," a migrant worker from Shandong told a reporter of a Shanghai newspaper.[54]

There are no easy solutions to the pressure of overpopulation, particularly surplus rural laborers and the increase of urban unemployment. A top Chinese leader recently said to the media: "Agriculture and state enterprises are the keys to developing a healthy economy and maintaining a stable society."[55] Unfortunately, both these key areas have been beset with serious difficulties.

"These two problems are like time bombs," said a 66-year-old retired schoolteacher with whom I chatted in Wuhan. "These problems can be contained now, as China has continuously had a good grain harvest for the past few years, and the Chinese economy generally grows well. But who knows what will happen if rural China experiences a famine, or if urban China suffers another major unemployment hit, or if the Chinese government deliberates too long in establishing a responsive social welfare system, or if a large number of state-owned enterprises are unable to pay their employees, or if migrant women all want to have more children as they were allowed to do during the Mao era, or if . . ."

The man kept adding hypothetical conditions to his "list of ifs."

I think his concerns are justified. I myself feel great anxiety about my native land, where 200 million people remain "surplus" or "floating." Due to the development of transportation and its low cost, distances are no longer a significant barrier to China's internal migration. The snowball effect will compound the problem as more surplus rural laborers flood into the cities. The multiple causes of China's surplus rural laborers and consequent large-scale internal migration also suggest that the Chinese government needs to adopt various measures to deal with these crises. The next chapter will look at some of the main characteristics and trends of China's internal migration and discuss the policies that the Chinese government could adopt.

8

"94ers: Eastward Ho!"

China's Internal Migration

As I stood on the platform in the Fuyang railway station, which was crowded with thousands of migrant workers, I was witnessing the unfolding of a profound human drama.

Located 700 kilometers northwest of Shanghai, Fuyang is a populous agricultural region of Anhui, a poor interior province. The government recently estimated that this region had 3 million surplus rural laborers. Many of them had already left the countryside and gone to cities like Shanghai as migrant workers. Virtually every day in the month after the Chinese Spring Festival in 1994, the Fuyang railway station was packed with people who wanted to catch any of the east-bound trains. The station was very small and could accommodate over 1,000 passengers each day. But the day when I was there, about 14,000 tickets were sold. Holding a ticket did not guarantee that one could get on the train. Many of the east-bound trains that stopped in the Fuyang station did not even open the doors because the trains were already filled with migrant laborers from elsewhere.

"I have been waiting here for two days, please let me in." A young man begged the passengers inside to open the window so that he could climb on the train.

"No way!" a person on the train responded. "There is absolutely no room inside. You could not find a space to stand, even in the toilet."

During the rush season, a tiny toilet on the train, I was later told by a train conductor, sometimes "accommodated" as many as seven passengers on the trains from Anhui to Shanghai.

Seven people in a train toilet? Incredible! The toilet in a Chinese train is as small as the ones on Amtrak in the United States. I could not believe what I heard until I saw a newspaper report that a toilet in Train No. 311 from Fuyang to Shanghai once held eight people!

Overloaded trains and huge crowds of people on platforms were not seen only in the Fuyang station. It was reported that in the railway station of a major city, about 80,000 travelers could not get on a train and had to stay overnight.[1] For those who "luckily" got on the train, the miserable conditions were difficult to bear. For instance, there was absolutely no space to stand on the train that I took back to Shanghai during the Spring Festival season—when I moved my leg, I could not find a place to put it down.

In one extreme case, conditions were so intolerable that a few passengers jumped out of the window of a moving train and were killed. The Ministry of Railway Transportation investigated 50,000 passengers on five trains and found that 115 passengers suffered mental disorders due mainly to the poor conditions on the train. Most of them (86 percent) were migrant laborers.[2] During the Spring Festival, the most important holiday in China, almost all migrants return to their native homes, where they spend about two weeks with their families. Then they go back to their work places in cities, usually bringing with them more surplus rural laborers from their home villages. This is what the Chinese call "the tidal wave of migrant workers" (*mingongchao*). Faced with this tidal wave, the entire railway system in China has almost shut down during the Spring Festival season in the past few years.[3] According to the Chinese authorities, China's railway system transported altogether 21 million migrant workers during the Spring Festival season of 1994. Another 5 million people were transported by buses and ships.[4]

"Twenty-six million people is roughly the population of Canada," a reporter for China's official newspaper, *People's Daily*, said to me. "Imagine all the people of Canada being relocated by train within a few weeks!"

"This is one of the largest migrations in human history," commented a demographer from the Chinese Academy of Social Sciences. "The scale and impact of China's current internal migration are surely as great as other major domestic migrations in the world, such as the nineteenth-century European industrial revolution and the 1849 gold rush in the United States."

An analysis of the direction of migration shows that an overwhelmingly large portion of interprovincial migrants moved from the west and the north of China to its east and south coast.[5] Just as "Westward Ho!" became a catchword for American "forty-niners," the idea "Go East" has inspired millions of Chinese "ninety-fourers"—the term I coined to refer to China's migrant workers. But unlike the American West in 1849, which was a primitive and relatively uninhabited area, China's east coast is the most developed region in China and one of the most populous areas in the world.

Chinese migrant laborers have created their own folk rhymes: *"Yao facai, pao Shanghai"* (If you want to make a fortune, run to Shanghai) and *"Dongxinanbei zhong, dagong dao Pudong"* (East, west, south, north, center, to find a job, go to Pudong). Pudong, a new district of Shanghai and the largest special economic zone in the country, has become a "realm of fantasy" for surplus laborers in rural China. About 4,000 construction projects have been started in Pudong since 1994, and most construction workers are migrants from other provinces.

Make no mistake, China's tidal wave of migrant workers did not start in 1994 but in the early 1980s. Furthermore, surplus laborers in rural China have not only migrated from west to east in the country, but also from north to south. Guangdong, a southern province, for example, had the largest percentage of migrant laborers in the country until 1990. The number of migrant laborers, however, increased sharply in the early 1990s. According to a study of Sichuan, Anhui, Hunan, Hubei, Henan, and Jiangxi, the number of rural laborers who left their farmland was less than 1 million in 1982 but had increased to 24 million by the end of 1993.[6] As of May 1994 the largest tidal wave of internal migration had already taken place. The east coast near Shanghai has become the main region where migrants seek to find jobs.

The uneven distribution of China's population is well known. As demarcated by Hu's line (see Map 8–1), approximately 94 percent of China's population inhabit the eastern and southeastern parts of the country, which account for only 46 percent of China's territory, while the western and northwestern parts of China account for 54 percent of the country's land area but only 6 percent of the total population.[7] In Shanghai, for example, the population density is 2,118 persons per square kilometer, compared with 2 persons per square kilometer in some inland provinces, such as the Xizang Autonomous Region (Tibet).[8] Qinghai, Xingjiang, and Nei Mongol have 5, 8, and 16 persons per square kilometer, respectively. These four provinces contain 50 percent of China's land area but only 4 percent of its population.[9] Chinese cities and towns are crowded within the eastern region of the country. Furthermore, the densely populated eastern and southeastern coastal areas—despite their high level of economic development—have inadequate deposits of natural resources, whereas the less developed western and southwestern areas of the country, with their sparse population, are richly endowed with natural resources.

An overwhelming majority of migrants, however, have flowed into cities and towns on the east and south coast, the most populous region of the country. They have joined what Chinese authorities call "the floating population" (*liudong renkou*). The floating population includes the rural-to-urban migrant laborers, but the two terms are not identical. The floating population also refers to children, aging people, and nonagricultural workers who flow from one place to the other, including urban-to-urban, rural-to-rural, and urban-to-rural migration. Some Western scholars and journalists, mistakenly, use these two terms interchangeably. The floating population refers loosely to those people who stay in places where they do not have a permanent household registration status. This category would include temporary residents, contract rural workers, short-term visitors, and people on business trips.

For Americans, moving from one state to another is quite a common phenomenon. The annual interstate rate of moving in the United States is 4 percent. But in China, the annual cross-province movement rate was as low as 0.12 percent in the 1980s.[10] Two major reasons account for the difference. First, China is traditionally not a mobile nation. In the past, only war or natural disaster could persuade Chinese peasants to leave their beloved farmland. Second, contemporary Chinese authorities have always controlled internal migration. The term "floating population" is uniquely Chinese. Citizens in democratic countries are free to move from one region to the other.[11] The Chinese Communist government adopted a household registration system soon after it came to power in 1949. Each family in an urban area had a household registration book (*hukoubu*). A copy was kept on file at the local police station. *Hukoubu* indicated legal permission for a family to live in an urban area. The family also needed this registration to receive certificates for grain, cotton, cooking oil, milk, sugar, meat, and other necessities.

But during the post-Mao era, the ration system dissolved because all products could easily be bought at slightly higher prices on free markets. Although the household registration system remains, it has lost its effectiveness as a means of controlling where people live. Rapid urban economic growth pulled more laborers from rural areas to join work forces in construction, commerce, and civil service in Chinese cities.

A recent study conducted by China's Ministry of Public Security reported that the floating population was 80 million in 1994.[12] Not all of this cohort comes from the countryside, although the dominant migra-

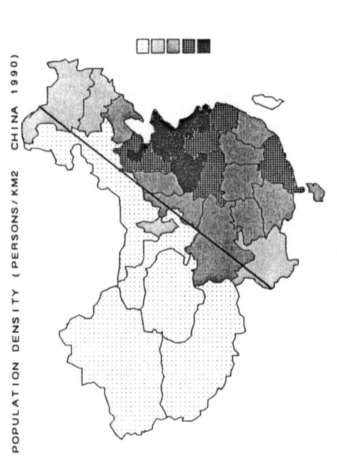

Map 8-1 Population Density of China (persons/sq km, 1990)
Source: China's Population Today, July 1994, 11.

tory pattern is the movement from rural areas to urban centers. Table 8–1 shows the migration distribution in terms of urban-rural direction. More than one-half of all migrants move from rural to urban locations. A 1990 nationwide survey of large cities showed that 60 percent of the floating population was from the countryside and the rest from interurban flows.[13] In addition, about two-thirds of the floating population are short-term visitors. If one also deducts the number of children and aging people combined (reported to be 6 percent) in the floating population, the figure becomes about 15 million—the estimated number of surplus rural laborers in the floating population. The figure seems too small, and it is only 7.5 percent of the total 200 million surplus rural laborers. This small number is inconsistent with findings of many other studies.[14] For example, Guangdong Province alone had 10 million migrant workers from other parts of the country in 1993.[15]

No reliable source exists to show how many surplus rural laborers have joined the floating population. This is partially because of the definitional confusion mentioned above and partially because of the fact that data on migrants are not systematically collected. China's Administrative Bureau of Population Registration estimated that 30 million migrant laborers flooded cities in 1995.[16]

Table 8–2 shows the population migration in China by province. The data are based on a national 1 percent sample survey in 1987 and the 1990 census. We can see three general trends from the table: First, almost all the coastal provinces have net migration; particularly evident is the net migration of Beijing, Shanghai, and Tianjin, China's three largest cities. Second, although the two surveys are only a few years apart (and actually

TABLE 8-1
Migration by Rural-Urban Differentiations Based on 1% Sample Survey in 1987

Direction of Flow	Percentage
From rural to urban	51
From urban to urban	26
From rural to rural	17
From urban to rural	6

Source: Gu Shengzu, *Feinonghua yu chengzhenhua yanjiu* (A study of nonagriculturalization and urbanization) (Hanzhou: Zhejiang People's Press, 1991), 131.

TABLE 8-2

Population Migration in China by Province (1982–1990) in millions

Province	1982–1987 (National 1% Sample Survey)					1985–1990 (the 1990 Census)				
	Intraprovince Migration	Outward Migration	Inward Migration	Gross Migration	Net Migration	Intraprovince Migration	Outward Migration	Inward Migration	Gross Migration	Net Migration
Beijing	54.9	10.1	32.3	42.4	22.2	7.8	12.2	62.1	74.3	49.9
Tianjin	4.9	5.7	16.0	21.7	10.3	4.0	8.2	27.8	36.0	19.6
Hebei	16.5	6.5	10.4	16.9	3.9	13.3	10.6	8.5	19.1	-2.1
Shanxi	29.0	6.7	6.1	13.8	-0.5	21.8	7.6	10.7	18.3	3.1
Neimenggu	27.7	10.0	8.1	18.0	-0.9	26.9	14.1	11.9	26.0	-2.3
Liaoning	25.8	6.1	8.3	14.4	2.1	22.4	7.5	13.7	21.2	6.2
Jilin	39.3	10.2	7.2	17.4	-3.0	24.8	14.4	9.6	24.0	-4.8
Heilongjiang	25.6	13.1	5.6	18.8	-7.5	30.0	17.3	10.4	27.7	-6.8
Shanghai	22.1	6.6	29.9	36.6	23.3	13.0	9.9	49.8	59.8	39.9
Jiangsu	21.3	5.1	7.5	12.5	2.4	17.7	9.3	11.8	21.0	2.5
Zhejiang	19.3	5.8	3.0	8.8	-2.8	19.3	15.3	8.1	23.3	-7.2
Anhui	16.2	4.7	3.1	7.8	-1.6	15.5	9.5	6.0	15.5	-3.5
Fujian	16.3	3.9	3.2	7.0	-0.7	24.1	7.9	8.4	16.3	0.4
Jiangxi	14.9	4.1	2.8	6.9	-1.2	19.5	7.8	6.0	13.7	-1.8
Shandong	19.1	4.3	6.9	11.2	2.6	14.1	6.3	7.2	13.5	0.9
Henan	11.3	4.0	3.3	7.3	-0.7	14.5	6.9	5.6	12.4	-1.3
Hubei	31.9	4.4	5.4	9.8	0.9	20.2	6.4	8.0	14.4	1.5
Hunan	21.2	6.5	3.8	10.3	-2.8	21.4	8.7	4.5	13.2	-4.2
Guangdong	34.7	2.4	4.6	7.0	2.2	42.5	4.0	20.0	24.0	16.0
Guangxi	16.8	5.3	1.5	6.8	-3.9	21.0	13.9	3.4	17.3	-10.6
Hainan						21.8	16.2	22.9	39.0	6.7
Sichuan	31.5	4.5	3.5	8.0	-1.0	21.9	12.3	4.1	16.4	-8.2
Guizhou	18.1	4.0	3.8	7.8	-0.2	14.3	9.7	5.9	15.5	-3.8
Yunnan	18.3	5.2	2.7	7.9	-2.5	19.8	7.5	6.7	14.3	-0.8
Shaanxi	25.4	9.2	7.2	16.4	-2.0	21.5	11.0	9.4	20.5	-1.6
Gansu	19.3	9.0	4.4	13.5	-4.6	20.1	12.5	8.8	21.4	-3.7
Qinghai	14.7	24.0	6.7	30.7	-17.4	33.9	22.9	25.8	48.7	2.9
Ningxia	21.1	11.8	21.1	32.9	9.4	26.4	12.2	19.7	31.9	7.6
Xinjiang	25.2	16.9	14.2	31.2	-2.7	23.8	18.3	22.5	40.8	4.2

Source: Li Shuzhuo, "Zhongguo bashi niandai de quyu jingji fazhan he renkou gianyi yanjiu" (A study on the development of regional economy and population migration in China in the 1980s), *Renkou yu jingji* (Population and economics), no. 3 (1994): 4.

overlap for three years), the rate of gross migration increased significantly during the more recent period. Third, both intraprovince and interprovince migration rates are high in both periods, but in the more recent period the intraprovince rate in most provinces declined while the interprovince migration rate in almost all provinces increased. This suggests the trend of migrant workers choosing a long-distance destination.[17]

Table 8–3 reaffirms the rapid increase in the floating population in China's major cities during the past few years. Migrants already constitute a significant portion of the population in China's major cities (see Table 8–4). In 1994, Shanghai's floating population reached 3.3 million, almost doubling the 1986 figure, according to statistics compiled by the Shanghai Public Security and Statistic Bureau. This means that there is one newly arrived migrant for every three residents in the urban area of Shanghai. The ratio between the floating population and the permanent population in these cities increased from 12.6 percent in 1984 to 22.5 percent in 1987 and to 25.4 percent in 1994. In Wuxi, Jiangsu Province, migrant laborers account for 38 percent of the total labor force of the city. In Foshan, Guangdong, 58 percent of workers are from elsewhere.[18]

Table 8–5 illustrates the mobility types of the floating population in terms of purposes in ten major cities. Not surprisingly, in all the cities seeking employment is the most important motivation of the rural-to-urban migrants.

Several studies show that most migrant workers are in their late teens or early twenties. About 80 percent have primary or middle-school education. Fully three-quarters are unmarried. About 70 percent are male.[19] In Shanghai, for example, a large number of migrants are engaged in construction work. Others work as waiters, maids, repairmen, furniture makers, factory workers, shop assistants, tailors, street peddlers, packers, haulers, road and lavatory cleaners, garbage collectors, and mortuary attendants.[20]

Although many other developing countries have been confronting the population explosion in their overcrowded cities, few countries in the world seem faced with such high population pressure as China. Chinese authorities admit that "social, economic, and environmental problems are an inevitable consequence of such pressures."[21]

"The tidal wave of migrant workers in China that we have recently witnessed is only the tip of the iceberg," said Dr. Han Jun, an expert on migrant workers in the country. "Over 80 million in the floating population in the past few years is the 'prelude' to a much larger number of surplus rural laborers and their families in the years to come."

Although it may still be the "prelude," the rapid growth of the migrant

TABLE 8-3
The Growth of the Floating Population in 10 Major Cities (10,000 people/day)

City	1980	1981	1984	1985	1986	1987	1988	1989	1992	1994
Shanghai	30	62	102		183		209			330
Beijing	30	39		90	105	115	131		150	167**
Guangzhou			50	50	80	114	117	130		
Tianjin			29	50	57	86	112			
Wuhan		25	35		81			75	120*	
Chongqing		16			48		67			
Chengdu		20	27	35		53		53		
Hangzhou	15		20	30	25	40		50		
Zhengzhou	8				23	31		37		
Taiyuan	8	10		13		26	29	36		

Source: Li Mengbai, "Liudong renkou pengzhang yu xiangcum laodongli zhuanyi" ("The explosion of migrant population in cities and the transfer of rural laborers), *Nongcun jiungji yu shehui* (Rural economy and society), no. 2 (1994): 23. Some more recent data are from *Shanghai Star,* 22 March 1994, 2; 15 April 1994, 1.

Notes: *This number refers to the floating population in Wuhan in 1990, not 1992.

**Estimated and not the final result of the investigation. *Cankao xiaoxi* (Reference news), 6 November 1994, 8.

TABLE 8-4
The Floating Population in Seven Chinese Cities and Their Percentage
of the Permanent Population

City	1984		1987	
	Floating Population (10,000 people)	Percentage of Floating Pop. in total Permanent Pop. (%)	Floating Pop. (10,000)	Percentage of Floating Pop. in total Permanent Pop. (%)
Beijing	70.0	14.60	115.0	22.03
Shanghai	102.6	15.25	183.0	26.18
Tianjin	27.5	6.27	66.1	15.59
Wuhan	35.0	12.07	65.8	21.79
Guangzhou	50.0	20.08	88.0	33.21
Shenyang	20.0	6.31	50.0	14.97
Chengdu	22.0	14.47	53.0	24.88
Total	327.1	12.62	620.9	22.50

Source: Gu Shengzu, *Feinonghua yu chengzhenhua yanjiu* (A study of nonagriculturalization and urbanization) (Hangzhou: Zhejiang People's Press, 1991), 135.

TABLE 8-5
Mobility Type of the Floating Population in Terms of Purpose
in Ten Major Cities in China

City	Total Number (10,000/Daily)	Mobility Type			
		Social %	Urban-Functional %	Employment %	Others %
Shanghai	209.0	19.3	32.6	41.3	6.8
Beijing	130.0	8.9	26.0	62.9	2.1
Guangzhou	91.4	6.2	34.9	54.6	4.3
Wuhan	75.5	14.7	16.6	68.0	0.7
Chengdu	53.0	12.7	34.8	47.1	5.9
Hangzhou	50.4	6.7	27.3	61.2	4.8
Zhengzhou	37.4	9.6	40.9	33.5	16.0
Taiyuan	35.8	17.8	22.7	46.8	12.7
Harbin	22.5	2.8	10.4	37.3	29.5
Jilin	7.3	31.6	13.0	46.6	8.8

Source: Li Mengbai, "Liudong renkou pengzhang yu xiangcun laodongli zhuanyi" (The explosion of migrant population in cities and the transfer of rural laborers), *Nongcum jingji yu shehui* (Rural economy and society), no. 2 (1994): 24.

population in the city has already placed tremendous pressure on urban infrastructure, housing, transportation (both within the city and across the country), health care, and social welfare. Mou Xinsheng, vice minister of public security, told the media in 1994 that the Chinese government should pay increasing attention to the sociopolitical implications of this great internal migration."[22]

Migrant workers could move freely from one city to another, but they might not always find jobs. In all the metropolitan cities I visited, for example, Beijing, Guangzhou, Wuhan, Nanjing, Hangzhou, Chongqing, and Chengdu, I always saw a large number of migrant workers waiting for jobs on the streets.

"I came here hoping that I could find a job and a better life,"said a migrant laborer from Hunan whom I met in Wuhan. "Instead, I found a lot of other people looking for the same thing here. I have waited here for a week but no one wants to hire me, even for a temporary job."

Frustration among migrant laborers due to the shortage of jobs is thought to be one major reason for the increase in crimes committed by migrants in the urban areas. According to statistics provided by the Ministry of Public Security, China's crime rate increased 6 percent annually during the past 10 years. Serious crimes increased as much as 18 percent annually. In 1992, about 1,540,000 crimes were reported in the country. A significant number of these crimes were committed by migrants. In Shanghai, Beijing, and Tianjin, migrants committed 50 percent of crimes; in Guangzhou and Shenzhen, over 80 percent.[23]

In Shanghai's Pudong district, the crimes committed by migrants increased from 33 percent in 1988 to 52 percent in 1991 and 70 percent in 1993. These crimes were usually committed by groups rather than individuals. For example, about 60 percent of crimes by migrants in Beijing during 1991 were group crimes.[24] The rapid increase in the crimes perpetrated by migrants also caused an increase in city residents' hate crimes against migrants.

"Everyone in Guangzhou is sick of the drifters," a Cantonese woman said to a Western reporter. "They are rascals. They come with hardly any money, are dirty, and don't have any skills. If they don't find work, they start begging or stealing. They are the reason crime is so bad."[25] In the spring of 1996, the Chinese government launched a nationwide campaign against crimes in urban areas and executed several thousand people within a few weeks. A large number were migrants.

The shortage of urban jobs leads some female migrants to become "karaoke singers," "nightclub escorts," and "massage girls." From mid-September to the end of October 1993, Guangdong Province, for example, closed 2,683 brothels, massage clubs, and other illegal businesses. Over 31,000 women who had worked in these places were not allowed to continue their jobs. Most of these women were migrants, and over 6,600 were sent back to their native regions.[26]

A large number of migrants in Shanghai have neither jobs nor places to live. They usually sleep in tunnels, under trucks and buses in parking lots, in the waiting areas of railway stations, in the shelters of construction sites, under bridges, and in other odd places. These migrants have become street people in Shanghai. It is unknown how many street people are in the city. During a recent "clean-up campaign" in a district of Shanghai, policemen caught over 500 vagrants (*mangliu* in Chinese) in a single day and immediately sent them back to their home villages.[27]

The most vulnerable among the homeless people are the children. According to a report released by the Chinese government, official institutions in Shanghai took in about 2,000–3,000 homeless children annually during the past few years.[28] The report stated specifically that "these homeless children came from all the provinces in China except Tibet." They made their living by various means—most of them (59.6 percent) by begging, 15.1 percent by working as child laborers, 13 percent by being pickpockets, 12.1 percent by collecting garbage, and 0.4 percent by prostitution.[29]

Wang Ping, a 14-year-old boy with whom I talked on Nanjing Road, Shanghai's most famous commercial street, is one of thousands of homeless children in the city. Born in the rural area of Changde, central China's Hunan Province, Wang went to school for three years. He quit school because his father had cancer, and Wang Ping had to take care of him.

"Did your father go to the hospital?" I asked.

"No, in our village, when one gets a serious disease like cancer, one just waits for death," replied Wang Ping. "Our family could not afford medical treatment. I started to work on the farm at 11 when my father died. Two years after my father's death, my mother remarried an old man in a neighboring village. My stepfather moved into our house, because his village was even poorer."

"So you didn't need to work on your family's land since your stepfather could do the job?"

"Yes, I became 'surplus' or 'useless' in my family. My stepfather started to swear at me. He even beat me when my mother was absent. I could not stand him and left Hunan three months ago."

"What made you decide to come to Shanghai?"

"Shanghai is China's new frontier and will be better than Hong Kong soon," the boy replied. "This is what everyone in our village said. We all heard that in Shanghai, Taiwanese and Japanese businessmen spend 10 yuan bills like using toilet paper!"

This was the first time I heard this expression.

"Adults in our village also said that Shanghai's Nanjing Road has 10 miles of neon lights and thousands of shops. In some restaurants you could drink Coca-Cola for free. Most importantly, there are so many jobs and opportunities waiting for you.

"I have lived in Shanghai for three months now, but I never had a 10 yuan bill. I did drink Coca-Cola, but just from the remains in the cans that people threw away. No one wants to hire me because I don't have an I.D. card. I end up as a beggar on the streets." In China, only those who are over 16 are entitled to have an I.D.

"Do you regret leaving your home and coming to Shanghai?"

"No, I just feel that the heaven has been unfair to me. Where else can I go? Hunan is not my home. I don't have a home. Shanghai is wonderful, but only for rich people." Wang Ping pointed to the neon lights on the street and said, "These neon lights belong to them."

The vast internal migration in China has caused or aggravated many other problems in the country. Public health care, for example, is an area that has been severely affected. The inadequacy of China's medical insurance system, the neglect of workplace safety, the lack of resources in urban areas, and the spread of contagious disease have all become acute under the pressure of the large-scale migration.

In Shenzhen, China's first special economic zone, many joint ventures or private firms have violated labor regulations. Although the municipal government enacted a minimum wage, some firms still paid workers less than the minimum. Some workers were paid only 5.5 yuan ($0.6) per day.[30] Furthermore, some owners in Shenzhen required contract workers to sign contracts stating that they would waive any compensation if an accident occurred. Workers called the contract *"maishenqi"*—indenture to the factory.[31]

Legally established workplace safety regulations are usually neglected by employers of migrant workers. One of the worst violations of workplace safety happened in Shenzhen on 19 November 1993, when 81 workers in a toy factory died in a fire. Among them were 79 young women; all were from other areas. They could not escape because the owners had sealed the windows and locked the gate of the workshop to "prevent theft."[32]

"No medical care, no health insurance, no work contracts, no trade union, no welfare benefits, no permanent residence permits, no workplace safety—we have virtually nothing but a little bit of money," said a migrant laborer whom I met on the train during the 1994 Spring Festival season. He was originally from Liaoning and was heading to Xuzhou, Jiangsu Province, where he worked in a railway station as a porter.

"My back was injured while I was moving a heavy box two weeks ago. But I couldn't ask for sick leave. If I did, I would lose my job for sure," the porter continued. "Fortunately, I could go home for my Spring Festival vacation three days after I hurt my back. Now I guess I can manage heavy work."

The bitterness of that porter is widely shared by other migrant workers. A Chinese researcher interviewed 610 migrant workers in Beijing and found that 60 percent of them felt that they had been discriminated against by employers, government officials, or local residents.[33] Not being permanent residents of the place in which they work, migrant laborers have less protection against injustice and exploitation. They are often treated as though they have only minimum maintenance needs, rather than as individuals with equal human needs and rights.

"We used to spend three months doing farm work, one month celebrating the Spring Festival, and eight months idle time every year," explained Wang Haitao, a 25-year-old migrant laborer from Henan Province I met in a restaurant in Suchou. Mr. Wang worked as a waiter and earned 400 yuan ($47) a month. Although working 14 hours a day, seven days a week, he seemed to be happy with his current situation.

"This is four times more than my monthly salary as a peasant in Henan," he said.

"Do you feel that you work too many hours?" I asked.

"No, it is better than sitting idly by watching people in cities getting rich," he answered.

"The conditions here are not bad at all. Color TV, electric heating, free meals—these are great," Wang continued. "What I like most here is that I can take a shower every day! I was not able to take a bath during the entire winter at home. It would be too cold to do so in the river."

"Is the owner of the restaurant nice to you?"

"Sure." He gave me an example. "Last month my younger brother came to Suchou to look for a job. My boss gave me two days off so that I could show him around the city. Actually my brother ended up working in this restaurant as a dishwasher."

Dorothy Solinger, an American scholar on Chinese politics, has observed that Chinese migrant workers, like immigrant laborers elsewhere, "are eager to earn money at any price, grateful for the chance to live in the city, vulnerable to threats of deportation, subject to enormous competition, and powerless because of the state's unwillingness to offer them rights, welfare, or security."[34]

Migrant laborers are not considered permanent employees of state-owned enterprises. In addition, they cannot benefit from cooperative medical service since they have left the countryside. Although some firms that hire migrant laborers provide them with limited medical insurance, a majority are actually not covered at all.

Earlier in my visit, I saw a young girl crying and burning joss sticks before the statue of the Buddha at a temple in Shanghai. I asked her why she was crying so sadly.

"My brother is in the hospital, and he will undergo a stomach operation. I am praying to the Buddha to help him—that the operation be successful, but not too expensive," she said.

She and her brother came to Shanghai from Anhui about a year ago. She worked as a maid and her brother as a construction worker. Her brother got a gastric ulcer because of the excessive workload. The young girl told me that her brother had not been willing to spend money for standard medical treatment. Instead, he purchased some pills from a street peddler. But as a doctor later told her, those pills were phony medicine that actually caused her brother to have a massive gastric hemorrhage.

"The hospital asked us to pay 10,000 yuan ($1,200) as a deposit for the operation. This is double the total amount of money that my brother and I have earned since we have been in Shanghai," she wept.

"Many of the Anhui natives here have kindly lent us money. But, as you know, 10,000 yuan is just the deposit. Only Buddha knows how much money the hospital will eventually charge us!"

Only about 110 million people, 10 percent of China's population or 25 percent of the entire labor force, benefit from medical insurance at present. This is one of the reasons that fake medicine has found its way into the market. According to reports published by a Chinese official newspaper, from 1985 to 1991, China found 45,600 cases of fake medicines. The number increased over the years, from 11,000 cases in 1985, to 13,650 cases in 1990, to over 15,000 cases in 1991.[35] As a vulnerable socioeconomic group, migrant workers are commonly victims of phony medicines.

"I am not concerned about fake medicines as much as about poor resources in the cities," commented an environmental scientist in Shanghai.

"The growing population has strained city resources and caused more pollution," he said. "But the municipal government seems not to be really aware of the potential environmental crisis."

"Potential environmental crisis?" I asked him to explain.

"Let me use water as an example," he said. "The Shanghai Tap Water Company predicts that the daily demand for tap water will reach a record 5.3 million tons this summer, while the company can produce only about 5 million. This means that people in Shanghai have to use 300,000 tons of 'unclean water' every day.

"At the same time," he continued, "the sewage disposal system in Shanghai is absolutely incapable of handling the rapid increase in domestic sewage. About 2 million migrant workers have been added to the population of the city in recent years, but Shanghai's sewage disposal capacity has not increased correspondingly."

In a recent study of China's internal migration and environmental problems, two researchers found that about 80 percent of domestic sewage in Shanghai is dumped into the Huangpu River without treatment.[36]

"I am worried that a massive epidemic of hepatitis A, similar to the one that occurred in Shanghai in 1988, will happen again," the environmental scientist said. During the 1988 epidemic, about 600,000 people in Shanghai caught hepatitis A mainly by drinking polluted water. The city was almost paralyzed for a few months.

"The municipal government," the scientist concluded, "should make great efforts to improve the living conditions of city residents, especially those of migrant workers." Migrant workers to metropolitan areas usually find it difficult to obtain living space in the overcrowded central city. They therefore rent or build slum dwellings in satellite towns or in the outskirts of big cities. They usually form their own community of people from the same province. "Anhui village," "Sichuan village," "Hunan village" have emerged in China's large cities.

In Beijing, about 10,000 migrant workers from Zhejiang have settled in Fengtai's Dahongmen district. The "Henan village" of several thousand migrant workers is in Haidian's Erlizhuang district. Local longtime residents in Beijing dub these new neighborhoods "Trash Villages." Some of the villages are indeed surrounded by garbage. In a village near the Fourth Ring Road in Beijing, only one toilet serves over 6,000 people. The sanitary conditions there are extremely bad.

Not many Shanghainese nowadays are interested in visiting Pengpu district, but for a reporter investigating the lives of migrant laborers, it is a compelling destination. Before I went, I had heard it described as a "newly established slum" and one of the largest communities of migrant workers in Shanghai.

I visited the Pengpu district on a sunny but windy day in late March 1994. At first I simply could not find the migrant laborer settlement. The residential quarter of Pengpu district was old, but no one in Shanghai would call it a slum. Thirty years ago, when the district was built, houseless newlyweds would consider it a dream to find a room there. In recent years, several new apartment buildings had been built in the residential quarter.

"Where do migrant workers live in this neighborhood?" I asked a girl who was selling eggs on the street.

"Over there," the girl pointed to a place about 200 meters away. "See that line of shacks in front of the new tall building?"

I had thought these were the temporary storage shelters for the construction team and never imagined that these tiny houses could be homes.

"Would you like to take a look?" A young man who had just bought eggs from the salesgirl was very friendly. He was willing to show me the shack in which he lived.

"Yes, of course." I was really grateful for his offer.

"May I know your name?" I asked.

"Liu Lin," he answered.

Aged 19, Mr. Liu came from Sichuan province. He arrived in Shanghai at the beginning of 1994 and found work for a construction company as a bricklayer.

"How much do you earn every month?" I asked on our way to the shack.

"It depends on how much work is available," he responded. He told me that he earned 1,000 yuan ($120) in the first month in Shanghai, 600 yuan in the second month, and expected to receive 1,200 yuan in March.

"Do you send money back home?"

"Yes, I spent 200 yuan per month here and sent the rest to my mother at home."

"Your mother will put the money in the bank so that you can use it when you get married, am I right?"

Liu Lin's face blushed with shyness. "I'm too young to think about marriage," he explained. "My parents' house in Sichuan is old, and we need to save money to repair it."

"Are you happy with your life here in Shanghai?" I asked.

"It's fine, although you may think that our living conditions are not so good, as you will see."

Walking along a bumpy, narrow passageway, we arrived at the line of shacks where Liu Lin and his fellow workers lived. The shacks were built with fired-brick walls, soil-stone floors, and asphalt roofs. Actually, there was only one large shack, which was separated into smaller "rooms" by cardboard and bamboo plates.

Liu told me that over 500 people lived in this 300-square-meter shack. It was difficult to believe that it could hold so many people. Liu brought a stool so that I could see the entire shack from above. This very low structure actually had two "floors"—some residents added hanging boards under the roof for sleeping.

Liu also showed me a six-square-meter "room" where 18 migrant workers lived. "We are so tired after work each day that we only need a space to lie down," Mr. Chen, 23, also from Sichuan, explained to me when I asked him how 18 adults could manage to live in this tiny room.

There was virtually nothing in the shack except the bedding. Some asphalt roofs had already been blown off by the heavy wind. The bedding was moist because late March is the rainy season in Shanghai. This shack could not provide shelter from wind or rain.

"People will get rheumatism if they have moist bedding," I said to Liu.

"Yes, I know," Liu pointed to the bedding hanging outside the shack, "we are drying them in the sun."

"But if the rain lasts for weeks . . ."

"We are not really concerned about too many things," Liu interrupted me.

"I do not complain about my situation here. The rent is low," Liu explained. "More importantly, I like to stay with my fellow Sichuan people. We take care of each other like brothers. We shoulder our hardship together, just as we share our dreams."

Liu told me that he had to go back to work. I thought I should pay him for the time he had spent showing me around. But I needed to do so in a respectful way.

"Do you smoke?" I asked.

"Yes."

"May I buy you several boxes of cigarettes?"

"No, you don't need to. You may just give me a cigarette now," he said.

"I'm sorry I don't smoke. But I can buy some nearby."

"No, don't worry about it."

Mr. Liu said good-bye to me and left. I took a taxi back to downtown Shanghai.

I really enjoyed meeting this 19-year-old young man. He was simple and honest, but at the same time also mature and sophisticated for his age. He did not have any sensational stories to tell; instead he actually told me a lot about the lives of migrant workers in Shanghai—their happiness and bitterness, their hardships and dreams. These are probably the common experiences and aspirations of many other migrant workers in China. Unlike the forty-niners in the United States, China's ninety-fourers do not necessarily want to be people of wealth. They are simply looking for a better life, an alternate way of life, a life beyond the countryside.

Mr. Liu's remarks also reminded me that we should look positively at the flow of migrant laborers. Xiao Yang, governor of Sichuan, also believes that the tidal wave of migrant workers is the third great undertaking

in China's rural reform, after the successes of the household contract responsibility system and the township and village enterprises. Xiao told
Chinese journalists that migrant workers have made three contributions:
(1) they have contributed to the economy of the place to which they have
moved; (2) they have brought advanced technology, experience, and a new
way of thinking to their native homes; and (3) they have sent money back
to their home villages.[37] In Sichuan province, for example, migrant workers have sent 5 billion yuan back annually—equivalent to the total amount
of money exchanged in China's stock market in one year. In Anhui Province, the income that migrant workers received in 1992 was 7.5 billion
yuan—2 billion yuan higher than the total revenue of the province.[38]

The major implication of China's internal migration, some scholars believe, lies in the impulse not only to reduce the segregation between rural
and urban areas institutionalized during the Mao era but also in the long
run to narrow the widening gap between rich and poor regions under
Deng Xiaoping. The availability of 200 million surplus rural laborers provides great human capital and is a positive factor for continuing rapid
economic growth in the country.

Regardless of the way in which people perceive the surplus issue, probably no one will disagree that the crucial question for China is how to
absorb this huge group. What measures can the Chinese government take
to respond to the pressure? The following list includes some measures
that the government could adopt to deal with this issue. Some of these
have been used since the 1950s, but they have recently become less effective. Some measures are currently in use or under consideration by policy
makers. Because of the large scale and multiple causes of China's surplus
rural laborers and internal migration, no easy solution is available, and no
single measure will be sufficient to deal with the complicated issues involved. It is, therefore, necessary to have a more comprehensive approach
to respond to the pressure. Not all of these measures are complementary—there are tensions and conflicts among certain policy measures.

- To reenforce administrative control (previously used measures)
  —The household registration system
  —Control of the supply of grain and cooking oil
  —The labor and employment system
- To absorb into urban state-owned enterprises
- To absorb into township and village enterprises
- To develop labor-intensive infrastructure projects
- To help migrant laborers settle down in small/medium-sized cities (to
  abolish the household registration system at the county-town level)

- To develop tertiary industry (service sector)
- To establish job information/service centers at all levels of administration and to facilitate various kinds of training programs
- To intensify farmland protection and establish both preventative and curative measures to protect the environment
- To increase the investment in the agricultural infrastructure
- To raise the prices of farm products to keep up with those of manufactured goods
- To reallocate financial resources and to increase funds for social welfare
- To create an early-warning mechanism for situations likely to cause protests by migrants, especially concerning violations of human rights

One can imagine that there is a powerful force within the Chinese government that advocates controlling and restricting the flow of migrant workers. From the 1950s to recent times, China's population has been relatively immobile geographically, due in part to the country's tight control on movement.[39] Some officials in major cities have advocated that local governments should adopt a more restrictive policy to limit the flow of migrant laborers, and some cities have done so. In 1994, the Shanghai municipal government issued a year-long and renewable "blue card" a work permit system to allow migrant laborers to work in the city. This new measure is intended to make it more difficult for those who lack blue cards to work in Shanghai. According to the new regulations of the municipal government, any firms that hire migrant laborers should offer jobs only to those migrants who have three cards—a work permit, a temporary household registration, and an I.D. But very few private firms in the city really adhere to the regulations.

The restrictive policy towards migrants has received much criticism from the public. Chen Zhenhui, a senior economist with the Guangdong Province Labor Services Company, argues:

> If the migrant workers are stopped, there would be at least a stagnation in the coastal areas. At worst, the economy of the coastal areas would collapse, causing the national economy to collapse. That will create far greater chaos in China, a much bigger threat than the disorder in the cities from the floating population. If we drive these people back to their home towns, they become different people. They cannot stay there peacefully. The whole country will become unstable.[40]

This does not mean that the government should not provide guidance for the direction of the flow of migrant workers. Major Chinese cities such as Shanghai, Beijing, and Guangzhou have already been over-crowded and are on the verge of paralysis. The state-owned enterprises in Chinese cities need to cut their work forces and certainly cannot absorb migrant workers. It would be strategically sound for the Chinese government to use policy measures to guide migrants to settle down in small and medium-sized cities. The government can, for example, abolish the household registration system at the county-town level, extend small cities, and help peasants pursue permanent residence there. One of the most salient characteristics of China's internal migration is that an over-whelming majority of migrants do not really settle down in the towns and cities where their new work places are located. They move back and forth from their old homes and new residences. To guide migrants to settle down in small cities could reduce the pressure caused by the influx of migrants to major cities, especially the pressure for transportation.

One of the most successful cases in absorbing surplus rural laborers in small cities and towns is southern Jiangsu. Over the past decade that region has absorbed a large number of workers, both from within the region and elsewhere, in its rural industries. The whole region has undergone rapid urbanization, and as a result, many new jobs have been created. During the mid-1980s, township and village enterprises in southern Jiangsu successfully transformed 3,360,000 agricultural workers, 65 percent of the total labor force in the region, to nonagricultural employees.[41] By 1993, Sunan had absorbed over 2 million surplus rural laborers from other areas to work in the region. This number does not even include the temporary workers hired without work permits or the floating population.[42] The experience of southern Jiangsu in absorbing surplus rural laborers from other areas is particularly remarkable, because southern Jiangsu itself is one of the most populous regions in China. Some scholars call southern Jiangsu's TVEs the "sponges" or "reservoirs" of these workers.

It would be a mistake, however, to assume that TVEs are unlimited labor reservoirs that could emply 200 million surplus workers. Many recent studies indicate that, although rural township enterprises continued to develop rapidly since the end of the 1980s, they did not necessarily create new jobs. The Chinese government could create jobs and remedy other major problems by reallocating resources to initiate labor-intensive projects to consolidate water and soil conservation and construct more railways and highways—the bottleneck of China's economic development. The shortage of highways has been particularly notable. The density of China's highways, for example, is only one-fifth of India's, one-seventh of the United States' and one-thirtieth of Japan's. According to a study conducted in 1992, the total capacity of China's five types of transportation (rail, highway, water, air, and pipe) was 2.07 million kilometers. This figure was even less than 50 percent of the capacity of high-way transportation alone in the United States in 1938.[43] The timing is ideal for the Chinese government to launch more labor-intensive trans-portation and infrastructure projects while millions of inexpensive sur-plus rural laborers are available.

One important policy measure that would absorb surplus rural laborers would be to encourage the development of the service sector in China's economy. The service sector, or what is also called the tertiary industry, accounts for only 13 percent of China's labor force; some experts estimate that if the percentage increases to 30 percent by the year 2000, 120 million jobs will be created. A comparative study of employed workers in tertiary industries in various countries shows that the percentage of employed laborers working in the service sector of the total work force in 1991 was 18.9 percent in China, 47 percent in Taiwan, 58.7 percent in Japan, and 71.6 percent in the United States.[44]

Meanwhile, the Chinese government should increase the protection of farmland and adopt a more constructive policy towards agricultural devel-opment. Investment in agricultural infrastructure accounted for only 1.7 percent of state expenditure in 1994, the lowest percentage in history. Some experts agree that the privileges accorded to urban residents, such as housing, social welfare benefits, subsidized food and public transport, education, and medical services must either be eliminated or extended to rural residents as well.[45]

The government should facilitate various kinds of service and training programs at all levels of administration to help migrant workers. A na-tionwide information center must be set up to inform migrants of their rights and obligations. Some priority should be given to social facilities.[46] Because of its tremendously large scale and scope, the issue of surplus rural laborers will confront China for many years, if not many decades, to come.

Migrant workers have already become a distinct group in China during the 1990s. They are an important socioeconomic force that has contrib-uted to the economic development of the country. But they are still largely treated as what a Chinese official has called a "community outside the system" (*tizhiwaiqunluo*). Like the forty-niners, Chinese migrant workers face many hardships. One of the biggest challenges for China in the years to come is how to integrate migrant workers into all aspects of urban life and to provide all the social welfare benefits that they deserve. To a certain extent, the future of China—its political stability, economic growth, and social progress—largely depends on how the government responds to this challenge. The issue of migrant workers is one that China cannot afford to deliberate upon for too long.

9

"Rome Was Not Built in a Day, but Zhangjiagang Was"

A Model of Urbanization

In his classic work on the development of American civilization, *The Age of Reform: From Bryan to F.D.R.*, Richard Hofstadter had the following opening remark: "The United States was born in the country and has moved to the city."[1] The history of the United States, in a way, is a history of urbanization. The level of urbanization in the United States (the percentage of urban population of the total population of the country) has increased greatly over the past two centuries—from 5.1 percent in 1790 to 77.7 percent in 1990.[2] By 1970, the United States already had 4,653 cities—there were 6.9 cities per 10,000 square kilometers. Urbanization is a process of economic change. It is usually defined as a transformation of the population from rural to urban residents. As people move from rural to urban areas, they also change their occupations from the traditional agricultural sector (the primary sector) to the modern industrial and service sectors (the secondary and the tertiary sectors).

America has experienced two broad movements in the urbanization process in its more recent history: the shift of emphasis from metropolis to small and medium-sized cities, from the East Coast and Midwest to the West Coast and the South. One certainly could find problems and draw lessons from the landscape changes in the United States over the past two centuries. But in general, prior to World War II, the urbanization of the United States paralleled and contributed to the American industrial revolution. In the postwar era, American urbanization has corresponded to the structural transformation of the U.S. economy and led to the rapid development of the tertiary sector.

China's urbanization, by contrast, had a slow pace and a far more troubling experience up until the 1980s. At the end of 1989, China had a total of 467 cities—0.49 cities per 10,000 square kilometers.[3] The percentage of the urban population in the total population of the country was 28.5 percent, which was about the average level of urbanization in the world in 1950 (28.7 percent), and much lower than 52 percent, the world average in 1990.

One of the main characteristics of the economic reform in post-Mao China, as discussed in chapter 5, is the rapid development of township and village enterprises in the rural areas. Over 100 million laborers have changed their occupations from agricultural to nonagricultural since 1978. But these nonagricultural workers usually remained in the same geographical location. This phenomenon differs from the process of urbanization in many countries, such as the United States and England, where geographical relocation of workers occurred prior to their occupational change.[4] Although millions of migrant workers have flooded into large cities in post-Mao China, few of them have settled permanently there. As a result, China's immense rural area has suffered industrial pollution caused by the random spread of TVEs, and at the same time large cities have become overcrowded. In general, urbanization has lagged far behind the industrialization of the country.

China's urbanization, however, has accelerated remarkably in recent years. Newly born booming towns and small cities have mushroomed along the east and south coast, particularly around the Yangtze River Delta near Shanghai and the Pearl River Delta near Guangzhou. The country's urbanization is now growing the fastest it ever has in Chinese history. In 1992 and 1993, for instance, 106 new cities have come into existence. The total number of Chinese cities is now 620, three times the number registered in 1978.[5]

Perhaps the most impressive new city in the country is Zhangjiagang (pronounced *chang-jia-gong*), Jiangsu Province. Zhangjiagang didn't have the status of a county-level city until the end of 1986. But within a few years, a modern city has been built in this backward region in Sunan. In 1992, Zhangjiagang's GNP increased 87 percent over the previous year, the highest growth rate in the country.[6] Zhangjiagang can well serve as a model for China's urbanization.

China's Urbanization: A Review

Many reasons explain the slow pace of China's urbanization during the first four decades of the PRC. Historically, China had an agrarian economy. As the most populous country in the world, maintaining agricultural sufficiency has always been the most important concern among the Chinese people. During the Mao era, the PRC government had a negative attitude towards urbanization and sent city dwellers to rural areas in the name of reducing the economic gap between urban and rural areas.

As a Chinese scholar noted, the Maoist government had three misconceptions.[7] First, in the view of the government, urban development would detract from rural development. The authorities therefore tried to constrain the former in order to ensure the latter. Second, the authorities believed that industrialization and urbanization were exactly the same thing. The government paid attention only to industrial development and ignored the development of urban infrastructure and the service sector. As a result, China's urbanization lagged behind the process of industrialization of the nation. The stagnancy of urbanization, in return, also restricted industrial development. And third, the government failed to understand that urbanization is not only the result of economic growth, but can also be its cause.

According to statistics from the Institute of Demography at Wuhan University, China's level of urbanization actually declined in the 1960s. The household registration system, which was adopted by the Chinese government in 1958, restricted the flow of population from rural villages to towns and cities. The total number of people who lived in towns, for example, decreased from 46 million in 1959 to 41 million in 1963. The town population in 1971 was lower than that of 1959.[8] During the Cultural Revolution, 1.7 million urban high-school graduates were sent to the countryside, further reducing the urban population.[9] Many urban factories moved to rural areas. Doctors, engineers, teachers, and many others were sent to rural areas, either permanently or temporarily. The percentage of the urban population in the nation's total population decreased from 18.4 percent in 1960 to 17.9 percent in 1978.[10]

China's economic reform, which started in 1978, has reversed the direction of internal migration. Table 9–1 shows the rapid increase in numbers of Chinese cities and towns from 1978 to 1992. The number of towns has increased faster than the number of cities. In Wenzhou, Zhejiang Province, for example, the number of towns increased from 33 in 1984 to 120 in 1992. About 2.4 million people have left their villages and settled in these towns. Over 40 percent of rural laborers changed their occupations from peasants to workers in the industrial or the tertiary sectors.[11] In the entire country, the percentage of the urban population out of the total population increased from 17.9 percent in 1978 to 28.5 percent in 1990. It is estimated that the figure will reach 35.7 percent by the year 2000—doubling in about two decades.[12]

TABLE 9-1
The Urban Development of China during the Reform Era (1978–1992)
(Number of Cities or Towns)

	1978	1992
Prefecture-level cities (*dijishi*)	91	191
County-level cities (*xianjishi*)	99	323
Towns in which township administrations are located (*jianzhizhen*)	2,176	14,500

Source: Shizhang cankao (Mayor's reference), no. 6 (1994): 2.

Six factors have contributed to the rapid development of China's urbanization. They are (1) the economic growth of the country, (2) the rapid development of rural and local industries, (3) the mobility of surplus rural laborers and more flexible government policy towards internal migration, (4) large state construction projects in cities, (5) the increase of foreign investment, and (6) the growth of satellite cities around metropolises.[13]

One of the fastest-growing regions in China's urbanization is Sunan, the enormous area under the jurisdiction of three prefecture-level cities: Wuxi, Suzhou, and Changzhou. As chapter 5 shows, the rural industrial revolution has brought a fascinating economic boom to this region—the so-called Golden Triangle. The rural area of the Sunan region has industrialized rapidly. At present, agriculture accounts for only 8 percent of the total industrial and agricultural output in the region, and industry accounts for 92 percent.[14]

This rural industrial revolution has significantly changed the labor structure of the region. The percentage of nonagricultural employment in the rural area of Jiangsu Province in 1989 was 39.1 percent, ranked fourth in all provinces and municipalities directly under the central government—after only Shanghai, Beijing, and Tianjin. Jiangsu's annual increase of nonagricultural laborers from 1978 to 1989 was 13.2 percent, ranked third after Zhejiang and Guangdong. According to one study, by 1990 the percentage of nonagricultural laborers in the rural area of Sunan had already reached 76 percent.[15]

The rural industrial revolution has led to the urbanization of the region. The mayor of a Sunan city used three terms to characterize the change in the development strategy of the Sunan region.

"In the 1970s we emphasized 'farmland development' [*zaotian*], and in the 1980s we placed our priority on 'factory development' [*zaochang*]," the mayor told me. "Now in the 1990s we have made great advances in 'city development' [*zaocheng*]."

Both the local governments and entrepreneurs in Sunan have indeed invested a large amount of money in the urban development of the region. In Wuxian County, for example, the annual investment in city infrastructure increased from 50 million yuan in the late 1980s to 95 million in 1991 and 250 million in 1992.[16]

"Rome Was Not Built in a Day, but Zhangjiagang Was"

One cannot discuss the rapid urban development in Sunan or the entire country without mentioning Zhangjiagang. "If there is any city that can make China proud of its urban development," a British sinologist commented, "Zhangjiagang should be the one."

At present, Chinese cities are generally notorious for their lack of green—few trees and little grass. With a few exceptions, such as Beijing and the former capital Nanjing, most cities have narrow streets, which have made traffic jams familiar to urban dwellers. But what one sees in Zhangjiagang is an unusual urban scene in China: trees and grass are planted everywhere in the city. Smoking is prohibited in public places and streets. It is not surprising that Zhangjiagang city has won the title of "National Sanitational City" every year since 1993.

Zhangjiagang County covers an area of 999 square kilometers, including 221 square kilometers of water and 778 square kilometers of land. The city has recently built 19 new boulevards, and planted 850,000 trees and 1.2 million square meters of green areas.[17] These newly built streets are usually over 50 meters wide. Highway Zhangyang and Highway Yanjiang, two roads that lead directly to the downtown area of Zhangjiagang, are each over 100 meters wide.

Rapid economic growth is easily visible on the streets of Zhangjiagang. Joint venture factories, fancy commercial centers, and elegant office and apartment buildings stand on both sides of spacious boulevards. On commercial streets small businesses are flourishing. Entertainment clubs, restaurants, and karaoke bars are filled with well-dressed entrepreneurs using cellular phones.

All these developments, however, were achieved during the past few years. Just a few years ago, most urban areas of Zhangjiagang were farmland or covered with reeds. Zhangjiagang was not even on the city map of China in the mid-1980s, because it was then a county. Called Shazhou County (with the nickname of "Sunan's Siberia"), it was a backward county in Sunan. Even in the early 1970s, a majority of the peasants in the county were almost as poor as peasants in Subei (northern Jiangsu). The site on which downtown Zhangjiagang is now located was a small town called Yangshe. Most of Zhangjiagang's urban construction projects took place after 1992.

"Rome was not built in a day, but Zhangjiagang has been," said a civil engineer in Zhangjiagang, describing the rapid rise of Zhangjiagang. The engineer originally worked in Shanghai but has now settled in Zhangjiagang, where he has been involved in a number of construction projects.

Zhangjiagang surely benefits from an ideal location. The city is on the southern bank of the fertile lower reaches of the Yangtze River, with Shanghai on its east, Suzhou on its south, Wuxi and Changzhou on its west, and Nantong on the other side of the Yangtze River. With 26 industrial satellite towns under its jurisdiction, Zhangjiagang County has a total urban and rural population of 820,000. Among them, over 100,000 live in Zhangjiagang city.

Zhangjiagang city is named after its impressive international open port—Zhangjiagang Port—situated northwest of the city. The port has a favorable site, and it never silts up or freezes over. Cargo vessels can be steered close to shore because of its deep water. Ships of less than 100,000 tons can tie up directly at the wharfs. The port has already opened 11 international routes and six containerized international shipping lines. It has 22 scheduled departures every month. The port has a freight transport business with over 100 international ports in more than 140 countries.[18] In 1993, its annual handling capacity reached 15 million tons. Zhangjiagang Port handles about 46 percent of the goods transported overseas in the whole Jiangsu Province.[19]

In 1991, Zhangjiagang was ranked seventh among the 100 economically strongest counties in the country. Its position in these supercounties rose to fourth in 1993, and second in 1995.[20] In 1993, the city's total industrial and agricultural output reached 36 billion yuan, higher than that of some inland provinces in China. At present, nine major branches of industry have been set up in the city: metallurgy, electronic components, construction materials, light industry, textiles, chemicals and medicines, wool weaving, knitwear, and arts and crafts.

In terms of attracting foreign investment and promoting foreign trade,

Zhangjiagang was ranked first in Jiangsu Province in 1993 when its foreign trade export purchasing value reached 72 billion yuan. Only in 1992 did the State Council approve the establishment of the Zhangjiagang free trade zone. At present, foreign funds pledged to contracts already total over $10 billion.

The city not only has over 1,000 joint ventures (including 379 foreign manufacturing enterprises and about 700 foreign-investment enterprises), but has also established 80 enterprises abroad (set up by parent companies in Zhangjiagang). More than 360 items are exported and sold to 80 countries.[21] All 47 province-level major corporations are export-oriented enterprises. Qin Zhenhua, party secretary of Zhangjiagang, told Chinese journalists in 1994 that all new production in the city should target foreign markets.[22]

The living standard of the people of Zhangjiagang, especially those who were peasants, has improved greatly. In 1991, the average income of people in the rural area was 2,140 yuan, 24 times the average income in 1962. In 1994, the average income of urban dwellers was 6,024 yuan, and average income of farmers was 3,108 yuan. The GNP per capita was 18,600 yuan, and the revenue was 1.03 billion yuan.[23] Over 70 percent of peasants have moved into new two- or three-story houses since 1978. The average housing space per person is 47 square meters.[24] From 1980 to 1991, Zhangjiagang had an average annual GNP growth of 19.6 percent. The total industrial and agricultural output value increased 24.1 percent annually, on average. From 1992 to 1994, the GNP of Zhangjiagang increased 68.3 percent annually on average (with an 87 percent growth in 1992).[25]

"China has had the fastest-growing GNP in the world in the past few years. In China, Zhangjiagang has the fastest-growing GNP," an official in the municipal government of Zhangjiagang said to me. "I dare say that no other county, in China or elsewhere, has achieved as high a rate of GNP growth as Zhangjiagang has."

"I believe you," I replied. "How could one surpass an 87 percent GNP rise in one year?"

When I told a friend in the United States about the GNP growth rate in Zhangjiagang, she commented, "We in the United States would be thrilled if our GNP achieved only one-tenth of Zhangjiagang's growth rate."

What Led to Zhangjiagang's Economic Boom?

How could Zhangjiagang achieve all this, transforming itself from a small town and a "fishermen's wharf" to a modern port city in such a short time?

Geographical location, especially that of the port, certainly has helped. During my visits to Zhangjiagang, many people told me the same story about how the mayor and Party secretary of the city went to Beijing to campaign for free trade zone status—they brought many young girls to Beijing with them and gave these girls to officials of the central government as maids or housekeepers. These officials didn't even need to pay the wages of these girls because the municipal government of Zhangjiagang took care of it. The only thing the officials in Beijing needed to do was simply to give approval for the establishment of the Zhangjiagang free trade zone.

"In the United States nominees for the cabinet or other top government posts are in big trouble if they only once fail to pay taxes for the maids working in their houses," said an American businessman with whom I traveled in Sunan. He asked a local official who told us the story, "Do the Chinese leaders feel awkward about failing to pay their maids?"

"Awkward?" the local official said. "No one felt awkward. Everyone got what they wanted—the leaders of the central government got maids for free, the maids made connections in Beijing, and Zhangjiagang city got approval. Why feel awkward if we could get things done? We local officials should work very hard to win favorable policies from *big men* in Beijing."

"You greased the wheel to make it run," said the American businessman.

"By the way," the local official continued, "if your American company decides to invest in Zhangjiagang, we can export a lot of maids to serve your CEOs and trustees. How about it?"

The American businessman laughed. "Is this Chinese gentleman serious?" he asked me in English.

"I'm not sure," I replied. "But the story that Zhangjiagang officials sent maids to their bosses in Beijing is well known in Sunan."

"The Zhangjiagang officials should be praised for their 'local initiative' and their creativity in establishing a 'reciprocal relationship' with the central government," the American businessman said.

"I agree," I responded.

Notwithstanding the ethical issue of the "maids diplomacy" (*baomu waijiao*) pursued by the local leaders of Zhangjiagang, the establishment of the free trade zone (*baoshuiqu*) has directly contributed to the economic boom in the city. So far, Zhangjiagang free trade zone is the only inland river free trade zone among all the duty-free zones approved by the Chinese central government.

The special policies carried out in Zhangjiagang, according to local officials, are even more flexible and favorable than those exercised in any other existing special or economic development zones. The Zhangjiagang free trade zone has attracted many domestic and foreign enterprises and agents, who are engaged in international trade, export-oriented storage, transportation packaging, entrepôt and transit trade, and export processing.[26]

"Geographical location, local leadership, and favorable policy in the free trade zone are all relevant to the rapid development there," said Lin Jiangong of Suzhou University. "But the most important factor behind the economic boom of the city is the role of township and village enterprises. TVEs are the driving force behind the rise of Zhangjiagang."

Professor Lin's interpretation is well supported by the statistics. In 1988, for example, the total industrial and agricultural output value of the city was 7.2 billion yuan, of which the TVEs' output accounted for 5.5 billion yuan (76.7 percent of the total). In 1991, the total industrial and agricultural output value reached 12.2 billion yuan, an increase of 18 times larger than in 1978 and 89 times higher than in 1962. The percentage of TVEs in the total output of Zhangjiagang was as high as 81.8 percent in 1991 and 87 percent in 1992.[27] Among China's top 500 TVEs in 1994, 47 were located in Zhangjiagang.[28]

Foreign investment has certainly played an important role in the rapid economic growth and urban development there, but the main source of capital thus far has come from Zhangjiagang itself—from the funds accumulated by TVEs in previous years. The rate of accumulation in Zhangjiagang was 68 percent in 1991, 14 percent higher than that of Suzhou and double that of the total country.[29]

Zhangjiagang as a Model for China's Urban Development

What sets Zhangjiagang apart from most other counties in which TVEs have developed rapidly is that Zhangjiagang is more willing to invest money in infrastructure and urban development.

"Although TVEs in Zhangjiagang achieved a high growth rate in the 1980s," said a top official in Zhangjiagang, who did not want to be identified, "we had four major problems by the end of the 1980s. First, TVEs were scattered here and there in villages and towns. They overlapped each other in terms of their products. Second, Zhangjiagang lacked natural resources. Most raw materials came from other regions. Third, transportation and infrastructure lagged far behind the economic growth of the region. The main means of transportation in Zhangjiagang had been water, which accounted for 80 percent, while road transportation accounted for only 20 percent. We haven't built a railway yet (the railway between Zhangjiagang and Wuxi is now under construction). And finally, like all other counties in Sunan, we had a shortage of capital as we planned to further our economic development. We desperately needed more foreign capital.

"We realized that the key to solve all these problems," the official continued, "was to accelerate urbanization and invest more in transportation. By doing so, we could attract TVEs to the city and would have a better environment for foreign investors."

"If TVEs have moved to cities, do you still call them township and village enterprises?" I asked.

"No," the official answered, "the TVE was a product of the Chinese rural industrial revolution. This revolution has two tasks: to industrialize part of China's vast rural area and to achieve rapid urban development. The rural industrial revolution may not achieve these two tasks simultaneously but urbanization should closely follow industrialization."

"Do you mean that the TVEs will fulfill their historical task and transform rural areas into urban enterprises?" I asked.

"Yes, people in TVEs use the expression 'leave the farmland but remain in rural villages; enter factories but not cities' [*litubulixiang, jinchangbujincheng*] to characterize the change in their occupation but the continuation of their rural identity. This phenomenon will no longer continue. They either remain in rural areas as peasants or go to cities or towns as nonagricultural workers."

"Will China have a shortage of grain if millions of peasants leave the farmland, and most of the country urbanizes?" I wanted him to reply to this important question.

"A shortage of grain in a country is often caused by many factors, such as domestic politics and the international economic environment," the official commented. "In the Mao era, especially during the early 1960s, millions of Chinese died of starvation. But over 85 percent of China's population then lived in rural areas. China will remain a poor Third World country forever if China does not transform itself from an agrarian economy to an industrialized nation.

"We officials in Zhangjiagang were criticized by many people elsewhere, including your people in Shanghai, for 'pulling too many peasants into urban areas' and 'abusing rural land for urban construction,' " the official continued. "They forgot that China has over 200 million surplus rural laborers. Zhangjiagang has actually absorbed a great number of migrants from other regions."

The official was quite right. In some economically advanced market towns in Zhangjiagang as well as in other counties in Sunan, the number of nonlocal laborers has surpassed the number of local residents.[30]

"People in Shanghai criticized us for building too many roads—too many wide roads," the official continued. "These narrow-minded people seemed too familiar with the narrow streets in Shanghai to understand in the long run there will be a great need to build broad roads.

"The most important thing that Zhangjiagang has contributed to Sunan and to the entire nation is neither its 87 percent of the GNP growth rate, nor its export-oriented economy, but its role model for China's urban development. This does not mean that the urban development here is perfect, but Zhangjiagang serves as a model for other small and medium-sized cities in the country. Do you understand what I mean?"

I did understand what the official tried to say. The role model of urban development is indeed very important to China. Since 1978, the Chinese government has adopted a three-part strategy for urban development: "To strictly control the growth of metropolitan cities; to rationally develop medium-sized cities; and to vigorously promote small cities."

But this strategy has been ineffective because small cities have lacked capital to develop, while millions of jobless peasants have rushed into major cities. According to Chinese government statistics from 1988, big cities accounted for 38 percent, medium-sized cities 16.5 percent, small cities 14.5 percent, and towns 31 percent of the total number of towns and cities in the country. There were too many big cities.[31] Post-Mao China has therefore confronted two seemingly contradictory major problems in its urban development. One is the lag of urbanization in contrast to the rapid industrialization in the country (*chengzhenhua de zhihouxing*), and the other is the deterioration of the urban environment of China's metropolises, or what some scholars call the "city syndrome" (*chengshibing*).

The Lag of Urbanization. Since the economic reform started in 1978, China has restructured its economic sectors and promoted the development of the industrial sector. Like many populous agricultural countries, China has long had a surplus of rural laborers. Urban industries' ability to absorb these laborers, however, is limited. Under these circumstances, China has chosen the road that emphasizes nonagricultural development (*feinonghua*) in rural areas. The boom of township and village enterprises over the past decade has reflected this. TVEs have absorbed millions of surplus rural laborers and contributed to the growth of the Chinese economy.[32] This strategy aimed to avoid the "massive exodus" that is still occurring in countries such as Mexico, where not only are millions of jobless peasants leaving the country, they are also rushing to cities. Approximately one-fourth of the population in Mexico, for example, lives in Mexico City.

Yet the Chinese way of development has its own costs and problems. An overwhelming majority of rural enterprises are scattered randomly throughout the countryside. Of the total 21 million TVEs in the country in 1992, only 1 percent were in the towns where county governments were located (*xiancheng*), 7 percent were in other towns, and an overwhelming majority of TVEs (92 percent) were scattered throughout the countryside.[33] Although the development of rural enterprises may contribute to the formation of townships, those places with a few TVEs are usually too small to support urban functions. According to a study of Chinese coastal towns, towns in which county governments are located have 26,000 people, on average, towns in which township administrations are located (*jianzhizhen*) have 2,600 people, on average, and market towns (*jizhen*) have only 398 residents, on average.[34]

The dispersal of township and village enterprises in China's huge rural area has not only made the infrastructure (e.g., water and electric supply, transportation and road construction, and waste disposal) there less efficient, it has also made the formation of cities more difficult. According to a recent study, the ratio between nonagricultural development and urbanization in China in 1990 was 1:1.52. This means that a significant portion of nonagricultural development took place outside cities and towns in the country.[35]

The lag of urbanization has led to a more serious consequence—the stagnancy of the tertiary sector of the Chinese economy. Characteristically, the development of this sector takes place in urban areas, or more precisely, it relies on the density of the population in cities. Businesses such as commerce, information, advertisement, telecommunication, entertainment, hotels, and restaurants usually develop most quickly in urban areas with sufficient residents. The dispersal of rural industry has generally failed to stimulate the growth of the tertiary sector. Therefore, the tertiary sector, which can potentially absorb millions of surplus rural laborers, is not well developed in China. In 1991, the percentage of the total population that worked in the tertiary sector was 18.6 percent, while the figure for advanced industrialized countries was about 60 percent.[36]

China's "City Syndrome." The second major problem of urban development during the post-Mao era has been the deterioration of the urban environment of China's metropolises as a result of both the natural growth of the population in cities and the internal migration of the country. Housing, transportation, and other infrastructure facilities such as water and electricity in China's major cities cannot meet the basic needs of the increasing number of urban dwellers.

The density of population in Shanghai during the 1980s, for example, was 19,900 per square kilometer, which was much higher than the figures of many other overcrowded cities in the world, such as Tokyo (5,400 per square kilometer) and New Delhi (4,000 per square kilometer) during the same period.[37] According to an official report, 899,900 families in Shanghai have insufficient housing (meaning less than four square meters per person), and among them 68,800 families simply do not have room to live.[38] But the government's priority during the past decade has been to construct office buildings, fancy hotels, and expensive villas for foreign and domestic business people, rather than to help the families with housing problems. An official from the Ministry of Urban and Rural Construction said in 1994 that the conditions of about 8 million households in China's metropolises should be improved immediately. Approximately 33 million square meters of dangerous dwellings should be torn down, and nearly 500 million square meters of decrepit housing should be renovated.[39]

The inadequacy of urban transportation is another serious symptom of China's city syndrome. In Shanghai, the number of bus passengers reached 4.6 billion annually in the 1980s, 18 times that of 1949, but the number of buses increased only fourfold and the road space only twofold.[40] In 1991, urban Shanghai had 200,000 cars, but three years later, the number had doubled.[41] Most of these cars, however, are often stuck along Shanghai's narrow streets. In Guangzhou, from 1978 to 1992, the GNP increased sevenfold, and the number of automobiles elevenfold, but only 2.4 times more urban road space was added.[42] Not surprisingly, the city transportation systems in many major cities such as Guangzhou and Shanghai have been on the edge of paralysis.

In addition, the infrastructure in China's major cities has lagged far behind the rapid growth in the urban economy and population. It has been common in China's metropolises to shut electric power down by district in turns. Among China's 479 cities in 1991, over 300 had water shortages.[43] The situation has actually deteriorated in recent years, as more city dwellers have installed air conditioners and showers in their residences.

Almost all major cities in China are seriously polluted. According to a recent environmental evaluation of world metropolises, Beijing and Shenyang rank among the seven most polluted cities on the globe. In Chongqing, one-third of residents have respiratory problems. In one-half of China's cities, tapwater is polluted. Qu Geping, chairman of the environment protection committee under the People's Congress, said that China has been losing $11.5 billion every year as a result of environmental pollution. That is about 3 percent of China's GNP.[44]

Despite all these problems caused by overpopulation, big cities have increased at a higher rate than have those of small and medium-sized cities during this decade. Table 9–2 shows that the percentage of cities with populations over 500,000 increased from 73.2 percent in 1981 to 80.6 percent in 1990 while that of cities with a population of below 500,000 decreased from 26.8 percent in 1981 to 19.4 percent in 1990. It seems that the overpopulation in China's big cities will become an increasingly serious problem in the years to come.

Challenges of Urbanization and China's Choices

Both the excessive urbanization in Chinese metropolises and the lag of urbanization in enormous areas of the country suggest the great challenges that China confronts at present. Meanwhile, these problems also contrast with the success of small and medium-sized cities and highlight the great importance of Zhangjiagang as a model for China's urban development.

One may argue that because of its port and other geographical advantages, Zhangjiagang is unique and thus unsuited to be a model. But one should also notice that Zhangjiagang was a poor county in Sunan in the early 1980s, and it lacked many natural resources. Thus, despite certain atypical characteristics, Zhangjiagang can still serve as a model for China's urbanization for various reasons—its urban size, its conducive environment for the development of TVEs, its efforts to avoid the dispersal of TVEs in rural areas, its emphasis on infrastructure and transportation in the city, its environmental and ecological concerns, its dramatic rise from

TABLE 9-2
Distribution of Urban Population by City Size (1981–1990)

City Population	1981		1985		1990	
	Number	%	Number	%	Number	%
More than 1,000,000	37	52.1	57	47.7	98	48.1
500,000–1,000,000	41	21.1	85	25.6	153	32.5
100,000–500,000	136	26.0	171	23.5	198	19.2
Less than 100,000	15	0.8	11	0.3	12	0.2

Source: Lin Yan, *Shanghai nongcun chengshi hua yanjiu* (Research on urbanization of Shanghai's rural areas) (Shanghai: Science and Technology Publishing House, 1993), 69.

a poor economic background, and its initiative in both getting favorable policies from the central government and attracting foreign investment.

China is currently undergoing one of the largest and fastest urbanizations in human history, as millions of surplus rural laborers leave their homes. In Pudong, for example, 150,000 peasants have become urban dwellers within 12 years. A similar scale of population change in the western part of Shanghai took place about 150 years ago.[45] In any country, including the United States, large-scale, rapid urbanization can be a painful experience. In India and Mexico, for example, many socioeconomic problems have been caused by urbanization. Three decades ago, the world had 19 cities that each had populations of over 4 million; now the number is 135. By 2025, about 5.5 billion people will live in cities. Eight-tenths of them, however, will be in developing countries.[46] In China, according to the government, the urban population is expected to hit 400 million by the year 2000 and 500 million by 2020.[47]

The crucial question that China faces now is how to absorb its huge number of surplus rural laborers. The country has three major options. The first is to absorb them into the major cities. However, the population of China's 15 largest cities is about 40 million. These cities clearly cannot absorb five times as many additional people into their already overcrowded urban areas.[48]

The second option is to encourage TVEs to create more job opportunities within rural areas. As discussed earlier, during the past 16 years, over 100 million rural workers have already been absorbed by 21 million rural industrial firms all over the country. But since the end of the 1980s, the number of new jobs created by township industries has decreased. The development priority for township industries is to attract capital and to upgrade technology rather than increase the labor force. More importantly, the dispersion of TVEs in China's huge rural area has not only made the use of resources and infrastructure less efficient, but has also constrained the development of the tertiary sector of the Chinese economy.

The third option is to set up and extend small and medium-sized cities and help peasants pursue permanent residence there. China has 300 smaller cities like Zhangjiagang (each with less than 200,000 people). These cities are located in all parts of the country and therefore can avoid transportation problems caused by the flow of the population from one distant area to the other. These smaller cities lack the heavy burdens of large cities, and therefore the social cost of hiring new laborers is relatively low. In addition, local governments have a great incentive to develop urban infrastructure in their own regions.

Zhangjiagang is a success story. However, it remains to be seen whether Zhangjiagang's method of urban development can be duplicated in other parts of the country. If not, how will China respond to the serious challenges of environmental deterioration both in overcrowded major cities and in rural areas where TVEs have been scattered randomly?

10

A Yangtze Three Gorges Adventure

Ever since my boyhood I have dreamed of taking a cruise to the Three Gorges (*Sanxia*). This 200-kilometer stretch of the Yangtze River gorges, starting from Fengjie in the eastern part of Sichuan Province to Yichang in western Hubei Province, is one of the great scenic attractions of China. Its gorgeous scenery and turbulent waters have not only fostered a number of legendary military tacticians, but have also inspired many of China's painters, poets, and philosophers.

I always remember a photo that my father showed me when I was a child. He took the photo during a cruise to the Three Gorges in the early 1960s. In the photo, scores of trackers (*qianfu*) lined the hilly riverbanks and hauled a big boat with long ropes against the current. The boat, as my father told me, was loaded with fish and other river products. Fishermen were transporting their catches to sell in nearby cities. My father also taught me a Chinese saying as he commented on the photo: "Those living by the mountain live off the mountain, those living near the water live off the water" (*kaoshan chishan, kaoshui chishui*).

My desire to visit this area and to see how the diligent Sichuan and Hubei people live and work became stronger with each passing year, especially when I heard that the Chinese government decided to build the Three Gorges Dam near Yichang, in central China's Hubei Province.

Controversies over the Three Gorges Dam Project

Full-scale construction of the Three Gorges Dam began in 1995, although preparatory work, which included clearing the construction site and evacuating residents in the area, started two years earlier. According to the proposal, the dam will be 1,983 meters long, 175 meters high, and 185 meters at its peak. Construction of this would-be world's largest dam is scheduled to take 17 years.

Such a huge project will certainly affect people's lives and the environment. According to a Chinese official newspaper, about 632 square kilometers—encompassing 2 cities, 11 counties, 140 towns, and 1,351 villages—will be displaced by the waters of the Yangtze River, as the water level will rise over 175 meters. At least 1,130,000 residents in Sichuan and Hubei Provinces will be resettled to make way for the project. The ecological system of the region and the Chinese landscape will fundamentally change after the construction of the dam. Many species of fish, for example, will disappear from the Yangtze.[1] The environmental effects, as an American observer illustrates, will be "comparable to those of damming the Grand Canyon or diverting Niagara Falls."[2]

What has worried scientists and citizens the most are the potentially catastrophic consequences of any major technical problem with the dam. If it is not built properly, if it were sabotaged by terrorists or foreign

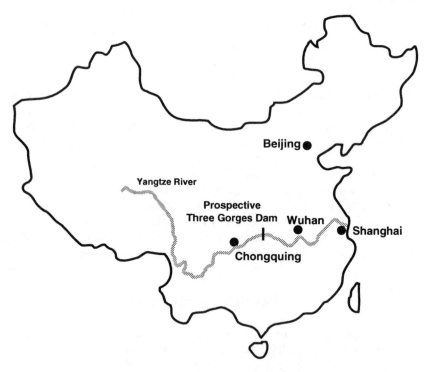

Map 10-1 The Yangtze River and the Location of the Three Gorges Dam

The Dragon Gate Bridge at the Daning River. Although this bridge seems to be far above the river, it will be inundated. The water level of the upper reaches of the Yangtze is supposed to be raised by 175 meters after the completion of the Three Gorges Dam project.

powers or damaged by an earthquake, the dam would flood the huge area of the middle and lower reaches of the Yangtze River, including some of China's major cities. Geographical studies have argued that the massive change brought by the building of the dam could induce earthquakes.[3] To put the matter bluntly, the lives of more than 380 million people, one-third of China's population, who live along its banks, will depend on the future safety of this gigantic dam.

The Chinese authorities have long restricted any open discussion of the project, but the controversies over the construction of the dam can be traced back to the early years of the Republic. In 1919, Sun Yat-sen, the founder of the Republic of China, initiated the idea of building a dam on the Three Gorges in order to prevent floods that might inundate the enormous area at the middle and lower reaches of the Yangtze River. From 185 B.C. to 1911, this area suffered a total of 214 floods—once every 10 years, on average. From 1911 to 1949, seven major floods took place in the Yangtze River area. In 1931 and 1935, for example, two floods hit the river's middle and lower reaches. Each of them killed about 140,000 people.[4]

Because of the civil war and the Japanese invasion, as well as a lack of capital, the Republican government did not turn the idea of the dam into an actual construction project. For decades, experts on irrigation works usually placed their emphasis on building small dams at the branches of the Yangtze River instead of the construction of a gigantic dam in the Three Gorges.

In 1953, Mao Zedong took a cruise along the Yangtze River. He ordered the reconsideration of the construction of the Three Gorges Dam. "The Socialist Three Gorges Dam project," said Mao, "should excel other major projects in Chinese history such as Qin Shi Huang's Great Wall and Shui Yang Di's Grand Canal."[5] Following Mao's order, Chinese scientists began to study the feasibility of the Three Gorges Dam. Those scientists and officials—for example, Chen Mingshu—who publicly raised doubts were persecuted as rightists. The project, however, did not move beyond the planning stages during the Mao era, primarily due to the Sino-Soviet conflict and the famine caused by the Great Leap Forward during the early 1960s. The country simply did not have the resources to build such a big dam.

Another main reason, according to some insiders in Chinese politics, was the private meeting between Mao and Li Siguang, a prominent scientist and minister of geological resources. Li told Mao that he would commit suicide if he could not stop the construction of the Three Gorges Dam. Li's strong criticism of the project finally called Mao's attention to the potentially catastrophic consequences of the dam.[6]

This story may be too dramatic for some people to believe, but it was by no means unusual for a scientist in China to fight for principles at the risk of his or her life.[7] During the construction of the Gezhou Dam, thus far the largest in China, the team that worked on the foundation of the dam did not do their job properly. A scientist who inspected the foundation found some serious problems. He reported to the authorities on the project and demanded that the foundation be rebuilt. This meant that the completion of the project would be postponed for a year. The authorities refused to consider his demand. With a strong sense of responsibility, the scientist decided to launch a hunger strike to protest. Five days after he began his fast, the authorities finally realized the potential danger if they did not rebuild the foundation of the dam. The scientist won the battle.

The critics of the Three Gorges Dam project, however, haven't won any of their battles. In the mid-1980s, China's new technocratic leaders led by Li Peng put the Three Gorges Dam proposal on their agenda. They organized 412 specialists to spend two years studying the feasibility of the dam. According to the report that these specialists presented to the authorities, the Three Gorges Dam project would have the following four major benefits:

- *Flood control and prevention.* The reservoir of the Three Gorges Dam would be able to contain 22.2 billion cubic meters of water. It holds promise of bringing a measure of flood control to the areas along the Yangtze River.
- *Electric power generation.* As the world's largest power station, the Three Gorges project could produce 84 billion kilowatt-hours of electricity a year—this is 10 times the capability of the Dawan Nuclear Power Station in Guangdong. The dam could thus greatly ease the shortage of electricity in central and eastern China.
- *Navigation capability.* The dam will inundate 650 kilometers of shoals between Shandoupin and Chongqing and as a result, heavily loaded boats will be able to navigate from Shanghai to Chongqing.
- *Water conservancy capacity.* The dam will be able to improve the water supply in a huge area of the country.

All these prospective benefits, however, have been challenged by many other scientists. They believe that the flood control function of the Three Gorges Dam will be very limited. It may prevent floods at several branches of the upper reaches of the Yangtze River, but it cannot control floods in the great area of the lower and middle reaches of the river.

Qian Weichang, a well-known Chinese scientist and president of

Shanghai University, wrote an article in 1991 in which he argued that it would be an unforgivable mistake if the Chinese government really decided to spend billions of dollars to build the Three Gorges Dam.[8] It is worth mentioning that Mr. Qian is generally in agreement with the government in the reform era and has been vice chairman of the Chinese People's Political Consultative Conference and one of the most influential advisors to the Chinese authorities.

In April 1992, when the National People's Congress convened a meeting to vote for the construction of the Three Gorges Dam, 177 deputies voted against the project, and another 664 deputies abstained. This meant that a third of the congress had reservations that they were willing to express about the dam project proposed by the Central Committee of the Chinese Communist Party and the State Council. In the People's Republic of China, deputies of the congress are supposed to unanimously support any Party proposal. It was the first time in the history of the congress that so many deputies voted against a proposal by the central government.[9]

Despite strong criticism from many people, especially environmentalists, both in China and abroad, the Chinese government made the final decision to start the project. I felt an urgent need to visit the Three Gorges before construction began. So when three former students of mine at Hamilton College, Alex, Tony, and Steve, invited me to spend a week with them during their journey in China, I immediately told them that I would join them for a cruise to the Three Gorges.

"The First Impression's a Lasting Impression"

I did not expect to hear from my traveling companions before we met at Chengdu Airport on 7 June. But the telephone in my apartment in Shanghai rang at midnight on 6 June. It was Alex.

"Professor Li," Alex said. "I am calling from Xi'an just to let you know that we are all fine."

"That's good." I replied politely, but I was wondering why he called me at midnight to say this.

"We also called our families in New York to report that we are okay."

"You did." I became even more puzzled.

"Tony's mother was so relieved to hear from him, because she had just watched the news about the crash in Xi'an on CNN," Alex continued.

"Crash in Xi'an!" I asked.

"Yes, you don't know about that?"

"No, I didn't watch the TV news," I said. "Besides, only the hotels that accommodate foreigners in China have CNN."

"What caused the accident?" I asked. But I immediately regretted asking such a silly question. It usually took years, if not decades, for the Chinese authorities to release information about the cause of an airplane accident. Such information is always a state secret. Similarly, in the summer of 1994 in Shanghai, over a hundred cases of epidemic cholera were diagnosed. But this was a state secret. The municipal government ordered doctors to call the cholera epidemic "Number Two disease" instead of its real name.

"I don't know the cause of the accident," Alex answered. "What I do know is that a Russian-made Tu-154 plane crashed 10 minutes after it took off from Xi'an airport and headed for Guangzhou this morning. The plane belonged to China's Northwest Airlines. All 146 passengers and 14 crew members on the plane were killed."

"The Xi'an airport was closed for a while, but we were told that it would be no problem for us to fly from Xi'an to Chengdu tomorrow," Alex continued.

"Yes, you should not worry about your flight." I tried to comfort Alex. Anyone who was going to fly from a city that just had an airplane crash must have some "psychological shadow."

"The Chinese airlines are usually fine." I told Alex a "reassuring lie." I knew that the Chinese airlines were quite often *not* fine. An international aviation organization recently ranked the Chinese airlines as one of the world's worst in terms of safety. Some of my friends in the United States do not want to visit China simply because they are afraid to take any Chinese domestic airlines when traveling within the country.

Chinese airlines' poor service is also notorious. The following day, for example, I took Flight 4502 of China's Southwest Airlines from Shanghai to Chengdu. When I received a boarding pass at the airport, I asked the woman working at the check-in desk to give me an aisle seat if possible.

"What do you want?" The lady seemed to be entirely unprepared for my request.

"May I have an aisle seat, please?" I repeated.

"No!" the woman said bluntly. "No one can select a seat on Chinese airlines, unless he is a VIP."

"Why?"

"It would be too much *mafan* [trouble] for us if every passenger wanted to select a seat," she answered.

"Is this a policy of the Chinese airlines?" I asked.

"If you want to discuss policies, go see my supervisor." The lady seemed to be angry with me. "Don't waste my time here. Look, there are many passengers who want to check in after you." So she assigned me a window seat and gave an aisle seat to the person after me. I almost wanted to yell at her, but I did not do so because, after staying in China for several months, I had learned how to be tolerant, not of different opinions but of various kinds of humiliation.

When I was entering the cabin of the plane along with the other passengers, we were stopped by the pilot. He told us to wait until the arrival of the stewardesses. Therefore, instead of the stewardesses welcoming the arrival of the passengers at the entrance of the plane, the passengers stood on the two sides of the plane gate waiting for the stewardesses.

"I have traveled on many international airlines, but have never experienced such lousy service as that of the Chinese airlines," a passenger from Hong Kong said.

"Do you trust a crew that even fails to be at their posts on time?" a middle-aged Chinese asked. No passenger wanted to answer that question.

During the flight, I had a brief conversation with a stewardess who was serving beverages to passengers. "Miss, how long have you been working on planes?"

"About six months."

"May I ask how old you are?"

"I'm nineteen."

"Do you like your job?"

"No, it's really boring. I am tired of asking passengers 'Tea or coffee?' "

"But this is an important job," I said to her. "For foreign guests, you represent China and the Chinese people. Your service and attitude can be a window through which foreign passengers see our homeland."

She did not say anything, but her facial expression clearly indicated that she did not care what I just said.

Although the plane was late in taking off, it arrived in Chengdu on time. The flight that my student friends took from Xi'an was about an hour late. We were very happy to see each other. They told me that a teenage Chinese girl who sat next to Alex was so nervous on the plane that she sat like a Buddhist—she didn't open her eyes—and prayed all the time during the flight.

"None of the passengers on the plane laughed at her," Tony told me.

The safety of the airplane is a matter of life and death. Is anything more important than life and death?

Things More Valuable than Human Life?

I arranged our Sichuan trip through a hotel in Guilin where a friend of mine was a manager. He told me that his colleague in the department of tourism at the hotel would be very helpful.

"Will your colleague earn a commission on our cruise tickets?" I asked my friend over the phone.

"No, absolutely not," my friend answered.

My experience in China told me that earning a commission (*huikou*) is prevalent in virtually all kinds of business in the country. I did not mind paying for service, but it did not make sense to let the agent, or in many cases, the agent's agent, earn a huge commission.

My friend's colleague in Guilin was indeed very helpful in arranging our trip to Sichuan. The hotels where we stayed in Chengdu and Chongqing—the Minjiang Hotel and the Chongqing Guest House—were nice and comfortable. The rates in both places were also very reasonable. However, as we later found out, my friend's colleague did draw a big commission from our cruise tickets.

Soon after we arrived in Chongqing on the morning of 9 June, a sales representative from the East International Travel Company came to our hotel to deliver the cruise tickets and receive payment. The representative, Ms. Li, was a young woman in her mid-20s. Like many professional businesswomen in the United States, she was dressed fashionably and worked efficiently. When she handed me the bill, I found that the charge for the three-day cruise had changed from $450 per person, the price that the folks in Guilin gave me, to $480 per person.

"Your original price for the cruise is already very expensive. Why do you charge an extra $30?" I said to her seriously.

"We are not going to pay any extra money," my American friends all agreed with me.

"Mr. Li, don't worry," Ms. Li said calmly. "If $450 was the price that the folks in Guilin gave you, you just pay that amount of money."

"I can show you the fax that they sent me." I gave her the fax.

Ms. Li looked at the fax and said that she would telephone Guilin immediately. She talked to my friend's colleague in Guilin and told him that she would take only $450 per person from us. What she really wanted to tell him was that she would solve the problem by deducting the difference ($120 for four of us) from the commission that she originally promised to give him. The telephone conversation lasted for about 10 minutes. I could sense that the person on the other end of the line was not happy with her solution. But she insisted that it was his fault for giving us a price

of $450 instead of $480. That $30 (250 yuan) was the average monthly
salary of a worker in Sichuan.

Ms. Li asked me what the relationship was between these Americans
and me.

"They were my students in the United States," I replied.

"Do you have a lot of American students or friends who come to
China?" she asked.

"Yes, four groups of my former students have already visited me since
I came to China last fall."

"Will more of your American students and friends visit China in the
future?"

"I guess so," I answered.

"Mr. Li, I would like to give you a commission," she said.

"Well," I said, completely unprepared for her offer. "I don't think it's
appropriate. As you know, they were my students. Now they have graduated from college, but I consider them friends."

"So what?" she said.

I explained my ethics to her.

"What if I give you a discount for your cruise ticket?" Ms. Li said to
me. "You can pay me $400 instead of $450. I hope that you will encourage
more foreign guests to take the cruise with our company in the future."

"I don't want to promise anything, especially when I haven't taken
your cruise yet."

"Anyway, I would like to give you a $50 discount this time," Ms. Li
said. I could sense the decision-making power in her voice.

"If you are interested in working with us in the future," she continued,
"you can get a big commission from us. I can hardly imagine that you
would refuse this good opportunity to make a lot of money."

I was about to tell her that there are a lot of things in life that are more
important than making money. But on second thought, I did not say so
because I doubted she would listen to my "old-fashioned propaganda."

Only after we boarded the cruise boat *East Goddess* did I realize why
Ms. Li was so enthusiastically trying to persuade me to introduce more
foreign guests to take the cruise. Three-fourths of the guest cabins on the
boat were empty. Only about 30 guests were aboard. Besides the four
of us, there were a tourist group from Malaysia, three journalists from
Singapore, a Canadian journalist who worked for the *Asian Wall Street
Journal*, an American couple, and a Chinese couple. Several Chinese officials who were in charge of China's river navigation and tourism were also
aboard, along with their relatives and friends. A Chinese official told me

that he had already taken this cruise quite a few times. He came this time to accompany a friend; both of them apparently received a free ride.

This three-deck boat has about 60 cabins with private bathrooms. It has central air-conditioning, an observation corridor and platform, restaurant, ballroom, karaoke bar, barber and beauty shops, clinic, laundry, and other amenities. The boat was nothing luxurious (despite Ms. Li's claim), but it was clean and comfortable. I heard that there were three really luxurious cruise boats on the Yangtze River, each with a swimming pool and a band that plays music while guests are eating. The cruise fare is about $1,200 per person—equal to the annual salaries of four Chinese workers. These three boats belong to a Sino-American joint venture run by one of Deng Xiaoping's daughters, who controls many other businesses as well.

I was really surprised that there were so few guests on our boat, because early June is usually peak season for the Yangtze River cruise. When I discussed this with a tour guide for the group from Malaysia, he asked me whether I had heard of a recent incident on the Lake of a Thousand Islands.

The Lake of a Thousand Islands is located in Chun'an County, in western Zhejiang Province. Its beautiful scenery has attracted thousands of tourists every year. On 31 March 1994, when a cruise boat carrying 24 Taiwanese tourists, along with eight crew members and tour guides, was sailing on the lake, three local young men in a motor boat boarded the cruise boat. They held hunting rifles, daggers, axes, and explosives. These three robbers first ordered the Taiwanese tourists to surrender their money and belongings and then forced all the people on the boat to enter the bottom cabin. They finally ignited the explosive and set the cruise boat on fire. All 32 people on the boat were killed.

The three accused robbers were arrested two weeks after the incident and executed about two months later. None of the relatives of the Taiwanese victims attended the trial, although they were invited by the Chinese authorities. Some relatives and journalists from Taiwan who investigated the incident had serious reservations with the way that the Chinese authorities handled the case. They found it suspicious that the principal criminal's elder brother was a first lieutenant in the armed forces in the area. The lieutenant intended to borrow money from his younger brother, and he admitted to harboring the robbed money. But the Chinese authorities insisted that the lieutenant was not involved in the robbery, and his case should be separated from the robbery case.

After the incident, the Taiwanese authorities banned travel agencies in Taiwan from organizing tourist groups to Mainland China. As a result,

China's tourist business fell by about 80 percent in the second quarter of 1994. In China's summer resorts such as the Yellow Mountains, luxurious hotels that used to attract many tourists from overseas were almost completely vacant.

One might think that the Chinese authorities, especially those in charge of tourism, would be more conscientious about the safety and the quality of their tourist business after that incident. But except for the lip service they have paid on TV or in newspapers, I have not seen any evidence of real improvement. During our three-day cruise on the Yangtze, for example, neither any crew member nor the tour guide told us anything about the safety of the cruise. The captain of the *East Goddess* appeared only once among the guests. He came to toast us during our first lunch on the boat.

"Welcome to our cruise. If you have any questions, please ask my assistants." These were the *only* words that he said and they were slurred.

"He must be drunk. I hope that his assistants are not like him," Steve said.

On the second day of our cruise, we temporarily changed to a small boat to explore the "Lesser Three Gorges" in Wushan County along the Daning River. It was difficult to navigate the river, which is famous for its turbulent rapids and numerous submerged rocks. But we did not even know where to get a life jacket in case of an emergency. Only after a Singapore journalist expressed her anxiety to a crewman did he show us where life jackets were stored.

"We are foreign guests here in China, and we are usually better taken care of than ordinary Chinese," the Singapore journalist said to me. "I'm concerned about what kind of protection ordinary Chinese receive on the job and in their lives."

The Singapore journalist's concern is valid. According to figures that were released by the Chinese government, industrial accidents that killed at least three people numbered 317 in the country during the first half of 1994, with a total death toll of 2,051. These two figures were, respectively, 40.2 and 38.1 percent more than those for the same period in 1993. The increase in industrial accidents, as the Chinese authorities admitted, was the "result of some managers pursuing production at the expense of safety." The slack implementation of regulations on work safety also contributed to the increase in accidents.[10]

"Some people apparently don't know which is more valuable, money or human life," another Singapore journalist commented.

"Of course money is more valuable than human life here in China," a Chinese passenger said sarcastically. "Let me tell you a real story that happened in Guangdong this summer. A newlywed helped to install an expensive Japanese-made air conditioner in a restaurant. During the installation, he fell with the air conditioner from the third floor, where the restaurant was located. The young man was killed, and the air conditioner was completely destroyed. The victim's wife received 4,000 yuan ($480) from her husband's company as compensation. But the owner of the restaurant wanted the widow to pay 8,000 yuan to the restaurant because the air conditioner was worth that amount of money."

"Which is more valuable, a 4,000 yuan Chinese life or an 8,000 yuan Japanese-made air conditioner?" the Chinese passenger asked. I could sense his sadness.

Things More Beautiful than the Scenery

The American couple on the cruise boat were from Springfield, Missouri. Both were in their early sixties.

"Is this your first time in China?" I greeted them with a routine question.

"No, it's my husband's second time and my third," the woman answered my question and introduced herself and her husband to me. Her name was Mary Slater Penry. Mary told me that her husband was a retired minister, and she was a social worker in a local organization. Mary spoke very slowly. The way she talked to a stranger suggested to me that she was a well-educated and warm-hearted woman.

"Do you come to China as missionaries?" I asked.

"No, we don't," Mary answered. "But my father did, though a half century ago."

"Your father came to China?"

"Yes, actually I was born in Nantong, a small city at the lower reaches of the Yangtze River. My father was a medical doctor of the American missionary team that was stationed in the city in the 1930s. My parents lived in China for almost 10 years, during which my brother and I were born."

"How many years did you stay in China?" I asked.

"Eight," Mary answered. "Our family had a Chinese *Ayi* [nanny]. Because both of my parents were very busy with their medical and missionary work, my brother and I were actually brought up by *Ayi*."

"Did you speak Chinese?"

"Yes, of course I did. I spoke like a native Chinese. I played with the children of *Ayi* and dressed like a Chinese girl. When I was seven, my parents sent me to an elementary school for the Chinese children rather than the school for foreign boys and girls."

"Do you still remember Chinese?"

"Unfortunately, I have forgotten the Chinese language completely except some children's songs that *Ayi* taught me."

"Really?" I found her story very interesting.

"My family left China when the Japanese came to occupy Nantong in the late 1930s," Mary continued her story. "My family returned to the United States, where we settled down in the Midwest. It was hard for both my brother and me to adjust to our lives in the United States. We felt we were treated like aliens. But we didn't want to be different. We wanted to be 'normal' like other American children. We threw out the Chinese clothes that we wore in Nantong and dressed like midwestern American children.

"I never forget the humiliation that I experienced during the first day of my first semester in an American school. A teacher said to the entire class: 'The little girl from China stand up, please.' "

"My gosh," I couldn't help saying.

"I stood up, and all the students in the class looked at me. I still could not understand why the teacher did that. Curiosity? Maybe. I cried when I got home that day. I told my parents that I would never ever speak in Chinese again."

"I now, of course, regret my childish decision then. Foreign children or American children with foreign experience in today's America probably do not feel embarrassed by foreign backgrounds. But this happened almost half a century ago."

"I understand how you felt then," I told Mary.

"I tried very hard to forget everything that was associated with China or the Chinese," Mary continued. "But in the bottom of my heart, I really missed *Ayi* and her children on the 'other end of the earth.'

"My father returned to China in the early 1940s, during World War II. That time he worked as a medical doctor in the United States Air Force. He was stationed in Chongqing for two years. When he returned home, my father told us that he didn't have a chance to visit Nantong, although he did see *Ayi*."

"How could it be possible?" I asked.

"This was precisely what we asked him," Mary explained. "When he was about to leave China, my father asked a pilot of a military helicopter to do a favor for him. The pilot and my father flew over Nantong to look at the place where *Ayi* lived. My father said that he did see *Ayi*, though from a far distance. None of us believed what my father said. But in 1991, when I visited *Ayi* in Nantong, she told me that she saw my father in a helicopter waving to her on 'a shining day about 40 years ago.' "

"Is it true?" I couldn't believe what I heard.

"Yes, absolutely," Mary said calmly.

"Is *Ayi* still alive?" I asked.

"Yes," Mr. Penry joined our conversation. "We are going to see her after the cruise. *Ayi* is over 90 years old now, but still in good health."

"As I just said, I saw her in 1991," Mary continued. "I also saw her daughters, the playmates in my girlhood days, who had already become grandmothers like myself. Our reunion was a very touching moment."

"I can imagine," I said. To tell the truth, I was also moved as I heard this story.

"Many people in Nantong knew our story," Mary said. "The journalists for local newspapers and television reported our reunion. We were warmly welcomed wherever we went in the city during that trip."

"I felt like the husband of the Queen of Great Britain," Mary's husband added.

"Was it difficult for you to find *Ayi* and her family after losing contact for decades?" I asked.

"Yes," Mary replied. "I spent several years looking for them in the mid-1980s, when China finally opened its door for foreigners. Some institutions also helped us look for them. *Ayi*'s family moved several times during those years."

"Did *Ayi* and her family suffer during that time?"

"Yes, *Ayi* was persecuted during the Cultural Revolution because of her close relationship with us, an American missionary family. I always felt responsible for the suffering that *Ayi* and her family went through during that terrible period."

"It's not your fault," I said to Mary.

"I know, but they suffered a lot," Mary said calmly, though I could feel the strong emotion underlying her narration.

"I told *Ayi* in 1991 that my husband and I would often come to see her," said Mary. "I said so not just to please her; I feel that I have two homes and two home countries. To use a Chinese expression, 'I grew up drinking the water of the Yangtze River.' I am concerned about the future of the people in this land. Their happiness as well as their difficulties are also mine."

My chat with Mary and her husband was interrupted by an announcement on the loudspeaker informing us that the cruise boat would soon enter the scenic area of the first gorge.

"We are going to see the beauty of the Yangtze River," Mary said to me. Mary probably did not realize herself that the story that she just told me—the friendship between her family and *Ayi's*—was even more beautiful than the scenery that we were about to see.

"Gorgeous Gorges!"

Sword-shaped precipices, sites of ancient palaces, the centuries-old plank road built on the cliff faces, inscriptions of ancient poems on crags, mysterious hanging coffins, shoals and rapids. All these great sights might be lost after the Three Gorges Dam is built . . . But you can keep them forever on your bookshelf with a large coffee-table book, *China's Three Gorges of the Yangtze River*, published, and on sale now, in the city.[11]

. . . a farewell visit by boat to the Three Gorges is recommended as soon as possible before the scenery changes forever.[12]

These words from a Shanghai newspaper are nothing but advertisements that lure people to buy the expensive "coffee-table book" about the Three Gorges or to take the cruise. But one message from these advertisements is accurate: many of the great sights in the Three Gorges will no longer exist after the construction of the dam.

The Three Gorges area includes many important historic sites, such as the Temple of Huang Ling, one of the most famous temples in China; Zigui and Baidicheng, where the greatest ancient Chinese poets such as Qu Yuan (340–278 B.C.) and Li Bai (701–762) wrote their masterpieces; and Fengdu, the "ghost city" that is filled with legends and cultural relics. Unfortunately, all of these places will be inundated by the dam project.

A working group has been organized to develop a comprehensive plan for archaeological study and protection of the relics. It is believed that some 8,000 historical sites will be submerged during the construction of the Three Gorges Dam.[13] Plans include moving some of the sites out of the areas that will be flooded. According to experts, this will be the largest clearance of relics and historical sites in human history. They have demanded a total of 4,500,000 yuan ($535,000) for the cultural project. But the government budget for protection of antiquities necessitated by the Three Gorges migration is only 460,000 yuan ($54,000).[14]

The Three Gorges refers to Qutang, Wu, and Xiling Gorges, which are, respectively, about 8 kilometers, 40 kilometers, and 80 kilometers long. The width of the gorges varies from 300 meters at their widest to less than 100 meters at their narrowest. As our cruise boat went downstream and entered the Qutang Gorge, towering mountains on both sides seemed to merge in front of our boat and block the surging water. But in several minutes, the swift current brought us to an enormous opening where the Yangtze River cuts its way through lofty mountains.

Some of the scenic wonders in the Three Gorges area are not only beautiful, but mysterious. Several times we saw some wooden cases in a series of crevices on a cliff face. We could not see them clearly because they were lodged there some 100 meters above the water. These wooden cases puzzled local people and passengers for hundreds of years. The mystery was not unraveled until 1971 when two people climbed to the lowest crevices and found these wooden cases were actually ancient coffins dating back as far as the Warring States period (457–221 B.C.).

Anthropologists believe that there was an ancient tribe in this area whose custom was to place the coffins of their dead in high mountain caves. This unique burial method is said to have later been spread to South China's Fujian Province by immigrants from the Three Gorges area. It is still a mystery to anthropologists how people who lived over 2,000 years ago were able to place these large coffins into the crevices of a cliff face 100 meters above the river.

Another mystery in the Qutang Gorge and the Wu Gorge is *zhandao*—the plank path built along the face of the cliffs. The construction of this famous path started as early as the Warring States period and was completed during the Kingdom of Shu Han period (221–263). The path stretched nearly 50 kilometers along the Yangtze River and its branches. According to historical records, this was the only land route into the hilly Sichuan area in ancient times. Whoever controlled this plank road would control the upper reaches of the Yangtze River, and many battles in the Kingdom of Shu Han period took place in this area. The plank path was destroyed centuries ago; what we saw now were only its traces: the manmade holes on the face of the cliffs that supported it.

"These holes are absolutely incredible," an oarsman said to me and other passengers during our cruise to the "Lesser Three Gorges" along the Daning River.

"All these holes are exactly the same size—about two feet in width, one foot in height, and two meters in depth," the oarsman explained. "It was really amazing that ancient people were able to make thousands of the holes precisely the same size, wasn't it?"

"Ancient people did not build this plank path on the ground, but on the face of the cliffs above the turbulent river," his junior fellow oarsman added. "Construction workers in our time would probably find it very difficult to do so, although they have advanced modern tools and techniques. It's ironic, isn't it?"

"It's even more ironic that the government in our time is going to destroy these priceless cultural remains," a Singapore journalist said to me in English.

"Those Living Near the Water Live Off the Water"

I chatted further with these two oarsmen. The older one, Dong Jinjia, was in his early fifties and the younger one, Zhang Anping, was 21 years old. Both were born and grew up in the Daning River area. Jinjia started to work as an oarsman for a tourist boat when he was a teenager.

"I have been working here for over 30 years now," he said. "In our own words, I have lived off the Yangtze River."

"Do you like your job?" I asked. This was the same question that I had asked the stewardess during my flight from Shanghai to Chengdu a few days earlier.

"How would it be possible for me to dislike my job after having done it for 30 years?

"My job is my life," Jinjia continued. "Bad weather or good weather, turbulent rapids or calm river—I have experienced a lot of different things and have an emotional attachment to my job and the river."

His junior colleague told me to look at Jinjia's fingers—they were mangled from arthritis. If I had contempt for that self-indulgent young stewardess, I had true respect for this weather-beaten oarsman.

"Have you experienced any accidents on the river?" I asked Jinjia. "I mean, did your boat ever capsize?"

"Please don't ask such a question while we are on the river," Anping said to me politely. "Boat people avoid using the word 'capsize' [*fanchuan*]."

I apologized to both of them for my blunt question.

"That's okay," Jinjia said. "I am not superstitious. Besides, I am very proud to tell you that my boat has never capsized in the past 30 years. I will really miss my job next year."

"You will miss your job next year?" I could not understand what he said.

"Yes, I have to quit my job and emigrate to another area because of the construction of the Three Gorges Dam." He told me that the village in which his family lived would be inundated in a couple of years.

"How do you feel about moving to a new place?" I asked.

"No one in our village really wants to leave," Jinjia replied. "For me, my home village is the place that I have lived for over 50 years. But this is

Dong Jinjia, an oarsman who took us in a small boat to explore the Lesser Three Gorges along the Daning River. Jinjia started to work as an oarsman for a tourist boat when he was a teenager. He loved his job, but had to move to another area soon. His house as well as the orange and rice fields that his wife has taken care of for decades will be inundated as the result of the construction of the Three Gorges Dam.

Several weeks before I left China, Anping, another oarsman whom I met on the same trip sent me a letter, telling me that Jinjia died in a fire in the spring of 1995. All the company boats that were berthed at the wharf were burned in a fire on a windy evening. Jinjia was sleeping in the boat. "This could have been avoided," Anping wrote, "if our families did not have to migrate because of the dam project and Jinjia could have stayed in his old house. It would not have happened if our boss had been concerned about our safety."

a government decision, and it's good for the whole country. We should sacrifice."

"Do you have any concerns?" I asked.

"To be honest, yes, I do. I am concerned about my two sons. Both of them are in a senior high-school in Wuxian County. They are smart and hard-working. As you know, I am just an oarsman, and my wife is a peasant. Neither of us received any formal education when we were school age. We hope that our children will go to college."

"How will the emigration affect your children's education?"

"I don't know what kind of jobs my wife and I will have in a new place. I'm not sure whether we can afford to support our children in college." Jinjia told me that his wife was a peasant who took care of over 100 orange trees and five *mu* of rice fields. He and his wife owned a small old house that they had renovated five years earlier. But his family will have to abandon both the house and the fields and move to the upper mountain in the neighboring county.

According to a government report, the area that will be inundated is the usually fertile land along the Yangtze River. What will remain is the hilly land 800 meters above sea level. Peasants will have serious trouble cultivating their new farmland. Jinjia told me that he doubted that his family would be assigned the good fields for orange and rice production. In addition, he probably would not work as an oarsman any more.

"Do you make a lot of money by working as an oarsman now?" I asked.

"Not really," Jinjia answered. "Each of us earns ten yuan [$1.20] per day if our boat has business with a travel agency, just as we take your group to visit the Lesser Three Gorges along the Daning River now. But we do not have business every day. Even if we do, sometimes the weather is so bad that we have to cancel the voyage."

"We usually earn 200 yuan [$24] a month," Anping added.

"Living expenses are low here, however. So I can manage to save some money for my children's education," explained Jinjia. "But I am really concerned about the future when we move to a new place and start a new life."

Jinjia's junior fellow oarsman, Anping, shared anxieties about moving, though Anping seemed more optimistic about the future than Jinjia. Anping had just graduated from a technical school in Wuxian County. He and his friends planned to go to Shenzhen, the most famous economic zone in southern China. The local governments of Shenzhen and Wuxian have an agreement that the former would accept migrant workers from the latter.

"What will you do in Shenzhen?" I asked.

"I don't know yet," Anping replied. "I should probably start to learn some new skills."

"Has the local government, either Wuxian or Shenzhen, provided you with some specific arrangements for your resettlement in Shenzhen?"

"Not yet."

"Do you speak the Cantonese dialect?" People in Shenzhen usually speak Cantonese instead of Mandarin.

"No, but I can learn."

"Mr. Li, were you born in the United States?" Anping asked me.

"No, I was also born along the Yangtze River, though not at its upper reaches like Sichuan where you were born, but at the lower reaches in Shanghai. I went to the United States when I was 29 years old."

"Was it difficult for you when you started your life there?" Anping was very curious.

"Yes," I replied. "I had three major problems. First, I did not have any money. Second, I had the language barrier and culture shock. And finally, I really missed my family and friends in China."

Anping listened to me with rapt attention.

"Like many other immigrants," I continued, "the only thing that could inspire me was a better future. But the future was not guaranteed to be better, and it was actually filled with uncertainties and anxieties."

"I guess I can understand what you felt then," Anping said. "I'm so glad that you have made it. What do you do now?"

"I am a teacher in an American college." I handed him my business card.

"Hamilton College." Anping looked at the Chinese characters of the translation on the card and asked, "Is the college named after Alexander Hamilton, the first treasury secretary in the United States?"

"Yes," I said. I was really surprised by his knowledge of American history.

Anping is young, intelligent, and energetic. He does not need to worry about supporting a family because he is still unmarried. He has a high-school education, and therefore it will be relatively easy to learn some new skills in a new environment. Although I talked to him for only about two hours altogether during the cruise, I was truly impressed by his intelligence and confidence. Even for him, a new life in Shenzhen will not be easy and he surely knows that. But what will happen to other migrant workers who do not have a good education or skills and who have heavy family responsibilities?

In Yichang, Hubei Province, I met a local official who told me the hardships that the residents in the area went through. A household that was ordered to move usually would receive 20,000 yuan ($2,380) for the settlement allowance, including the expense of building a house in the new area. Because of the rapid price increase of construction materials in the country, 20,000 yuan is far from enough to build a decent house.

Local people usually felt reluctant to leave their lifelong homes. However, many residents were ordered to leave on short notice. In a small village called Zhongbaodao, 23 households had to relocate their homes within four days after they received the notice to move. Some local officials, for example, the township head, deputy head, and Party secretary of Shandoupin, the town in which the Three Gorges Dam will be located, were all replaced by higher authorities because they had reservations about the government's policy concerning the resettlement of the residents.[15]

A resident who is ordered to move will receive a government subsidy of 43.50 yuan ($5.20) monthly during the year following the move. Many migrants cannot find a job within a year. This means that they will have no income after the year is over and they no longer receive the government subsidy. Some enterprises in the migrants' new residence have requested that newcomers should invest 10,000 yuan in the enterprise. This will entitle them to a job. But this amount of money will not be refunded to migrants if the enterprise does not do well financially.

According to an official Chinese newspaper, the PRC has built 86,000 reservoirs in the past four decades at a cost of forcing more than 10 million people to leave their homes. About one-third or 3 million of them still live with problems related to resettlement—poor living conditions, unemployment, and the psychological alienation resulting from a new environment.[16] The migration caused by the construction of the Three Gorges Dam is the single largest migration for a dam project in the country. In Sichuan and Hubei Provinces, 1,130,000 residents will be resettled to make way for the project within a few years. In addition an estimated 137,000 fishermen make their livelihood fishing the waters of the area. The construction of the dam will greatly reduce that plentiful resource.[17] It remains to be seen whether the Chinese government is sensitive to various kinds of problems confronting migrants.

A year after my Three Gorges trip and prior to my return to the United States, Anping, the junior oarsman who settled down in Yixing, Jiangsu Province, instead of in Shenzhen, sent me a letter, telling me that Jinjia died in a fire in the spring of 1995. All the company boats that were berthed at the wharf were burned in a fire on a windy evening. Jinjia was drunk and sleeping in the boat. "This could have been avoided," the junior oarsman wrote, "if our families did not have to migrate because of the dam project, and Jinjia could stay in his old house, or if our boss had any concern about our safety."

"Damn Dam!"

Because of the great impact on the environment, on cultural relics, and on people who must migrate because of the dam project, critics argue that it would be rational to construct small and medium-sized hydroelectric power stations along the Yangtze River instead of building the big dam in the Three Gorges. The construction of smaller hydroelectric stations would be technically easier and less risky than the Three Gorges Dam. In addition, local governments will have more incentive to raise money for the construction of hydroelectric power stations in their homeland.[18]

Fund-raising is a big problem for the dam project, especially during the first 11 years of the project that are marked as a pure input period. Chinese authorities assert that one-half of the budget will come from a rise in the price of electricity nationwide, another portion from the revenues of the Gezhou Dam, 17 percent derived from loans emanating from the State Development Bank, 7.5 percent from the initial electricity generated by the project, and a final 4.5 percent from foreign investment.[19] The Chinese government has issued stocks and bonds and made use of foreign investment to collect much-needed funds for the project. But it is still unclear how much money it will require to build this would-be world's largest dam. The Chinese government has claimed that the project requires a total investment of 95.4 billion yuan ($11.4 billion).[20] A recent study, however, indicates that it may cost as much as 285.4 billion yuan ($33.9 billion).[21] An official from the Three Gorges project committee recently said that during the first 11 years of the project there will be a shortfall of at least 20.8 billion yuan ($3.57 billion).[22] No one knows how much money the Three Gorges Dam project will eventually cost. In China today, as elsewhere, the real cost of a project can diverge widely from the projected cost.

The main reservation of critics of the Three Gorges Dam project, however, centers on the potential problem of mud and sand that would accumulate as a result. The mud and sand silted in the area could further raise the water level at the upper reaches of the Yangtze River. This could threaten to inundate Chongqing, one of the largest cities in China. According to critics, large-scale landslides that often occur after the construction of a dam may aggravate the situation. In addition, silted mud and sand will change the ecology of the entire Yangtze River and damage both great areas of farmland and city ports near the lower reaches of the river.[23]

Li Rui, who was a personal secretary of Mao and former vice-minister of the Ministry of Water Conservancy and Electric Power, wrote to top leaders of the Chinese Communist Party in March 1993, listing serious problems that were unsolved, and probably insolvable, concerning the project. He particularly criticized some government officials who deliberately ignored these serious problems, such as silted mud and sand, ecological balance, navigation, and migration. Li Rui also collected the names of 81 well-known scientists who opposed, or had serious reservations about, the Three Gorges Dam project.[24] During my interview with Li Rui in June 1995, he told me that he would continue to write to current top leaders such as Jiang Zemin and Qiao Shi, hoping that Chinese authorities will eventually stop the dam project.

In April 1992, when the People's Congress decided to vote on the Three Gorges Dam project, Huang Shunxing, a Taiwan-born standing member of the congress who had long opposed the construction of the dam, requested an opportunity to speak to the congress according to the procedures of the meeting. His request, however, was denied. To lodge a protest, he walked out of the meeting hall. He later told foreign journalists that he was shocked by the carelessness and irresponsibility of the Chinese authorities toward such a titanic project.

Not all critics could voice their reservations about the dam project as freely as Li Rui and Huang Shunxing did. Dai Qing, a leading critic of the Three Gorges Dam and the author of *Yangtze! Yangtze!,* a collection of articles opposing the dam by several Chinese scholars and journalists, was denounced in China. Her book was officially banned, and 30,000 copies were destroyed.[25] It was reported in the Western media that in May 1992, Chinese authorities arrested 179 members of an organization in Kai County, Sichuan, and "charged them with counterrevolutionary activities aimed at sabotaging the progress of the Three Gorges project."[26]

"Damn Dam!" A Chinese journalist who investigated the Three Gorges Dam project in the late 1980s and who later was forced into exile in the United States once used this strong phrase to express his resentment about the project. He believed that the Three Gorges Dam project would be a new and equally disastrous Great Leap Forward for China.

The Great Leap gave undue prominence to heavy industry at the expense of agriculture and light industry. Heavy industry grew by 230 percent between 1958 and 1960. Peasants were ordered to abandon their cultivated land and engage in steel production. Consequently, the agricultural labor force decreased by over 20 percent in 1958. Grain rations declined significantly during the years of the Great Leap Forward. When famine occurred in the early 1960s, the entire country was starving, and millions of people died. In Sichuan Province alone, altogether 7 million people— about 10 percent of the population of this "rich province" of China then—died during this famine.[27]

In China, the first three years of the 1960s were inappropriately called "the period of three-year *natural* disaster." But it was primarily a man-made disaster, or indeed a Mao-made disaster. It was Mao's radical policy that aggravated the shortage of grain and caused such a human tragedy. The Great Leap Forward glorified human will, advocating that popular mobilization was an effective method for resolving problems in all spheres of action. "We learn from history that men never learn anything from history," the Chinese journalist said to me, quoting George Bernard Shaw.

Critics' views and voices, however, were inundated by the overwhelming praise the dam project received in China's mass media. An official in charge of the Three Gorges Dam project suggested during the early 1990s that construction workers should speed up the project so that they could dam the river by 1997. He said to the public, "This will make the year of 1997 a year of double celebrations [*shuangqing zhinian*]." The other celebration in 1997 that he refers to is, of course, the return of Hong Kong to China.[28]

This official's remark, ridiculous as it sounds, is nothing new. It reflects the political concern of Chinese leaders behind the dam project. According to Karl Marx, Max Weber, and many other social scientists and historians, Chinese feudalism and strong authoritarian rule were prolonged so long largely because of China's substantial irrigation projects. The construction of dams and other irrigation works has always been a symbol or demonstration of the feudal power of Chinese rulers. The completion of any project, in return, usually helped consolidate both national integration and authoritarian rule in the country.

Human Life and Human Responsibility

Our cruise on the Yangtze ended soon after the *East Goddess* passed through the Gezhou Dam. We got off the cruise boat in Yichang, where we took a train to Wuhan. With a population of over 3 million, Wuhan is a major industrial city in central China. The city was so polluted that both Alex and Steve felt sick as we walked down the street. While in Wuhan, we visited Mao Zedong's residence, which was recently opened to the public. Mao's residence, called the Meiling Villa, is located on the famous East Lake. The villa was built in 1958, during the Great Leap Forward. Mao always stayed there whenever he came to Wuhan. As tourists, we were allowed to see only part of the villa, which is incredibly large.

We saw an indoor Olympic-sized swimming pool, which was specially built for Mao. The tour guide told us that Mao swam there only three times. The villa has a huge park. When we walked along the small path that cut through the forest in the park, we were amazed that Wuhan had such a nice place—clean, quiet, and spacious. We all noticed the sharp contrast between Wuhan city and Mao's villa, although the latter was located right in the center of the former. I wondered whether the late chairman was aware of the pollution and other problems of Wuhan when he came to stay in this luxurious villa in the city. If he was, did he really care? Similarly, current technocratic leaders in China, for example, Premier Li Peng, must also have a lot of "more important things" to worry about than some local problems or environmental issues. They are surely more concerned about "grave matters" such as a power struggle in the Party, China's position in the world, and their own positions in Chinese history.

A Western philosopher once said, "Nothing is more surprising to those who consider human life as the most valuable thing and human responsibility as the most important human task, than to see the ease with which both human life and human responsibility are neglected."

During my trip to the Three Gorges, the philosopher's words returned to me repeatedly. The events and episodes that I witnessed or heard during the journey—for example, the lousy service of the Chinese airlines, the neglect of safety concerns by the travel agency and other business institutions and, most important, the various losses caused by the ongoing Three Gorges Dam project—all became more meaningful as I saw them in the light of the philosopher's words.

For the same reason, many individuals—the rude woman at the airline's check-in desk, the self-indulgent stewardess on the plane, the drunken cruise-boat captain, the merciless restaurant owner, and the dam project official who wanted to "make the year of 1997 a year of double celebrations"—all became comprehensible.

I am neither a scientist nor an engineer by training. I know almost nothing about dam construction or irrigation works. Yet common sense as well as many seemingly trivial things that I witnessed or heard of during the journey have made me suspicious and even cynical about the dam. But what can I, as a citizen of China, do to stop this besides writing of human life and human responsibility?

Part IV

Incongruities

In Pudong, the newly established economic zone of East Shanghai, dozens of skyscrapers are going up simultaneously. The entire city of Shanghai is like a construction site.

A view of the Bund. The land and buildings on the Bund are now "for lease" and "for sale" to foreign investors. The building on the far left of the picture used to be the Shanghai Club, which was built in 1910 by the British. It is now a Kentucky Fried Chicken restaurant.

11

"Shanghai: City for Sale"

Construction Fever and Land Leasing

> All the land up to a line somewhere five miles inland had been bought up. Money had been borrowed, quick profits had been realized. Speculation was the motto of the day, and whoever had a few shillings to risk was bound to make a fortune. Millions of dollars were squeezed out of the yellow mud. Wild griffins saw themselves burdened with heavy bank accounts. Money circulated freely, and Shanghai grew, . . . grew more rapidly than Sydney or San Francisco; grew like a tumor.[1]

These words are from *Shanghai: City for Sale*, written in 1940 by Ernest O. Hauser, an American journalist. The book covers a century of Shanghai's history, from the arrival of British colonists in 1843 to the coming of Japanese soldiers in 1937. Throughout this period, "foreign devils," the *Taipans* (the wealthy foreign owners and managers in Shanghai), corrupt Chinese officials, and local speculators were all madly, sometimes violently, involved in the real estate boom of Shanghai. These speculators found, as the author described, that there was more money in Shanghai's "inconspicuous mud than in the whole sea-going trade of this commercial emporium."[2] All these greedy people "smelled an opportunity—a typical Shanghai opportunity—to make much money in little time."[3]

Hauser was absolutely right as he described the correlation between real estate speculation and the rapid rise of modern Shanghai. In Chinese, Shanghai literally means "up to the sea." Although there is evidence of human settlements in this area since around 4000 B.C., it was a small fishing village, and it did not become a commercial center producing cotton and textiles until the sixteenth century. Shanghai rose to importance much later than other Chinese cities—over 150 years ago, rather than at the dawn of Chinese history.[4] Foreign presence since the 1840s, especially the establishment of foreign "concessions" (foreigners owned the land and lived under their own laws), turned Shanghai into a cosmopolitan city—"a paradise for adventurers." Fifty-five years have passed since Ernest Hauser wrote that book. History, however, seems to have come full circle. After all the great changes that took place in China over the past half century—the civil war, the Communist victory, the rural land reform, the nationalization of the urban economy, the socialist transformation, the Great Leap Forward, the Cultural Revolution, and the economic reform—Shanghai is "for sale" again.

According to the policy of the Shanghai municipal government, both foreign and domestic investors can purchase—or, in the official term, "lease"—land in the Shanghai area for up to 70 years. During the past few years, not only the large land area of the newly established economic zone in Pudong (East Shanghai) has become the primary target for industrial investment,[5] but also "for sale" is the property along China's busiest and well-established commercial streets in downtown Shanghai, such as Nanjing Road.

Make no mistake, this time no foreign country is forcing China or its largest city, Shanghai, to sell its land. China is undoubtedly an independent and emerging economic power. The primary goals of property development in Shanghai today are to attract foreign investment and to raise capital for the reconstruction of the city. During his tour of Shanghai in early 1992, the paramount leader, Deng Xiaoping, urged the municipal government to achieve a "change in the appearance of the city every year and a great change every three years." Because of Deng's order, Shanghai has been engaged in the largest urban reconstruction plan in the PRC's history.

"What's going on in Shanghai, and up and down the China coast," as a *Wall Street Journal* reporter described it, "might be the biggest construction project the planet has seen since coral polyps built the Great Barrier reef after the last Ice Age."[6] Greater Shanghai, Morgan Stanley's 1993 report on China noted, is "three times the size of Singapore and growing at least twice as fast."[7]

With the property boom of the past few years, Shanghai has witnessed the springing up of over 1,000 skyscrapers taller than the 78-meter Park Hotel, the highest building in the city for almost half a century.[8] An estimated 9.7 million square feet of office space, mainly for foreign companies, will be available in 1995, and that amount doubled in 1996.

What is even more remarkable, however, is the sociopolitical impact of property development on the residents of Shanghai. Just as the establishment of foreign concessions profoundly changed the lives of local residents and aroused antagonism between colonists and local dwellers over 100 years ago,[9] the ongoing large-scale relocation of Shanghai residents causes much anguish and resentment. As some foreigners in Shanghai observed, the "mass eviction of local families to bleak suburbs has fueled more resentment in China's largest city" in the past few years than even inflation and factory layoffs.[10]

According to a top official of China's Ministry of Construction, over 1 million households in Chinese cities have been relocated during the last few years because of land leasing and urban reconstruction.[11] Problems involved in the leasing of land and the relocation of residents are emerging as one of the most sensitive political issues in Shanghai, as well as in many other cities in the country.

The "Transfer of Land-Use Rights"

In the People's Republic of China, the state owns the land in both urban and rural areas. During the early decades of the PRC, no one—individual or institution—could sell or lease property to individuals, foreign joint ventures, or domestic companies. The ownership of private houses was completely eliminated by the state during the Cultural Revolution.

Since 1978, when economic reform started, Chinese peasants have been able to lease farmland in rural areas from the state for up to 50 years. In urban areas, owners of private houses (except those that were confiscated in 1949) regained their property rights. Urban residents are allowed to own houses, although the land legally belongs to the state.

Since the early 1980s, land leasing, or what the Chinese call "the transfer of land-use rights (*tudi pizu*)," has become a new way to raise capital for the government. The transfer of land-use rights first appeared in Shenzhen and other economic development zones in the southern provinces. According to government regulations, investors, both foreign and domestic, can lease a plot of land for between 40 and 70 years (40 years for entertainment facilities, 50 for office buildings, and 70 for residential use).

Land leasing and the use of foreign capital in major infrastructure projects have been controversial among political leaders in Shanghai. In 1980, four years before the establishment of the Shenzhen economic zone, some officials in the Shanghai municipal government began proposing the establishment of special economic zones to attract foreign investors. But some political leaders rejected the proposal to resume foreign concessions in Shanghai and criticized those who wrote it.[12]

The Shanghai municipal government did not allow land leasing until 1988, when a plot in the Hongqiao economic development zone was sold to foreign investors for commercial use. From 1988 to 1991, only 13 plots of land were leased in Shanghai. Although land leasing in Shanghai started slowly, it has developed very quickly in recent years. In 1991, the Shanghai municipal government launched an ambitious plan to sell state property and to lease urban land in the city to foreign investors. In 1992 alone, a total of 201 plots of land (about 20 million square meters) were leased. The city received $2.665 billion and 1.528 billion yuan. In the same year, 755 real estate companies, including 48 foreign-owned companies and 153 joint ventures, were established in Shanghai.

By the end of 1993, the municipal government of Shanghai claimed that the city had 1,425 real estate companies, among which 208 were foreign and 217 belonged to governments of other provinces or departments under the state council.[13] Virtually all state banks have set up financing and leasing companies that venture into property development.

An estimated 5 million square meters of residential housing were sold to foreigners and overseas Chinese between 1994 and 1996.[14] In 1993, Shanghai's "sales volume of garden villas to foreigners surpassed Guangzhou and Shenzhou, ranking first in the country."[15] The cost for a villa with an area of 250 to 400 square meters ranged from $300,000 to $1 million. Real estate speculation in Shanghai, once again, has become the quickest way to make money.

Although elegant hotels and office buildings have flooded the market in recent years, the price of real estate in Shanghai is still rapidly increasing. For example, in early 1995 rents at the Portman Shangri-La Hotel, where many foreign offices are located, went from $5.58 per square foot a day in 1993 to $8.36.[16] The average rent for office buildings has increased almost fourfold from 1985 to 1993 (see Table 11–1).

Investment in property development in Shanghai has increased significantly in the past few years, from 759 million yuan in 1991 to 1,251 million yuan in 1992, to 8,778 million yuan in 1993, and to 11.76 billion yuan in 1994.[17] Foreign investment is the main source of real estate development in the city. In 1993, for example, 51.8 percent of the capital for land-leasing projects was from overseas (see Figure 11–1).

Shanghai's land leasing in 1993 doubled that of the previous year in terms of square meters of land for lease. The land in Pudong (China's largest special economic development zone) has attracted big investors. In 1992, for example, Shanghai received $2.67 billion and 1.53 billion yuan

TABLE 11-1

Change in the Index of Average Rent for Office Buildings in Shanghai (1985–1993)

Year	1985	1986	1987	1988	1989	1990	1991	1992	1993
Index (%)	100	120	93	97	99	148	174	263	383

Source: Shanghai fangdichan shichang 1994 (Shanghai real estate market) (Shanghai: Zhongguo Tongji Chubanshe, 1995), 47.

FIGURE 11-1
Financial Resources of the Land-Leasing Projects in Shanghai (1993)

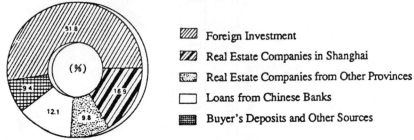

Source: *Shanghai fangdichan shichang 1994* (Shanghai real estate market) (Shanghai: Zhong-guo Tongji Chubanshe, 1995), 77.

for land leasing, of which $1.925 billion was from foreign investors. That was equivalent to 60 percent of Shanghai's total fixed investment that year.[18]

Property developers from foreign countries have flocked to the real estate industry in Shanghai. In 1992, only a year after Shanghai launched its campaign to attract overseas property investment, virtually all the major Hong Kong property companies had a foot in the city, including Sun Hung Kai Properties, Shun Tak Holdings, Sino Land and Hang Lung Development Corp., Li Ka-shing's Cheung Kong Holdings, and Hutchison Whampoa.[19]

"The property boom in Shanghai has been driven by Hong Kong and Taiwan speculators," noted a manager in a real estate company in Pudong. "People in Hong Kong and Taiwan believe that the meteoric rise in real estate prices in both places in the past two decades will also happen in Shanghai."

The gap between property prices in Hong Kong and Shanghai, inadequate housing supply in Shanghai, rising local incomes, the increase in the population of the city, rapid economic growth along the lower Yangtze River area, and lax government regulations all have helped encourage property speculation in the city. In 1993, for example, investment from Hong Kong accounted for 49 percent of the total number of foreign investment projects, 51 percent of the total amount of intended investment, and 40 percent of foreign capital in use in Shanghai.[20] Meanwhile, urban construction and the real estate business have become main attractions for foreign investment in the city.

Sales on the Bund

Before the Communist takeover in 1949, Shanghai hosted over 200 foreign banks and other financial institutions. Many of them were located in Western-style buildings on the riverfront "Bund" (an Anglo-Indian word meaning river embankment). After the "liberation," all these bank buildings were confiscated by the Communist government. The Hong Kong & Shanghai Bank building, for example, was used as the headquarters of the municipal government for over four decades. This building was constructed in the early 1920s by the British firm of Palmer and Turner and was the second-largest bank building in the world at that time.[21]

Now this building, along with 18 others on the Bund, has a "For Sale" sign. They are being leased to foreign financial institutions through competitive bids. The city's English-language newspaper, *Shanghai Star*, repeatedly printed large, bold headlines on its front page, "SALES ON BUND DUE," "FOR SALE SIGNS UP," to lure potential foreign buyers.[22] *Jiefang ribao*, the official newspaper in Shanghai, had a lead article in May 1995 stating that all major banks in the world are racing to have a site on the bank of the Huangpu River.[23] The municipal government claims that the Bund will regain its past glory as the city's financial hub and China's Wall Street.[24]

By early 1995, Shanghai had a total of 130 offices of foreign banks, insurance companies, and other financial institutions. This was 30 times higher than the number in the prereform period. Foreign financial institutions had capital resources of $3 billion in Shanghai in 1993, 185 percent greater growth than in the previous year.[25]

Several foreign banks and financial institutions have indeed signed leases with the Shanghai Bund Building Function Transformation, the company authorized by the municipal government to take charge of "redeveloping" properties in the Bund area. Banque Indosuez, a major French bank, for example, is going to return to its previous address on the Bund. The Hong Kong & Shanghai Bank is negotiating with the municipal government to move back to its old headquarters.

"The Shanghai municipal government," a senior official in the government told the foreign media, "is very pleased to return the buildings on the Bund to their former owners."

"The Chinese government does not really *return* the buildings to former owners," growled a Dutch businessman I interviewed in Shanghai. "Chinese authorities confiscated our properties in Shanghai after 1949, and now they want us to *purchase them back*. The sale price of some of the buildings on the Bund is as high as 2 billion yuan [$244 million]. How

The newspapers of Shanghai, both Chinese and English, are often filled with bold headlines of "Sales on Bund Due" to lure potential foreign buyers.

can we be sure that they will not confiscate our properties again in the future? It's disgraceful for the Chinese government to sell the buildings on the Bund to us now, isn't it?"

Not only foreign investors consider Chinese authorities who sell the land of Shanghai shameful; local residents in the city have even stronger resentment toward the municipal government's decision to relocate residential areas in downtown Shanghai as a result of land leases to foreigners.

In addition to leasing the Bund to foreign banks, the state-owned enterprises that are situated in downtown Shanghai are often eager to lease out their factory sites and move to the suburbs. According to a World Bank report, it is anticipated that 25 percent of Shanghai's core-area factories will move out of the inner city within a few years.[26] David E. Dowall, an analyst from the World Bank, recently completed a study of urban land markets in China. He noted that the typical industrial relocation project usually costs 1,700 yuan per square meter of vacated land area. While old factory sites in the inner city can be sold for more than 2,000 yuan per square meter, a site located within the "Golden Mile" of commercial streets can be as high as 12,000 yuan per square meter.[27]

For these state-owned enterprises, land leasing has become the best way to get rid of heavy debts and other financial difficulties. In Shanghai's Huangpu District where the Bund is located, for example, rental revenue derived from commercial land is 5,086 yuan per square meter, about 20 times that derived from land for industrial use (256 yuan per square meter).[28]

"Construction Fever" and "Relocationphobia" of Urban Residents

The ongoing large-scale urban construction and land leasing in Shanghai usually do not bring good fortune to the residents of the city. Instead, the government policy regarding the relocation of downtown households and factories has caused great anguish among Shanghai citizens.

"All the government wants is money; it has no shame," a local resident told a foreign journalist reporting a street protest against the demolition of an old city neighborhood.[29] The protest occurred in the spring of 1995. Hundreds of protesters blocked Huaihai Road, the second-largest commercial street in the city, to voice their anger and frustration over the ruthless way that the local government had handled the matter.

Residents in the area were told by local officials that they had to move out of their apartments by the beginning of the summer to make way for a commercial development. The local government gave residents in the old neighborhood only two choices of new residential areas into which they could move. Both were located in bleak suburbs with no hospitals, schools, post offices, or vegetable or grocery markets. In addition, residents had to pay a large amount of money to the government if they wanted more space in their new homes.

The relocation of residents along Huaihai Road is only one of many such projects in this construction-crazy city. Property development is so frantic in Shanghai, as someone described it, that residents are afraid of returning home after work "lest they find the dreaded relocation notice nailed to their doors."[30] Government statistics show that about 200,000 households have been resettled over the past several years.[31] According to the government plan, another 200,000 households will have to go within a few years. Residential areas in the Huangpu District and in certain streets in Jingan, Luwan, and Xuhui Districts will be changed to exclusively commercial areas by the end of the 1990s.

"If every household has four people, 400,000 households have a total of 1.6 million people," a technocrat from the Urban Construction Commission under the Shanghai municipal government proudly told me. "Just imagine that 1.6 million people are being relocated within a decade! No other city in the world has experienced such a quick and massive reloca- tion of its residents. Only our socialist country can accomplish such dras- tic urban reconstruction!"

What that technocrat probably did not know about, or didn't care about if he knew, is the anger of Shanghai residents and the frequent street protests such as the one that took place on Huaihai Road. During the past two years, residents' protests have occurred many times in front of the headquarters of the municipal and district governments. The government, however, quickly used force to quell them.

Some residents refused to move, but construction workers were still ordered to tear down the houses where they lived. In the fall of 1994, my friend Andrew Browne, Reuters's bureau chief in Shanghai, and I saw a resident standing on the roof of a three-story house to protest while construction workers approached him. This middle-aged man had two rooms in the house, which was located on the corner between Nanjing Road and Tongren Road, near the Portman Shangri-La Hotel. He had to use one of the two rooms as a small shop, selling souvenirs to tourists, as well as food and drinks. For him, to move out of the downtown area also meant closing his business. He was so frustrated that he decided to refuse to leave even though all his neighbors had already gone.

"We must tear down all the houses in the area by today," an official of the construction team said. The area was leased to a Malaysian commercial company. Consequently, about 2,000 families were ordered by the district government to move to a rural suburb. "Otherwise, we have to pay the Malaysian company 200,000 yuan [$24,000] a day according to our con- tract," the official explained to the spectators. "This is as much as the cost of an Audi car. We cannot afford to wait."

The scene attracted a big crowd. Almost all of the spectators sympa- thized with the resident. They asked the construction workers to be pa- tient and shouted:

"Don't drive that resident crazy!"

"Stop tearing down the house!"

"He will jump off the roof if you try to catch him!"

The construction workers decided to tear down other houses first and let the man stay on the roof for the moment.

Browne and I went to a nearby restaurant for lunch. When we returned, all the houses in the area, including the one with the man on the roof, had been torn down. The construction workers and spectators, as well as the resident who had refused to move, were all gone. Later I found a witness who told me that the man had finally given in when the construction workers pushed him to the edge of the roof.

"The workers took him down to the ground and beat him up," the witness told me.

"Why?" I asked.

"They said that the man had scared them and delayed their work," the witness explained. "Some spectators stopped the beating and took the man to a hospital."

"Tears and tantrums, letters and petitions, street protests and even the veiled threat of violence failed to prevent their homes from being flattened like tens of thousands of others in this construction-crazy city," commented Browne, who has written several reports on the relocation of Shanghai residents.[32]

In the fall of 1994, Browne interviewed a couple who lived near the Great World Amusement Hall, the central downtown area of Shanghai. The couple worked for a state-owned tour company, which was located nearby. They were resentful of the government's decision to demolish the neighborhood in which they lived. To protest, they brandished a pellet rifle to defy officials trying to move them out. But in the end, the couple, like the resident who stood on the roof, were no match for local housing

A resident stands on the roof of a three-story building to protest its destruction.

authorities. They had to move to the newly opened Pudong area, beyond the reach of public transportation.[33]

Very few people in Shanghai would go as far in defying authorities as the couple with the rifle and the man on the roof, but most residents are resentful of them for their heartless efforts in driving them out of downtown.

"It is understandable that the municipal government wants to build a new downtown Shanghai to attract foreign investment," a former high-school classmate said to me. "As you know, the living conditions of most families in the downtown area are not good at all. Many of them live in tiny attic rooms with no bathroom or kitchen. They don't mind moving from their cramped homes in old houses to spacious apartments in the suburbs. But what has frustrated them is the fact that the government does not pay any attention to their concerns. Authorities are concerned only about vacating the old neighborhood, not about the facilities in new residential areas. They have never thought of the problems and pains that local residents have experienced in changing their homes."

In the summer of 1995, I sublet a two-bedroom apartment from an old friend of mine. She and her parents used to live in a neighborhood block on busy Chengdu Road and Nanjing Road. Because of the construction of a new overpass on Chengdu Road, they moved out of the area in 1993. During the past two years they had crowded in with relatives in the city while waiting for the completion of the apartment assigned to them. In May 1995, my friend's family was finally able to move into an apartment in the Zhenbei residential area, located in the northwestern suburbs of Shanghai. My friend let me rent the apartment for the final month of my fellowship in China.

There were about 50 apartment buildings in this newly built residential area. Each building had six floors, and each floor had eight apartments. But like many other new residential areas in the suburbs of Shanghai, this large community had no school, no hospital, no post office, no department or grocery stores. The entire neighborhood had no telephone or gas connections. Garbage was spread everywhere outside apartment buildings because there was no sanitary service in the area. Mice were hunting for food among the garbage even during the day.

"You live in this area?" asked a colleague from Hamilton College who visited the apartment. "This looks like land deserted after a war or natural disaster," she said.

"If Shanghai people can live here, so can I," I replied. "About 2,400 families and a total of 10,000 people live in this neighborhood. From the official viewpoint, this is probably not a bad new residential area at all. At least it has water and electricity."

During the day of her visit, however, the water supply to the apartment was shut off all day without advance notice.

Most residents in the area had to commute between their new apartments and old work places. But there was no direct bus linking the area to downtown Shanghai. Although a minibus line connected the area to the center of the city, it ran only from 6 A.M. to 5 P.M. During a minibus ride, I met a nurse working in the Jingan District Hospital in downtown Shanghai. She told me that many employees in the hospital have moved to this Zhenbei residential area. They now have to spend three extra hours on the road every day.

"We panic when we cannot finish work by 5 P.M.," the nurse said. "If we miss the minibus, we need to take a taxi, which usually costs 40 yuan, to go home. Forty yuan is about 5 percent of my monthly salary! How can I afford it? To be honest, I cannot even afford to take the minibus. Four yuan for a round-trip minibus daily costs 100 yuan per month. This means I must spend one-eighth of my salary on bus fare." She was angry.

"Things will surely get better," I said.

"Do you really think so?" the nurse responded. "Shanghai's traffic jam, for example, will never get better, only worse. That's why people who live in Shanghai often say, 'I'd never give up a bed in downtown for a room on the outskirts.'

"Things will never get better for ordinary people like me," she added. "My husband and I have not only used up all of our savings, but also borrowed 20,000 yuan for moving expenses and the interior decoration of the apartment.

"Things will get better only for rich and powerful people," she continued. "Life for those speculators in the real estate business and property developers in Shanghai will surely get better. Many of them are the children or relatives of high-ranking officials. They can easily get loans from the state bank, which they use to speculate in the real estate business. This is one of the ways that they become incredibly rich. Only these people can enjoy newly opened elegant stores and luxurious restaurants on Huaihai Road and Nanjing Road. The property boom is actually dividing the city and widening the gap between rich and poor."

Resentment against the government was widely shared by residents of Shanghai. "The government wants to attract foreign investors and property developers who sell to rich entrepreneurs," a retired textile worker said. "Everyone wants to make big money and no one cares about us—we are 'small potatoes' [*xiaorenwu*]." The retired worker told me that she used to shop on Sichuan Road, which was famous for small shops selling cheap odds and ends. Now the small shops are being torn down to make room for high-class department stores.

According to an official report, about 900,000 families in Shanghai had insufficient housing (meaning less than 4 square meters per person); among them, 70,000 families had no room at all to live.[34] "The government should build more roads, schools, hospitals, and low-income housing instead of providing loans for the construction of luxurious villas, nightclubs, expensive shops, or golf courses," said a teacher in the primary school that I attended as a young boy. A major part of the school has now become an elegant nightclub mainly used by people from Hong Kong and Taiwan.

One of the largest plots that has been leased to foreign developers is a 1.24-square-kilometer area between the Shanghai Railway Station and Suzhou Creek. A Hong Kong property company paid $131 million to lease this area for 50 years. The area is now named "Nightless City" (*buyecheng*). When it is completed, there will be 40 skyscrapers with a total of 324,000 square meters of commercial space.[35]

The central government seems to notice some of the problems involved in the property boom. The State Council sent out a circular to local governments in June 1995, claiming that the construction of expensive office and apartment buildings, garden villas, entertainment centers, nightclubs, and golf courses has taken too much capital from the construction of residential housing.[36]

Shanghai residents particularly complained that the children of Deng Xiaoping, Chen Yun, and other leaders, as well as some local officials, have made huge sums of money by leasing land in the city. A real estate official in Shanghai told a journalist from Hong Kong that children of high-ranking officials now move to Shanghai from Beijing to speculate in real estate. They simply told local officials in Shanghai, "My father is so-and-so—give me land."[37] If you take a bus in Shanghai these days, you will hear many similar stories or rumors about corruption and power abuse involved in property development in the city.

Xu Yin, a well-known Shanghai writer, wrote an article in *Jiefang ribao* comparing Li Hongzhang, a top bureaucrat known as a "running dog" of foreign power at the end of the Qing Dynasty (1644–1911), with current government officials who received commissions by leasing land to foreign companies. The difference between Li Hongzhang and current leaders, Xu concluded, was that the former did not receive kickbacks (*huikou*) from foreigners, but the latter did.[38]

Some local officials have been punished for wrongdoing involved in land leasing. For example, a deputy head of the Luwan District Government who was in charge of property development on Huaihai Road was sent to jail in 1994 because he had received bribes from Hong Kong and

Taiwan investors. According to Shanghai gossip, the deputy head was only a scapegoat for high-ranking officials in the country.

Construction Fever or Destruction Fever?

"Both Chinese officials and foreign property speculators in Shanghai are shortsighted," said an economist from Fudan University whom I interviewed in Shanghai. The economist, who did not want me to use his name, has done several studies of the real estate industry in Pudong. "The undersupply of fancy hotels and office buildings in the city," he said, "will soon become an oversupply. Property prices will drop in a few years when many of the new buildings are available. Only a very few people can afford these expensive apartments and offices. The credit crunch and other problems that occurred on Hainan Island [the most overbuilt area in China] will also occur in Shanghai.

"I'm afraid that Shanghai is experiencing a new version of the Great Leap Forward," the economist continued. During the Great Leap Forward in the late 1950s, millions of Chinese people were ordered by Mao and Communist officials to build a 'furnace in the backyard' to produce steel at the expense of the development of agriculture and light industry.

"The ongoing large-scale construction of elegant residential districts and luxurious shopping malls is also achieved at the sacrifice of thousands of ordinary Shanghai residents," the economist commented. "Recent visitors to Shanghai are usually so impressed by the construction boom in the city, especially the mushrooming of skyscrapers here in Shanghai, that they tend to overlook some serious problems caused by reconstruction."

One of these problems is the deterioration of the environment. According to one investigation, of the 89 public parks and gardens in the city, 27 are going to be leased, either partially or entirely, to foreign companies within a few years.[39] They will no longer be public or parks. The lack of green landscape is becoming a distinguishing feature of Shanghai. When a plot of land is leased, property developers tend to build higher buildings to obtain more space.

"Green land serves as the lungs of a city," Luo Xiaowei, a distinguished Chinese architect and director of the Shanghai Architecture Society, told the Chinese media. "Some believe that a green belt around the city will be enough. That's like cutting out a person's lung and replacing it with a tube outside the body. It just won't work. Shanghai should have a healthy lung."[40]

"The changes taking shape in Shanghai mean different things to different people," said Erh Dongqiang (Deke Erh), a Shanghai-born and -based freelance photojournalist. "Some see most of the changes as a necessary process if Shanghai is to become an economic, financial, and commercial center in the Far East. Others see most of the changes as a destructive force that is undermining the unique characteristics and cultural fabric of the city."

Erh Dongqiang was not enthusiastic about what he called the "destruction fever" in Shanghai. In a recent book coauthored with Tess Johnston, a former American diplomat in Shanghai, he observed:

> new victims of urban renewal are now sweeping through Shanghai like a scythe: facades defaced by smoked glass and garish additions, classic old buildings pulled down to make way for widened streets or high-rise complexes.[41]

The book, which includes approximately 250 photos of Shanghai, is appropriately titled *A Last Look: Western Architecture in Old Shanghai.* Old Western-style architecture is disappearing very quickly in the construction boom. The authors state explicitly that they want to give the reader "one last look" before it is too late.

"The Cultural Revolution destroyed many cultural relics in Shanghai, but the ongoing construction fever is probably even more destructive," Erh said. "It will wreck the architectural characteristics of the city. I'm afraid that Shanghai is going to lose its sense of style, its reminders of the city's past, and indeed, its sense of history."

In addition to taking photos of the old buildings in Shanghai and tracing their histories, Erh Dongqiang has been collecting handicrafts in both urban and rural Shanghai. He has purchased two old houses on the outskirts of the city and established a small folk art museum—probably the first private folk art museum in the country.

In another newly published book, *German Architecture in China*, Torsten Warner, a German graduate of Shanghai's Tongji University, traces the German residential complex in Shanghai. The complex, which was completed in 1929 at the corner of today's Huashan and Yanan Roads, comprised the German Community Center, the Kaiser Wilhelm School, the German Protestant Church, and other buildings. The church, designed in the Expressionist style, was demolished during the Cultural Revolution. Buildings for the German Community Center and the Kaiser Wilhelm School were dismantled in recent years. On their sites now stand the Hilton Hotel and the International Equatorial Hotel—two tall and styleless buildings.[42]

"Who said that Shanghai does not have style and character?" an old Chinese man said sarcastically.

"I call it the 'Marlboro City.' Look at these Marlboro advertisements," the old man pointed to the advertisements on the tall buildings around the park. "These Marlboro advertisements—a strong and handsome American cowboy on horseback with a canvas coat, sporting jeans, and cowboy hat—are everywhere in Shanghai."

This man was in his early eighties. I met him in a tea house at the People's Park in downtown Shanghai in the spring of 1995. He refused to tell me his personal background, but he seemed like a well-educated person. He did tell me, however, that he was born in Shanghai and had spent his entire life there.

"Can you find a better image for Shanghai than the Marlboro City?" the old man challenged me.

The old man might sound too cynical, but Marlboro has indeed become a well-known American icon and a symbol of the Western way of life. Like the old man in the tea house, an article in the *New Yorker* referred to Shanghai as "a city of Marlboro."[43]

What the old man said also reminded me of the article published in *Cankao xiaoxi*, one of the largest newspapers in China. A Chinese reporter wrote, "The U.S. government has discouraged its citizens from smoking cigarettes, but it encourages Japan, Taiwan, South Korea, and Thailand to open their tobacco markets." Even more unfortunately for people in East Asia, the reporter said, "China has now become the largest cigarette market in the world."[44] According to scientists at Oxford University, the number of Chinese men who will die from lung cancer will increase from 30,000 in 1978 to 900,000 in 2025.[45]

"Over 150 years ago," grumbled the old man in the tea house, " 'foreign devils' [*guilao*] exported opium to China. Now they are selling cigarettes to the China market. Some foreign biochemical factories here have not only polluted China's environment, but have even sold banned medicine to the Chinese people."[46]

"After the Liberation in 1949, everyone in Shanghai was familiar with a popular song" the old man started to hum the tune. "*Socialism is wonderful . . . the imperialists ran off with their tails between their legs.*"

"Now," the old man said, "someone has rewritten the words of the song: *Capitalism is wonderful . . . the imperialists are back with wallets under their arms.*" I told the old man that I had heard this "new version" of the song at a popular music concert.

"Are you optimistic or pessimistic about Shanghai's future?" I asked the old man.

"What do you mean by optimistic or pessimistic?" the old man responded. "Everyone is talking about changes in Shanghai, for better or for worse, but no one has ever asked about the meaning of these changes. I don't know about the future, nor can I even understand the past and present.

"You are a professor of Chinese studies," the old man challenged me once more. "Can you tell me the meaning of all these changes happening in Shanghai or China over the century?"

"Hum . . . well . . . ," I said, then realized I could not say anything meaningful.

"Some believe that the world is becoming worse, and some think it is getting better," the old man concluded. "In my view, the world is just turning around as usual."

On the Road to Subei

The Transportation Bottleneck in China's Development

"The bus leaves Nantong for Dafeng at 6 A.M." A friend left this telephone message on the answering machine in my apartment in Shanghai.

"The time we get up in the morning depends on the distance of our hotel in Nantong from the bus station," the message continued. "There are a few hotels near the bus station if you don't mind keeping fleas and cockroaches company. The most decent hotel in the city, Nantong Grand Hotel, is located about five kilometers away from the bus station. It will take at least an hour and a half for us to walk to the station since it is difficult to get a taxi that early in the morning. This means that we need to get up at 3:30 A.M. and leave our hotel around 4 o'clock. Does that make sense to you?" my friend concluded sarcastically.

To get up at 3:30 A.M.! It did not make sense to me at all. Only pilgrims, I thought, would get up that early for a journey. We were not going to Mecca or Jerusalem; we just wanted to visit a small village-run enterprise in Dafeng.

Dafeng, a county under the jurisdiction of Yancheng city, is located in the northern part of Jiangsu Province, or what people there call "Subei." It is about 400 kilometers (250 miles) north of Shanghai. In the United States, it usually takes half a day to drive 250 miles. But here in China the number of expressways (*gaosugonglu*) is extremely limited, even in economically well-developed coastal regions like Jiangsu and Shanghai. Thus, it takes at least 11 hours to travel that far, either by car or by bus. There is no train between Shanghai and Yancheng. Actually, until recently there was no railway at all in the vast area of Subei, with the exception of

Xuzhou and Lianyungang, two cities in the northernmost part of Jiangsu Province.

I had never been in Nantong or Dafeng or any other part of Subei before. While traveling in Sunan (southern Jiangsu) and witnessing the economic boom in this, the fastest-growing region in the country (as presented in chapters 5, 6 and 9), I thought it would be interesting to visit Subei, the other part of Jiangsu Province, which has lagged notably far behind Sunan. So when Guo Qiang, a good friend of mine who is a manager of a copper factory in Shanghai, told me that he was going to Subei on business, I asked Guo to take me with him.

Neither my friend nor I wanted to take an 11-hour bus ride, especially on a bumpy road, directly to Yancheng from Shanghai. Instead, we planned to break our journey into two parts. First we would go to Nantong by boat and stay there for a night, since Guo also planned to visit a state-owned factory in Nantong. Then we would take a bus to Dafeng in the early morning of the following day so that we could arrive in the afternoon. We would visit a village-run enterprise in Dafeng that has business dealings with my friend's factory in Shanghai.

Because of his business connections in Subei, Guo was very familiar with the region, especially its socioeconomic condition. I was very happy with our travel plans until I learned that we had to get up at 3:30 A.M. in Nantong! I had not expected all the inconveniences of travel in this part of the country. Subei is located on China's east coast and is not far from the nation's most developed regions.

In general, Jiangsu is an economically prosperous province. Within the province, however, is a big gap between Sunan and Subei in terms of economic development. The Yangtze River divides Jiangsu Province into two parts. While the southern side of the river (including the Nanjing and Yangzhou areas) has 40 percent of the population and 33 percent of the total land of the province, it contributes 64 percent to the total GNP and has 73 percent of the total industrial output.

Although Subei has also achieved moderate economic growth during the reform era, the gap between Sunan and Subei has increased greatly during the 1980s. In 1980, the difference between Sunan (Suzhou, Wuxi, and Changzhou) and Subei (Xuzhou, Huaiying, Yancheng, and Lianyungang) in terms of industrial and agricultural output was 8.08 billion yuan. But in 1990, the number increased to 49.62 billion yuan. The difference in GNP in 1980 was 1.29 billion yuan, but in 1990 it increased to 9.64 billion. The difference in a peasant's average annual income between

Map 12-1 Subei (Northern Jiangsu)

Sunan and Subei increased from 60 yuan in the 1980s to 799 yuan in 1991.[1]

According to a 1993 investigation of three poverty-stricken villages in Binghai County in Subei, for example, 20 percent of households did not have a supply of grain stored; 18 percent did not have enough clothing; 54 percent still lived in houses made of grass and soil. Three villages had a total of 766 households, 3,024 people, and 3,407 *mu* of cultivated land. Average annual income in these three villages was 364 yuan ($64). Eighty-six men who were in their thirties to mid-fifties could not afford to get married. Many women married men in the richer Sunan area or elsewhere. Also because of the poverty, the primary school enrollment was only 61

percent in the villages. Among the total of 1,264 laborers, about 400 had
left the villages seeking jobs elsewhere during the early 1990s.[2]

Why do Subei and Sunan, two neighboring areas in the same province,
display such a sharp contrast in their economic development? The differences between the two areas are the result of specific historical conditions
or different starting points in economic development. But many success
stories of China's economic reform, including those in Sunan, suggest
that local conditions themselves can change.[3]

Among the reasons for the gap between Sunan and Subei—e.g., the
geographical advantage of the former and the lack of entrepreneurship in
the latter—the most convincing one for me is the difference in the condition of the transportation infrastructure in these two regions. In addition
to lacking a railway, Subei has far fewer highways, especially well-main-
tained highways, than Sunan. There are 2,547 kilometers of first- and sec-
ond-grade highways in Subei, which account for 14.8 percent of its total
highway kilometers versus 22.8 percent in Sunan. Good-quality surface
roads in Subei account for 36 percent of its total roads, compared to 61.5
percent in Sunan.[4]

The economic growth of Subei has been constrained by the lack of
power, railways, and roads. Subei's Peixian County, for example, can produce 5 million kilograms of peaches annually, for a potential total of 20
million yuan in profit. But because of the poor transportation, most of
these peaches cannot be conveyed promptly to markets in other regions.
As a result, many peaches are unsold and thus spoil.[5]

While township and village enterprises in Sunan have brought economic prosperity to much of this region, TVEs in Subei are beset with
infrastructure bottlenecks. According to a recent report, many TVEs in
Subei have no electricity for about 150 days annually due to the lack of
coal-transport capacity in the region.[6] In China, coal accounts for 70 percent of China's power generation. Meanwhile, railways are a dominant
mode of coal transport in the country.[7] Shortages and inefficiency in the
transportation and energy sectors in Subei, especially the absence of railways, have become major obstacles to economic growth. Development
of these elements of infrastructure is necessary for all other economic
activity.

A trip to Subei, I thought, might be a good opportunity to investigate
transportation bottlenecks in China's economic development.

Three of us, Guo Qiang, his assistant Ren Min, and I, arrived in Nantong in the early afternoon after a three-hour journey by speedboat. This
speedboat line between Nantong and Shanghai was recently opened. Nan-

tong, with a population of about 600,000, is a major port city in the lower Yangtze River Delta. Nantong is over 1,000 years old. During the Qing Dynasty (1644–1911), Nantong became a commercial city as a result of the rise of the textile industry. The city had a great reputation for its cultural and economic development during the early decades of the twentieth century. China's first teachers' college, first textile school, first folk museum, first drama institute, and first Chinese-run school for the deaf and blind were all established in Nantong.

The city was one of the "14 open coastal cities" that the PRC government established in the mid-1980s. Nantong, however, has not done nearly as well as the cities in Sunan, such as Jiangyin and Changzhou, in terms of GNP growth and foreign investment. As the speedboat approached the port, I did not see signs of the kind of economic boom that I had noticed in the Sunan area. The Nantong port looked small and old.

We took a bus to a hotel near the bus station. We preferred to stay at a nearby hotel, although it might be a flea-pit, rather than at Nantong Grand Hotel. A clean and comfortable hotel five kilometers from the bus station did not appeal to us if this meant that we needed to get up at 3:30 in the morning. We checked into a 15-story hotel right next to the bus station. The hotel, called the Tian Nan Hotel, turned out to be pretty good. The bed sheets were clean, and there were no signs of fleas, although we spotted a couple of cockroaches. The hotel even provided its guests with hot water for showers from 7 to 10 P.M.

After a quick lunch, we headed to the Nantong Aluminum Fabrication Plant, the state-owned factory from which my friends would claim a payment due (chapter 13 describes our memorable visit to this factory). The plant was a 15-minute walk from the hotel. Mr. Ren Min, who had visited the plant a few times before, showed us a shortcut. The so-called shortcut was actually a small pond. There was a small boat tied with a steel cable across the two ends of the pond. Ren Min and Guo Qiang pulled the cable so that the boat could move forward. I had never taken this kind of "ferry" before. I was amazed that this primitive mode of transportation was still being used in a big city like Nantong. The pond was apparently polluted, because its water was almost as black as coal.

The following morning, we arrived at the bus station at 5:50 A.M., 10 minutes before the scheduled departure time, but the bus did not actually leave Nantong for Dafeng until 6:45 A.M. The reason for the delay, as the conductor explained it: the engine needed to be warmed up. Only fools would believe his explanation. Everyone knew that the driver and conductor did not want to leave until all the seats were filled on the bus. They wanted to make as much money as possible for the trip.

During the reform era, China's public transportation has been managed in various ways. While urban bus transportation has usually continued to be run by the state, intracity minibuses and long-distance buses connecting cities are often owned and managed by private companies or individuals; in some cases, they are managed by private companies under contract with the state. Privatization of China's long-distance buses has stimulated the material incentives of the people who work for the public transportation service and has resulted in the opening of many new long-distance bus lines. In Sichuan, for example, fewer than 7 percent of townships had bus service at the beginning of the 1980s. But since the mid-1980s the province has experienced a "rapid growth of cooperative and private bus and freight services."[8] This change, however, has caused new problems. Some conductors arbitrarily raise bus fares. It has become common for conductors to give a "discount" to passengers who do not want bus tickets or receipts.

In addition, the schedule of long-distance buses is often ignored. In the summer of 1994, I took a minibus from the foot of the Yellow Mountains, a famous resort in Anhui Province, to the Tunxi airport to catch an airplane back to Shanghai. But the driver kept picking up passengers at various scenic spots at the foot of the mountains. About two hours after I got on the minibus, I found that I was back where I started.

"Why didn't you get off earlier?"

"Why didn't you change to another bus?"

"Did you tell the bus driver that you were going to the airport to catch a plane?"

These are the questions that the people to whom I described this experience often asked. What they mean to say is that I was foolish to stay on that minibus for so long.

I was naive enough to believe the bus driver, who kept saying that the bus would leave for the airport in a few minutes. Like many other passengers on the bus, I protested. But I did not see the point in taking another bus because it seemed to me that all the other buses were doing the same thing. Eventually I did get off and took a taxi to the airport. The one-hour taxi ride to the airport actually cost me more than the one-hour airplane ride from Tunxi to Shanghai.

"If I were you, I would have hijacked the minibus with a knife or given counterfeit foreign currency to the taxi driver!" an American friend joked.

One probably does need to bring a knife or counterfeit money when one travels in some inland provinces in China today, but not for hijacking. In the spring of 1995, I traveled in to Henan Province by bus from Pingdingshan to Zhengzhou. In the county seat of Yuzhou, three young men in their early twenties got on the bus. With knives in their hands, they attempted to rob the passengers. The passengers, however, were not intimidated. We fought the robbers.

We seized the robbers, but the driver let them get off the bus instead of sending them to the police. He explained that these robbers were neighborhood villains, and he did not want to get in trouble when he passed this place next time. "Besides," the driver said, "these robbers have friends in the local police station."

"I suspect," a passenger who sat in front of me said in a low voice, "that the bus driver is also a friend of the robbers. He did not even ask them to pay a fare when they got on the bus."

"Robberies have occurred frequently on this bus line," added another passenger who often traveled between Pingdingshan and Zhengzhou.

Another serious problem in China's long-distance bus service is that in order to make more money, some drivers drive continuously for over 12 hours. As a result, the number of traffic accidents in the country has significantly increased in recent years. During a nine-hour bus journey from Zhengzhou to Shanmenxia, Henan Province, that I took recently, I noticed that the driver did not take a rest at all, not for even one minute, throughout the entire trip.

The bus that took us to Dafeng, however, stopped for about an hour and a half after it left Nantong. This was not to pick up more passengers, but because of technical problems.

"The engine must have overheated in the bus station in Nantong," Guo Qiang joked.

We waited for about 15 minutes. Then the driver told the passengers that the bus had serious problems that he could not solve. He asked us to get off and catch the next bus to Dafeng.

"How long will we have to wait for the next bus?" a passenger asked.

"It will be only a few minutes," the driver answered.

"Don't believe him," Guo Qiang said.

I told the driver that he should call the bus company and ask them to send another bus to pick up the passengers. I explained to him that in the United States, if an airplane, a train, or a bus has an accident or a serious technical problem, the company usually sends a substitute from the nearest location to the site of the accident in order to convey the passengers to their destination.

The driver looked at me for a while and then said, "This is China. No company could afford to do so."

"It is not a matter of whether the transportation company can afford it," I said. I wanted to finish even though I knew it would not make a difference. "What matters is whether the company has a sense of responsibility for its passengers."

"Do I need to pay a bus fare again for the next bus?" a passenger, apparently a peasant, asked the conductor.

"No," the conductor answered. "You will have no problem if you show your ticket to the conductor of the next bus."

I suspect that the conductor immediately regretted what he had said, because those passengers who had had a "discount" in the bus fare in the form of a waiver of tickets now started to claim tickets from the conductor.

After waiting on the road for about an hour, we finally caught a bus heading toward Dafeng. We showed our tickets to the conductor and were told that we had to buy tickets again because the two buses belonged to different companies. All the seats of the bus were taken, and we had to stand. It was 9:30 A.M. It would take two more hours from there to our destination. Standing for two hours on a bus was certainly not comfortable, but it was at least better than waiting on a road that led nowhere. We needed to be in the county seat of Dafeng before noon to catch a local bus to the village that we planned to visit.

But again, unexpectedly, the driver announced that he would take all the passengers to a restaurant on the road for lunch. I looked at my watch—it was 10:30 A.M.

"Why does the driver want the passengers to have lunch here and now?" I asked Guo Qiang. "Dafeng is only an hour away. People can have lunch there."

"Isn't it obvious?" Guo replied. "The owner of this restaurant will give the driver a kickback if passengers spend money here."

I told Guo and Ren that I was really learning a lot about the "entrepreneurship" of Chinese bus drivers during this trip.

My friends and I were not hungry. Moreover, we did not want to let that driver earn even a penny from us. Ren Min suggested that we stand on the side of the road while waiting. He hoped that we could catch another bus to Dafeng.

This time we were lucky—there were even seats available on the bus that we stopped for a ride. But our luck did not last long. About 10 minutes after we got on the bus, it had a flat tire. The bus driver asked all the passengers to get off temporarily so that he could replace the tire.

I looked at the bus as I got off. It looked very old, like one made in the 1950s. But the bus driver told me that it was a 1990 bus. He might be right, because the poor road conditions of China's highways, as well as the lack of maintenance of public transportation vehicles, often make buses look older than they actually are.

I told my friends that the United States has a wonderful long-distance bus company called Greyhound. It runs across the entire country. The physical appearance of Greyhound buses is in sharp contrast to China's buses—the former give passengers the impression of speed and safety while the latter seem sluggish, vulnerable, and unreliable.

"Do you want to change to another bus?" Ren Min asked Guo and me.

"No," Guo replied, "this is already the third bus that we have taken this morning. I'm so tired that I don't want to do anything. God knows what will happen to our fourth bus—if there is a fourth one!"

At this point I decided to write a report about our "adventure" on the road to Subei.

"Your readers in the United States will not believe all these incidents could happen to us on a three-hour ride in a coastal area of east China," Ren commented.

"American readers will think you made up the stories to make a point," Guo added.

"But we will be your witnesses as long as you buy us two Greyhound bus tickets across America," Ren said teasingly.

My friends were quite right. For people in the United States, a country with an excellent highway system, some of the incidents on China's highways that I have reported here probably seem unbelievably dramatic. But for those Chinese who often travel by bus, these things are usually too common to mention. The accidents that I witnessed during my bus rides in China—the lack of concern for safety, the highway robbery, the overcharging of bus and taxi fares, the arbitrary delay of the bus schedule, the overuse of transportation vehicles—all reflect the problems of poor management in China's public transportation system. The government has not made enough effort to deal with these problems.

The poor quality of the public transportation system on China's highways has not only made people's lives less convenient, but also has become a bottleneck in China's flow of economic development. Our visit to Sanlong Metal Processing Plant, a village-run enterprise in Sanlong town of Dafeng County, shows the ways in which poor transportation has prevented the enterprise from further economic growth.

The plant is located 30 kilometers from the county seat of Dafeng. When the bus with a new tire arrived in the county seat at 1 P.M., the local bus to Sanlong had already left. That was the last bus for the day. There were, however, several motor tricycles available. After negotiating the fare, we took one big motor tricycle and headed to Sanlong. All three of us wanted to take a nap on the tricycle, but we were never able to do so because the road was very bumpy. We saw a number of buses and cars parked in the middle of the road because of mechanical problems.

The motor tricycle that we took, however, did not cause us any more trouble. The director of the factory, Mr. Jiang Yaolong, and his three deputies welcomed us into the office of directors. All of them were dressed in military-style uniforms—khaki cloth, brass buttons, even epaulettes.

I was amazed at their old-fashioned clothing. During my visits to Sunan, I had never met a local official or a director of a township and village enterprise who wore a military-style uniform. Rich businessmen and local officials in Sunan virtually all wear Western-style suits. Based on their clothing, people in Sunan and Subei seemed to live in two different worlds.

"Are you all discharged military men?" I asked Mr. Jiang.

"No, actually only one of us served in the army," Mr. Jiang explained. "We bought the uniforms because there was a military-uniform sale at the town market. They were much less expensive than Western-style suits."

Jiang told us that they had been waiting for us for over three hours. Some of them had not even had lunch because they wanted to treat us. "We have seldom received people from Shanghai," Li Gui, a deputy director of the factory, said to us. "You are our honored guests."

When Ren told them that I was a professor in the United States, they all wanted to have a photo taken with me. They were delighted that a Chinese-American professor would visit their small factory. Mr. Jiang asked the clerk in the office to go to his home to get a can of Coca-Cola for me. He thought people from America must only drink Coca-Cola or "Seven Happinesses" (the Chinese translation for the soft drink 7-Up). I told him that the tea that they served me was just fine. I found these people kind and sincere.

The Sanlong Metal Processing Plant had a total of 400 employees. About three-fourths of the laborers in Sanlong village work in this village-owned enterprise. Mr. Jiang, the director of the plant, is also head of the village.

The plant developed very quickly in the 1980s. It is a joint venture with a small Hong Kong firm. But the Hong Kong firm actually did not contribute anything except the initial $50,000 capital. Because it is a joint venture, the Sanlong Metal Processing Plant receives some tax waivers from the state. Mr. Jiang told us that his factory had already paid the $50,000 back to the Hong Kong firm.

This village-run industrial enterprise has improved the living standard of the people in the village. While many poor laborers in neighboring villages and towns migrate to urban areas to seek jobs, no one in Sanlong village has left. The plant produces 4,500 tons of aluminum goods annually. Housed in an area of 19,000 square meters, this firm had 6 million yuan in fixed assets and 3.5 million in working capital in 1994.

But the plant is faced with several serious constraints to further development. "We not only need capital and technical expertise to upgrade the technology of our plant," Mr. Jiang said frankly, "but we also should reduce the cost of our products because of increasing competition with other enterprises."

"Our plant is not in a good location to attract foreign investment," Mr. Jiang explained. "The village, like other rural areas in Subei, is geographically isolated because of poor transportation. Also, because of the high cost of transportation for our products, we have lost a lot of customers."

"In addition, engineers or college graduates in cities are unwilling to work here," Mr. Li added. "None of the 400 employees here has a college education. There are only two high-school graduates in the plant."

"We are very grateful to you to have traveled all the way from Shanghai to provide us with technical guidance, information, and machines," Mr. Jiang said to Guo and Ren.

"To be honest, we are equally delighted that you are going to purchase our machines," Guo responded.

Not surprisingly, it took only half an hour for Mr. Jiang and Guo, on behalf their respective factories, to sign the contract for technical cooperation and the sale of machines. After signing the contract, Mr. Jiang said that he and his colleagues would host a banquet for us. Guo told him that we would not have time for dinner since we would like to go back to Yancheng that night. Instead, Guo asked Mr. Jiang whether they could show me the workshops in their plant.

"Of course, we would be delighted to show the Chinese-American professor anything that he wants to see," Mr. Jiang said. "We just hope that he will not laugh at us for the primitive conditions in our plant."

"No, I won't," I said. I was really moved by his frankness and friendliness. "Honesty is something admirable, not laughable," I thought.

Mr. Ni Chongming, another deputy director of the plant, showed us two workshops in the factory. These were, of course, not like the modern workshops with advanced machinery that I visited in Sunan. Most work was actually done half manually and half by machine. A chimney at the plant was releasing black smoke. As with the TVEs in other areas, environmental pollution is also a major problem here.

Unlike many state-owned factories where employees do little or have no work to do, the workers in this small village-run enterprise were all busy with their assignments even in the late afternoon. Mr. Ni told me that the average salary here is 400 yuan per month. Several years ago the average income in this rural village was less than 100 yuan because most villagers worked on farms.

After showing us the plant, Mr. Ni and his two colleagues took us on the back seats of their motorcycles to the county seat of Dafeng, where we could catch a bus to Yancheng. Mr. Ni told us that they owned the motorcycles privately.

"It was a good investment," I said.

"Yes, the motorcycle is very helpful," said the young man who gave me the ride. "Previously, it would take about two hours if we wanted to go to the county seat by bicycle. Now, it takes only 20 minutes. The only problem is that the road is still too bumpy."

"Why don't people here build better highways?" I asked.

"Please ask officials of our local government about road construction," the young man replied.

We did not talk at all during the entire ride down the dusty and bumpy roads. But the young man's words—"Please ask officials of our local government about road construction"—occurred to me repeatedly after the trip to Subei.

The transportation problem, especially the shortage of roads and highways, is not a problem confined to Subei. It has increasingly become a bottleneck hampering China's economic development. Even the official Chinese media have recently admitted that transportation has not been given enough attention from both central and local governments for too long.[9]

During the 1960s and 1970s, the Chinese government invested 200 billion yuan in construction on "three fronts" (China's military-industrial complex). About 29,000 large state firms were established in China's inland provinces. These firms were usually far from cities and main transportation networks. Investment in the transportation infrastructure was marginal during the first three decades of the PRC.[10] From 1950 to 1986, for example, China's railways returned a total of 115.6 billion yuan to the state—this amount was actually 40 percent more than the total amount of money that the state invested in China's railways during the period.[11]

According to a 1992 study, the total distance covered by China's five types of transportation (railway, highway, water, air, and pipe) was 2.07

million kilometers. This figure was less than 50 percent of the capacity of highway transportation alone in the United States in 1938.[12]

The transportation infrastructure completed in China a couple of decades ago cannot meet the rapid growth in demand. When the Beijing subway was completed in the early 1970s, it had only 700,000 passengers per month. Now, it carries 1.25 million passengers per day.[13]

The shortage of highways has been particularly notable. Highways per square kilometer in China, for example, amount to only one-fifth of India's, one-seventh of the United States', and one-thirtieth of Japan's. Huang Zhendong, China's minister of transportation and communication, has admitted that the average daily volume of transport on the nation's highways has surpassed the designed capacity by 20 percent. The transport volume of trunk lines on the national highway system has surpassed the transport capacity by over 100 percent.[14] Meanwhile, the number of cars in China has increased at a rate of 15 percent per year.[15]

In addition, more than a third of China's roads are unpaved or in poor condition.[16] The rural road system has come under particular stress because China's rural area has faced a rapidly increasing flow of goods and migration of peasants. Yet as late as 1993, over 2,000 towns and 190,000 administrative villages nationwide were not connected by buses.[17]

Vincent Benziger, an American scholar who deals with China's rural road system, recently noted that in Sichuan Province the type of bus passengers during the early 1980s changed from a ratio of three peasants to every seven urbanites to seven peasants to every three urbanites.[18]

"With the greatly expanded flood of bicycles, tractors, and other slow-moving vehicles, stemming from the success of the agricultural reforms, these roads were simply overwhelmed," Benziger observed. The Chinese government has allocated resources to improve major intercity roads during the reform era, but rural roads have been "left largely without a system of support."[19]

Railways, the country's main transport arteries, can meet only 60 percent of the demand for both cargo and passenger transport. According to China's transportation authorities, major railway trunk lines such as those from Beijing to Guangzhou, Beijing to Shanghai, and Lianyungang to Lanzhou, can handle only 40 percent of the transport requirements. In addition, 75 percent of China's 55,000 kilometers of railways are single-tracked, and 80 percent are not electrified.[20]

To be fair to the Chinese government, the state investment in transportation infrastructure has significantly increased in the past few years. For example, the government poured 71.2 billion yuan in 1993 into "infrastructure projects and basic industries in a major endeavor to ease strains in the transport, energy, and raw materials sectors."[21] In 1994, a total of 33.2 billion yuan ($4 billion) was invested in railway construction and 3,346 kilometers of railway lines were completed. According to government officials, the country's total length of rail lines has increased by 26 percent over that of 1970.[22] The government has also decided to inject over 100 billion yuan during the next three years to add over 10,000 kilometers of railway lines nationwide.[23] China's infrastructure shopping list for the next decade, as some foreign business people calculate it, is eye-popping: "40 airports, 14 metropolitan subways and light-rail systems, scores of ports, power plants, roads, and bridges."[24]

In Jiangsu Province several new railway lines, including the one that will connect Lianyungang to Yancheng and Nantong, are under construction. The Jiangyin Bridge on the Yangtze River is going to be built later this year. This will be the first bridge that links Sunan and Subei, connecting Jiangyin County on the south side and Jingjiang County on the north side of the Yangtze River. These projects are expected to reduce bottleneck effects and to stimulate economic growth in both the Sunan and Subei regions.

But the increase of state investment in the transportation infrastructure, according to experts, is still insignificant, especially considering the great need to improve poor transport in both rural and urban areas. According to a recommendation made by the United Nations, investment in urban infrastructure should account for 1.5 percent to 4 percent of GDP of a country, but China's budget on urban infrastructure in the early 1990s was only about 0.14 percent to 0.87 percent.[25]

Chinese authorities have often used financial constraints as an excuse for not investing enough money in transportation infrastructure. According to Liu Zhongli, China's financial minister, China would need $50 billion to upgrade infrastructure over the next decade.[26] The main question, as Minister Liu asked, is how China can raise such a large amount of money. Loans from foreign banks and foreign direct investment are certainly two major sources. Over the past decade, six loans totaling $1.63 billion were acquired from the World Bank to finance 10 railway projects. In 1995, more than $4.5 billion in foreign funding (from Japan, Australia, and the World Bank) is expected to be spent on railway projects.[27]

Foreign companies, however, are often reluctant to invest in China's transportation infrastructure.

"I wouldn't touch infrastructure projects in China," a direct-investment fund manager told a Hong Kong journalist. "They can change the rules any time, and you can't take a road with you."[28]

Problems such as the absence of a legal system, the uncertain political future of the country, rigid bureaucratic management, official corruption, and low economic return have driven potential investors away.

"The main problem concerning China's infrastructure development," a scholar from Jiaotong University in Shanghai said, "is not the shortage of capital, but the poor management of financial resources. During the reform era, especially in the past few years, too much money has been spent on building luxurious hotels and fancy department stores in major cities. Urban reconstruction in large cities has been achieved at the expense of some more needed projects of improving the transportation infrastructure in smaller cities and rural areas."

In a recent article on the strategy of China's economic development, an author found it ironic that China claims to be a front-runner in scientific and technological development worldwide in fields like nuclear technology, and rocket and satellite development, but the government cannot even deal with some basic problems such as traffic congestion in cities and the shortage of roads in rural areas.[29]

Government officials often argue that China will not be able to inject a large amount of money in transportation projects until it becomes a rich country.

"This argument is completely wrong," an economist from Nanjing University told me. "China is of course not a rich country. But the point is that China will never become a wealthy country unless it has a well-developed transportation system.

"In the early decades of this century, people in the United States built a large number of expressways, not because they were rich," the economist continued. "They were rich partly because they had built these expressways, which led to the boom of industry and commerce in the country."

My friends and I stayed in Yancheng that night. The following morning we boarded a bus back to Shanghai. In a few towns or market places, we saw several hundred young adults waiting on the road—not for buses, but for jobs. They were surplus rural laborers from poor counties in the Subei region. They waited on the road hoping to be picked up by anyone who could offer them jobs, temporary or otherwise.

This scene was not new to me. I have seen this kind of "labor market" in Zhengzhou, Xi'an, Shanghai, Beijing, Guangzhou, Hangzhou, and many other places. As shown in chapter 7, there are probably 200 million surplus rural laborers nationwide. I cannot help but ask the following questions: Why hasn't the Chinese government launched more labor-intensive transportation and infrastructure projects to absorb these surplus laborers? Is there anything more essential to China's economic development than the improvement of infrastructure and transportation? Or more important to social and political stability than absorbing millions of idle laborers?

13

Unresolved Issues of State-Owned Enterprises

Visiting an SOE and Claiming an IOU

Most people in English-speaking countries know the meaning of IOU (I owe you), but probably very few are familiar with the abbreviation SOE (state-owned enterprise). For students of Chinese industrial enterprises, however, SOE has almost become a synonym of IOU; a majority of state-owned enterprises in China today have heavy debts.

I read and heard many stories about the problems associated with SOEs during my stay in China, but a visit to a state-owned factory in Nantong gave me firsthand knowledge about the scope and scale of the problems. As described in the previous chapter, I journeyed to Subei with Mr. Guo Qiang, a former high-school classmate of mine, and his colleague Mr. Ren Min. The purpose of their trip was to claim an IOU from the Nantong Aluminum Fabrication Plant on behalf of their factory in Shanghai.

The Nantong Aluminum Fabrication Plant is located in the downtown part of the city. What astonished me first, as we arrived at the plant, were several steel plaques hanging on the wall near the front gate of the plant. These awards had been presented to the plant by the provincial government of Jiangsu during the previous several years. Some plaques recognized the achievement of the plant management or granted the title of "Clean Factory" to the plant. One was awarded for the good credit record of the plant.

"How can a factory win the title 'Clean Factory' while the factory's pond is heavily polluted?" I asked Guo Qiang. The pond water was as black as coal.

"It's even more ironic that the factory received an award for a good credit record at the same time it has failed to pay our factory for products purchased," Guo said.

"Credit," said his colleague Ren, "is not important in the world of Chinese business people, especially among managers of SOEs. They are far more interested in things like 'network' [*guanxi*] and 'kickback' [*hui-kou*] rather than 'credit' [*xinyong*]."

Guo told me that the Nantong Aluminum Fabrication Plant has owed their factory, the Hujiang Copper Plant in Shanghai, 32,000 yuan for two years. Guo had telephoned the director of the Nantong plant numerous times to claim payment but was always told that the aluminum plant would pay when its financial situation improved. A few days before our trip to Nantong, Guo informed the director that he was coming to collect the money in person.

"They will never pay if we don't go to claim the money," Guo explained.

We went directly to the director's office, but the door was locked. We told a clerk in the next room that we were from Shanghai and had an appointment with the director of the plant. Upon our request, the clerk phoned the places where the director might have gone, but could not find him.

While waiting for the director in the corridor outside his office, I noticed that the factory was very quiet. There was no sound of machinery running. Guo and Ren sat on the floor and took a nap. I started to read a Chinese novel I had brought with me.

We waited for about an hour. A young man appeared and introduced himself as an assistant director of the factory. He told us that the director knew we were coming that day, but he didn't know where the director was at the moment. He asked us to rest in the director's office.

"I have a hunch the director has been hiding from us," Guo said to Ren and me.

"Will he eventually appear today?" I was really anxious to know.

"I'm sure that he will come to see us," Guo said, "though I don't know whether he will pay us."

"It is increasingly unlikely," Ren said.

"How do you know that?" I asked.

"If he were going to pay us today," Ren said, "he would have given us the check right away. Letting us wait is a message that we will not get the money today."

"Ren and I have visited many factories to claim IOUs," Guo said to me. "We are familiar with the psychology of managers whose factories are in debt."

"How do you know that he will eventually appear? If I were he, I would be so embarrassed that I would hide all day," I said.

"If he did not want to see us," Ren said, "he would not let us travel all the way to Nantong from Shanghai in the first place."

"But it's really rude to keep us waiting for hours," I said.

"In China," Ren commented, "other people's time is not valued." Ren likes to make generalizations. Most of these generalizations, however, are based on his personal experience.

"Let's wait and see what will happen," Guo said to me mysteriously. I did not ask any more questions. I trusted my friends' knowledge.

Instead, I asked the assistant director why the factory was so quiet on a work day. "There is not enough work," he replied. "Only one of the six workshops in the factory has enough work for its employees. If we do not receive new orders for goods in the coming months, some of the workshops will completely shut down.

"This problem is not unique to this factory," the assistant director continued. "The lack of orders is a common phenomenon in state-owned enterprises in Nantong."

"Previously, such problems were covered by state subsidies, low-priced raw materials, and the state monopoly over sales," Guo explained to me. "The government, however, is increasingly unwilling to subsidize the factories, and most of these SOEs do not know how to survive in a market economy."

Guo's explanation is actually very similar to the official view of the problem. A recent article published in *China Daily* asserted:

> For over forty years, state-owned enterprises have played a dominant role in the country's economy. As the country dismantles its centrally planned economy in favor of a market economy, many state-owned enterprises are unable or reluctant to adapt to the new economic system. As a result, a majority of enterprises are running in the red.[1]

These SOEs have survived largely because of state subsidies. In 1992, for example, state subsidies cost as much as $90 billion.[2]

"Our factory has been beset with heavy debt," the assistant director said. He seemed to have a good understanding of the problems that the factory faces.

"Last year," he continued, "Nantong city alone owed 120 million yuan in taxes to the central government. The SOEs in the entire Jiangsu Province, most of which were in Subei, owed 1.2 billion yuan in tax."

The assistant director told us that Zhu Rongji, who has been in charge of China's economy, visited Nantong in December 1994 and raised the issue of debt during a meeting of the directors of state-owned large and medium-sized enterprises. Zhu was not satisfied with the current situation of SOEs in Nantong and urged the local officials to improve their performance.

Zhu's dissatisfaction with the poor performance of SOEs is well known among Chinese officials. In a meeting on the transformation of China's SOEs, Zhu Rongji said pointedly that the most important feature of the Soviet accounting system, which China has used for four decades, is that "one can never figure out whether an enterprise is making a profit or not."[3]

"Are SOEs in Nantong going to pay their debts this year?" I asked the assistant director.

"I don't think so," the assistant director replied. "How can SOEs in Nantong raise such a large sum of money? Many other coastal cities such as Shanghai can raise capital by leasing their land to investors, both foreign and domestic, or they can issue stocks and bonds. But business people are usually reluctant to invest in Nantong because the city is not even connected to others with a railway. The highways in the region are usually unsatisfactory.

"Besides owing tax to the state, many firms also owe money to other enterprises," the assistant director went on. "Our factory, for example, owes 2 million yuan to Suzhou Metal Machine Factory and 1 million yuan to the Suzhou Aluminum Fabrication Plant. Meanwhile, our factory has invested 40 million yuan in our production lines, of which 36 million yuan is a bank loan. This means that we need to pay about 650,000 yuan as interest to the bank every year. This amount of money is already a heavy burden for us. In addition, we need to pay our factory's 700 employees' salaries and to pay pensions to over 100 retired workers."

The debt problem that the assistant director described is certainly not unique to the Nantong Aluminum Fabrication Plant. *Baokan wenzhai*, one of the largest newspapers in China, recently listed 10 major problems in China's economic development. The problem of debts of state-owned enterprises was on the top of the list, followed by the banks' dead loans (see Table 13–1).

According to statistics recently released by the state council, China's cabinet, the total assets of national SOEs are now 2.5 trillion yuan ($300 billion). This figure actually includes two parts: (1) 800 billion yuan ($95 billion) in net assets; and (2) 1.7 trillion yuan ($205 billion) in debts.[4]

TABLE 13-1
Ten Major Problems of China's Economic Development
(ranked by importance)

Rank	Problems
1.	Debts of State-owned enterprises
2.	Banks' dead loans
3.	Financial deficits
4.	Loss of State assets
5.	Foreign deficit
6.	Waste of State property
7.	Decline of school enrollment, esp. in countryside
8.	Unemployment
9.	Lower income of peasants
10.	Environmental problems

Source: Baokan wenzhai (Newspaper and magazine digest), 17 February 1994, 1.

State-owned enterprises, which number 70,000, owed a total of 1 trillion yuan ($120 billion) to banks last year. That is 40 percent of the nation's total bank credits.

Because at least 60 percent of state-owned enterprises are running in the red, bad debts have become a nightmare for Chinese banks. Official statistics show "bad debt made up one-third of the nation's total bank loans" in 1994.[5]

"These state-owned enterprises cannot repay their debts because they earn too little but have borrowed too much," said Ding Ningning, a senior research fellow with the Department of Enterprise Economic Research under the state council.

Many enterprises repay their debts by obtaining new loans. Some simply deny debts owed to other enterprises and banks through mergers or bankruptcy. A recent article in *China Daily* reported that "some local governments encourage local enterprises to refuse to pay loans obtained from banks in other regions."[6] The author of the article argued that such practices threaten the security of bank depositors, most of whom are individuals.

"Business people in the West often fantasize about China's economic boom and the country's huge market, but they don't understand the bizarre ways their Chinese partners can behave," Ren commented. I had to agree with him. If the Chinese SOEs could refuse to pay loans borrowed from banks in other regions, they could certainly do the same thing to foreign creditors.

"Does your boss acknowledge the debt that your factory owes to Guo's factory in Shanghai?" I asked the assistant director.

"You should ask my boss," the assistant laughed. Guo and Ren also laughed, though somewhat awkwardly.

"Seriously," the assistant director continued, "we acknowledge the debt that we owe you just as we hope those firms that owe debts to us will do the same."

"Do other enterprises owe debts to your factory?" Ren asked the assistant director.

"Oh, yes," the assistant director replied, "actually, according to our records, other enterprises owe our factory a total of several million yuan. Our factory is really in the typical situation of what people call 'chain debt' [*sanjiaozhai*]."

Chain debt is another common problem of Chinese enterprises. Large uncollected accounts at many state-owned enterprises force them to delay payments to their own creditors. According to an expert's estimation, the total chain debt in the country in 1994 was about 200 billion yuan.[7] Wuhan Steel Company alone, for example, had a total of 8 billion yuan in uncollected accounts. Chain debt often takes a large part of the enterprises' working capital and prevents firms from receiving funds needed to purchase raw materials or to produce more goods.[8] Chain debt has jeopardized the business relationship among Chinese industrial enterprises.

In response, the Chinese government established a special fund with a few billion yuan in the early 1990s in order to save those SOEs locked into chain debt. But this plan soon proved utterly inadequate.

"One cannot put out a burning cartload of faggots with a cup of water [*beishui chexin*]," said a general manager of a large SOE in Shenyang, using a Chinese proverb to describe this failed government plan. As a result, all the money in this special fund was used up while most SOEs remained in red.

Since 1993, the central government has changed its strategy to restrict chain debt among SOEs. The government issued an order that no enterprise could purchase raw materials such as coal, petroleum, and natural gas through credit or IOUs. Major industries such as electricity and metallurgy were required to request immediate payment from their customers.

The government has tried to adopt more comprehensive measures to deal with problems such as stagnant sale of products, financial deficits, and undercapacity operation. Among these measures: (1) state-owned enterprises are encouraged to experiment with the modern corporate system (*xiandai qiye zhidu*), which means transforming SOEs into firms that offer shares of stock; (2) loans are restricted to those enterprises with marketable products; (3) an effort is made to tighten credit policy and control the amount of investment in fixed assets and the issue of currency; (4) enterprises under poor management will be forced into bankruptcy; and (5) the state will control the scale of infrastructure construction, institutional spending, and the rapid rise of workers' incomes.[9]

While these measures may prevent the increase of the debts of SOEs, the government continues to take a lenient policy towards debt-laden SOEs. As an official newspaper in China recently noted, the Chinese government passed the bankruptcy law nine years ago, but it is still not really enforced.[10]

In addition, some SOEs often give false reports of their financial situation. In 1994, for example, a large enterprise with 2,000 employees in Shanghai had a deficit of 60 million yuan, but had claimed to be making a profit for the previous five years. This factory therefore received a loan of $150,000 from the Bank of China, but this money was not reported on the factory's financial balance sheet. The enterprise was even named as a model enterprise, and the factory director was rewarded. The false report was found only after the factory director retired.[11] Some other SOEs, however, tried not to report the profit of their firms because they wanted to use their firms' profits rather than pay more tax to the state.

The most important reason for the Chinese government's continued leniency toward money-losing SOEs is that SOEs have 70 million employees—a large segment of the labor force in urban China.[12] In the absence of a broader social safety net, the bankruptcy of a large number of SOEs would be politically dangerous for the government. An unofficial survey in Shanghai showed that in 1994 about 200,000 people in the city were looking for jobs. A 1994 report in *Jiefang Daily*, an official newspaper in Shanghai, predicted another 50,000 to 100,000 workers would join the city's unemployment force in the near future as many SOEs were compelled to reduce the number of their workers.[13]

Neither government officials nor SOE managers fail to understand the political threat to them if they decide to lay off a large number of SOE employees.

Guo and Ren were right. The director did finally appear, although he kept us waiting for over two hours.

"I'm Ge Dihua. Sorry to keep you waiting for so long." The director shook hands with each of us.

I noticed that he spoke in the Shanghai dialect. Mr. Ge was in his late forties. He told us that he was born and bred in Shanghai. He came to Nantong to attend a technical school when he was 18. After graduation, he started to work in this plant, first as a technician and then as an engineer. I looked at the business card that he handed to me. His professional title is chief engineer of the plant.

"I had a busy day," he explained.

"Sure, we can imagine," Guo replied.

"I spent the whole afternoon in the accountant's office and in the bank," Ge said. "I'm terribly embarrassed about the small amount of money that I have to pay you today," he said to Guo.

"How much?" Guo asked.

"It is certainly not the amount that you expect," Ge responded.

"How much?" Guo repeated his question bluntly, though both he and Ge were smiling as this conversation went on.

The director showed his index finger.

"*Yiwan* [10,000 yuan]?" Guo asked.

"No, how about *yiqian* [1,000 yuan]?" Ge replied.

"Director Ge," said Guo, in a serious tone that emphasized his disappointment, "three of us traveled all the way to Nantong to collect 1,000 yuan? Our travel expenses exceed that amount. Your factory owes my firm only 30,000 yuan. That amount should not be a big deal for your plant, which has fixed assets of 30 million yuan."

"But this is the maximum that I can raise right now. Representatives of two factories in Suzhou also came to our plant to claim IOUs today. What I did to them was simply to update and re-sign the contract, acknowledging the amount that our plant owes them," Ge said humbly. "I promise that we will repay the total amount that we owe you as soon as possible."

"We don't want 1,000 yuan today," Guo said to the director. "We just hope that you will give our factory top priority when you repay your debts in the future."

"I appreciate your understanding," Ge responded quickly. "I will try my best."

It was 5:30 P.M. Guo, Ren, and I looked at each other and decided to leave.

"But I have arranged dinner at a restaurant for you," the director said to us. "We cannot repay our debts today, but at least we can afford to treat you to a casual meal."

To be honest, I was glad that the director would host us for dinner, because it would be a good opportunity for me to chat with him. Guo and Ren certainly understood my intention. We therefore accepted his invitation. What I did not expect was that this "casual meal" would turn out to be a 12-course banquet.

The dinner was held in a small but elegant restaurant near the plant. Ge told us that a former employee of the plant had opened this restaurant. He and his colleagues liked to host guests of the plant there.

"We had lunch with people from a Suzhou factory at this restaurant today," his assistant added.

"Will Ge receive a kickback from the owner of the restaurant by hosting the banquet there?" I asked Ren privately.

"Sure," Ren replied. "Ge is the real 'winner' today."

Altogether, there were nine people at the dinner. In addition to three of us from Shanghai and one person from Suzhou who also came to claim an IOU, Ge also brought four colleagues. His assistant, however, did not join us because he said that he "ate too much at lunch" and did not feel well.

I was amazed that four of Ge's colleagues attended the dinner. Neither my friends from Shanghai nor the person from Suzhou knew any one of them. They did not even talk during dinner except to raise their cups and say "cheers" (*ganbei*). They did that to each other, because none of the guests liked alcohol.

I have no idea how much money the host (the SOE of course) spent for the banquet, but it must have been terribly expensive because rare seafood and a famous brand of liqueur were served. It was truly beyond my imagination that the director of a debt-laden factory would behave like this. My friends Guo and Ren did not see the absurdity of this—they had probably experienced similar events too often.

The use of public or SOE money for private entertainment has been a common practice in China during the reform era. The Chinese government has issued as many as 36 orders in recent years to prevent local officials and managers of SOEs from using public money (*gongkuan*) for private entertainment, especially for banquets.[14] According to a study, 100 billion yuan ($18 billion) of public money was spent on dinner parties in 1992 alone, 2.5 times that of 1984.[15]

A new Chinese jingle vividly reflects the extent of the problem: "Workers, farmers, merchants, officials, and soldiers, all are crazy about eating and drinking; east, west, south, north, and central, everywhere spending public money." Mao once had a famous saying "Revolution is *not* having a dinner party." Now it is irreverently changed to "Revolution is *having* a dinner party."

Some local officials in rural areas spend most of their time giving dinner parties. People make fun of them, calling them "specialized households of eaters and drinkers" (*chihe zhuanyehu*). In urban areas, local officials and managers of SOEs often spend public money for entertainment in nightclubs. A 1994 study of nightclubs in a coastal city showed that about 80 percent of the income in these nightclubs was from state and public money.[16]

A columnist for Shanghai's *Wenhui Daily* believes that the use of public money for private entertainment reflects a systemic problem of SOEs. Directors of the SOEs usually are appointed for four to five years. They are more concerned about their short-term popularity than the firms' long-term economic interests. Managers fix their eyes only on profits gained during their term of management, also ignoring the firms' long-term well-being. As a result, directors of SOEs often "eat up, use up, and distribute all the assets of their enterprises [*chiguang, heguang, fenguang*]" during their tenures as SOE directors.[17]

Using public money for private entertainment, however, causes far less social concern in the country than other kinds of loss of public property, especially the widespread phenomenon of official corruption. The heavy loss of state assets has become one of the most serious side effects of China's economic reform. According to the Chinese government, the state currently loses an average of 100 million yuan per day. It was estimated that from 1985 to 1992, a total of 500 billion yuan of state assets were lost.[18]

There are numerous channels for the loss of state assets. For instance, managers of SOEs do not evaluate state assets when establishing joint ventures or shareholding companies. Many SOEs split off part of their firms and turn them into collectively owned firms. State assets, including both capital and equipment, are often transferred to these collectively owned firms without charge.[19] While the state is losing assets, governmental officials and SOE directors have been making fortunes for themselves. In the first 10 months of 1992, for example, 64,000 cases of official corruption were reported by the government. The total amount of bribes exceeded $370 million.[20]

What has not been reported by the Chinese government, however, is that some high-ranking officials and children of revolutionary veterans have turned China's large international corporations into their private firms. They spend state money as if it were their own money. Officials at all levels have indulged in bribe-taking, reselling state property for their own profit.[21]

A son of Rong Yiren, vice-president of China, for example, personally owns a several-dozen-room mansion in a suburb of London where he has hired a housekeeper, two gardeners, three chefs, and several maids. The grandchildren of the late Marshal Ye Jianying, though they are only teen-agers, own luxurious houses on New York's Long Island. According to Xu Jiatun, the former head of the Xinhua News Agency in Hong Kong who later defected to the United States, in the late 1980s there were al-ready about 200 members of the "princes party" (children of high-rank-ing officials) in business in Hong Kong.[22]

Compared to the amount in bribes that China's high-ranking officials have received, the luxuries that managers of SOEs such as Director Ge have—hosting banquets and accepting kickbacks—are really insignificant. During the banquet with us, Director Ge himself complained about the corruption of high-ranking officials and their children.

"The central government," Ge said, "neither intends to deal with large-scale corruption of officials at the top, nor plans to fundamentally change China's ownership system. Instead, the government has often blamed di-rectors of SOEs and attributed chain debt and other problems of SOEs to the poor managerial behavior of enterprise directors.

"State-owned enterprises," Ge continued, "do have heavy deficits and owe chain debt to each other, but they continue to play a major role in the Chinese economy: they account for roughly two-thirds of fixed investment and 69 percent of government revenues. Each year we give over 90 percent of our profits to the government as tax. Because we can keep only a small proportion of profit (usually less than 8 percent) for our firm, we do not have enough money for technological innovation and new product exploration. In addition, we cannot afford the increasing medical and insurance expenses for both our employees and retired workers."

"SOEs are caught in the middle of the transformation from the planned economy to the market economy," said Ren.

"China's economy is neither a planned economy nor a market econ-omy," Director Ge responded. "I think a more appropriate term for Chi-na's economy is 'policy economy' [*zhengce jingji*]. We SOEs are caught in constant changes of government policies. No one knows what the gov-ernment policy will be towards SOEs tomorrow."

Director Ge's comments reflect the concern and dissatisfaction of man-agers of SOEs in general. Although the SOEs' share of national output value dropped from 78.5 percent in 1979 to 44 percent in 1993, SOEs still produced about 80 percent of the basic industrial products in the early

1990s.[23] In 1991, the large and medium-sized SOEs gave 94.8 percent of their profits to the government as tax.[24]

Most of China's large and medium-sized state-owned enterprises were established in the 1950s. This has two implications. First, they have heavy social burdens due to their retired employees. According to a recent survey of 16 cities including Shanghai and Tianjin, there were altogether 3,547,000 retired employees, which accounted for 29.2 percent of the total employees (12,510,000) in these cities. In Shanghai alone, retired employees accounted for 50 percent of total employees.[25] Second, equipment of these SOEs is increasingly out of date. But they do not have enough working capital to purchase new machines and equipment. According to a 1989 study, only 13 percent of large and medium-sized SOEs had equipment that met the standards of the 1980s.[26]

"Are you saying that SOEs would do well with better equipment and less social burden?" Ren asked Director Ge.

"Yes," Ge replied.

"Can you give an example of an SOE, in Nantong or elsewhere, that is really doing well?" Ren asked.

"Well," Mr. Ge answered, "there are many stories about model SOEs, which are publicized by the official mass media."

"Do you really believe these stories?" Ren continued, "These model SOEs, just like the false model of Dazhai under Mao's era, could not survive without heavy government subsidies. If you go to northeastern China, many model SOEs cannot even pay the salaries of their employees on time."

Director Ge did not say anything, but smiled.

Ren's generalization is widely shared by people who are familiar with SOEs in China. A relative of mine is a deputy director of a model SOE factory in Shanghai. Official newspapers in both Shanghai and Beijing reported how this factory has successfully repaid a large portion of its debts. But my relative told me that his factory did that by selling the site of the factory, which is located in downtown Shanghai, to foreign investors. His factory is fortunate enough to have land to sell, but the sad truth is that this sale is probably the last chance for the factory to survive.

"It is said there is only one kind of SOE that is doing remarkably well," said Anita Chan, a sinologist at the Australian National University. "These are China's prison factories. The prison factories are of course state-owned enterprises. They do not have labor cost, nor social burden." Dr. Chan recently conducted comprehensive research on labor relations in factories with various ownership forms in urban China.

When I repeated what Anita Chan told me about the success story of the prison factory to Guo, Ren, and Director Ge, they all laughed.

"I wish I was the director of a prison factory," Ge said jokingly.

"The top leaders of China may share the same idea with you," Ren responded. "It would be much easier to rule the country if everything was severely controlled, as it was during the era under Mao's rule. Now the Chinese economy has become so complicated. Any simplistic solution to the problems of SOEs is doomed to fail."

I found Ren's remarks insightful. Many sophomoric economists in the West, however, think that they have the answer to China's economic problems, especially those associated with SOEs. Some argue that rapid privatization is the key, while others believe that no major change is needed. Dwight H. Perkins, a Harvard economist, summarized some of the Western views:

> There are two schools of thought on the reform of Chinese state enterprises that argue either that nothing can be done about their reform or that nothing needs to be done. . . . Neither view is very realistic in the Chinese case.[27]

I am suspicious about any proposal for a quick remedy for SOEs. The Chinese government is faced with a dilemma: they must seriously deal with problems such as chain debt, loss of state assets, and inefficiency of SOEs, but any effective measures will not only challenge bureaucratic interests, they will weaken the government's power base, lead to large-scale urban unemployment, and produce social unrest.

The successful transformation of SOEs will require concerted effort and fundamental changes in all aspects of China's economic system, including the banking system, tax system, accounting framework, urban housing system, social insurance system, labor market and unemployment welfare, and most importantly, the legal system. China seems to have a long way to go to improve all these systems. But the problems of SOEs, like time bombs, may explode prematurely and blow the country in a different direction.

Director Ge asked us whether we would like to go to a nightclub to enjoy karaoke after the banquet. I told him that I was tired and wanted to go to sleep. My friends said that they would go back to the hotel with me.

I had a nightmare that evening—I dreamed that I was on a large, luxurious ocean-going ship on which everyone was drinking and dancing. But the ship hit a rock and started to sink. No one knew how to save the ship or to save the lives on the ship. We awaited our destiny, hopelessly.

Part V

Implications

This photo was taken, not during the Cultural Revolution, but in the fall of 1994. There are a number of restaurants in Beijing that are decorated with Mao's portraits and Cultural Revolution posters. These restaurants are usually very popular among Beijing residents.

"We are not really nostalgic about the 'good old days'—there never were such days," said a middle-aged man with whom I talked in a restaurant called "Black Earth." "But life was much simpler in the old days," he continued. "We didn't need to worry about the future, because the future would be the same for everyone. But now I don't know where I will work the next month and how much my salary will be. It is certain, however, that my boss earns 20 times more than I do."

The entrance to Huaxi village is a large square with bleachers with a capacity of more than 10,000 people. Huaxi Square is shadowed by a 25-meter-high, 15-meter-wide, 500-meter-long gigantic dragon—a good omen representing power and prosperity. For people in Huaxi, the dragon is both the witness and the "patron saint" of the economic boom.

14

Is a Rich Man Happier than a Free Man?

Huaxi Village, China's "Mini-Singapore"

I had been skeptical about comparing the socioeconomic development of Singapore and China until the fall of 1994 when I visited Huaxi (pronounced *wah-shee*), a village in southern Jiangsu Province.

Previously, I thought it was inappropriate to draw a parallel between Singapore, a city-state of 2.8 million people, and China, a mainly agrarian country with 1.2 billion inhabitants. Scholars have often attributed the rapid economic growth of both Singapore and China to their "common political and socioeconomic environments." But the ways in which these two countries have achieved their economic miracles are hardly identical. Singapore's success, as Singaporeans themselves have acknowledged, is due mainly to its ideal location on the busy sea routes between East and West. China, however, owes its economic revival largely to changes of economic structure that occurred during the reform.

Politicians in both Singapore and China enjoy talking about their identical "Asian ways of life" and shared "Confucian values." In the international arena, they have often acted as debating partners against the West, especially the United States. But only a couple of decades ago, Singapore and China considered each other threats ideologically. They did not even have diplomatic relations until 1990.

Recently, political leaders from both nations have argued that the West should cease its efforts to impose its own concept of human rights on Asian nations. Furthermore, they have asserted that other countries in the world should learn from Asian Confucian states because these states provide moral guidance for the twenty-first century.[1] But ironically, during the earlier decades under Lee Kuan Yew's rule, the Singaporean people

243

were ordered by the authorities to speak English instead of Chinese or other languages, because Lee (who did not speak Chinese himself) noted that "the English-educated do not riot."[2]

Similarly, in China today it has become fashionable for both young and old to watch Western TV programs, to listen to Western music, to eat Western fast food and to wear Western-style clothing. As some Chinese intellectuals have observed, there has been an erosion of spiritual and moral values as a result of both Mao's Cultural Revolution and Deng's economic reform. Confucian influence cannot compete with the increasingly powerful influence of Western culture on the Chinese people.

All these reasons led me to believe that the heated discussion of the "Asian way," or the praise of Confucian values in both Singapore and China, was "all a political ploy by certain ruling elites" to preserve their authoritarian rule.[3] But I am now somehow less confident about my previous rejection of any comparison of Singapore and China. This does not mean that I believe in the "Asian way" or find justification for authoritarian rule. What I witnessed and learned in Huaxi tells me that the political and socioeconomic changes in certain regions of China have become increasingly similar to those of Singapore.

As far as I know, no one in China or elsewhere has ever compared Huaxi village with Singapore, although Singaporean companies, with the guidance of the Singaporean government, have invested heavily in the Sunan region in which Huaxi is located. Singapore has recently started to build an economic and technological development zone—an entirely new town with 600,000 people and 70 square kilometers of land—in Suzhou. The construction of this new town, which is expected to be completed in ten years, will be largely based on the Singapore model.

The question that has interested me is how and why the political and socioeconomic life of Huaxi resembles that of Singapore. An analysis of similarities between Singapore and a newly developed region on China's coast, such as Huaxi, is important, both intellectually and practically, because it will not be a small matter if the land of China becomes more and more like Singapore.

The Richest Village in China

Huaxi village is located in a suburb of Jiangyin, which is about 300 kilometers northwest of Shanghai. Huaxi occupies an area of 0.96 square kilometers, including about 600 *mu* of arable land. There are altogether 320 households and 1,475 residents, including 918 laborers, in the village. In recent years, the village has absorbed over 3,000 migrant laborers from neighboring counties or provinces.[4]

Such a small village, of course, does not find its way onto the general map of Jiangsu Province, let alone the map of China. But Huaxi has recently received nationwide recognition and has been considered a model for China's rural development. During the past few years Huaxi has frequently appeared on the cover of many magazines in China, such as *Beijing Review* and *Rural World*. Top leaders of the country, Premier Li Peng, for example, visited the village in 1992. Li even wrote an endorsement for local officials, describing Huaxi village as "the place where the hope of rural China lies." Since the late 1980s, Huaxi has attracted thousands of visitors, both from within China and abroad. Many people came to study what has made this small town soar economically in such a short time.

What has made Huaxi village nationally famous is its rapid economic growth in the 1980s and 1990s. When it was founded in 1961, the village owned only 25,000 yuan collectively. But in 1992 Huaxi had amassed 230 million yuan of fixed collective assets, more than $40,000 per person, about 9,000 times the 1961 figure.[5] The total industrial and agricultural output value of Huaxi in 1992 was 516 million yuan, 85 times that of 1982.[6]

The living standard of the Huaxi people has improved dramatically in recent years. In 1993, average household savings were 87,500 yuan ($15,350) and per capita household fixed assets were 720,000 yuan ($126,000).[7] In 1994, the average output value per person was 1 million yuan and the portion of village revenue paid to the state per person on average was $10,000.[8] Not surprisingly, officials in Huaxi have claimed that their village is the richest village (*shoufucun*) in the country.

In both rural and urban areas of China today, a minuscule number of people own private cars. But in Huaxi, about 80 percent of families own Volkswagen Jettas, which each cost 175,000 yuan ($30,700). For Chinese workers whose annual individual salary was 3,000 yuan on average in 1993, 175,000 yuan is an astronomical amount.

"This is one of the most exciting events ever in our village," a village official told a Chinese reporter when the first 50 new Volkswagen Jettas, out of a total of 250 Jettas ordered, were delivered from a Changchun-based automobile factory to Huaxi.[9] This event was widely publicized in the Chinese media. When I visited some homes in the village, I noticed many of the families cherished a photo showing these just-arrived Jettas, all the same red color, lined up in orderly fashion along the village square.

Villagers in Huaxi were also very enthusiastic about showing visitors

Fifty Volkswagen Jettas, of a total of 250 cars ordered, were delivered from the Changchun-based automobile factory to Huaxi. These just-arrived Jettas, all in the same red color, are lined up in orderly fashion along the village square.

their newly built homes. The previous single-story thatched-roof houses have all been replaced. About 80 percent of the families of Huaxi now live in three-floor, nine-room houses, all with kitchens, several bathrooms, garages, and balconies. Per capita living space in Huaxi is 35 square meters.

I am truly impressed by the prosperity and wealth of the Huaxi people. Like other wealthy villages and towns in Sunan, the success of Huaxi is due to the great economic achievements of township and village enterprises. As explained in chapter 5, rural industrial revolution has brought all these fascinating changes. What interests me the most in Huaxi, however, is the pride and the sense of superiority that the Huaxi people demonstrate.

"We have already exceeded Hong Kong and Japan in terms of per capita living space and have surpassed Singapore in terms of per capita ownership of cars," a Party Committee member in the village explained to me. "If we calculate the indexes of living standard and economic growth by square meters, our village is usually ranked 'Number One'—the best in the nation. In China's countryside, our village has the highest personal savings, the highest per capita fixed household assets, and the largest per capita living space."

I couldn't figure out whether or not his "Number One" status of Huaxi was based on an accurate calculation. Frankly, I didn't care about all these hierarchical rankings at all. But the way that the Party official described Huaxi immediately reminded me exactly of the way in which Singaporean officials characterized the virtue and the superiority of their country.

At an international conference on the economic cooperation of ASEAN countries held in Hanoi in September 1994, a young and arrogant bureaucrat from Singapore said to other delegates that "Singaporean people are very proud of themselves and their country because we have the best quality and the best kind of life in the world. When one figures world living standard indexes in terms of square kilometers, one finds Singapore is always ranked Number One."

None of the participants in the conference, myself included, bothered to argue with him. On many other occasions, both formal and informal, I have heard similar remarks from Singaporeans. Every time, I felt sorry for my Singaporean colleagues. Couldn't they, I wondered, add any more interesting ideas to the conversation than praises for the "paradise of Singapore?"

I surely admire the Singaporean people for the great economic achievements they have made, but I find the Singaporean insistence on being "Number One" both awkward and distasteful. Unfortunately, people in China's fastest-growing economic regions, such as Huaxi village, seem to have adopted a similar attitude.

It is certainly not new that people in China and other Confucian societies view things from a hierarchical perspective. As some foreign observers have noted, Oriental societies are accustomed to viewing others as superiors or inferiors, but rarely as equals or peers.

People in free and democratic countries are usually suspicious of assertions about the "best quality of life," let alone the "best kind of life." To evaluate one's life is a highly subjective matter. It cannot, and should not, be determined simply by living-standard indexes. Ironically, for over three decades under Mao, including the period of the Cultural Revolution—the dark age of Chinese history—many people in China sincerely thought that they lived the best life in the world and were the "happiest people on earth." What is really dangerous is the mentality—and quite often, the illusion—that one's quality of life is superior to all others.

Dramatic changes in Huaxi have already made a strong impact on people's attitudes there—the way in which people in the region interpret these changes and evaluate their new life. Economic prosperity naturally leads to a search for a new identity, a new way to make sense of the people's new environment. It is under these circumstances, I believe, that village officials in Huaxi have brought back Confucianism.

The Resurgence of Confucianism

Visitors to Huaxi can hardly escape being impressed by the overpowering presence of Confucian doctrine in the village. The entrance to the village is a large square that can hold over 10,000 people. Similar to Sentoza Park, the most famous park in Singapore, which is centered around a huge dragon, Huaxi Square is also shadowed by a gigantic dragon—a good omen representing power and prosperity. The head of the dragon is 25 meters high and 15 meters wide. Its body is 500 meters long, functioning as an indoor passageway.

This 500-meter covered passageway leads directly from the square to the residential area of the village. Along the passageway are dozens of restaurants, stores, entertainment rooms, and tea houses. The largest restaurant in the passageway can accommodate over a thousand people. The stores offer a large variety of goods—from Mocca coffee to Heineken beer, from Nike sneakers to Giordano tee shirts, from Sony air conditioners to Minolta video cameras. Just a decade ago, no one could imagine that these products would find their way into rural China. I had never expected that such a small village would have a big commercial and entertainment center.

The Western influence, however, is not as strong as the presence of Confucian doctrine in the village. In front of a modern-style, air-conditioned tea house, I saw an announcement about a lecture on "Confucian Thought and Spiritual Civilization in the New Era." Although it was an hour before the start of the lecture, several dozen people were already in the room, sitting on comfortable sofas and drinking tea.

"This lecture is part of a series on Confucian moral education," said a 25-year-old tour guide who escorted me in Huaxi. "I attended the series a couple of times before. The speakers were professors from Shanghai and Nanjing. They were excellent." He told me that Huaxi officials established a company called "Huaxi Development Company for Spiritual Civilization."

"I have never heard of such a thing," I responded. "What does the company do?"

"The company, with its 5 regular staff members and 20 volunteers, organizes seminars and lectures, spreading traditional values of Chinese culture," he replied.

"I wish that I could attend the lecture," I said. "But I would like to see more of the village and its people."

"Don't worry," the guide told me. "Confucian moral education has penetrated everywhere in our village."

I soon realized what he meant by this penetration as we entered the Huaxi Farmers' Park. The park contains dozens of life-sized statues that represent Chinese historical figures. In the northern part of the park there are the "Twenty-Four Filial Piety Pavilions." Each pavilion has a few human-sized statues in ancient garb, representing a figure in a story based on a fable or a real historical anecdote. All these stories emphasize the virtue of filial obedience.

The Pavilion of Guo Ju, for example, is a story about Guo Ju, a poor farmer in Linxian, Henan, during the Han Dynasty, who lived in poverty with his aging mother, his wife, and his three-year-old son. His mother's health deteriorated because she often saved her food for the small boy. Guo Ju said to his wife:

> I feel shamed that I am not able to support my mother. In addition, our son is taking away my mother's portion of food. We now have to bury our son in order to support my mother. We can have another son in the future, but we cannot have another mother.[10]

The wife did not dare disobey Guo Ju. Therefore, the couple started to dig a tomb for their son. But to their surprise, they found gold as they were digging. Therefore, not only was their son saved, but also the couple used the gold to support Guo's mother. Most other filial piety stories are as peculiar as that of Guo Ju. These stories seem to make the point that one should observe filial piety under all circumstances.

In addition to "Twenty-Four Filial Piety Pavilions," there are five "Longevity Pavilions" (*changshouting*) in the Farmers' Park, representing the ages of 60, 70, 80, 90, and 100 years. When a senior villager reaches any of these ages, his or her children will organize a birthday party in honor of the aging villager in an appropriate pavilion. Huaxi village has an unwritten rule: when a villager celebrates his or her 100th birthday, the village will not only build a tower in honor of the birthday villager, but also offer 10,000 yuan to each and every one of the villager's children and grandchildren.[11]

"Through both material and nonmaterial incentives, villagers in Huaxi learn how to respect the elderly," commented a Chinese scholar I met in

Huaxi. He told me that in Huaxi, all retired people can live on a pension, and medical expenses are all paid.

Filial piety is of course not the only Confucian value that is disseminated in the Huaxi Farmers' Park, which a friend of mine called the "Exhibition Park of Neo-Confucian Values." Social hierarchy and obedience, the emphasis on collectivism and the neglect of individuality, diligence and work ethics are among the values that are highlighted in this extraordinary park.

Confucian doctrines exhibited in Huaxi's Farmers' Park demonstrate what one should do and what one should not do. One thing that is strictly forbidden in Huaxi is gambling. In the mid-1980s, village officials announced that anyone who gambled would be expelled from the village.[12] Anyone who reported gambling to the village administration would receive a 1,000 yuan award. Since then, no such award has been made. As in Singapore, any one who violates "public morality" will be severely punished in Huaxi.

The authorities in Huaxi claim unambiguously that the village is like an extended big family. Because it is a family, patriarchal behavior is not only acceptable, it is also necessary. The village authorities, therefore, enjoy a tremendous amount of power in determining the sociopolitical life of villagers. One individual, Wu Renbao, the patriarch of Huaxi, has been firmly in control of the village for the past three decades. It is no exaggeration to say that Wu Renbao is to Huaxi what Lee Kuan Yew is to Singapore.

Wu Renbao: "Huaxi's Lee Kuan Yew"

Just like Lee Kuan Yew, who has run Singapore since its independence in 1959, Wu Renbao has been the "boss" (*dangjiaren*)—the Party secretary in Huaxi—since 1961, when the village administration was established. He is now concurrently general manager of the Huaxi Industrial Corporation (HIC), which handles all industrial, agricultural, and commercial affairs in the village.

A native of Huaxi, Wu Renbao was born to a peasant family in 1929. His father also worked as a cobbler when the farm work was not too heavy. At the age of seven, Wu Renbao started to help his parents in the field. With financial support from his relatives, Wu studied in an old-style private school (*sishu*) for a couple of years. Because of his father's illness, Wu Renbao had to quit school and work as a migrant laborer in Wuxi. Later, he married a Huaxi girl who worked in a textile factory in Wuxi.

After the Communist victory in 1949, Wu returned to Huaxi, where he served as captain of the militia and head of the co-op, a Chinese commune organization. He joined the Chinese Communist Party in 1957. He was the first secretary of the Huaxi co-op (the predecessor of the village) and has held that post ever since. The Party Committee of Huaxi has five branches, with a total of 137 Party members. They account for 15 percent of the labor force in the village. Under Wu's leadership, Huaxi was known nationally during the early 1970s for its steady high grain yield. During the Mao era, Wu was selected as a deputy to the 10th National Party Congress. From 1975 to 1981, Wu served as Party secretary of Jiangyin County. He earned the title "National Model Worker" in 1989. During the recent National Conference of Rural Industries, Wu was selected as one of the top 10 heroes of township and village enterprises in the country. Now he is a deputy member of the People's Congress of China.

Although Wu is already in his late 60s, he does not intend to step down in the foreseeable future. In his recent talk at Qinghua University, he told the audience that he will not retire until he is 80. This seems highly possible, because in Huaxi no one can challenge Wu's authority.

Wu has four sons and a daughter. All of his sons and his son-in-law hold important leadership positions in the village. Just as Lee Hsien Loong, Lee Kuan Yew's son and currently the first deputy minister of Singapore, is expected to be the top leader of the country in the near future, Wu's oldest son, Wu Xiedong, currently the first deputy Party secretary of Huaxi and deputy general manager of the Huaxi Industrial Corporation, is a designated successor to Wu Renbao.

Wu's second son, Wu Xiede, also deputy general manager of the Huaxi Industrial Corporation, once headed the Huayuan Guest House, a 150-room hotel in Beijing run by the HIC. He is now general manager of Huahong Pipe Fittings Limited Company, a joint venture with Hong Kong. The third son, Wu Xieping, is general manager of Nanyuan Hotel, a high-grade 150-room hotel located in Huaxi. The fourth son, Wu Xie'en, a demobilized soldier, was in charge of industrial production supply in the village for a number of years. Now he is director of Huaxi Aluminum Products Factory. Wu Renbao's son-in-law, Miao Hongda, is deputy executive general manager of the Huaxi Industrial Corporation.

Wu Renbao and his "princes" are in firm control of political and economic power in Huaxi. Two sons and a son-in-law have occupied top leadership posts in both the Party Committee of the village and the executive committee of the Huaxi Industrial Corporation. Huaxi, in a way, can be identified as "Wu's family kingdom."

The phenomenon of strong family ties and nepotism is quite common in China's rural industries. In a recent article published by *Township and Village Enterprises of Southern Jiangsu*, an author used the term "power circle of relatives and friends" (*qinpen quanliquan*) to describe the prevalence of nepotism in Jiangsu's TVEs. According to the author, this power circle has destroyed the incentives of a majority of workers in the enterprises and has not been conducive to the effort to fight against corruption.[13] This phenomenon also raises the question of who really owns township and village enterprises. Many enterprises in Sunan claim to be collectives, but they are actually owned by directors of the firms, who are usually members of the same family.

Officials in Huaxi usually receive a large amount of money as bonuses because the village adopted a contract system for the distribution of profits in 1987. According to this contract system, 20 percent of the profits of an enterprise go to the Huaxi Industrial Corporation while the other 80 percent are distributed within the enterprises in a ratio of 1:3:3:3. This means that 10 percent of the remaining profits go to the director of the enterprise, 30 percent to other managers and technicians, 30 percent to workers, and the other 30 percent are saved as enterprise assets. In 1989, some directors of Huaxi received over 100,000 yuan as an annual bonus.[14]

Wu Renbao once told the Chinese media that he was not, and would not be, the wealthiest person in the village. His salary was not the highest in the village. He claimed that he and his wife were among the last group of people in Huaxi who moved into new houses. But in 1994, a delegation of Hong Kong journalists visited the house of Wu Xieping, Wu's third son. They were surprised to find what a luxurious life his son lived. The dining room of Wu Xieping's house, where they had lunch, could accommodate five banquet tables with seats for over 60 people. According to Hong Kong journalists, the house was much better than the houses of the middle class in Hong Kong and Singapore.[15]

I did not have a chance to interview Wu or any of his sons because they were all out of the village during my visit. Instead, I asked the villagers I met what they thought of Wu Renbao.

"He is great," a 50-year-old woman villager replied. "He has brought all these changes to our village."

"How?" I asked.

The woman did not answer my question right away, but instead looked at me for a while, making me feel that I had asked an absolutely dumb question, or the answer was too obvious for her to address.

Eventually she broke the silence. "You could not imagine how poor we were 30 years ago, or even 20 years ago."

"But Wu Renbao was also the 'boss' [*dangjiaren*] in Huaxi 20 or 30 years ago, wasn't he?" I asked.

"That's true," the woman answered, "but anyway, he was the leader who led us out of poverty in Huaxi."

Most people with whom I chatted in Huaxi seemed to share her view about Wu and other village officials. The satirical attitude toward officials and the resentment over corruption, which I had heard so many times in other parts of China, seemed not to exist in Huaxi. It occurred to me that corruption might not be a serious problem in Huaxi, just as it is not in Singapore. In addition, the dramatic improvement in the life of villagers over the past decade has been credited to local officials.

"When I was young, my entire family was crowded into one room," Hu Fenghu, a 54-year-old accountant at the village's steel strip factory, said to a Chinese reporter. "The annual individual income in Huaxi in the late 1960s and early 1970s was less than 100 yuan. We did not have enough grain and during those days we had to wear shoes made of straw."[16]

But now his family lives in a three-story house with 400 square meters of living space. The house has modern facilities such as a telephone, air conditioner, washing machine, refrigerator, and hot water heater. His wife, son, and daughter-in-law all work in Huaxi's village enterprises. The family's annual income surpassed 70,000 yuan in 1994. His two grandsons attend the village kindergarten for free.

"Wu Renbao has required officials, at both village and enterprise levels, to follow two important guidelines," a 30-year-old factory director in Huaxi told me. "They are: one, 'to keep our hands clean' [*lianjie*] and two, 'to know our jobs well' [*donghang*]."

"Yes, I do receive 10 percent of the profits as a bonus," the director explained to me, "but according to our village's regulation, I must deposit the bonus in my account in the enterprise. The money will be reinvested. This means that the growth of the enterprise is as important as our personal development. We aim at collective prosperity rather than just individual wealth."

In his recent address to a conference on the ideological work in provinces of East China, Wu Renbao claimed that Huaxi has successfully avoided the disparity between rich and poor. According to him, in Huaxi, the lowest savings account in a household is more than 50,000 yuan, and the highest is about 500,000 yuan.[17] In his view, there is neither any "poverty family" (*pinkunhu*) nor a single "tycoon family" (*baofahu*) in today's Huaxi.

A study of household income distribution of Huaxi village conducted in the early 1990s seems to confirm Wu's argument (see Table 14–1). According to the study, about 50 percent of the households in Huaxi had incomes ranging from 5,000 to 7,000 yuan. The study also showed that

TABLE 14-1
The Household Income Distribution of Huaxi Village (1989)
(Total: 403)*

Income Level (yuan)	Number of Households	% of Total
1000 and below	11	2.7
1001-2000	14	3.2
2001-3000	26	6.4
3001-4000	36	8.9
4001-5000	34	8.4
5001-6000	138	34.2
6001-7000	62	15.4
7001-8000	21	5.2
8001-9000	15	3.7
9001-10000	20	4.9
10001 and above	26	6.5

Note and Source: Lu Yinchu and others, "Yige xiangdang fada de xiandai nongcun shequ" (A well-developed rural community), in Lu Xieyi, ed., *Gaige zhong de nongcun yu nongmin* (Countryside and peasants in the age of reform) (Beijing: Central Party School Press, 1992): 341.

*This number may include some migrant households.

the salaries of Huaxi's top officials are only about 173 percent of the average salaries of employees of rural industries in the village.[18]

These data on salary distribution in Huaxi can be misleading because a large amount of income usually comes in the form of bonuses, which are not included in the study. Yet the income gap in Huaxi is indeed very small compared with other regions in the country. According to a nationwide survey, the income ratio between the top and bottom 20 percent of urban residents stood at 1.7:1 in 1981 and 2.8:1 in 1992. In rural areas the ratio grew from 2.9:1 in 1981 to the present 5:1.[19]

"Not only is there a narrow gap between rich and poor in Huaxi," an official in the municipal government of Jiangyin explained to me, "but also people in Huaxi reach out to help poor people in other areas." Huaxi has guaranteed more than 7 million yuan in loans to neighboring villages and towns. In addition, as Wu Renbao announced in 1994, the village committed itself to help 100,000 people in midwestern China live above the poverty level.[20]

What makes Huaxi officials well respected in the village, as people I met there told me, is not so much that they "keep their hands clean" as that they "know their jobs well." A majority of officials in Huaxi did not receive much formal schooling. Wu Renbao himself, for example, did not have even an elementary-school education. The educational level of villagers of Huaxi is the same as the average of the region. According to the 1990 census, Huaxi had only one graduate of a four-year college (see Table 14-2).

Despite their lack of formal education, Wu Renbao and other village officials understand the importance of science and technology in rural development. They have worked to help villagers receive technical training, to attract talented people from outside to work in Huaxi, and to encourage younger people to pursue higher education. The village not only provides tuition for students in elementary and junior high schools, but also offers scholarships for senior high and college students.

In 1994, four years after the census, the educational attainment level in Huaxi had already improved significantly. By then 86 percent of the labor force in Huaxi had received education above junior high school. Among them, 213 people had graduated from senior high, and 128 had gone to

TABLE 14-2
Educational Levels of Huaxi Villagers (1990)

Educational Level	Number	% of Total Village Population
4-year college	1	0.1
2-year college	3	0.2
Technical school	3	0.2
Senior high school	98	8.1
Junior high school	468	38.6
Elementary school	512	42.2
Illiterate (above 12-year-old)	128	10.6
Total	1213	100.0

Source: Lu Yinchu and others, "Yige xiangdang fada de xiandai nongcun shequ" (A well-developed rural community), in Lu Xieyi, ed., *Gaige zhong de nongcun yu nongmin* (Countryside and peasants in the age of reform) (Beijing: Central Party School Press, 1992): 357.

college.[21] Meanwhile, about 400 engineers and technicians from other regions have worked in Huaxi. Among them, 120 people have decided to continue long-term residence in the village.

Wu Renbao recently told the Chinese media that Huaxi is going to invest 17 million yuan to establish a college in the village, which will be called Huaxi University.[22] This is a joint venture with the Northern University. When it is built, the college will recruit students from Jiangyin and other counties in Sunan.

From Huaxi Village to "Huaxi Inc."

The most impressive "job" that village officials have accomplished is, of course, the rapid development of rural industries in Huaxi. As discussed in chapter 5, a majority of people in the huge rural part of Sunan have experienced a fundamental change—an occupational change—in their lives during the past decade. Because of the rural industrial revolution, rural Sunan has become quite a diversified reality. Huaxi, like many other villages in the area, is no longer a traditional, agriculture-oriented village.

Laborers in the village are no longer necessarily peasants. As a matter of fact, 97 percent of the labor force in the village consists of nonagricultural workers. The percentage of Huaxi's agricultural output of the total declined from 23.1 percent in 1975 to 0.3 percent in 1989, and the industrial output increased from 50.4 percent in 1975 to 99.1 percent in 1989 (see Table 14-3).[23]

Only seven people, 0.8 percent of the total labor force in the village, are engaged in agricultural work. Huaxi has three characteristics of modern agriculture: (1) specialized production (*shengchan zhuanyehua*), (2) mechanized cultivation (*gengfan jixiehua*), and (3) merchandised grain (*liangshi shangpinhua*). Although only seven people work on the farm, the total grain output has continuously surpassed 500,000 kilograms for nine years. During the harvest season, however, all the people in the village are available to help with farm work.

The village administration seems to understand the importance of grain production in a time of rural industrialization. The village has declared over 600 *mu* of grain fields a "protective agricultural area," which cannot be used for any nonagricultural purpose. In addition, 18 villagers in Huaxi, 2 percent of the total labor force, are engaged in sideline production. They have formed four groups, and each group specializes in vegetable planting, fish raising, domestic animal raising, or fowl raising.

The other 97 percent of the laborers work in industrial and commercial

TABLE 14-3
Distribution of Output Value of Agricultural, Sideline and
Industrial Sectors in Huaxi Village
(Percentage)

Year	Total Output Value	Agriculture	Sideline	Industry
1961	100	100	0	0
1975	100	23.1	26.5	50.4
1978	100	26.6	10.0	63.4
1985	100	1.0	9.3	89.7
1989	100	0.3	0.6	99.1

Source: Lu Yinchu and others, "Yige xiangdang fada de xiandai nongcun shequ" (A well-developed rural community), in Lu Xieyi, ed., *Gaige zhong de nongcun yu nongmin* (Countryside and peasants in the age of reform) (Beijing: Central Party School Press, 1992): 335.

sectors. There are 40 factories in Huaxi, among which 5 are joint ventures and 10 state-collective affiliated enterprises. Their products include textiles, wool sweaters, metals, chemicals, aluminum goods, copper products, plastic decorating board, steel pipes and strips, and metal flange. These products are sold to almost all provinces in China and to 12 countries.

All these factories are under the administration of the Huaxi Industrial Corporation that Wu Renbao heads. Leading officials of the village are concurrently executive managers of the Huaxi Industrial Corporation. It seems appropriate to say that Huaxi village has now become "Huaxi Inc."

Huaxi did not have any industry until the early 1970s, when 20 villagers with a total of 6,000 yuan in capital established a hardware factory, which mainly repaired agricultural machinery. Village officials supported this experiment at the risk of being criticized for "taking the capitalist road." The factory made profits of 50,000 yuan in the first year and then more than 200,000 yuan annually in the following years.[24] This experiment brought in both capital for further development and confidence in the industrial development of the village.

In the 1980s, the village not only set up many more factories, but also was engaged in a number of horizontal joint ventures with Shanghai, Beijing, and other regions. Huaxi Copper Products factory, Huaxi Aluminum Products factory, and Huaxi Cold-Rolled Belts steel plant, which were founded in 1985, 1986, and 1987, respectively, have had joint ventures with Shanghai factories. Huaxi Copper Products factory had an output value of 24 million yuan in the late 1980s. Joint ventures with foreign companies also emerged in Huaxi during the 1980s. Hua'an Flange Limited, which has an annual output of 5,000 tons of flange, is a joint venture with a hardware company in Singapore.

Since the beginning of the 1990s, Huaxi officials have made efforts to enlarge the size of village enterprises and have moved toward group consolidation on an extensive scale. For example, Shenhua Wire Rod factory, a steel-wire rod plant with a total investment of 60 million yuan and an annual capacity of 300,000 tons of wire rod, the largest wire rod factory in east China, was founded in 1993. More rural industries have taken an export-oriented approach. One enterprise in Huaxi has even established a branch company in Singapore.[25]

Huaxi Industrial Corporation, which was established in 1992, has functioned as an enterprise group (*qiye jituan*), coordinating the development of TVEs in the village. In 1994, Huaxi Industrial Corporation was ranked sixth in China's top 1,000 most efficient TVEs (HIC was first in Jiangsu Province). The HIC, with its 13 branch companies and over 40 TVEs, has become an economic giant in the region and it is expected to "annex" neighboring villages and towns through "regional horizontal cooperation" in the years to come.

Huaxi's large-scale industrial enterprises have brought even faster economic growth to the village. Huaxi's total output value has increased from 516 million yuan in 1992 to 1 billion yuan in 1993, 2 billion yuan in 1994, and 3.5 billion yuan in 1995.[26] Wu Renbao recently announced to the Chinese media that in 1996, when the village celebrates its 35th anniversary, the average household assets in Huaxi will exceed 1 million yuan.[27]

"We've been pioneering our work step by step," Wu said proudly. "We've accomplished plans ahead of schedule before. Our aim is to give villagers happier lives."[28]

"To give people happier lives—isn't this what Lee Kuan Yew has been saying for decades in Singapore?" a colleague of mine in Shanghai commented as I told him Wu Renbao's "grand plan."

Is a Rich Man Happier than a Free Man?

On a few occasions during my visit to Huaxi, I wanted to ask villagers if they were really happy in this model village of the country, but each time I eventually decided not to. It seemed impossible that I would get an answer other than "yes." In addition, I didn't want to be embarrassed again, as I was while asking the woman how Wu Renbao has brought changes to Huaxi Village.

But for me, the question about happiness is real. I am, of course, impressed by the achievements that the people of Huaxi have made. One can hardly imagine that a village would increase its assets 9,000 times within a single generation. There is no doubt that Huaxi village is a great success! But perhaps because of my education and experience in the United States, I feel something important—something fundamental—is missing in this model village. It is the absence of freedom and individuality. I am skeptical about the neoauthoritarian assertion that the rich man is happier than the free man.

Huaxi, despite its undeniable vigor and vitality, seems like a living machine. No matter how well they live in a material sense, people there actually live in a world of alignments and conformities. For me, it was hilarious to see all the villagers in Huaxi driving the same color Volkswagen Jetta and about 300 families living in the same style house, but nothing seems more depressing than to listen to "neo-Confucian doctrines" offered by "know-it-all" Huaxi officials.

Nonetheless, the visit to Huaxi was a great eye-opener for me. It is one thing to know that the rural industrial revolution has changed China's landscape, but quite another to see how this revolution has brought about changes at a village level. The economic growth of Huaxi is astonishing. The village's experience has put to rest any doubts about China's southern Jiangsu as another economic miracle in East Asia. Yet a less visible but no less salient dimension of Huaxi's experience is that it has become the model that Chinese authorities use to articulate a new identity and try to justify a neo-Confucian authoritarian rule.

I have come to realize, after this trip, that the Singaporean way of life— and way of thinking as well—has indeed found its way to China, especially in its rich coastal area. The Singaporean way of life emphasizes communitarianism rather than individualism. The individual counts for little in the society; the individual is far less important than the community.[29] In Lee Kuan Yew's words, Confucian societies have demanded certain values, such as hard work, thrift, discipline, loyalty, obedience, and social coherence. Both Lee Kuan Yew and Wu Renbao have suggested that cultural values are the strongest driving force behind their successes.

Yet I am still not sure whether the success stories of both Singapore and Huaxi can really be attributed to these values. Fareed Zakaria, the managing editor of *Foreign Affairs*, was right as he criticized the cultural explanation for East Asian miracles.

"If culture is destiny," he argued, "what explains a culture's failure in one era and success in another?"[30] The Mao era, for example, also emphasized things like hard work, thrift, discipline, loyalty, obedience, and social coherence. But a majority of Chinese people, including those in Huaxi village, lived in poverty throughout the Mao era. These values are also very similar to the old Protestant work ethic to which many people in the West attributed the great gains of England and the United States in the nineteenth and early twentieth centuries.

Confucian culture, I believe, is more relevant as a tool for political elites to use in order to justify their rule than as a force to achieve an economic miracle. During my journey to Huaxi, I was absolutely astonished by the local officials' efforts to reinforce Confucian doctrines to villagers. The gigantic image of the dragon, the Filial Piety Pavilions, and the Huaxi Development Company of Spiritual Civilization are just a few cases in point.

One may reasonably argue that there is nothing new about all these activities as exemplified in Huaxi. In China's millennia-long history, political elites have always relied on these cultural doctrines to maintain their dictatorships. Yet I believe there is an important difference between the past and present: China today is on its way to becoming an economic giant in the world.

Twenty years ago, in 1975, the American writer Jan Morris visited Singapore and concluded the following:

> I felt I was experiencing, if only vicariously, something new in the world—a new energy of the East with which, sooner or later, the Western peoples will come to grips, if not physically, at least philosophically. It is a sort of mystic materialism, a compelling marriage between principle and technique which neither capitalism nor Soviet communism seem to me to have achieved.[31]

What has happened in the relationship between Singapore and Western countries in the past few years precisely confirms Jan Morris's prediction.

In a sense, I feel that I experienced the same thing in Huaxi during this trip that Jan Morris did in Singapore 20 years ago. Huaxi, however, is only a village. I don't want to jump to the conclusion that Huaxi's today will be China's tomorrow. In fact, Huaxi does not even represent the Sunan region. Many other villages in Sunan that I visited seemed more lively and less rigid than Huaxi.

Yet I have a hunch that Huaxi is going to become a model for China in the future, just as top leaders such as Li Peng have claimed. As a native Chinese, I wish my motherland to be economically wealthy, politically stable, and internationally respected. But honestly, I am not enthusiastic about the arrogance, conformity, lack of individualism, nepotism, and strong family ties in business and politics as reflected in the development of Huaxi village. I am probably too much an adopted child of a free and democratic society to tolerate the neglect of individualism and the lack of political freedom.

15

China's "Yuppie Corps"

Meet Mr. Zhang, a Chinese Technocrat

"I will tell you how China has changed and how it is going to change further," Mr. Zhang said to me on the telephone, agreeing to see me when I told him that I was visiting Beijing.

"Tell me where you are staying in the city."

"Do you know where the China World Hotel is located?" I asked.

"Of course I know that luxurious hotel. Actually, I was one of the officials who approved construction of that joint-venture hotel along with the World Trade Center project nearby." Mr. Zhang's pride crackled through the telephone.

I first met Mr. Zhang (not his real name) in 1985, when both of us had just arrived in the United States. I was a graduate student in Asian studies at the University of California at Berkeley while he was a visiting scholar in the engineering school there.

A native of Beijing, Mr. Zhang went to an elite engineering university in the capital in the early 1960s. He remained at the university as an instructor after graduation. During the Cultural Revolution he was sent to a factory in northeastern China, where he was a worker, a technician, and an engineer, successively. After the Cultural Revolution, Mr. Zhang returned to his alma mater and resumed his teaching post. Under a Sino-American educational exchange program, he spent four months studying at Berkeley.

Mr. Zhang and I happened to live in the same neighborhood in Oakland, California. Both of us had very little money then, and we could not even afford to take the bus to school. It was nice, especially at night, to walk for about three miles with a companion. Therefore, we became good friends. During those early morning and late night walks, we often had rambling chats about everything under the sun. But what we talked about most often were our concerns about China's future and our views of the United States.

We hadn't seen each other since he left for China at the end of 1985. During the past nine years, we corresponded only once a year as we exchanged New Year's greetings. I heard that he was promoted to full professor and chairman of the department soon after he returned to China. He left this educational institution and was appointed to the posts of Party secretary and director of an industrial bureau in Beijing in the late 1980s. Now, at 51, he is a deputy minister–level official (*fubuji ganbu*) and is in charge of several major industrial projects in China.

I was not surprised by the dramatic change in my friend's political life. His personal experience actually reflected a profound change under way in China since the mid-1980s—the "meteoric rise" of technocrats in Chinese leadership.

The term "technocrat" does not have a universally accepted definition. In the United States, people usually consider elites like Michael Dukakis and Ross Perot, two past presidential candidates, as technocrats. Ross Perot, for example, is an engineer by training, always favors "computer chips" rather than "potato chips," and is interested in power, although he is hesitant to admit it. In China, a technocrat is a person who has specialized training, a professional occupation, and holds a leadership position. In other words, three traits—technical education, professional occupation, and leadership position—are all basic criteria in the definition of technocrats.

Few leadership posts in China were filled by such people in the early 1980s. The Chinese Communist Party rose to power as a military organization, the majority of whose leaders were peasants. These peasants-turned-revolutionaries became important members of the ruling class when the People's Republic of China was founded in 1949. During most of the Maoist era, recruitment to leadership positions was generally based on class background, seniority in joining the Communist Party, and political loyalty—rather than on technical training or administrative competence. During the Cultural Revolution, technical experts were often accused of being "Soviet revisionists" for their technocratic orientation.

But dramatic shifts in cadre policy under Deng promoted technocrats, whom people sometimes call China's "Yuppie Corps," to almost all levels of China's leadership within a decade. The percentage of college graduates among Chinese leaders at various levels increased rapidly during the 1980s, for example, from 2 percent to 78 percent among municipal and county heads; from 4 percent to 58 percent among military leaders; and from 20 percent to 59 percent among governors and provincial Party secretaries.[1] New leaders are much younger than their predecessors. In Shenzhen, China's frontier city in terms of economic reforms, for example, districts and bureaus are often headed by 30-year-olds.[2]

Qian Xuesen, former chairman of China's National Committee of Science and Technology and now vice chairman of the Congress, even proposed as early as 1983 that by the year 2000, all cadres must be college graduates, all leaders at the county and bureau level must hold M.A. degrees, and all full or deputy ministers and provincial governors must hold Ph.D. degrees.[3] We may find it hard to conceive how anyone could imagine a country run by Ph.D.'s—but Qian's proposal was widely publicized in China.

Although it is not clear whether by the year 2000 China's cabinet will be filled with Ph.D.'s, the speedy advance of technical specialists to political leadership posts in the past decade is truly impressive. According to official data, between 1982 and 1988, more than 550,000 better-educated younger cadres rose to leadership positions above the county level. At the same time, more than 2,870,000 senior cadres retired under a program of leadership reform.[4]

All cabinet ministers, governors, and provincial first Party secretaries, as well as 97 percent of the members of the 14th Central Committee of the Party, are newcomers who were promoted after the mid-1980s. This is not only the largest turnover of leadership in modern China, but also probably the most massive and rapid change of elites within any regime in human history.

These data are even more striking if we consider that the proportion of college graduates in the Chinese labor force in 1986 was only 0.8 percent. Most of these college-educated elites majored in engineering and natural sciences. For example, about three-fourths of ministers and deputy ministers are engineers or natural scientists by training. The same pattern can be found among Chinese mayors.[5] An overwhelming majority of new Chinese political leaders, therefore, have come from the engineering profession—a very small portion of the population.

The rapid emergence of technocrats in post-Mao China, however, has not received the serious attention that it deserves. Western "China watchers" have tended to underestimate the significance of the technocratic orientation in the country. The crucial role of Deng and other aging veteran revolutionaries in Chinese politics has led foreign observers to characterize the Chinese leadership as gerontocratic rather than technocratic.

Four top leaders of China—Party Secretary General Jiang Zemin, Premier Li Peng, and two Politburo members, Li Tieying and Ding Guangeng. You might notice the similarities in their appearance—all wearing glasses and dressed in Western suits. Even more similar among them are their political and educational backgrounds. All came from revolutionary veterans' families, majored in engineering, and studied in the former Soviet Union or Eastern European countries.

Indeed, they are all technocrats. [Photo Source: *China Daily*]

Meanwhile, most of the Chinese dissidents who wrote about social and political issues during the past decade themselves came from technocratic backgrounds. Fang Lizhi, an astrophysicist who is known as "China's Sakharov," was a Communist Party official prior to the student movement in 1987. He was a radical advocate of technocracy for a long time. He constantly argued that a "knowledge elite" should be the ruling class in our time because the knowledge elite is *the* primary progressive social force in the contemporary world. Fang and other dissidents preferred identifying their opponents, for example, Li Peng and Jiang Zemin, as Communist hardliners rather than as people who might be identified as their peers, at least in terms of political and educational background, if not social values.

No one can completely ignore the vital importance of veteran revolutionaries' role at present. But it is unrealistic to assume that old men make all the decisions for the country. One may reasonably assume that these technocrats will not need a patron figure like Deng and will play an even more important role as China enters the twenty-first century. This suggests a historical transformation from charismatic-revolutionary leadership to managerial-technocratic leadership.

Does a change of leadership type lead to a change of leadership style? What are the characteristics and values of Chinese technocrats? Do changes in leadership composition reflect broad social, economic, and political changes? What implications does the dominant presence of technocrats in the Chinese leadership have for the country's future development?

These are the questions that I have wrestled with in the study of Chinese politics during the past few years. I have authored and coauthored a number of scholarly articles, exploring the technocratic orientation in post-Mao China. What I mean by the technocratic orientation refers to a four-point scenario: (1) the dominant role of technocrats in power, (2) dissemination of technocratic views and values in society, (3) the government's emphasis on economic and technological development, and (4) a focus on the role of experts in decision making.

Yet until now, I hadn't had a formal or informal interview with a technocrat that covered a variety of issues. I therefore really looked forward to seeing Mr. Zhang and to listening to his explanation of "how China has changed and will change."

"You have become an American millionaire, haven't you?" Mr. Zhang asked me first as I greeted him in the lobby of the China World Hotel. "Only rich business people stay in this extravagant hotel in Beijing."

"No, I am not a rich businessman." I explained to him that a multinational corporation invited me to a meeting held in the hotel, and I didn't need to pay the bill myself.

I thanked him for coming to the hotel to see me. As a high-ranking government official, he must have been very busy.

"My pleasure," he said. "You are my friend, and I certainly wanted to see you. Besides, I love the cafe in this hotel, which has the best cappuccino in the city."

I remembered that Mr. Zhang became fond of drinking nice coffee in California. When he was about to return to China, he said to me humorously that learning to enjoy the good taste of coffee was one of the few things that he had learned during his four months of study at Berkeley.

We went to the cafe in the hotel and ordered two cappuccinos.

"Li Cheng, when you come to China from the United States next time, would you please bring me a cappuccino coffeemaker?"

"Sure," I said. This was the first time that I had heard that one could buy a cappuccino machine for home use.

"I will give you an antique-style Chinese teapot in exchange," Mr. Zhang added.

"Okay, a deal." It occurred to me that Mr. Zhang must be a very good business negotiator.

"Tell me what you are doing here in China. Are you working for an American business firm?" he asked.

I told him that I had a fellowship from the Institute of Current World Affairs, which allowed me to do research in China for two years. I have been interviewing people from different fields and writing about many aspects of the country. My monthly reports from China were being circulated among hundreds people in various fields in the United States and elsewhere, including many CEOs of business firms.

"Are you going to interview me?"

"Yes, may I?" I noticed the subtle diminution in his enthusiasm about our meeting.

Mr. Zhang took a quick look around the cafe and seemed to worry that someone might be watching. After a while, he said to me "I don't mind being interviewed by you, but I do want you to promise three things."

"What are they?"

"First, please don't release my name or identify my post. Secondly, don't take any photos or have our conversation recorded, though you may take notes. And finally, we should talk about economic issues *only; no political matters should be discussed.*"

"I understand your concerns. I certainly can promise the first two points," I responded. "But how can we be restricted from talking about politics while you are a political leader, and I have the title of 'political scientist'?

"You told me on the phone," I reminded Mr. Zhang, "that you would tell me all the changes that have occurred in China in recent years. Do you mean there have been only economic changes, but no political changes in the country?"

"No, this is not what I meant," Mr. Zhang responded quickly. "What I meant by political matters are topics such as human rights, political succession after Deng, and legal systems in China. You Americans always want to discuss these issues."

"Why not? Aren't they important issues?"

Mr. Zhang did not respond to my question directly. "You Americans often criticize China . . ."

"Please don't use the term 'you Americans,' " I interrupted him. "First of all, I am not an American citizen. Second, Americans differ from one another, and they do not necessarily agree with their government's policies. And finally, I prefer to be identified as 'a China-born U.S. resident who has a global consciousness.' " I said my final point jokingly.

"This identification is 100 percent 'PC' [politically correct]." Mr. Zhang made fun of the identification that I had chosen for myself.

Both of us laughed.

"I of course would like to tell you about the political changes happening in China as well," Mr. Zhang continued. "I disagree with the prevalent assumption in the West that China has made great progress economically, but has lagged far behind former Communist countries politically."

I asked him to elaborate on his statement.

"Let's just look at our own personal experiences. Could you imagine during the Mao era that you would have gone to the United States to study political science and then would have come back to write about Chinese politics?"

"No, I couldn't," I said.

"Me neither. I could not imagine then that I would become a high-ranking government official today. During the Cultural Revolution, college-educated people were all branded *choulaojiu* [the "stinking ninth category"] and were considered bad elements in society like landlords or counterrevolutionaries. Don't you think that those changes in our personal life reflect significant political development in the country?"

Mr. Zhang's point was well taken. China's political progress in the reform era becomes more comprehensible and concrete when seen through personal experience.

"As you know," Mr. Zhang continued, "during the Mao era, political leaders did not know much about economics or scientific and technological issues. They were only fond of revolutionary campaigns, class conflicts, and ideological indoctrination. We who are the new leaders, especially technocrats, however, favor pragmatism and build our legitimacy on the basis of economic and technological development in the country and choose policies that make rapid growth a top priority."

"Are you saying that technocrats are more popular in society than their predecessors or leaders from different backgrounds?" I asked.

"Of course, the fact that technocrats are playing important roles in society suggests a change in society's definition of the most desirable leadership qualities."

Mr. Zhang went on, "We live in an information age; the modern economy has become so complex that only specialists can estimate the implications of a decision. In other words, growing industrialization and rapid technological development calls for our expert governance."

I was really amazed by Mr. Zhang's argument because I had read similar arguments written by Western scholars such as John Kenneth Galbraith, Jacques Ellul, Daniel Bell, and Zbigniew Brzezinski. I was not sure whether Mr. Zhang had ever read these Western scholars' works on technocracy, but the technocratic argument was basically the same in both the East and the West.

"Let me give you an example." Mr. Zhang thought I was puzzled by his argument because I seemed to be immersed in deep thought. "If you had a disease, would you like to get advice from a doctor specializing in that disease or from an ordinary person? Of course, from the doctor, right?"

"Yes, but politics and engineering are totally different branches of knowledge; technical issues and political problems are fundamentally different," I said. "Can you tell me why an expert in engineering can assume to be an expert in public administration as well?"

"If one is really smart in one profession, probably he will also do well in other professions," Mr. Zhang defended himself.

"Even Michael Jordan is not that sure," I responded.

"Michael Jordan?" Mr. Zhang did not know who Michael Jordan was. Nor did he know that Michael Jordan left his extremely successful basketball career to become a professional baseball player, a field in which he is far from top-notch.

Intelligence and diligence help in life, but connections, or *guanxi*, are what really count. As the popular saying goes, "it's not what you know, it's who you know." Chinese technocrats in power are not necessarily "the best and the brightest" of the nation. Some case studies show that those trained engineers who later came to power were usually academically average or mediocre while they were college students.[6] Since the late 1950s, training students to be both "red and expert" became a guiding principle of all institutions for higher education in China. The emphasis, however, was on the "red"—politically obedient. The student political activists, despite being mediocre academically, usually received good grades, were sent abroad for further education, and were assigned good jobs after graduation. Some of them are now top technocrats in government.

The success of their political careers depends on institutional networks or their college ties more than on their academic performance. A large number of civilian leaders in the Chinese government are graduates of Qinghua University, while China's high-ranking military technocrats are graduates of the National Defense University.[7] Institutional networks, particularly college ties, have played a crucial role in the emergence of technocrats.

"Belonging to an elite college network is far more essential for politicians than having an elite college degree," a professor at Qinghua University explained to me.

College ties seem to carry more weight in the elite selection process today than other kinds of networks formerly considered crucial, that is, those based on shared revolutionary experiences or field army affiliation. The ties that bind graduates from Qinghua and the National Defense University, however, are only partly new. They are much like the ties that bind groups based on other loyalties: to field armies, revolutionary experience, geographic places, class origins, or particular patrons. Like their predecessors, technocratic elites form their own networks—"groups of people who help each other along in life, in ways that mystify and infuriate those excluded," as a British reporter pointed out in the *Economist*.[8]

"It is inappropriate for the United States government to use human rights improvement as a precondition for the renewal of the most-favored-nation [MFN] status with China," Mr. Zhang picked up the topic again.

"Why?" I was eager to hear his argument.

"I think that the politicians in the West have used human rights issues as a weapon to intimidate the Chinese government. They either deliberately want to be hostile to the Chinese or do not understand China's situation at all."

I asked Mr. Zhang to explain his statements.

"The Chinese people," Mr. Zhang argued, "should be suspicious of the intention of those foreign politicians who claim to be interested in human rights and democracy in China. The British government, for example, has recently started to talk about establishing democratic institutions in Hong Kong at the same time the region is ending its colonial rule. I wonder why those British democrats did not introduce democracy to this colony during the first nine decades of their governance?"

"It is ironic," I agreed with him.

"China is a developing country," Mr. Zhang continued. "The primary concern of the Chinese people at present is to achieve economic development and social stability. I would say this is a human rights concern. As Premier Li Peng said: 'a life free from poverty and debt is an inalienable human right.' "

"I have no problem with what you have just argued," I said, "but I don't see how economic rights contradict other basic human rights such as freedom of speech and the right to be free from arbitrary political persecution or imprisonment."

"Economic development and social stability are sometimes incompatible with 'uncontrolled political progress' in a given country," Mr. Zhang said straightforwardly. "What American politicians have meant by human rights in China are actually the rights of a small number of Chinese dissidents. It was the intent of these dissidents to lead China into a chaotic situation so that they could undermine the current government. No country could really develop under chaos."

Although I was not sure whether he could make such a generalization concerning the intention of Chinese dissidents, I did understand that Mr. Zhang's statement reflected the concerns of the Chinese government, which were probably valid.

"If my memory is correct," Mr. Zhang went on, "it was you who told me nine years ago that there were some correlations between economic structure and political progress, between economic wealth and political democracy."

"Yes, I remember that I often discussed with you what I had just learned in class during our 'Long March' between Berkeley and Oakland," I said to him.

I first heard the correlation between economic wealth and political progress, known as the theory of economic precondition for democracy, in a sociology class at Berkeley. The sociologist Seymour Martin Lipset argued that "the wealthier a nation, the greater the chances that it will sustain democracy." His argument was supported by the empirical phenomenon that the vast majority of high-income industrial countries were democratic.

In an article published in the mid-1980s, Samuel Huntington further elaborated on the theory of economic precondition for political development in the following four aspects: (1) a wealthy economy makes possible higher levels of literacy, education, and mass media exposure, which are conducive to democracy; (2) a wealthy economy moderates the tensions of political conflict because alternative opportunities are likely to be available for unsuccessful political leaders; (3) a highly developed, industrialized economy cannot be governed efficiently by authoritarian means; (4) since democracy means majority rule, it is only possible if the majority is a relatively satisfied middle class.[9]

"Is Deng Xiaoping a better student of the Western theory of economic growth and political development than Gorbachev?" Mr. Zhang wanted my affirmation.

Mr. Zhang was probably right. Deng has said on many occasions that the top priority for China is economic growth and market reforms. In order to achieve rapid economic development, China needs the political stability that could provide a favorable environment. This does not mean that China should pursue only economic reforms, not political reforms, but that the political reforms should be under the control of the government and the Communist Party. Russia, by contrast, has been more successful in political development, but democratic victory might be undermined because of slow economic growth there.

"I understand your point, Mr. Zhang," I responded, "but China is now faced with political crises. The authority has problems with its legitimacy. Moreover, as has happened in many parts of the world, a technocratic-authoritarian regime, which achieved great economic growth, would not automatically insure political progress. In many cases, technocrats tended to block democratic development."

"All of the assumptions you have just made are wrong. Let me tell you why." Mr. Zhang asked the waiter to bring him another cup of cappuccino, indicating he wanted to present his arguments in a more pointed way.

"First of all," he said, "people have already put the Tiananmen incident behind them."

"Really?"

"We preferred that the Tiananmen incident would have been solved peacefully, but the government did not have an alternative then. Besides, only a small number of leaders from the central authority made the decision. It would be unfair to blame the entire leadership, especially provincial and ministerial officials who were not responsible at all.

"It is also too simple-minded," Mr. Zhang said frankly, "to believe that technocrats tend to block democratic development in a given country.

"Do you think that Taiwan is a democratic state?" Mr. Zhang asked.

"Well, yes," I answered, "if you define democracy as a political system that, first, offers genuine political choices through regular elections, second, permits civil liberties and freedom of the press, and third, is based on rational respect for law."

"But how do you explain the fact that actually technocrats have dominated the government of Taiwan for a long time?" Mr. Zhang asked.

I have certainly been aware of the dominant presence of technocrats in the Taiwanese leadership. I coauthored an article in 1989, discussing the identical process of elite transformation on both sides of the Taiwan Strait. In the 1988 cabinet of the KMT government, almost 60 percent of its members held Ph.D. degrees and another 25 percent held M.A. degrees.[10]

Most of them were trained as engineers and natural scientists. They were also widely known for their elitist and technocratic views of modern governance. Technocrats actually dominated the first direct presidential election in Taiwan in May 1996.

The recent political development in Taiwan, however, has led some scholars to believe that technocrats actually contributed to democracy on the island. This view is straightforwardly expressed in a recent issue of the *National Geographic:*

> It is true that without American economic and military aid in the 1950s and 1960s Taiwan would not have become an economic powerhouse. However, economic and military aid alone did not create a democratic Taiwan. That was largely due to American universities educating Taiwanese graduate students. The best examples are President Lee (a Cornell Ph.D.), Prime Minister Lien (a University of Chicago Ph.D.) . . . These leaders, together with tens of thousands of United States–educated civilians, have brought real democracy to Taiwan.[11]

The relationship between the dominant role of technocrats in government and democratic development seems a complicated one. Technocracy and democracy, as they have emerged in the contemporary world, represent not a simple synthesis, but rather a complex and conflicting set of institutional processes and ideological standpoints. Technocratic values are incompatible with democratic ideas. Technocrats believe in a political system that emphasizes their own role in society and that provides no role for the masses or other social groups that lack technical expertise.

Yet this does not necessarily mean that technocrats in power will never change their attitudes and behaviors. As situations elsewhere demonstrate, democracy does not just develop from noble ideas but mostly from the lessons learned from recent experience. In other words, democracy may grow from the practical experiences of elites who come to recognize the limits of what they can do and the defects in technocratic politics.

Mr. Zhang and his technocratic colleagues in Mainland China, however, seem not to realize their own limitations on this point. On the contrary, they are still elated by their "success."

"During the last few years," Mr. Zhang said pointedly, "our government has brought the Chinese people one of the greatest increases in living standards in human history. More than 100 million Chinese peasants were lifted out of poverty during the past decade. This is over one-half the population of America. Look at what the U.S. government has done to help poor people there or to improve the living standards of middle-class Americans."

"Probably not much," I added.

"I wonder how American politicians dare blame the Chinese government without looking at their own poor performance at home."

I told Mr. Zhang that people in the United States have made similar observations. For example, a *New York Times* article noted that the American government has periodically complained about the Chinese government's abusing its citizens, "yet there is no question that the Communist Party is overseeing a far greater rise in prosperity and general well-being than any Democratic or Republican administration has ever achieved in such a short time."[12]

"But the question is," I asked, "how much credit the technocratic leadership in China should get for the increase in living standards of the Chinese people."

"Although the hard-working Chinese people deserve credit," Mr. Zhang responded, "China's economic miracle has been achieved largely because of the right decisions that we technocrats have made. Through government initiative, the proportion of private ownership was increased in cities, the People's Commune was abolished, the influence of market forces was enhanced. We have attracted much more foreign investment to the country; we have encouraged scientific and technological breakthrough, we . . ."

I interrupted him by adding more "achievements" to his list: "you have constrained official corruption; you have emphasized environmental protection; you have reduced military expenditure; you have decreased the unemployment rate; you have controlled inflation; you . . ."

"Stop!" Mr. Zhang was not happy with the ironic remarks that I made.

I apologized to him for my sarcasm, but I wanted to make my point clear: "No government should claim credit only for positive developments and evade responsibility for problems."

"Tell me which government really behaves like the one you have just described," Zhang asked, "the U.S. government?"

"Well . . ." I was not ready to respond to his question.

"The difference between the current Chinese government and the U.S. government," Mr. Zhang said, "is that the former is often criticized by some 'superior Western democratic governments' and the latter is always condemning 'authoritarian' governments of foreign countries."

"Don't nondemocratic regimes deserve more criticism from the international community?" I asked.

"This is not just a matter of criticism, but interference in other countries' internal affairs. I don't think the U.S. government has the right to flagrantly interfere in Chinese domestic affairs. To be honest, I don't understand why Americans are so concerned about human rights in China. They are even willing to risk losing great trade opportunities with China. Li Cheng, could you tell me why?"

"Let me give you an analogy," I said. "If your neighbor brutally beat his small child, would you interfere by stopping your neighbor?"

"No, I wouldn't," Mr. Zhang answered, "Chinese tradition does not encourage anyone to interfere in the family affairs of one's neighbors. Parents can do what they think is appropriate in bringing up their own children. It's none of their neighbors' business." Mr. Zhang looked triumphant because my analogy seemed not to work in the Chinese context.

I apparently needed a better case to argue with him.

"Let's suppose," I said, "that you are arrested by the Chinese police after our meeting today, being falsely accused of selling state secrets to a foreigner. You are sentenced to imprisonment for life."

"It is impossible." Mr. Zhang became defensive.

"This is exactly what happened to many Chinese dissidents and other people. A Hong Kong journalist was recently sentenced to 15 years in prison. Everyone in China knows that poor man did not do anything illegal. He was just a journalist."

Mr. Zhang did not respond.

"If that kind of mistreatment happens to you," I continued, "do you hope that foreign governments will voice their resentment of the false charges and, indeed, the human rights violations?"

Mr. Zhang kept silent.

"No one can be really safe in a country where human rights are not lawfully protected," I said.

Mr. Zhang looked at his watch and told me that he was expected to attend a meeting in his office. I thanked him for so openly discussing various issues with me. I told him that I would send him a copy when I completed this interview report. He could judge whether or not I fairly and accurately presented his views.

Technocrats have already emerged as the principal force in China's political life. They will likely play an even more important role when Deng and other revolutionary veterans die. It is important, both intellectually and practically, to understand the visions of the technocratic leadership in China. Mr. Zhang is only *one* technocrat. His arguments and concerns may or may not represent those of other technocrats. But I also found that some of his views and values are widely shared among his peers.

Technocratic views are, of course, not uniquely Chinese. At the beginning of this century, an American, Frederick Taylor, created a set of scientific methods, known as "scientific management," to run a factory and then extended it to govern society. In his view, society, like a machine, could be examined by scientists and engineers. Engineers and efficiency experts were inherently bound to discover and solve problems of the "machine" and to increase productivity. The broader implication behind this scientific management was a "social engineering" that adjusted men and women to the functional requirements of a machine.

Technocratic views have influenced people in the West, but Western intellectual criticism of technocracy has been much greater. This is in sharp contrast to China, where social criticism of technocratic values has been absent during the post-Mao era, and genuine democratic ideas have been weak among the Chinese people, including dissidents.

This is precisely why I felt the need to debate with Chinese technocrats like Mr. Zhang. Among the many things I have learned during my stay in the United States is that I have come to understand that social engineering, whether Communist or technocratic, is fundamentally incompatible with the governance of human society. No master science exists to solve the many dilemmas caused by conflicting human values.

To what ends should China's political development be directed? How should social dialogue among competing interest groups be promoted? In what way should the country adjust its traditional culture to respond to modern challenges in an increasingly integrated world? How can the country achieve rapid economic development without the expense of environmental degradation? Will the technocratic orientation in today's China lead to a new kind of Great Leap Forward tragedy, such as a possible catastrophe resulting from the ongoing Three Gorges Dam project? These are certainly not the *technical* issues, but the *political* ones that China faces at the turn of the millennium.

I promised Mr. Zhang that I would bring him a cappuccino coffeemaker when I come to Beijing next time. However, I wonder whether I can bring him a better gift from America. It seems far easier for my "Yuppie" friend to enjoy nice coffee than to appreciate democratic values!

16

New Thinking of Chinese Intellectuals

Meet Dai Qing, a Woman of Ideas and Action

Few writers, in China or elsewhere, in this or any other age, have had more dramatic or bizarre political experiences than Dai Qing (pronounced *dai ching*). A child of an anti-Japanese martyr, an adopted daughter of a Communist marshal, a Red Guard in the Cultural Revolution, an engineering student specializing in intercontinental ballistic missiles, an intelligence agent for the People's Liberation Army (PLA), a prominent investigative journalist, an activist in the 1989 Tiananmen protest movement, a political prisoner in China's maximum security jail, a spokesperson for environmental protection and other social movements in the country, Dai Qing undoubtedly has had an extraordinary career.

Even more extraordinary, however, is Dai's courageous character, her strong sense of social responsibility, and her thought-provoking ideas about China's future. After the Tiananmen massacre, many dissident intellectuals and student leaders escaped to foreign countries. The cultural attaché at the German Embassy in Beijing offered Dai the opportunity to go to Germany, ostensibly to take part in a cultural exchange program. But Dai told the German diplomat that as a public intellectual in China, she was concerned about something more important than her own safety.

When Dai was released after 10 months of imprisonment without trial and was allowed to travel to the United States, two American lawyers asked Dai whether she would like to request political asylum or pursue permanent residence in the United States. Dai responded that she enjoyed the intellectual freedom and material comforts in America, but as a writer with a focus on Chinese society, she should live in China and keep in touch with the Chinese people.

Dai Qing: A prominent woman intellectual and dissident who has been a spokesperson for various social movements in China.

Dai's decision to remain in China has embarrassed and angered both the Chinese government and dissident intellectuals exiled in Western countries. Chinese authorities would prefer to let Dai stay abroad forever. Her presence in China represents potential trouble, a time bomb, for the authoritarian regime. But authorities cannot find an excuse to expel or arrest her. For dissident intellectuals, however, the fact that Dai has continued her work in China makes them look like cowards and their exile status somehow unjustified.

While both the Chinese government and the overseas dissident movement try to limit her influence, Dai has continuously been very active, as a writer, a government critic, and a spokesperson for various social movements such as environmental protection, the preservation of indigenous culture, and the independence of women.

An Independent Intellectual and a Woman of Action

Soon after she was released from jail in the spring of 1990, Dai started to work as chief editor of *ECHO*, a Chinese magazine focusing on the popular and indigenous cultures in Mainland China and Taiwan. The main purpose of the journal has been to guard against the destructive impact of modernization upon folk customs and indigenous cultures in Chinese society.

Recently, Dai established a private data collection and translation center focusing on environmental issues in China. It collects information about environmental problems and protection in the country, translates the information into English, and sends it, through electronic mail, to nongovernmental organizations (NGOs) around the world. The center also publishes a monthly journal, *Environmental Protection Digest*. Twenty issues had been published by 1995. As one foreign journalist noted, the center itself plays the role of a genuine NGO in the country.

Dai's book *Yangtze! Yangtze!*, a critique of the massive Three Gorges Dam project which was banned by Chinese authorities after its 1989 release, was translated into English and published in 1994 (by both Probe International Publications and Earthscan Publications). In the first half of 1995, Hong Kong's Mingbao Press published Dai's three new books, including *My Life at the Qingcheng Prison*, a personal recollection of her experience in jail and a moral criticism of the Communist authoritarian rule. All of these books became best-sellers in the Chinese-speaking world outside Mainland China.

During the past few years, Dai frequently traveled abroad, giving talks in the United States, Canada, Australia, New Zealand, Germany, Norway, Switzerland, Sweden, Taiwan, Hong Kong, and other countries. Her topics ranged from "thought reform" in the Mao era to "economic reform" under Deng, from the anti-intellectualism in China during the early period of Communist rule to the technocratic orientation of the new Chinese leadership, from a reexamination of the 1989 Tiananmen protest movement to the problems of Western misunderstanding of Chinese politics, from women's issues to the green movement.

Dai's contributions to Chinese society have gradually gained international recognition. The *Times, Economist, New York Times, Christian Science Monitor, Wall Street Journal, Reader's Digest* and many other publications interviewed her or published feature articles about her. Dai has also received numerous awards and fellowships, such as the 1992 Golden Pen for Freedom (Prague), the 1993 Goldman Environment Award, the 1993 Condé Nast Environmental Award, the Nieman Fellowship at Harvard University, the Freedom Forum Fellowship at Columbia University, and the Humanities Research Fellowship at the Australian National University.

I had never read her books before I returned to work in China in the fall of 1993. Although all of her books are banned from publication or reprint in China today, those published prior to the 1989 Tiananmen protest movement, for example, *The Last Oval, Expel the Devil and Clasp Onto God, Oral History of Contemporary Chinese Women, Chu Anping and "Total Party Domination," Out of the Modern Superstition and Conversation with Scholars*, are available in many public libraries in the country.

Most of her books are collections of nonfiction essays and reports. The stories in these collections show why Dai Qing is celebrated. I was impressed by her sharp criticism of the political establishment, her rich observation of Chinese character, her capacity to analyze complicated sociopolitical issues in a simple but not simplistic way, and her deep concern about the human condition in China and the world. Reading these books left me wondering—why isn't the author more famous?

I first met Dai Qing in 1995, when we were both visiting fellows at the Contemporary China Center in Canberra, Australia. Dr. Jonathan Unger, head of the center, suggested that I write a report about Dai Qing for ICWA readers. I was excited by the idea. During the first year of my fellowship in China, I had completed several intensive interviews with people in different occupations, e.g., a technocrat, a migrant worker, and a peasant-turned-industrialist. But I had not written a story about a Chinese public intellectual—someone with a university degree who is engaged in public affairs.

It would be a good idea, I thought, to interview a Chinese intellectual and write an article about his or her perspective on the transformation of contemporary China. There can be no deep understanding of Chinese society and politics without paying attention to intellectuals—men and women of ideas.

I had difficulty, however, finding the right person in China. Many intellectuals had been caught up in the rapid change of economic conditions. The effort to survive financially kept them from engaging in serious intellectual endeavors. Some were reluctant, for understandable reasons, to discuss sensitive political issues with a writer from the United States.

A friend of mine suggested that I interview a dissident intellectual in exile. But to be frank, I found most Chinese dissidents in exile to be political opportunists. Fang Lizhi, an astrophysicist who was known as "China's Sakharov," and Chai Ling, a student leader in the 1989 Tiananmen protest movement, for example, were considered, in the West, heroes of China's democratic movement. But even before the government crackdown on 4 June, Fang went to the American embassy with tears in his eyes and asked for political asylum. Chai was already hiding outside Beijing. These "spiritual leaders" of the "democratic movement" left thousands of protesters to encounter the tanks and machine guns of the Chinese army while they were hiding out or pursuing political asylum at a foreign embassy.

Some well-known exiled politicians, Yan Jiaqi and Chen Yizi, for example, had served as political advisors for Zhao Ziyang, former secretary general of the Chinese Communist Party. They were advocates for authoritarian rule while Zhao was in power. But after the Tiananmen incident, they claimed all of a sudden to be "long-time fighters against Communism and spokesmen for Chinese democracy." I felt that these dissidents would not honestly face their own past. In addition, they were out of touch with current Chinese society. A recent foreign visitor to China observed that people in China today display nothing but contempt for these dissidents.[1] I certainly would not waste my time listening to their nonsense.

Dai Qing, however, is quite different. In fact, unlike many exiled Chinese dissidents who had served as government officials, Dai has never held any official post in her life. "The Chinese people like to mention one's *highest official post* in an obituary. The highest official post in my obituary will be," Dai Qing once said to me sarcastically, "no higher than the deputy team leader of the Young Pioneers [a children's organization in elementary schools in the People's Republic of China]."

I found Dai to be much more honest about her past than those "Chinese democrats in exile." She does not deny her privileged Communist family background and political activities, including her experience as an intelligence agent for PLA. Dai, as some of her friends described her to me, is a writer not only willing to explore her own mistakes and weaknesses, but also dedicated to challenging her readers to see their own lives and worlds from new and different perspectives.[2]

Dai Qing seemed to be an ideal person to interview on the subject of Chinese intellectuals. She is from a privileged Communist class background, but betrays and mercilessly denounces the Communist ruling class. She is both an intellectual with a sense of history and a vision of the future and a woman of action who has her feet firmly planted on the ground of Chinese society. Dai Qing's experience not only reflects, but also affects in a profound way, China's political development.

From Intelligence Agent to Investigative Journalist

Dai Qing readily agreed to be interviewed. "But I don't think that you should call me 'an extraordinary woman,' " Dai corrected me when I referred to her in that way.

"I admit, however," Dai added, "that my political background is unique, and my life up till now has been filled with dramatic tales."

Dai's life has surely been filled with dramatic changes. She was born in Chongqing, a city in southwestern China, during the anti-Japanese war. Her father, an intellectual who received a university education in Moscow in the early 1920s, was a member of the first generation of Chinese Communists. Her mother, who was born into a well-known scholar's family in Beijing at the end of the Qing Dynasty, once studied in Japan, where she became interested in the Communist movement.

Her parents married at the liaison office of the Chinese Communist Party in Chongqing, the capital of the Nationalist government during World War II. As intelligence agents for the Far East Division of Communist International (CI), her parents were sent by CI to their home city, Beijing, which was then under Japanese occupation. They were later arrested by the Japanese, and her father was executed when Dai Qing was only three years old.

Dai was adopted by Ye Jianying, a Communist marshal who later became chairman of China's People's Congress and one of the most powerful figures in the country in the late 1970s. Dai grew up a privileged member of the Communist ruling class. She entered a public middle school in Beijing, which had previously been a religious boarding school. Even under Communist control, this school emphasized aesthetics and a liberal arts education. As Dai later recalled, the humanitarianism taught and the liberal arts education that she received then had a strong impact on her. In her years at middle school, Dai became interested in literature, especially British and French works.

But like many other children of high-ranking officials, Dai did not choose to study the humanities in college. Instead, she entered the Harbin Institute of Military Engineering, one of the most prestigious and elite universities in the country, in 1960, studying the automatic control system of intercontinental ballistic missiles. Soon after her graduation, the Cultural Revolution took place, and she joined the Red Guards. When the Red Guards' movement declined, Dai was sent to the countryside in Guangdong Province and then Hunan Province to work as a farm laborer. In the early 1970s, Dai returned to Beijing to work as a technician in a factory run by the public security department. This factory specialized in surveillance and other technical equipment.

After the Cultural Revolution, Dai attended the PLA Institute of Foreign Languages to study English. While in the language program, Dai was recruited into the Chinese army's intelligence service.[3] In her spare time during these years, Dai started to write and publish short stories and soon became an eminent young novelist. Because of her training in foreign languages and her talent in literature, Dai was assigned by the PLA to the Chinese Writers' Association as a full-time interpreter and part-time spy. Her task was to make foreign contacts and to keep watch on the international exchange program of the association.

Because a male colleague of hers in the PLA intelligence service divulged a list of personnel to a young lady in the CIA, Dai and her other colleagues had to give up intelligence work. In 1982, Dai left the PLA and worked as a journalist for *Guangming Daily*, a leading national newspaper whose readers were mainly intellectuals. During her seven years' tenure at the newspaper, Dai became the country's best-known woman journalist and one of the boldest investigative reporters in the history of the People's Republic of China. She traveled all over the country and reported on many extremely sensitive political issues.

In 1985, for example, Dai went to Guangxi Province, in southern China, to report on the Sino-Vietnamese war. As she interviewed Chinese soldiers at the China-Vietnam border, Dai found that, in contrast to the government's propaganda, the army's morale was very low. Chinese soldiers complained that the authorities did not value their lives at all. Dai did not write the reports that the authorities expected. Instead, she wrote two articles—one satirizing the foolishness of the war and the other challenging the government's decision to go to war. Both articles were banned from circulation. Because of her disobedience, Dai lost her chance for promotion at the newspaper.

In 1987, Dai went to Heilongjiang Province, in northeastern China, to cover stories on the prolonged forest fire in the region. Dai and several other Chinese journalists wrote eyewitness reports displaying how human error—the authorities' disdain for human life and lack of environmental concern—had led to the forest fire, which lasted many months. Because of the political sensitivity of these reports, the authors could not publish them in the newspapers and journals for which they worked. Dai Qing therefore edited and published these reports as a monograph, which had an unusual and revealing title, *! and ?*. This was the first time in PRC history that Chinese journalists had a "horizontal coalition" (*hengxiang jiehe*) to enable them to voice dissent.

In 1989, prior to a scheduled People's Congress's special meeting on the proposed Three Gorges Dam project on the Yangtze River, Dai compiled and published a collection of interviews with essays on and statements by China's public intellectuals, scientists, and journalists who opposed the dam project. The publication of this collection, as the Hong Kong journal *Far East Economic Review* noted, was a watershed event, as it represented the first time in PRC history that ordinary Chinese people decided not to keep silent about a massive project that would profoundly affect their lives.

Because of the events at Tiananmen in 1989, the People's Congress postponed the meeting on the proposed dam project. In April 1992, when the National People's Congress convened to vote for the construction of the dam, 177 deputies voted against the project, and another 664 deputies abstained. This meant that one-third of the Congress had reservations about the dam project proposed by the Central Committee of the CCP and the State Council. As I noted earlier, in the PRC, deputies of the Congress are supposed to unanimously support any proposal by the Party. It was the first time in the history of the Congress that so many deputies voted against a proposal by the authorities. Dai's book certainly made the deputies more aware of the problems involved in the dam project.

All these journalistic activities by Dai Qing are truly remarkable if one considers the Chinese authorities' firm control over mass media in the country. It is incredible that Dai alone covered so many important issues and voiced her dissent on major government policies. Many people believe that Dai's background as an adopted daughter of Marshal Ye Jianying protected her. But according to Dai, when she started her writing career,

Marshal Ye had already left the center of power and then soon died. When Dai became an investigative journalist and published some controversial reports in the mid-1980s, she had already split off from the power circle.

It was courage, not family background as some foreign observers said, that distinguished Dai Qing from many other public intellectuals in China. Dai's courage was evident because she was constantly under the threat of being expelled from her journalistic job.

"Everywhere in the world, including Western democratic countries," Dai said to me, "investigative journalists are often faced with threats. But in democratic countries, freedom of the press is legally protected. Chinese journalists do not have legal protection. From the first day of my employment at *Guangming Daily* to the day that I was forced to leave the newspaper, I had to constantly struggle, through both words and deeds, for the independence of journalism and freedom of the press in China.

"The Chinese Communist Party considers journalism 'a mouthpiece of the Party,' " Dai explained, "so the main task for Chinese journalists is to propagate the Party line. I told my boss at *Guangming Daily* on the first day I worked there that I had a special request—I would refuse any assignment to report on a Party meeting. In the country where all major policies are already made by a small number of leaders before being presented at a meeting for discussion, it is a waste of time to report on any official meeting. My boss actually accepted my request, although he could not figure out why I would not accept this kind of 'hot' assignment."

Since the mid-1980s, Dai Qing has more openly expressed the need for freedom of the press in China. Dai wrote many articles on this subject in various newspapers in the country, such as the *World Economic Herald*, a liberal newspaper in Shanghai. During the 1989 Tiananmen rally, Dai not only participated in the protest movement, but also played the role of a mediator between students and the government, trying to persuade student protesters to leave Tiananmen and calling on Chinese authorities not to crack down on students by force. When she found that the mass protest movement was being used by politicians, both old and young, to advance their power interests, she withdrew from the movement. On the day that authorities used violence on the protesters, Dai quit the Chinese Communist Party.

"It was emotionally a tough decision for me," Dai Qing said. "My life up till then had been really tied to the Chinese Communist Party in 101 ways. My father gave his life to the Party when his three children were only three, one, and still unborn. My mother escaped execution because of her pregnancy. Also as a devoted CCP member, my mother was so infatuated with the Communist revolution that she cared more about the affairs of the Party than about her children. I grew up as a daughter of the Party."

"Does your decision suggest that as an insider of the CCP power circle, you had a better understanding of the problems and the loss of the 'mandate of heaven' of the Chinese Communist Party?" I asked.

"Yes," Dai replied, "but this was only part of the reason. Although I grew up under the influence of Communist doctrines, I became interested in Western literature at an early age. Humanism, which is immensely reflected Western by authors such as Dickens, Hugo, Singer, and Bellow, had a strong impact on me.

"More importantly," Dai continued, "my job as a journalist gave me a great opportunity to understand the lives of ordinary people—their hardships, vulnerability, and frustrations. Meanwhile, I observed how the Communist Party fabricated history and fooled the people. Over the years, I came to realize that my journalistic integrity and the CCP doctrines were as incompatible as fire and water. My loyalty to, my trust in and, indeed, my illusions about the Party were completely destroyed after the 1989 Tiananmen event."

The Lessons of Tiananmen and the Problems of Chinese Intellectuals

It happened to be the sixth anniversary of the Tiananmen Massacre when I saw Dai Qing again to continue my interview. This time I saw Dai at her apartment near Beijing University. Four policemen were assigned to stay outside her apartment building day and night to keep watch on her. Foreigners were not allowed to enter the apartment building. Chinese authorities were obviously very sensitive to the activities of dissident intellectuals like Dai during this "eventful period of the year."

"Do these policemen outside the apartment bother you?" I asked, to start the interview.

"No, not really," Dai replied, "my family and I are already used to this kind of 'protection.' I sometimes even make fun of these policemen. Yesterday morning, my neighbors and I saw these policemen arranging their lookout spot using a broken van outside my apartment building. One policeman asked me, 'You will not go out today, will you?' 'I will not go too far away,' I responded, 'probably only to nearby Beijing University to inflame students.' At first all the policemen were shocked and then they laughed as they realized that I was just kidding. But anyway, they said they would report to top leaders in Beijing immediately."

"The Politburo of the Chinese Communist Party probably had an emergency meeting because of your joke," I said, laughing.

Chinese authorities, however, might have reason to be cautious. Beijing residents' resentment against corruption is much stronger now than it was even six years ago. Zhou Guanwu, a close friend of Deng Xiaoping and the head of the Capiton Iron and Steel Corporation, one of the largest enterprises in China, was forced to resign. Zhou's son, a rich bureaucrat who was sent by the Capiton Iron and Steel Corporation to Hong Kong as chief representative, was called back and arrested. Wang Baosen, vice mayor of Beijing in charge of foreign investment in the city, committed suicide because of the scandal caused by his embezzlement of $20 million. His boss, Chen Xitong, a Politburo member and Party Secretary of Beijing, has also been in trouble. Chen was a notorious Communist hardliner during the Tiananmen Massacre.

Meanwhile, about 40 prominent Chinese intellectuals had just signed an open letter to Jiang Zemin, Deng's appointed successor, suggesting a more serious effort to punish corrupt high-ranking officials and asking Jiang to release all political prisoners in the country.

"Are you among the intellectuals who signed the open letter?" I asked Dai Qing.

"No," she replied.

"Why?"

"I have mixed feelings about what is happening in Beijing," Dai explained. "On one hand I am thrilled to see these corrupt officials step down; on the other I feel disappointed with my colleagues, or so-called dissident intellectuals. It seems to me that they are doing exactly the same thing that they did six years ago. As you know, during the 1989 protest movement students had a hunger strike, and prominent intellectuals signed the petition. Protesters at Tiananmen thought that they were able to achieve their objectives because of the conflict among the Chinese leadership and the weakness of authorities. Top politicians in the country, however, also wanted to use the protest movement to advance their own political interests.

"Six years have passed [*liu nian le*]," Dai raised her tone for emphasis, "since the 1989 Tiananmen protest movement, but my colleagues seem not to have learned any lessons from the movement. This time, again, they think that they can take advantage of the ongoing power struggle in the center and make democratic progress in the country. But actually, at most they are only the tools of politicians in the center."

"But they have some specific political demands this time, haven't they?" I said.

"Yes," Dai replied. "In an open letter, these intellectuals appealed to Jiang Zemin to solve the problem of official corruption and to constrain the growing power of the children of revolutionary veterans. But anyone who has a basic knowledge of Chinese politics should realize that no individual—Jiang Zemin, Qiao Shi, or anyone else—can solve the problem of official corruption today. This is a problem that is deeply rooted in the political and socioeconomic conditions of the country at present. In my view, these intellectuals can achieve nothing except attracting attention from foreign media."

"In retrospect," I asked, "what are the lessons that the Chinese people, especially Chinese intellectuals, can draw from the 1989 Tiananmen protest movement?"

"Almost all the forces involved in the event made serious mistakes," Dai responded. "Deng Xiaoping made the most obvious mistake by readily adopting violent means to deal with the crisis. Foreign journalists—most of whom had just arrived in China to report on Gorbachev's visit—also played a negative role in the event. These foreign journalists 'made a stormy sea stormier.' Their ignorance about Chinese politics and society, their simplistic dichotomy in portraying good guys and bad guys, their impatience toward the transformation of the Chinese Communist regime, and their journalistic interest in sensational stories all led them to push both sides—the Chinese government and student protesters—to extremes. Meanwhile, student protesters at Tiananmen were led by nothing but their emotions. They did not know how to achieve their objectives. More precisely, they did not even know what their objectives were."

"Did these mistakes have an equal effect on the course of this tragic event?" I asked.

"No," Dai replied quickly. "I believe that the most serious problem lay in ourselves, I mean China's public intellectuals. We Chinese intellectuals as a whole should have taken the main responsibility for the tragic result of the Tiananmen incident."

I asked Dai to elaborate.

"To give you a better answer," Dai said, "let's see what the 1989 Tiananmen movement really was. People both in China and abroad often identify the Tiananmen rally as a democratic movement, a cultural movement similar to China's May 4th Movement in 1919, or a social movement with concrete objectives from which certain social groups could benefit. I believe that the 1989 Tiananmen movement was none of these. First, it was a big mistake to identify the 1989 Tiananmen protest as a democratic movement. Public intellectuals actually disseminated a lot of *demagogic noise* rather than *democratic values*."

I certainly agree with Dai. Soon after the Tiananmen incident, I coauthored an article in *Modern China*, criticizing the common wisdom in the West about the nature and characteristics of China's 1989 protest movement.[4] My coauthor Lynn White and I noticed that the political demands from Tiananmen were generally not structural. They were often presented in emotional words and through traditional petitions, not through means that would assure more permanent benefits for social groups, nor were they translated into specific calls for broad electoral and other democratic procedures. Constitution-makers were noticeably scarce in 1989 Beijing. It was interesting for me to hear a similar evaluation from Dai, one of the most important participants in the movement.

"Secondly," Dai continued, "intellectuals and students in the movement claimed that they were inspired by the May 4th Movement, an antifeudal and new cultural movement led by intellectuals during the second decade of this century. Protesters in Tiananmen identified themselves as spiritual successors of the May 4th Movement. But public intellectuals in 1989 interpreted the nature of that movement in the same way that Chinese Communists did. They appealed for revolutionary change and violent confrontation [*gemin he douzheng*]."

"People in the West, however," I commented, "overlooked the fact that some protesters were also prone to violent confrontation."

"Yes," Dai said. "The readiness for violent confrontation deviated from the main characteristic of the May 4th Movement, which emphasized a fundamental cultural change through evolutionary means. China's public intellectuals, with few exceptions, neither wanted to seriously reexamine Chinese culture and reject its negative aspects, nor really study the essence of Western democracies. For over seven decades since the May 4th Movement, public intellectuals were still eager for quick success and were more interested in the transition of political power and other superficial changes in the country. The motivation of many dissident intellectuals at Tiananmen was no more than to become revolutionary leaders like their Communist predecessors. In my view, the Chinese intellectuals' effort to change China's political system without a change in Chinese political culture was doomed to fail.

"Thirdly," Dai continued, "China's 1989 Tiananmen movement was not a social movement, but only a political movement, or even simply a political event."

I asked Dai to distinguish between a social movement and a political movement.

"The difference," Dai explained, "is in the objectives of the movements. A political movement is power-oriented. The objective of a political movement is usually to replace a government or one group of ruling elite by another. A social movement, by contrast, aims to achieve some concrete objectives for certain social groups. An environmental movement, for example, aims to maintain ecological balance.

"As a political movement, the best possible consequence from Tiananmen in 1989 would be that a group of more 'liberal' and popular elites won over conservative hardliners. Some dissident intellectuals such as Yan Jiaqi and Chen Yizi would probably join Zhao Ziyang's new cabinet if protesters in Tiananmen had kicked Li Peng and other hardliners out of power. But I doubt this kind of change would affect, in a fundamental way, China's political system and Chinese society.

"The most important lesson that we can learn from the 1989 Tiananmen incident," Dai concluded, "is that Chinese intellectuals should be more conscious of their intellectual integrity and dignity [*zhishi fenzi de duli renge*]. In traditional China, intellectuals generally attached themselves to 'bigwigs' [*quangui*], especially to those with political power. This tradition continued in the Mao era. Although intellectuals occasionally played the role of critics of political authorities, this role was often restricted for three reasons. First, authorities did not tolerate criticism from intellectuals. Second, intellectuals financially depended on the Communist Party-State. And third, some intellectuals were interested in power, and they became political elites in the Party."

"These three factors still exist, don't they?" I asked.

"Yes," Dai replied, "but to a far lesser degree today. The capacity of the Communist state to control society has significantly declined. Intellectuals are not necessarily employed by the state. They can work for the private sector or even be self-employed. Of course, there will always be some intellectuals who have personal ambition for power and who are willing to sacrifice intellectual integrity and dignity to promote their own careers. But only shortsighted intellectuals believe that the Communist Party will run China forever."

"How can Chinese intellectuals make progress and improvement as a social group?" I asked.

"I think that Chinese intellectuals should do more down-to-earth kinds of work. Individually, each intellectual should first fulfill his or her professional role in society. If you are a journalist, you should seek truth; if you are lawyer, you should fight for justice; if you are a scientist, you should oppose environmentally catastrophic projects such as the construction of Three Gorges Dam; if you are a teacher, you should advocate freedom and democratic values to your students."

"What about the collective role of public intellectuals?" I asked.

"As a social group," Dai replied, "intellectuals should make efforts to study the political procedures and structural measures of Western democracies, to disseminate democratic values in society through all means, to reexamine and renew Chinese culture, and most importantly, to more actively participate in various social movements."

"Are these the tasks that you have been performing in recent years?" I asked.

"Yes," said Dai. "What an individual intellectual can do is always limited, but I want to try my best to do some concrete work in areas with which I am familiar. Currently, I have been engaged in several book-length projects, for example, biographical studies of some distinguished public intellectuals in contemporary China. I hope that the courage, integrity, and scholarship of older generations of Chinese intellectuals will serve as role models, inspiring younger generations."

The Independence of Women and Women's Organizations

"As a distinguished woman intellectual writing about social issues," I said to Dai, "you have also served as a role model for Chinese women, especially for women intellectuals."

"A role model? No!" Dai laughed. "The All-China Women's Federation [ACWF] has long considered me a troublemaker, a bad example for Chinese women."

"But you were elected a delegate to the All-China Women's Federation Conference in 1988?" I asked.

"Yes, I was," Dai answered. "It was during that conference that I confronted the All-China Women's Federation and its chairperson."

I asked Dai to tell me the story.

"The All-China Women's Federation," Dai said, "like many other national organizations in China, serves as a tool for the Communist authorities instead of representing the interests of Chinese women. Not surprisingly, this conference did not have any substantial discussion of serious issues such as discrimination against women in employment and education, the loss of social welfare for women, sexual harassment in the work place, the increase of child laborers and child prostitution, and the reemergence of concubinage. Instead, almost all the conference documents were about how the Chinese Communist Party was deeply concerned about women, how Chinese women were grateful to the Party, and how the delegates of the conference were thrilled to meet top leaders.

"The All-China Women's Federation Conference," Dai continued, "attempted to accomplish nothing but a big show. Everything was already decided by the Communist authorities before the meeting. I was particularly disappointed with the leaders of the federation. Chen Muhua, chairwoman-designate of ACWF [nominated by the Party], for example, was so sure that she would be elected that she did not even bother to attend the group discussion of the conference to meet with delegates. Instead, she went to play golf."

"In China," I said, "the admission fee to a golf course costs a senior professor two months' salary."

"Yes," Dai responded, "but more importantly, the money was not from her own pocket, but from public funds."

Chen Muhua, the highest-ranking female politician in China, does not have a good reputation. In the late 1980s, when she traveled to a Western country, she used the whole chartered plane to transport furniture for her family. On another occasion during her travel abroad, she refused to take a seriously sick athlete back to China in her chartered plane. It is said that the athlete died because of improper treatment.

"On the final day of the conference," Dai continued, "when delegates were about to vote for the executive members and chair of ACWF, I raised my hand. The executive chair of the conference had probably never expected that one of the delegates would raise her hand before voting, although any delegate had the right to do so. The chair asked me, 'What's wrong with you?' "

"Did she really say this?" I said.

"Yes," Dai explained. "For any election in the People's Republic of China, delegates would routinely check their ballots or would unanimously raise their hands during the vote, but not prior to the vote. A delegate who eagerly raised a hand prior to the vote therefore must have something wrong—maybe a personal emergency."

"I told the chair that I wanted to have a microphone to ask a few questions. The chair said 'okay' but I had to go to the platform to use the microphone there. It was unheard of that any delegates would want to use a microphone at their seats. The chair asked me what questions I wanted to ask. I said that as a delegate I would like to ask Chen Muhua, nominated by the ACWF for chair, two questions before voting."

"Did the chair of the conference allow you to speak?" I asked.

"The chair talked to Chen for a few minutes and then said that the conference did not have a session for questions and answers. She was afraid that if more delegates wanted to ask questions, the conference 'would not move smoothly and successfully.' I immediately responded that I could not understand why democratic practice would prevent the 'complete success' of the conference."

"How did other delegates at the conference react to your confrontation?" I asked.

"When I spoke, I received applause from a small number of delegates. But a majority of delegates seemed not to support me. For many, to attend this national women's conference was a good opportunity to advance their political careers in the future. They might think that I was foolish because I ruined my career by challenging the leadership of ACWF. Some delegates even yelled, 'Get off the platform!' 'Don't answer her questions!' 'We don't have any questions!' When my request for asking questions was finally denied, most delegates in the hall even started to sing songs. My effort to exercise democratic rights at China's national conference for women completely failed."

"What were the two questions that you planned to ask Chen?" I asked.

"First, I wanted to ask Ms. Chen how she could persuade us to vote for her since her previous administrative performances were very disappointing. During the years when she was minister of foreign trade, China had large deficits in foreign trade. During her tenure as governor of the People's Bank of China, the inflation rate was much higher than the bank interest rates in the country. Now Chen was nominated to be the chair of the All-China Women's Federation, but as far as I knew, she had never written any articles or delivered any speeches on women's issues. There was no evidence indicating that she had a good understanding of the problems concerning Chinese women. I wanted to give her a chance to explain why she would not perform as poorly in her new post as she had in her two previous posts. Secondly, I was about to ask her to explain why she refused to take the sick athlete in her chartered plane."

"It would have been really exciting," I said, "to see how she would respond to these questions."

"Delegates at the conference, however, never knew what my questions were," Dai said. "I did give these two questions to Chinese journalists who covered the conference. But no newspaper or magazine in China ever released this news. This shows the strict control of the Chinese Communist Party over the mass media. Chen Muhua, of course, was elected to be chair of ACWF, although she lost 40 votes out of a total of 300 voting members."

Chen still holds the highest position in ACWF. She was also the chair of the Chinese delegates who attended the Fourth World Conference on Women in Beijing in September 1995.

"We are going to see another big show, aren't we?" I said, referring to this conference.

"Yes," Dai replied, "the Chinese authorities have no idea about the women's movement in the world. They host this conference mainly to enhance China's status and improve its image in global affairs. Since Beijing was selected to host both the Fourth World Conference on Women and the parallel meeting of nongovernmental organizations, hundreds of 'nongovernmental' women's organizations have been established in China. But I call them 'GUNGOs' (government-organized nongovernmental organizations).

"To improve China's image in women's affairs, the Chinese authorities have lately appointed more women to leadership posts in the country," Dai continued. "But what good is it if the Central Committee of the CCP has 20 percent female members instead of 10 percent, but these women members still do not speak for women? Those who are selected to leadership posts are usually the women who fawn on authorities. Chen Muhua's qualification to be the chair of ACWF, for example, is simply the fact that she is a woman among the Communist top leaders, and she would always say 'yes' to her male bosses in the party."

"What will be the most important step for Chinese women if they want to join the international women's movement?" I asked Dai.

"We should realize the awakening of women's consciousness as individuals and independence as a social group," Dai replied. "In a country where the women's organizations are supposed to be the tool of political authorities, one cannot really expect these organizations to defend the interests of women, nor can we make genuine progress toward equality between men and women."

I agree with Dai. The lack of independence has prevented women's organizations from playing an important role in the country at the time of rapid socioeconomic change. Economic reform in the Deng era has had a strong impact on family, marriage, and social norms. According to a Shanghai newspaper, during the past three years about 300 women in Shanghai asked the women's organizations for help because they were suffering from domestic violence. But in most of these cases, they did not get much help, and their husbands continued to abuse them.[5] Meanwhile, China had about 909,000 divorces in 1994, three times more than the figure in 1991.[6]

In 1994, China's public security reported 143,000 cases of prostitution, involving about 288,000 people. The police closed 4,917 places of prostitution and arrested about 29,000 people.[7] The Chinese government recently admitted that local police bureaus usually punish or arrest only those people without official backgrounds. Those who have high-ranking official status or connections with public security are often the main customers and patrons of sex industries in China. These people often avoid any punishment.

The Crucial Role of Intellectuals in the Ongoing Transformation of China

"In a way, the problems of Chinese women are similar to the problems of Chinese intellectuals—the lack of a concept of independence," Dai said. "The Chinese people always attribute China's political problems to rigid authoritarian rule. But a deep-rooted cause probably lies in Chinese cultural values—in people's minds. The rigid authoritarian system has spawned people with subservient personalities. People with subservient personalities, in turn, help to consolidate rigid authoritarian rule."

"How can the Chinese people break out of this 'vicious circle?' " I asked.

"Some of my friends," Dai answered, "write many lengthy books on this subject and make the issue more complicated than it is. I think that, because of foreign interventions and civil wars over the past hundred years, China has lagged far behind developed countries. The explosion in population and the degradation of natural resources in the country have also aggravated China's problems. Chinese intellectuals should recognize the backwardness, both in the country and within themselves. They should catch up and lead China to join the world community for peace and development."

"Why do you single out intellectuals among various social groups in China?"

"China is undergoing rapid socioeconomic change," Dai explained. "Chinese politicians, however, are not clear about what economic system China should establish, how far the Chinese political reform should go, and what role China should play in international affairs. Intellectuals can play a crucial role by providing a vision for China's future. Recently, people in the West have become concerned about the 'China threat.' For the West, both a strong authoritarian China and a weak, disintegrated China can cause a lot of trouble in the world. In my view, this dilemma can only be solved when a majority of Chinese intellectuals become mature, independent, pro-democracy, and pro–world peace."

I'm not sure whether Dai overemphasizes the role of intellectuals in the ongoing transformation of China. At present, both Chinese authorities and Western China watchers seem to pay more attention to other social groups in the country than to intellectuals. No one will fail to see the increasingly important role of new social groups in Chinese society, that is, dissatisfied workers in the troubled state-owned enterprises, urban unemployed people, rural surplus laborers, migrants across the country, rural industrialists, urban entrepreneurs in private enterprises, bureaucratic capitalists in the state sector, and technocrats in government. In contrast to the late 1980s, when Chinese intellectuals and students were in the limelight, today intellectuals seem to be marginalized, on the edges of society.

Yet I found Dai Qing's perspective on intellectuals revealing and her own political experience inspiring. Theodore Draper, an American scholar who studied intellectuals and politics, once made the following remark about intellectuals in Western societies:

> They [intellectuals] are not to be trusted as much as before, but society and government are likely to be just as dependent on them in the foreseeable future. The reason is that the intellectuals are but the most articulate, self-conscious repositories of the accumulated learning and experience of a society. If the intellectuals are in trouble, they are not the only ones; the society is in trouble.[8]

This remark seems to be relevant to what has happened in China during the past decade. Dai Qing's perception of the important role of intellectuals in Chinese society also echoes Draper.

In many aspects, Dai Qing's political experience is unique and her character extraordinary. Yet, as Dai told me a few times, she is an ordinary Chinese woman and an ordinary Chinese intellectual. Her personal experience often reflects major political events and broad social changes in the country. Her courage, her self-criticism of past mistakes, her strong belief in intellectual freedom, and her remarkable contributions to various social movements all suggest the regeneration and the new thinking of Chinese intellectuals.

My interview with Dai Qing in her Beijing apartment was constantly interrupted by telephone calls. Apparently, Dai was very busy with social contacts.

"I don't have a regular job," Dai told me. "In official terms, I am unemployed. But I have a full working schedule filled with interviews, meetings, traveling, reading, and writing." She told me that she had several appointments after our interview that morning. In the summer, she planned to travel to the Yunnan Minorities Autonomous Region, in southern China, to do research and interviews for a book that she has been writing.

"The book," Dai told me, "is about how to resolve religious and nationalistic conflicts through compromise and negotiation. I believe that this is one of the most important issues facing the post–Cold War world."

"Will the policemen outside your apartment follow you while you are traveling?" I asked.

"I don't know and I don't care," Dai replied. "I have been enjoying my work. I cannot afford to be distracted because of the harassment of political authorities.

"To live is not to breathe; it is to act." Dai concluded our meeting with a quote by Rousseau.

"To live is not to breathe; it is to act." Does this quote tell us, better than any other words, the character and experience of Dai Qing—an "ordinary" Chinese woman intellectual who has many extraordinary accomplishments? If more Chinese intellectuals perceive their role in the same way as Dai, what changes will they bring to China's political system and Chinese society in the years to come?

17

China's Future and
Prospects for Sino-American Relations

In May 1990, when the former Soviet Union was undergoing fundamental changes, Walter Laqueur, a student of Russian politics, wrote an article entitled "Forecasting the Soviet-Russian Future" in the British journal *Encounter*. The author expressed his hesitance to make political predictions about the Soviet Union:

> Political predictions are easiest to make when they are least needed, when the political barometer points to continuity. They become more difficult at a time of rapid and violent change. For those putting safety and caution above everything else, comment on the present situation in the Soviet Union is a subject to be shunned.[1]

I feel exactly the same way as I try to assess China's future. During the first few decades of the People's Republic of China, nothing seemed possible except perpetuation of the status quo. No one had the slightest doubt that socialist planning would continue in China's economy and that the Communists would rule political life. Today, however, there are a variety of possibilities.

Paradoxes and Complexities of China's Development

When I was about to finish my fellowship in China in August 1995, an American journalist friend said to me: "You will miss the opportunity to write on the spot when 'X day' finally comes." We used "X day" to refer to the day when Deng goes to see Marx. Indeed, I had a sense of unfulfillment. The remarkable changes that I observed during the two years I had been there were only part of the human drama unfolding in the country. Greater changes are probably yet to come.

The fact that I would not be able to observe "X day," however, did not really bother me. That day would certainly be important to China because the departure of Deng, like the death of Mao, will represent the end of an era and the beginning of another. But Chinese history, like all human histories, is a continuing process. Sociopolitical development, in a sense, is a process of wave formation—each succeeding wave owes something to the strength of what went before. Some socioeconomic changes in China that I wrote about while I was there, for example, structural changes in the economy, internal rural-urban migration, and occupational mobility, are far more monumental than the life and death, or the rise and fall, of a charismatic leader.

What really perplexes me, however, is a sense of uncertainty about the future of this most populous country in the world. As described in the preceding chapters, many contending economic and sociopolitical forces are at work simultaneously. Their roles in China's future development, however, are ambiguous, as economic reform has deepened and become more complicated. Technocrats and entrepreneurs, for example, are two important, rising elite groups in post-Mao China. Technocrats have contributed to the major policy shifts during the reform era—from the emphasis on political campaigns, class conflict, and ideological indoctrination that characterized the Mao era to the present priority on economic development and ideological pragmatism. But at the same time, the technocratic mentality of new leaders has led to some radical and thoughtless projects, such as the large-scale relocation of urban residents in coastal cities and the ongoing Three Gorges Dam project on the Yangtze River. In a way, this technocratic mentality may lead to tragic consequences as the idea of social engineering did during the Great Leap Forward.

The presence of Chinese entrepreneurs has been a direct reason for the economic boom in the country. Some of the socioeconomic changes that they have brought to the country may accomplish a political result that the 1989 Tiananmen protest movement failed to achieve. But the rise of the *"nouveaux riches"* has also led to increasing disparity and social tension in Chinese society. We need to be aware of some moral dilemmas involved in the process of change in China today. The changes brought by market reform in the PRC, similar to those in many former Communist countries in East Europe, may cause capitalist exploitation and other new problems. Those new problems may further bring cries for relief and demands for new directions. As James Rule, a student of former Communist regimes, has noted, the "institutional forms through which these tensions will be expressed are not yet in place" in most post-Communist states.[2]

All these contradictory phenomena suggest the paradoxical nature of many dynamic socioeconomic changes in China during the reform era. Anyone who predicts China's future using a single scenario seems not to have a solid understanding of the country's complexities. An emphasis on the difficulties in predicting China's future may disappoint those who expect certainties, but it can also be seen as an intellectual challenge and an encouragement to those who search for possibilities. As Walter Laqueur has reminded us, "If a man will begin with certainties, he shall end in doubts [Francis Bacon's words]. If he starts with possibilities, however, he may end in probabilities."[3]

Nicholas Kristof, after completing his five-year tenure as the *New York Times*'s Beijing bureau chief, wrote an imaginative article for that newspaper prior to his 1993 departure. In this predictive and semifictional piece, Kristof described three possible scenarios in China for the year 2000: (1) an authoritarian and military regime, (2) a quasi-democratic state, and (3) a country under civil war and vast upheaval.[4] In the first scenario, the post-Deng regime would even more systematically violate human rights in order to maintain its dictatorship, although under the cloak of anti-Communism and anticorruption. The second scenario would be the emergence of a "prosperous quasi-democracy." Deng's death may well accelerate and consolidate the process of rapid-fire economic development and more measured political liberalization in the country. China in the year 2000 would be like South Korea or Taiwan in the late 1980s. In the third scenario, China would fall apart just like a broken vase. Millions of people would die in a civil war. At the same time, a disintegrating China would flood millions of refugees over the entire Pacific-Asian region.

Some people in the West have criticized Kristof for his effort to make "sensational journalism," which is believed to be "mostly apocryphal." But I do not think any of his three scenarios is entirely impossible or groundless. Rather, he has focused our attention on the importance of political succession in China and its various possible consequences.

But to my surprise, recently, many American China experts, after a week-long visit to Beijing, came back and made all kinds of positive comments about China's political succession. One prediction is that China's post-Deng leadership succession is already completed, and Jiang Zemin is, and will be, in control. I did not get that impression during my stay in China, even in Shanghai, which is Jiang's power base. Instead, I heard numerous jokes about him and other Chinese leaders (such as the joke about "heart" and "brain" told earlier in the volume). Jiang currently holds the highest posts in the Party, government, and army. Probably he will not immediately lose all these positions when Deng dies. But the question is: how long can he remain in power?

Jiang Zemin does not have the respect of the people because he has not accomplished anything good for the country. The only thing that he did in Shanghai was to ban the city's liberal newspaper during the 1989 democratic movement. He recently purged corrupt Beijing municipal leaders, but most think this was only because he wanted to get rid of his political enemies. This action actually caused much resentment among many provincial and central leaders. Meanwhile, Jiang's relationship to the military—the "kingmaker" and one of the primary institutions determining China's future—is dubious.[5]

Chinese political leaders themselves cannot claim with any certainty that they know the way in which political factions will form or that they can predict the characteristics of post-Deng China. Any ambitious and wise politicians in the Chinese leadership have likely kept their political desires and visions hidden during this time of uncertainty. Two previously appointed successors to Deng, Hu Yaobang and Zhao Ziyang, successively lost their jobs because they had been "out of touch with China's political reality." If American China experts continue to be so optimistic about the leadership succession and the political system in the country, they will be in for another shock, similar to the one they got in 1989, not to mention the one in 1976.

Although it is impossible to predict how China will be ruled next year and who or which group of leaders will succeed Deng, one can comment with greater conviction about broad political and socioeconomic trends in the society. More importantly, an awareness of many uncertainties concerning China's future should not prevent us from rejecting some prevalent misconceptions in Western studies of China.

Three Major Western Misconceptions about China

The West is suffering under three serious misconceptions about events in China. The first misconception is the view that post-Mao China has remained a strictly Communist state and has been able to resist the pressure of political reform despite, or because of, tremendous progress in economic reform. This situation, according to some experts, is unlikely to change in the near future. The second misconception is the conventional view that the continuation of China's economic reform is inevitable, because this reform has brought about one of the greatest developments in human welfare in Chinese history. And the third misconception is the prediction that China is on the way to becoming an economic giant and therefore a threat to the West, particularly to the United States. While acknowledging some validity in these views, I believe all of them are basically wrong. Unfortunately, these misleading views have strongly influenced the general public, business people, academic studies, and governmental policies in the United States.

I would like to illustrate the Western misconception about the Communist government in China with an anecdote. In the spring of 1995, I went to Australia to give a talk. During the trip, I met a retired Australian bureaucrat. He asked me where I came from. I told him that I grew up in China and immigrated to the United States, but currently worked in China.

"Oh," he said, "it must have been bloody tough for you to live under Communists again. What do you think of these bloody, conservative Communists?"

"Well," I replied, "I haven't seen even one Communist during my journey across China. Instead I saw so many bloody, greedy capitalists there."

I was not joking. Throughout my two years in China, I did not see the kind of Communists with whom I had been so familiar as I grew up. Party officials in China I interviewed often identified themselves as chairmen of the board of trustees. I received about two thousand business cards in China. Believe it or not, none of them identified a position in the Communist Party, although some of the cards listed more than 10 administrative or professional titles. Actually I seldom heard the word Communism mentioned while I was in China, except on CNN and VOA.

Unfortunately, the prevalent view of China in the West is still ideology-laden. As the political scientist Chalmers Johnson has noted, one important lesson to emerge from the end of the Cold War is that English-speaking social science is in many cases as ideological as the Marxism-Leninism of the Communist world.

Socialism, capitalism, and Communism used to be essential concepts in the social sciences. The world split into two major blocs during the Cold War era because of these conflicting ideologies. Millions of Chinese people—whether Communists or anti-Communists—died for their ideological beliefs and/or political identities. Today, Communist ideology is becoming irrelevant in China. Many Western sinologists, however, still believe that the main conflict among Chinese leaders in the post-Mao era has occurred between Communist hardliners who want to maintain a socialist planning economy and the Western-influenced liberals who intend to move towards capitalist democracy. The 1989 Tiananmen incident, for example, was described as the struggle between "gerontocratic Communist bumpkins" and "younger well-educated reformers."[6]

The main issue for the Chinese leadership is not about the choice between returning to the previous socialist-planning economy or transforming to a conventional capitalist market. The real concern for the post-Mao
leaders is the problem of transition—transition to whatever kind of mixed
economy and whatever form of political system that can support the rapid
economic changes.

People in the West have often seen a sharp contrast when comparing
the former Soviet Union and China—the collapse of Communism in the
former and the prolonged continuation of Communism in the latter.[7] But
it can also be argued that the rejection of Communism occurred in China
a decade earlier than the collapse of the former Soviet Union. The stock
market, a notably capitalist phenomenon, has played an important role in
the Chinese economy during the reform era. The Shanghai Stock Exchange, which was established in the mid-1980s, was the first stock exchange in the world to be approved by a self-proclaimed Communist government. Private entrepreneurs in both rural and urban areas have already
formed a sizable capitalist class in China, which is in many ways more
active and influential than its counterparts in Eastern Europe and the former Soviet Union. China is no longer a Communist country in any meaningful sense.[8] The Chinese Communist Party has lost its mandate and its
ideological coherence.

It is also too simplistic, if not entirely wrong, to assume that post-
Mao China has made tremendous progress in economic reform but less
in political reform. One cannot really separate economic reform from
political change. The ongoing urban privatization, for example, is considered economic reform, but has brought about fundamental political
changes in Chinese society. In addition, decentralization of power at all
levels of government, the rise of technocrats in leadership, the experiment
of an independent legal system, and more genuine grassroots and local
elections are some of the important political reforms that have been taking
place in China.

I don't mean that all the political changes are constructive. Earlier, I
suggested that a large number of government officials are Communists in
name, but capitalists, or bureaucratic capitalists, in fact. To elaborate on
the political ramification of official corruption: the point is that students
of China should not be preoccupied with meaningless ideological jargons.
This preoccupation has distracted China watchers from asking the right
questions at the right time and with the right emphasis.

Whether the ruling elite continues to call itself Communist, as Andrew
Nathan has argued, is "the least important of the many questions that we
can ask about China's future."[9] In present-day China, disparity is up,

trust is down; Communism is out, markets are in. No one seems to doubt that the old political system has to go. The irony and hypocrisy within this so-called Communist state has strong implications for our assessment of China's future. Chinese leaders cannot continue to identify themselves as Communist while enthusiastically embracing capitalism. The current Chinese government is extremely unpopular and will surely be faced with challenges in the years to come.

This leads me to the second Western misconception about China. According to some Western China experts, the continuation of economic reform is inevitable because it has brought about one of the greatest improvements in human welfare in Chinese history. When I started my fellowship in China, I thought this as well. When my relatives and old friends complained, I always asked them, "Are you better off now than during the prereform era?" Some of them responded that this was not a fair question. They said that, although their standard of living had improved, they missed the old days under Mao—poorer, but simpler and more equal.

"We are not really nostalgic about the 'good old days'—there never were such days," said a middle-aged man with whom I talked in a restaurant in Beijing. "But life was much simpler in the old days," he continued. "We didn't need to worry about the future, because the future would be the same for everyone. But now I don't know where I will work the next month and how much my salary will be. It is certain, however, that my boss earns 20 times more than I do."

Chinese peasants, who were the major beneficiaries during the earlier years of the reform, now find they have lagged far behind urban dwellers. Many have migrated to urban areas. Migrant workers have already become a distinctive group in China, but they are still largely treated as a "community outside the system." Most of them have no medical care, no health insurance, no work contracts, no welfare benefits, no permanent residence permits, no workplace safety. Furthermore, their newly won freedom to move from rural to urban areas is often threatened by a more restrictive government policy.

Residents in urban areas now eat and dress better than they did during the old days of the Mao era and are enjoying a wide variety of goods in the marketplace that they could not imagine just a few years ago, but they are by no means satisfied with the current situation. They are resentful of the pressing problems such as corruption, inflation, and polarization. These problems have grown to such a serious degree that many people worry that they may ruin all of the achievements made during the past decade.

China's reform programs have been targeted at solving the old problems of socialism, but now many of these solutions are becoming new
problems. In chapter 11, I discussed the property boom in coastal China.
This development has attracted foreign capital and stimulated local economic growth. But it can also be seen as a destructive force that is undermining the cultural fabric of the city and causing tremendous disruption
for local residents. In the United States, it usually takes several decades
for large numbers of residents to move from the city to the suburbs. But
it took only months for Shanghai to move 100,000 households out of the
downtown area. Most of the new residential areas are located in bleak
suburbs without hospitals, schools, or grocery markets. People's resentment against the government is widespread. They complain that local
governments are more interested in building fancy hotels and office buildings, luxurious villas, nightclubs, expensive department stores, or golf
courses, than in building much-needed roads, schools, and homes for
low-income families.

Probably the most politically sensitive problem in China is the rampancy of official corruption. Speculation with public money and official
profiteering have become so prevalent during the reform era that a new
term, *"guandao,"* was created to refer to this phenomenon. Few issues in
the PRC over the past several years have generated as much public resentment and social tension as *"guandao."* Chinese authorities do not deny
the penetration of official corruption. Corruption has grown to such huge
proportions that Jiang Zemin warned that it would ruin the Communist
Party itself, and Li Peng recently depicted corruption as a "life and death"
issue for China.[10] The Chinese Communist Party came to power with an
anticorruption appeal; now this image is completely gone.

In 1994, officials of China's Supreme People's Procurator told two
Western political scientists that that agency alone had received an average
of 1,250,000 reports by citizens of official corruption each year during
the last few years.[11] From 1988 to 1993, the Discipline Inspection Committee of the National People's Congress investigated more than 870,000
official violations at various levels, 730,000 officials were disciplined, and
150,000 expelled from the Communist Party.[12] Corruption scandals were
also found in the Chinese army. Beginning in the mid-1980s, the People's
Liberation Army (PLA) was allowed to do business on its own. Over
10,000 army-run companies have been officially registered, and many
thousands more are known to operate without approval from the logistics
chiefs.[13]

But interestingly, those who have been punished are usually low- or
medium-level government officials and junior military officers. Less than

a handful of high-ranking leaders (at the ministerial or provincial level) have been caught during the past decade. A local saying in Shanghai, reflecting the hypocrisy and the problem of governmental anticorruption campaigns, says: "A big embezzler lectures about governmental anticorruption campaigns, a medium-sized embezzler listens to the lecture, only a small embezzler goes to jail."

"If the high-ranking officials were ever punished, they were punished not because of their crimes," said a 60-year-old engineer I met in Shenyang in the summer of 1995, "but because they lost a power struggle within the Party."

His view was widely shared by many people in Beijing. Two large scandals involving official corruption were exposed in Beijing in 1995. In the first case, Zhou Guanwu, chairman of Shougang, known as the Capital Iron and Steel Corporation, one of the largest state-owned enterprises in the country, was under investigation, and his son, Zhou Beifang, Chairman of Shougang's Hong Kong–based investment subsidiary, Shougang Concord Holdings, was arrested. The Chinese authorities have not spelled out the alleged crimes of the father-and-son team, but some press reports suggested that the investigation centered on Shougang's 1992 purchase of an iron-ore mine in Peru. The company paid $312 million—at least twice that of competing bids. The younger Zhou was accused of receiving a huge kickback.[14]

The second scandal was exposed because of the death of Wang Baosen, who was vice mayor and treasurer of Beijing. He was found dead with a "gun and scores of cigarette butts beside him."[15] Wang's boss, Chen Xitong, Politburo member and the head of the Communist Party in Beijing, was forced to resign and was under house arrest. According to official sources, Chen Xitong and his associates in the municipal government made a large fortune for themselves through fund-raising for the bid to host the Olympic Games in 2000 and by leasing the city's downtown areas to foreign investors.

Chen Xitong and his associates in the Beijing municipal government were caught because Jiang Zemin and his "gang of Shanghai-based leaders" wanted to expel their own political enemies. Otherwise, Chen would have remained a Politburo member, and Wang would not have died.

Before I left for the United States in 1985, most corruption in China consisted of petty bribery of a few hundred dollars; now officials steal several million or even several hundred million dollars. Chen Xitong was accused of embezzling over $1 billion. Some high-ranking government officials and children of revolutionary veterans have turned state property, including China's large international corporations, into their own private firms. The distinction between public firms and private companies has often become blurred.

"Before the 1949 Communist Revolution," a middle-school teacher with whom I chatted on a bus ride in Guangzhou said, "there were 'Four Big Families' [*sidajiazu*]—the wealthiest bureaucratic-capitalist families in the country. Now China has 'Four New Big Families.' New big families are far more wealthy than the old ones in the Nationalist government."

"The Four New Big Families," the school teacher told me, refer to the families of Deng Xiaoping, Wang Zhen, Rong Yiren, and Chen Yun. Children of Chen Yun, a revolutionary veteran who died in 1995, hold important business posts in the country. Chen Yun's son, Chen Yuan, is first vice governor of the People's Bank and his third daughter, Chen Weili, is vice president of China Venturetech, a state-backed investment firm, which is well known for its speculation in Shanghai's property market.[16] The use of the term "Four New Big Families" reflects the widespread resentment of official corruption in Chinese society today.

Official corruption has undoubtedly become one of the most destructive side effects of China's reform. According to a comparative study of corruption, recently released in the *New York Times*, out of 41 countries surveyed, China is ranked second next to Indonesia, in terms of the rampancy of corruption.[17]

"If the ultimate result of the reform is the resurgence of bureaucratic capitalists and enormous disparity in society," a Chinese historian in Shanghai said to me, "I would say that the reform is a complete failure. What China really needs is perhaps a revolution, not a reform."

I found this historian's remark to be thought-provoking. Problems such as the growing disparity between rich and poor, a huge pool of 200 million surplus laborers, and the large-scale rural-urban migration, the lack of a social safety net, urban public unrest caused by the mass eviction of local families to bleak suburbs, and especially the rampancy of official corruption are all the issues that the Chinese authorities cannot afford to deliberate upon for too long. These are tough issues, and none has an easy solution. It is not inevitable that China's reform program will proceed down the path it has begun. I suspect that Chinese leaders are particularly uneasy about what has happened recently in South Korea—a verdict of guilty for two former presidents. As some have observed, people in East Asian countries will not be lenient toward corrupt and dictatorial leaders, even if they have presided over a booming economy.

The third major misconception of China in the West is the prediction that China is on the way to becoming an economic giant and therefore a threat to the West, particularly to the United States. There is no doubt that the economic development in China during the reform era, especially in the coastal area, is remarkable. Never in history have so many people made so much economic progress in a single generation as residents of coastal China. Four chapters of this volume provide stories about the fascinating development in Sunan, with a focus on a region, a city, a village, and an individual entrepreneur, respectively. This previously agrarian area has now become a frontier of economic development as the result of the rapid development of rural industries. In 1993, for example, the GNP of the region grew 35 percent over the previous year, and in Zhangjiagang city, 68.3 percent. In Huaxi village, about 80 percent of the families own private cars—Volkswagen Jettas, each costing 175,000 yuan ($30,700).

During my stay in China, I met several dozen rich, rural industrialists, visited their homes, and listened to their life stories. Almost every time, I felt as if I was listening to a Chinese Carnegie or Rockefeller. Chapter 6 introduced readers to Mr. Chen, a 45-year-old peasant-turned-industrialist in Wujiang. For the first 30 years of his life, Mr. Chen and his family lived in a straw shed. Now he owns a huge, three-story mansion. I call it a "mansion" because it has so many rooms that his wife has to number them—201, 202, 203, 213, and so on. This mansion has three dining rooms, one banquet room, and a ballroom that can accommodate 80 people. Mr. Chen made his fortune during the past 10 years by manufacturing fiberglass, a construction material in great demand in the country. I visited Mr. Chen's house a number of times, once with a partner of Goldman Sachs. The American businessman asked me three times: "Is this a private house?" When assured that it was, he said to me, "That Chinese *dahu* is rich enough to be a senior partner of Goldman Sachs."

Stories about Sunan, Zhangjiagang city, Huaxi village, and Mr. Chen are by no means unusual in coastal China. Yet I do not want to give the wrong impression that the entire Chinese population is, or soon will be, as wealthy as people in Sunan. As I traveled across China, especially to northwestern and central China, I got the strong feeling that China will remain a poor country for decades to come. Make no mistake, living standards have also improved in these remote areas. There is no hunger or starvation, both common during the Mao era and still prevalent in many other poor countries in Africa and Asia. When the reform started in 1978, China's economic condition was extremely backward. Today it is still backward in terms of GNP per capita. It is important to know that if the United States increases GNP by 1 percent, per capita income in the United States will increase by $180. By contrast, if China's GNP increases 10 percent, per capita income in China will increase only $30.[18]

Is it truth or myth that China is becoming a new economic giant? My answer is that it is both. China's coastal area has already become a global economic powerhouse. But as a whole, as noted, China will remain poor for many decades. China has been, and probably will always be, a nation of many faces. The nation's economic progress is real, but so is its backwardness.

A China Threat? Cultural and Military Challenges to the U.S.?

Recently in the United States we have heard a lot of discussion about the "China threat" and the argument for containing China.[19] This concern is understandable. In the contemporary world, the rapid economic growth of a nation or a geographic region, for example, nineteenth-century Europe, post–World War I America, and the Soviet Union after 1945, often aroused suspicions and anxieties among other countries and regions. Today, there is growing suspicion in many parts of the world about the rapid rise of China and its intentions and aspirations. This suspicion is probably most strongly felt in the United States, the remaining superpower after the collapse of the Soviet Union.

In a 1993 article, Samuel Huntington, a political scientist, tried to characterize the nature of world politics in the coming decades. What global politics is likely to be, in his view, is this: "A West at the peak of its power confronts non-Wests that increasingly have the desire, the will, and the resources to shape the world in non-Western ways."[20] According to Huntington, Confucian culture, or the Oriental civilization that East Asian countries have embodied, will form an economic and political bloc. The bloc, which is likely to be centered in China, will be a major threat not only to the political and economic power of the West but also to its value system—Western civilization.

At first glance, the observations made by Huntington seem valid because politicians in Asian Confucian countries including China did explicitly claim the "superiority of their value system." Throughout the 1980s, top leaders of authoritarian regions such as China, and Singapore protected the value systems of Asia and rejected the interference of foreign countries. They called their economic success the "way of Asia." These Asian values include a strong sense of family, respect for authority, and the harmony of individual with collective interests. A Korean political leader recently argued that Confucian culture has emphasized collectivism, while the Western culture has respected individualism. In his view, today's world is entering an era of collectivism, for example, the European Union and NAFTA. The cultural renaissance of East Asia will lead to a Confucian-oriented world. Leaders in this region often claim that East Asians have their own concept of human rights; in order to deal with the West they should be united.[21]

The main problem with Huntington's thesis lies in its simplistic interpretation of East Asian values. He puts undue emphasis on certain aspects of the so-called Confucian civilization. What he failed to understand is the *yin* and *yang* of Chinese culture and society.[22] Confucianism may foster a strong nationalistic, hierarchical, and self-centered mentality. But Chinese tradition includes Taoism, Buddhism, and other value systems, in addition to Confucianism. Taoism, for example, advocates almost exactly opposite world views. In today's words, Taoism emphasizes environmental and global concern.

It is inappropriate, therefore, to assume that people in Confucian cultures are homogeneous in terms of their values and world views. Nationalistic and *Realpolitik* world views are certainly strong in Confucian societies. Yet unconventional and globalist values are increasingly articulated in the region. Global problems—such as environmental degradation, resource depletion, population explosion, international refugees and migration, international human rights, nuclear proliferation, narcotics, and the spread of AIDS—have begun to receive much attention among Chinese scholars. This is impressive because until very recently, mainstream international studies in China (and in Western democratic countries as well) did not give much attention to most of these global issues.

"Some Westerners assume that people in East Asia have a strong sense of ethnic superiority," a Chinese scholar said at a 1995 conference in Shanghai, "but I think that these Westerners display their own sense of ethnic superiority when they claim that Oriental people don't know what human rights are."

"This claim actually presumes a special access to justice and truth through cultural background," a young Chinese scholar added. "It's probably true that Americans are more concerned about global environmental problems than we Chinese are at present. But, ironically, so much energy and so many resources are wasted in the United States every day." The young Chinese scholar was absolutely right. It seems that *yin* and *yang* forces also coexist in the United States.

Undoubtedly, great differences exist between China and the United States for historical, geographical, and socioeconomic reasons. Yet we are all human beings, and all societies are faced with the problems of modern administration and the challenges of technological development. William

Butler Yeats made an insightful remark as he commented on the comparison of different cultures. He wrote: "Talent perceives differences, genius unity."

The central question is whether the lines between different civilizations have become blurred or clearer as the world moves towards a new millennium. I have seen an integration of civilizations rather than a clash of civilizations. Anyone who studies post-Mao China is surely aware how much the Chinese have learned from the West—not only its technology, but also its administrative skills, economic methods, social norms, lifestyles, and political values. It is truly ironic that Huntington sees a resurgent Confucianism at the very time when "spiritual deterioration and moral degradation are eroding China's cultural foundation," as a well-known Chinese writer has observed.[23] Although Confucian influence still exists, it cannot be compared to the increasingly forceful influence of Western culture on the Chinese people during the reform era. The threat of Confucian civilization is totally unfounded. To predict a "clash of civilizations" will only add to the tension and lead to more mutual misunderstanding.

Will an economically powerful China become a military challenge to the United States? It is true that Chinese nationalism is rising—a recently published best-selling book entitled *China Can Say No* reflects the anti-American sentiments among some young Chinese intellectuals.[24] But this does not necessarily mean that the Chinese authorities or even Chinese radical intellectuals intend to take an aggressive and combative stand towards the United States. A radical and xenophobic foreign policy probably requires a radical and charismatic leader, but I do not see such a leader emerging now or in the foreseeable future. Economic development remains China's primary objective, and to risk economic and political isolation with an attack on Taiwan would seem very irrational to the pragmatic technocrats who now run the country. Besides, the Chinese leadership has huge internal problems to worry about.

Some Westerners like to criticize the Chinese people for their strong nationalistic fervor and "middle kingdom mentality," but nationalism is on the rise in many Western countries and Eurocentric views are evident there. Nationalism—in many cases subnationalism—has caused or accelerated ethnic violence and even war in Western countries.

As in other countries, the Chinese leadership consists of both doves and hawks. It has been reported that hardliners in the Chinese military are becoming increasingly influential in decision-making circles. In 1993, for instance, several American naval ships stopped a Chinese cargo vessel on the high seas in order to inspect the cargo for banned weapons. In response to this incident, 50 Chinese generals wrote a joint letter to Jiang Zemin, calling for a tougher policy towards the United States. The generals claimed that the Chinese government should not sacrifice military interest and national security for the sake of maintaining foreign trade with Western countries.[25] But I doubt that they will receive much support from other elites and from the people. At present, the Chinese are in the mood to make money, not enemies. More importantly, both Chinese officials and people, especially entrepreneurs like Mr. Chen, want to have a peaceful and cooperative international environment, which will be conducive to continuing economic growth at home.

The United States, of course, should be alerted to the growing technocratic thinking of Chinese hardliners. Technocrats usually rationalize their foreign policies with a careful calculation of national resources and military capacity. But at present one should not exaggerate China's military strength. China's defense spending in 1995 was only about one-tenth that of the United States.[26] As some statistics show, with an out-of-date arsenal and poorly trained forces, China's military doesn't even have the capacity to invade Taiwan, let alone challenge the United States.[27]

Sino-American relations are obviously not in good shape. The United States has been critical of China's tough positions regarding Taiwan and the South China Sea, its nuclear proliferation and sale of arms, the repression of political dissidents, and human rights violations. This criticism, in my view, is justified. But the Chinese government has its own valid concerns. Look at today's world—how many governments are really willing to lose the territory that they claim? China is certainly not the only country that has been engaged in nuclear proliferation and the sale of arms. The Chinese government is very sensitive to political dissidents because it cannot afford to face another Tiananmen protest movement. This does not mean that the United States should avoid discussing these issues with the Chinese. The United States should tell the Chinese leaders that respect for human rights and for international law is important. But the United States should do so through dialogue, both privately and publicly, not through efforts to contain China. We should not be too cynical about the effectiveness of dialogue. For instance, the term "human rights" (*renquan*), which the Chinese used to consider an example of Western hypocritical ideas, now has become a positive notion. There is hope that the liberal forces within China will eventually prevail.

Containment cannot change any of the tensions in the region. It will only help Chinese hardliners justify their actions. Nothing could be more counterproductive than to establish an American alliance against China. As James Baker said, "the best way to make an enemy is to look for one."[28] The United States should be aware that China has an important and constructive role to play in the Asia-Pacific region. The two countries share many interests, such as regional security, economic cooperation, and environmental protection. It is in the interest of the United States to insure a secure and cohesive China, rather than an unstable and fragmented China.[29]

Meanwhile, the United States should not take an isolationist position by withdrawing from its involvement in East and Southeast Asia. This is not only because America has so many economic interests in the region, especially in China, but mainly because China's economic condition and social stability are not only internal issues. They are, and should be, global concerns. China's neighbors and the entire world community will share the pain if China experiences chaos. The real danger for United States–China relations, I believe, is not so much China's military threat as our failure to understand the contradictions and complexities involved in the ongoing transformation there.

In the early 1960s, during the Cold War, Rabindranath Tagore, a Nobel laureate, expressed his disappointment about the Cuban missile crisis and the conflict between East and West. He believed that the West did not show any real effort to resolve the crisis. In his view, the "West had not sent out its humanity to meet the man in the East, but only its machines."[30]

Now, the Cold War is over, and the two conflicting blocs of West and East no longer exist. The scientific and technological revolution greatly blurs cultural and territorial boundaries. People in different countries are able to more freely exchange their views and ideas. Sol M. Linowitz, an American diplomat, once wrote: "The best way to send an idea around the world is to wrap it up in a person."[31]

I was privileged to be in China for two years and to share the ideas and values that I had acquired in America with my fellow Chinese. At the same time I had the opportunity to learn from them, to know their bitterness and happiness, their frustrations and aspirations, which are evident throughout this book. My journey through China as presented here demonstrates the great need for a meeting of "East" and "West."

Notes

Note: The exchange rate during the 1980s and 1990s fluctuated greatly, from approximately 1.5 Chinese yuan per U.S. dollar to 8.4 Chinese yuan per U.S. dollar. The amount is indicated in U.S. dollars when identified by the source; otherwise no conversion has been made.

Chapter 1

1. *Economist*, 18–24 July 1992, 24.
2. Henry Grunwald, "Home Is Where You Are Happy," *Time*, 8 July 1985, 100–101.
3. Fernand Braudel, "History and Social Science," in *Economy and Society in Early Modern Europe: Essays from Annales*, ed. P. Burke (New York: Harper & Row, 1972), 24.
4. *Economist* "A Survey of China," 28 November–4 December 1992, 1–18.
5. *Economist*, 29 May–4 June 1993, 13–14.
6. John K. Fairbank, "The New China and the American Connection," *Foreign Affairs* 51 (October 1972): 36.
7. Quoted from Saylen and Masyrene Masters, "Foreigners in the Wonderland of China," *China Daily*, 15 February 1994, 4.
8. Morgan Stanley International Investment Research, *China! Report on the Morgan Stanley Tour of China*, (New York: Morgan Stanley International Incorporated, Autumn, 1993), 1.
9. Ibid., 15.
10. *China News Analysis*, no. 1556 (15 March 1996): 3.
11. I have derived this comparison from a thought-provoking article by Timothy Tung, "Changing China, A Personal Observation," *US-China Review*, (summer 1993): 12.

Chapter 2

1. James Fallows, "Shanghai Surprise," *Atlantic Monthly*, July 1988, 76.
2. James Fallows, "The Joys of Japan," *Atlantic Monthly*, July 1993, 104.

3. Ross Terrill, "Hong Kong" *National Geographic*, February 1991, 113.

4. Yang Dongping, *Chengshi jifeng: Beijing he Shanghai de wenhua jingshen* (City monsoon: the cultural spirit of Beijing and Shanghai) (Beijing: Dongfang Press, 1994), 314.

5. James P. Sterba, "A Great Leap Where?" *Wall Street Journal*, 10 December 1993, R9.

6. *Jiefang ribao*, 3 October 1993, 1.

7. Ibid.

8. Paul Theroux in 1993 traveled to China's southern provinces. He found the area fascinating because, in his words, this is the land "where only local knowledge matters and word of mouth is everything." Paul Theroux, "Going to See the Dragon," *Harper's*, October 1993, 33.

9. *Cankao xiaoxi*, 2 January 1994, 8.

10. Václav Havel, "The Post-Communist Nightmare," *New York Review of Books*, 27 May 1993, 8.

11. James Kenneson, "China Stinks," *Harper's*, April 1982, 15.

12. *Shanghai tongji nianjian* (Statistical yearbook of Shanghai) (Beijing: Zhongguo Tongji Press, 1995), 123.

13. *China Daily*, 13 July 1994; Wang Shan, *Disanzhi yanjing kan Zhongguo* (China through the third eye), 3rd ed., (Hong Kong: Mingbao Press, 1994), 214.

14. By the end of 1993, Shanghai had 805 commercial dance halls (2.12 times more than in 1992?), 1,539 karaoke bars, 1,020 KTV (karaoke television) clubs (including 4,895 KTV rooms). *Jiefang ribao*, 9 August 1994, 3.

15. Wang Shaoguang, "Siren shijian yu zhengzhi: Zhongguo chengshi xianxia moshi de bianhua" (Private time and politics: changes of the leisure patterns in urban China), *Zhongguo shehuixue jikan* (Chinese social sciences quarterly), (summer 1995): 108.

16. Ibid., 113. Also, *Information on Social Development in China, 1992* (Beijing: China Statistics Press, 1992), 114.

17. Ibid., 110. And also *Zhongguo qingnian* (China youth) 12 (1960): 30–31.

18. *China News Analysis*, no. 1310, 15 May 1986, 1.

19. *China News Analysis*, no. 1462, 15 June 1992, 2.

20. Yang Dongping, *Chengshi jifeng*, 12.

21. *Beijing Review*, 25 November–1 December 1991, 34.

22. Hong Lanxing, "Shanghai Boom in Cultural Studies," *Beijing Review*, 19–25 March 1990, 46.

23. Yu Tianbai, *Shanghai: xingge ji mingyun* (Shanghai: Her character is her destiny), (Shanghai: Wenyi Press, 1992); Yu Qiuyu, *Wenhua kulü* (The bitter travel of culture), (Shanghai: Zhishi Press, 1992); Yang Dongping, *Chengshi jifeng*, op. cit. For a review of these books, see Cheng Li, "Rediscovering Urban Subcultures: Contrast between Shanghai and Beijing," *China Journal*, no. 36 (July 1996): 139–153.

24. The essay "Shanghairen" was reprinted in many magazines and newspapers in the country. Yu Qiuyu, *Wenhua kulü*, 150.

25. Ibid., 151.

26. "The Special Style of the Shanghaiese," *Shanghai* 5 (January 1995): 1.

27. Yu Tianbai, *Shanghai: xingge ji mingyun*, 10.

28. Ibid.

29. Michael Berenbaum, *The World Must Know: The History of the Holocaust as Told in the United States Holocaust Memorial Museum* (Boston: Little, Brown, 1993), 59.

30. Yang Dongping, *Chengshi jifeng*, 122.

31. Michael Buckley and others, *China*, 4th ed. (Hawthorn, Australia: Lonely Planet Publications, 1994), 453.

32. Yu Tianbai, *Shanghai: xingge ji mingyun*, 235.

33. Tian Fang and Zhang Dongliang, *Zhongguo renkou qianyi xintan* (New approach to the study of China's population) (Beijing: Zhishi Press, 1989), 304.

34. Ibid.

35. *Xinmin wanbao*, 27 September 1993, 1.

36. Ian Buruma, "The 21st Century Starts Here," *New York Times Magazine*, 18 February 1996, 8.

37. *Baokan wenzhai*, 23 March 1995, 1.

Chapter 3

1. *Wenhui bao*, 11 January 1994, 7.

2. *Renmin ribao*, 9 January 1994, 8.

3. *Jiefang ribao*, 7 January 1994, 11.

4. *China News Analysis*, no. 1560 (15 May 1996): 5.

5. Ibid.

6. *Guangming bao*, 22 March 1996, 4.

7. *Renmin ribao*, 25 August 1995, 2; and 16 October 1995, 10.

8. *China News Analysis*, no. 1560 (15 May 1996): 9.

9. *New York Times*, 20 February 1996, 1.

10. Ibid., A6.

11. *Asian Wall Street Journal*, 28 December 1995, 1.

12. *Renmin ribao*, 1 February 1994.

13. *Jiefang ribao*, 10 January 1994, 2.

14. *Jiefang ribao*, 14 December 1993, 1.

15. *New York Times*, 6 September 1993, 5.

16. *China Daily*, 27 December 1993, 1.

17. *Economist*, 25 December 1993–7 January 1994, 26.

18. *Cheng ming*, no. 10 (October 1993): 14.

19. *Wenhui bao*, 28 November 1993, 7.

20. *China News Analysis*, no. 1560 (15 May 1996): 1.

Chapter 4

1. A. Doak Barnett, *China on the Eve of Communist Takeover* (New York: Frederick A. Praeger, 1963).

2. *New York Times*, 6 September 1993, 5.

3. *Baokan wenzhai*, 13 January 1994, 1; also, Eliana Cardoso and Shahid Yusuf, "Red Capitalism: Growth and Inflation in China," *Challenge* 37, (May–June 1994): 55.

4. *Economic Information Daily*, 31 May 1994, 4; *Renmin ribao*, 11 January 1995, 2; and *China News Analysis*, no. 1529 (15 February 1995): 2.

5. *Beijing Review*, 18–24 September 1989, 25.

6. Solomon M. Karmel, "Emerging Securities Markets in China: Capitalism with Chinese Characteristics," *China Quarterly*, no. 140 (1994): 1105–1120.

7. *Wenhui bao*, 1 November 1993, 2.

8. Orville Schell, "Shanghai Daze," *Los Angeles Times Magazine*, 18 June 1995, 15. In addition, another stock exchange in China, the Shenzhen Stock Market, listed 73 companies worth 2.8 billion yuan in circulated capital stock and 130 billion yuan in total market value. See Liu Chunlin, "Review of China's Stock Market in 1993," *Beijing Review*, 28 March–3 April 1994, 20.

9. Karmel, "Emerging Securities Markets," 1111.

10. Ibid., 1109.

11. *Renmin ribao*, 23 February 1992. For the English translation of the editorial article, see Fang Sheng, "Opening Up and Making Use of Capitalism," *Beijing Review*, 23–29 March 1992, 18–20.

12. *China Daily*, 13 November 1993, 4.

13. *Renmin ribao*, 23 February 1992; and also, *Economist*, 29 February–6 March 1992, 35.

14. *China News Analysis*, no. 1501 (1 January 1994): 2.

15. *China Daily*, 11 November 1994, 4.

16. *China Daily*, 13 July 1994, 4.

17. *China Daily (Business Weekly)*, 22–28 May 1994, 1.

18. *Shanghai Star*, 1 November 1994, 3.

19. *China Daily*, 3 March 1994, 1; Li Xinxin, "Zhongguo siying jingji fazhan zhong de wenti ji duice" (Problems and measures in the development of China's private enterprises), *Jingji yanjiu* (Economic research), no. 7 (1994): 42.

20. *China Daily*, 3 March 1994, 1.

21. *China Daily*, 11 November 1994, 4.

22. Li Ding, "Woguo siying jingjin fazhan de ruokan wendi" (Issues concerning the development of the private economy in China), *Jingjixue dongtai* (Economic trends), no. 1, (1994): 48.

23. *Shanghai Star*, 3 June 1994, 2.

24. *Jiefang ribao*, 2 November 1994, 1.

25. *Jinji gongzhu tongxun*, (Economic work newsletter), 15 November 1994, 10–11.

26. *Shanghai Star*, 13 January 1995, 7.

27. *Far Eastern Economic Review*, 7 May 1992, 50; Li Xinxin, "Zhongguo siying jingji fazhan zhong de wenti ji duice," 43.

28. Li Ding, "Woguo siying jingjin fazhan de ruokan wendi," 48.

29. Quoted from *China Daily*, 11 November 1994, 4.

30. *Wenhui bao*, 19 November 1993, 5.

31. This definition is based on Zhang Houyi, "The Position of the Private Entrepreneur Stratum in China's Social Structure," *Social Sciences in China* 16, (winter 1995): 33.

32. Zhang Houyi, "The Position of the Private Entrepreneur Stratum in China's Social Structure," 29.

33. *Caifu* (China rich), no. 8 (1996): 1.

34. Ibid., 5.

35. Mu's company is not 100 percent private; the state has backed his company for many years, especially when it had financial problems. Many large private enterprises in China have close ties with the government and state-owned enterprises.

36. *China Daily* (*Business Weekly*) 28 November–4 December 1993, 1.

37. Chen Baorong, *Jiushi niandai Shanghai geti siying jingji fazhan yanjiu* (Study of the development of private economy in Shanghai during the 1990s), working paper, Shanghai Academy of Social Sciences, 1994.

38. Shi Xianmin, "The Classification of Private-Owned Small Businesses in Beijing," *Social Sciences in China* 15, (spring 1994): 97.

39. Lu Xueyi and others, "Woguo siyou qiye de jingying zhuangkuang yu siyou qiyezhu de qunti tezheng" (Operational conditions of private enterprises in China and the group characteristics of private entrepreneurs) *Zhongguo shehui kexue* (Social Sciences in China), no. 4 (1994): 70. Also see chapter 6.

40. *China Daily*, 19 July 1994, 2.

41. *Shanghai tongji nianjian* (Statistical yearbook of Shanghai) (Beijing: Zhongguo Tongji Press, 1995), 123.

42. *China News Analysis*, no. 1560, 15 May 1996, 6; *Wenhui bao* (Hong Kong), 30 April 1996, A6.

43. *China Daily*, 13 July 1994, 4.

44. *Baokan wenzhai*, 12 May 1994, 2.

45. *Baokan wenzhai*, 13 January 1994, 1.

46. *China Daily*, 23 December 1994, 2.

47. *Wenhui bao*, 26 July 1994, 1. By the end of 1992, China had approved altogether 90,109 foreign companies in China, with capital investment amounting to $108.9 billion. Among the world's 500 largest transnationals, only 54 do business in China, including 24 in Shanghai. *Shehui kexue bao* (Social sciences weekly), 11 November 1993, 3.

48. *Shanghai Star*, 26 July 1994, 4.

49. *Shanghai Star*, 18 April 1995, 1.

50. *New York Times*, 7 July 1995, D2.

51. *Shanghai Star*, 25 February 1994, 1.

52. *Shehui kexue bao*, (Social sciences weekly), 11 November 1993, 3.

53. *China Daily*, 18 May 1994, 4.

54. *Shanghai Star*, 5 July 1994, 4.

55. *Far East Economic Review*, 18 April 1996, 70–71. Quoted from *China News Analysis*, no. 1560 (15 May 1996): 8.

56. Gao Ruxi and Yu Yihong, "Shanghai jingji: tingzhi yu zaiqifei, 1953–1993" (Shanghai economy, 1953–1993: Stagnation and take-off), *Ershiyi shiji* (The twenty-first century), no. 8 (1994): 154.

57. Liu Weihua, "Wenzhou jixing" (A journey to Wenzhou), *Nanjing shehui kexue* (Social sciences in Nanjing), no. 5 (1994): 59–60.

58. *Gongdang wenti yanjiu* (Studies of problems in the Chinese Communist Party) 20 (July 1994): 61.

59. Ibid.

60. Ibid., 62–63.

61. Kristen Parris, "Local Initiative and National Reform: Wenzhou Model of Development," *China Quarterly*, no. 134 (June 1993): 251.

62. Medical expenses of China's public health services increased from 2.7 billion yuan in 1978 to 55.8 billion yuan in 1994. *China News Analysis*, no. 1562 (15 June 1996): 6.

Chapter 5

1. Ma Hong and Sun Shangqing, eds., *Zhongguo jingji xingshi yu zhanwang* (Economic situation and prospect of China), white paper 1992–93 (Beijing: The Chinese Development Press, 1993), 12.

2. *Weishi* (Truth), no. 8 (1993): 7.

3. *Jiefang ribao*, 10 December 1994, 5.

4. *China Daily*, 19 January 1994, 3.

5. *Wenhui bao*, 2 February 1994, 1.

6. Michael Buckley, and others, *China*, 4th ed., (Hawthorn, Australia: Lonely Planet Publications, 1994), 518.

7. Ibid., 525.

8. *Economist* "A Survey of China," 28 November–4 December 1992, 11.

9. *Suzhou daxue xuekan*, (*Journal of Suzhou University, Social Sciences & Philosophy Edition*), no. 2 (1993): 27.

10. *Jingjixue dongtai*, (Recent trends of economic research), no. 1 (1994): 51.

11. Kristen Parris, "Local Initiative and National Reform: Wenzhou Model of Development," *China Quarterly*, no. 134 (June 1993): 251.

12. *Economic Statistics Yearbook of China, 1992.*

13. Wang Haijun, "The Development of Township and Village Enterprises in China and Their Structural Adjustment," *Social Sciences in China* 14, (winter 1993): 49.

14. *Baokan wenzhai* (Newspaper and magazine digest), 20 December 1993, 1.

15. *Qoushi xuekan* (Seeking for truth), no. 5 (1993): 45.

16. *Baokan wenzhai*, 31 October 1994, 1.

17. Sun Daiyao and Wang Wenzhang, *Julong de suxing* (Dragon wakes) (Beijing: Wenjin Publishers, 1993), 198.

18. Nicholas D. Kristof and Sheryl Wudunn, *China Wakes: The Struggle for the Soul of a Rising Power* (New York: Vintage Books, 1994).

19. Sheryl Wudunn and Nicholas D. Kristof, "China's Rush to Riches," *New York Times Magazine*, 4 September 1994; italics are mine.

20. *Jiefang ribao*, 7 June 1994, 5.

21. *Zhongguo gaige* (China's reform), no. 6 (1994): 16.

22. *Chengshi guihua* (City planning), no. 2 (1994): 39–40.

23. *Chengshi guihua huikan* (Journal of city planning), no. 2 (1994): 57.

24. *Zhongguo xiangzhen qiye* (China's rural enterprises), no. 11 (1987): 10.

25. *Weishi*, no. 8 (1993): 6.

26. For a discussion of the "floating population," see chapter 8.

27. *China Daily*, 31 August 1994, 4.

28. *Chengshi guihua huikan* (Journal of city planning), no. 4 (1994): 30.

29. Gong Yiming, *Mingongchao de qiluo* (The tidal wave of migrant workers) (Wuhan: Hubei People's Press, 1994), 18.

30. *Weishi*, no. 8 (1993): 6.

31. *Shanghai Star*, 7 June 1994, 10.

32. *Chengshi wenti*, (Urban problems), no. 4 (1994): 35.

33. Lin Yan, *Shanghai nongcun chengshi hua yanjiu* (Research on the urbanization of rural Shanghai) (Shanghai: Science and Technology Press, 1993), 17.

34. *Chengshi guihua huikan* (Journal of city planning), no. 2 (1994): 59.

35. Wang, "The Development," 55.

36. He Ciping, Han Hualin, and Qiu Weimin, eds., *Xiangzhen qiye hongguan guanli yu chanye jiegou tiaozhen* (Macromanagement of rural enterprises and structural adjustment) (Shanghai: Academy of Social Sciences, 1989), 45.

37. *Zhongguo xiangzhen qiye* (China's rural enterprises), no. 10 (1993): 10.

38. *Jiefang ribao*, 15 October 1994, 5.

39. *Jiefang ribao*, 11 July 1994, 1.

40. *Shanghai Star*, 7 June 1994, 10.

41. *Shanghai Star*, 3 June 1994, 3.

42. *Zhongguo xiangzhen qiye* (China's rural enterprises), no. 3 (1994): 36.

43. Ibid.

Chapter 6

1. Based on an interview report with Chen Jinhai published in a local newspaper, *Zuojia yu qiyejia* (Writers and entrepreneurs), 20 June 1985, 1.

2. Li Xinxin, "Zhongguo siying jingji fazhan zhong de wenti ji duiche" (Problems and measures in the development of China's private economy), *Jingji yanjiu* (Economic research), no. 7 (1994): 43.

3. Jia Ting and Qing Shaoxiang, *Shehui xinqunti tanmi—Zhongguo siying qiy-ezhu jieceng* (An exploration of new social groups) (Beijing: Zhongguo Fazhan Publisher, 1993).

4. *Wenzhai zhoubao* (Digest weekly), 26 December 1994, 1.

5. Hu Xianzhong, "Naoti daogua xintuan" (Further exploration on the problems of unbalanced payments for intellectuals and workers), *Jilin daxue xuebao* (Jilin University journal), no. 5 (1993): 8.

6. David S. G. Goodman, "Economic Reform: China's New Rich: Wealth, Power and Status," *Access China*, December 1992, 19.

Chapter 7

1. Although the exact number of surplus rural laborers in China is difficult to estimate, several recent studies conducted by research institutes in the country all confirmed 200 million—the number given by the Chinese official. *Mingbao* (Ming daily), 21 February 1994; *Jinji cankao bao* (Economic reference news), 14 September 1993, 4.

2. *Chengsi wenti* (Urban problems), no. 1 (1994): 47.

3. Martin Cadwallader, *Migration and Residential Mobility: Macro and Micro Approaches.* (Madison, Wisconsin: University of Wisconsin Press, 1992), 3.

4. Jack A. Goldstone, "The Coming Chinese Collapse," *Foreign Policy*, no. 99 (Summer 1995): 35–52.

5. Jim Landers, "A Crisis in Motion," *Dallas Morning News*, 6 February 1995, 1A.

6. Gu Shengzu, ed., *Dangdai zhongguo renkou liudong yu chengzhenhua* (Population mobility and urbanization of contemporary China) (Wuhan: Wuhan University Press, 1994), 1.

7. Fei Xiaotong, "The Course of Development in China's Urban and Rural Areas," *Social Sciences in China* 15, (summer 1994): 76. Translated from *Zhongguo shehui kexue*, (Social science in China), no. 1, (1993).

8. Alan P. L. Liu, "Economic Reform, Mobility Strategies and National Integration in China," *Asian Survey* 31, (May 1991): 393–408.

9. Dorothy Solinger, "China's Transients and the State: A Form of Civil Society?" *Politics & Society* 21, (March 1993): 97–98.

10. Wang Shan, *Disanzhi yanjing kanzhongguo* (China through the third eye) 3rd ed. (Hong Kong: Mingbao Press, 1994). Jiang Zemin, secretary general of the Chinese Communist Party, was reported to have endorsed the book, which had been banned earlier. The book was published both on the Mainland and abroad and reprinted many times.

11. Wang, *Disanzhi yanjing kanzhongguo*, 35.

12. *Xinmin wanbao* (Xinmin evening news), 6 December 1994, 3.

13. *Inter Press Service*, 26 December 1995.

14. *Independent*, 7 December 1995.

15. For example, Wen Lang Li and Ning Xu, "Socioeconomic Development, State Intervention and Urban Migration Patterns in China: 1982–1987," *American Asian Review* 12, (fall 1994): 81–118. The article uses some mathematical measurements to test the equilibrium theory, but the findings seem to restate the obvious: cities with better qualities of life tend to have greater increases in immigration, and urban areas have a much higher net migration gain than rural areas. Some of the exceptions are contained in Lincoln H. Day and Ma Xia, eds., *Migration and Urbanization in China* (Armonk, New York: M. E. Sharpe, 1994). This collection of essays is based on data derived from the 1986 large-scale survey of urban migration in China. See also Kam Wing Chan, "Urbanization and Rural-Urban Migration in China since 1982: A New Baseline," *Modern China* 20, (July 1994): 243–281; Harry Xiaoying Wu, "Rural to Urban Migration in the People's Republic of China," *China Quarterly*, no. 139 (September 1994): 670–698.

16. Judith Banister, *China's Changing Population*, (Stanford: Stanford University Press, 1987), 297.

17. Hui Feng, "Dui dalu laodong jiuyi wenti zhi tantao" (An exploration of the employment problems on the Mainland), *Zhongguo yanjiu* (Studies of Chinese communism monthly), no. 10 (1994): 61.

18. George P. Brown, "Arable Land Loss in Rural China: Policy and Implementation in Jiangsu Province," *Asian Survey* 35, (October 1995): 922.

19. Li Debin, "The Characteristics of and Reasons for the Floating Population in Contemporary China," *Social Sciences in China* 15, (winter 1994): 70. Originally from *Shehuixue yanjiu*, (Sociological studies), no. 4, 1993.

20. *Jingbao Monthly* (The Mirror monthly), no. 12 (1994): 35; also Marivic Bariga-Babiano, "Development and Destruction: China's Environmental Crisis," *China Currents* 4 (January–March 1993): 3.

21. Qu Geping and Li Jinchang, eds., *Population and Environment in China* (Boulder, Colorado: Lynne Rienner Publishers, 1994), 1.

22. For a comprehensive analysis of China's land resources, see Chen Baiming, ed., *Zhongguo tudi ziyuan shengchan nengli ji renkou chengzailiang yanjiu* (The land resources production capability and population-supporting capacity in China) (Beijing: People's University Press, 1992).

23. Hu Feng, "Dui dalu nongye he nongcun wendi zhi tantao" (An exploration of the rural economy of Mainland China), *Zhonggong yanjiu* (Studies of the Chinese Communist Party), 5 November 1994, 45.

24. Li Debin, "The Characteristics of and Reasons for the Floating Population in Contemporary China," 70.

25. *Chinese Rural Economy*, April 1994, 8; *Rencai kaifa* (Human Resources), no. 6 (1993): 7.

26. State Statistical Bureau of the People's Republic of China, *China Statistical Yearbook*, 1990 and 1993, (New York: Praeger, 1991, 1993); Gu Zhaolin, *Zhongguo chengzhen tixi—lishi, xianzhuan, zhanwang* (China's urban structure: past, present, and future) (Beijing: Shangwu Press, 1992), 343.

27. Lin Yifu, *Zhidu jishu yu zhongguo nongye fazhan* (Institution, technology and agricultural development in China) (Shanghai: Shanlian Press, 1994).

28. *Baokan wenzhai,* 17 January 1994, 1. Of the total of 460 million peasants, 420 million work in grain, 14.69 million in cotton, 6.7 million in vegetables, 3.16 million in tea, fruit, and silk, and the rest in other agricultural products.

29. Chen Xiwen, *China's Rural Reform: Retrospect and Prospect,* (Beijing: Zhishi Press, 1992).

30. *Chinese Rural Economy,* (April 1994): 8; *Rencai kaifa* (Human resources) no. 6 (1993): 7.

31. *China Daily,* 19 October 1994, 4.

32. *Jiefang ribao,* 23 November 1993, 5.

33. *Wenzhai zhoubao* (Digest weekly), 19 December 1994, 1.

34. *China Daily,* 13 July 1994, 4.

35. *China Daily (Business Weekly),* 22–28 May 1994, 1.

36. *China Daily,* August 31, 1994, 4. In Shengze, a town famous for silk production in Wujian County, two-thirds of the workers in the silk and cotton mills are from other regions. *Chengshi guihua huikan* (Journal of city planning), no. 4 (1994): 30.

37. Ching-kwan Lee, "Production Politics and Labour Identities: Migrant Workers in South China," paper presented in a seminar at University of Hong Kong, March 1995.

38. *Zhongguo shibao zhoukan* (China times weekly), 16–22 January 1994, 65.

39. *China Daily,* 4 November 1993, 1.

40. *China Daily,* 20 December 1993, 1; *Baokan wenzhai,* 7 February 1994, 1; *Shanghai Star,* 29 April 1994, 7.

41. *Cankao xiaoxi* (Reference news), 27 May 1994, 8.

42. *Yatai jingji shibao* (Asian Pacific times), 9 December 1993, 4.

43. *Baokan wenzhai,* 21 March 1994, 2.

44. *Juece tansuo* (Decision-making studies), no. 7 (1993): 26.

45. *Shanghai Star,* 24 May 1994, 11.

46. Tian Fan and Zhang Dongliang, *Zhongguo renkou qianyi xintan* (A new exploration of China's population migration) (Beijing: Zhishi Press, 1989).

47. Chen Xiwen, *China's Rural Reform,* 78.

48. Gu Shengzu, *Dandai zhongguo,* 3.

49. *Juece tansuo,* no. 7 (1993): 6.

50. *Baokan wenzhai,* 16 January 1995, 3; *Zhongguo renkou bao* (China population news), 6 January 1995.

51. *Renkou yanjiu* (Population research), no. 5 (1992): 42.

52. *Jiefang ribao,* 7 July 1994, 3.

53. *Jiefang ribao,* 27 March 1994, 10.

54. *Xinmin wenbao,* 7 April 1989.

55. *Shanghai Star,* 24 May 1994, 11.

Chapter 8

1. *Xinmin wanbao* (Xinmin evening news), 21 April 1994, 12.

2. *Liaowang,* no. 36 (1993): 18.

3. Even during the regular season, China's railway transport can meet only 40 to 60 percent of national demand. Zhou Zongmin, "China All Out to Ease Economic Bottlenecks," *New China Quarterly*, no. 30 (December 1993): 9.

4. *Renmin ribao*, 18 April 1994.

5. Lynn T. White III, "Migration and Politics on the Shanghai Delta," *Issues and Studies*, (September 1994): 63–93.

6. Gu Shengzu, ed., *Dangdai zhongguo renkou liudong yu chengzhenhua* (Population mobility and urbanization of contemporary China) (Wuhan: Wuhan University Press, 1994), 1.

7. *China's Population Today*, July 1994, 11.

8. Ibid.

9. Judith Banister, *China's Changing Population* (Stanford: Stanford University Press, 1987), 297.

10. *Renkou yu jingji* (Population and economy), no. 3 (1992): 13.

11. *Shehui* (Society), August 1993, 39.

12. *Baokan wenzhai*, 23 May 1994, 2.

13. Kam Wing Chan, "Urbanization and Rural-Urban Migration in China since 1982: A New Baseline," *Modern China* 20, (July 1994): 267.

14. For example, according to a recent study, about 10 million people joined China's floating population annually in the first three years of the 1990s. *Shehuixue yanjiu* (Sociological studies), (July 1993): 65. Some Chinese demographers estimate that the number of migrants nationwide topped 100 million in 1992; *China's Population Today*, July 1994, 12.

15. Ching-kwan Lee, "Production Politics and Labour Identities: Migrant Workers in South China," paper presented in a seminar at University of Hong Kong, March 1995, 3.

16. United Press International, 3 April 1996.

17. This discussion is based on Li Shuzhuo, "Zhongguo bashi niandai de quyu jingji fazhan he renkou qianyi yanjiu" (A study on the development of regional economy and population migration in China in the 1980s), *Renkou yu jingji* (Population and economy) no. 3 (1994): 3–8.

18. Gong Yiming, *Minggongchao de qiluo* (The tidal wave of migrant workers) (Wuhan: Hubei People's Press, 1994), 18.

19. *Zhongguo renkou nianjian*, (Yearbook of Chinese population), 1990, 553; *Shehuixue yanjiu*, (Sociological studies), (July 1993), 68. For a comprehensive analysis of age, gender, education, and occupation distribution, see Sha Jicai, *Gaige kaifang zhong de renkou wenti* (Population problems in reform and opening) (Beijing: Beijing University Press, 1994), 208–217.

20. *Shanghai Star*, 22 March 1994, 2; and 15 April 1994, 1.

21. Qu Geping and Li Jinchang, eds., *Population and Environment in China* (Boulder, Colorado: Lynne Rienner Publishers, 1994), 1.

22. *Baokan wenzhai*, 23 May 1994, 2.

23. Ibid.

24. *Renkou yu jingji* (Population and economy), no. 4 (1993): 37.

25. *South China Morning Post Magazine*, 12 December 1993, 23.

26. *Wenzhai bao*, 28 November 1993, 3.

27. *Xinmin wanbao*, 6 December 1994, 3.

28. In Guangdong, the number of homeless children who were taken in by government institutions increased from 5,172 in 1989 to 6,887 in 1990, to 8,700 in 1991. Wang Guangzhen, Zhang Bingshen, and Zhao Ruizhang, eds., *Zhujiang sanjiaozhou jingji wenhua fazhan yanjiu* (A study of economy, society, and culture of the Pearl Delta) (Shanghai: Shanghai People's Press, 1993), 452.

29. *Weile ertong* (For the children), no. 10, (1994): 26.

30. According to an investigation of Zhuhai city, Guangdong Province, the payment per day of a temporary worker is 4.5 yuan. Wang, Zhang, Zhao, *Zhujiang sanjiaozhou*, 450–451.

31. *Baokan wenzhai*, 3 February 1994, 1.

32. *Zhongguo xinxi bao*, 21 January 1994, 3; *Jiefang ribao*, 21 November 1993, 5.

33. *Zhongguo laodong bao* (Chinese labor daily), 30 October 1993, 3.

34. Dorothy Solinger, "China's Transients and the State: A Form of Civil Society?" *Politics & Society* 21, (March 1993): 97–98.

35. *Jiankang bao* (Health daily) 16 May 1992, 19 November 1994.

36. Tian Fan and Zhang Dongliang, *Zhongguo renkou qianyi xintan* (A new exploration of China's population migration) (Beijing: Zhishi Press, 1989), 305.

37. *Dangdai* (Contemporary), 15 August 1994, 70–72.

38. Gu Shengzu, *Dandai zhongguo*, 4.

39. Judith Banister, *China's Changing Population*, 350.

40. Jim Landers, "A Crisis in Motion," *Dallas Morning News*, 6 February 1995, 8A.

41. *Zhongguo xiangzhen qiye* (China's rural enterprises), no. 11 (1987): 10.

42. *Weishi*, no. 8 (1993): 6.

43. Zuang Jian, "Zhongguo disan chanye de fazhan yu wenti" (The status and problems of the development of China's tertiary industry), *Zhongguo disan chanyi nianjian* (Almanac of China's tertiary industry) (Beijing: Zhongguo Nianjian Publishers, 1993), 969.

44. Ibid., 991.

45. Guang Hua Wan, "Peasant Flood in China: Internal Migration and Its Policy Determinants," *Third World Quarterly* 16, (June 1995): 194.

46. Guang Hua Wan, "Peasant Flood in China," 194.

Chapter 9

1. Richard Hofstadter, *The Age of Reform: From Bryan to F.D.R.* (New York: Alfred A. Knopf, 1959), 23.

2. *Chengshi wenti* (Urban problems), no. 4 (1994): 54.

3. *Gaige yu zhanglüe* (Reform and strategy), no. 6 (1993): 38.

4. Gu Shengzu, ed., *Dangdai zhongguo renkou liudong yu chengzhenhua*

(Population mobility and urbanization of contemporary China) (Wuhan: Wuhan University Press, 1994), 276.

5. *China Daily*, 3 September 1994, 4; and *Baokan wenzhai*, 17 October 1994, 1.

6. *Chengshi guihua* (City planning), no. 2 (1994): 39.

7. *Gaige yu zhanglüe*, 38.

8. *Renkou yu jingji* (Population and economy), no. 6 (1993): 18.

9. *China Daily*, 22 June 1994, 5. The total number of urban dwellers who were forced to migrate to the countryside in the late 1960s and early 1970s, however, is still unknown.

10. *Chengshi wenti* (Urban problems), no. 1 (1994): 46.

11. Sun Daiyao and Wang Wenzhang, *Julong de suxing* (Dragon wakes) (Beijing: Wenjin Publishers, 1993), 260.

12. *Shizhang cankao* (Mayor's reference), no. 6 (1994): 2.

13. In 1987, the Chinese Academy of City Planning and Design published a report that listed five factors behind China's urban development: (1) the location of large state construction projects, (2) the growth of big cities and their satellites, (3) rural industrialization, (4) the input of foreign investment, and (5) the development of local industries. *Nankai jingji yanjiu* (Nankai economic research), no. 1 (1994): 24.

14. *Chengshi guihua huikan* (Journal of city planning), no. 2 (1994): 57.

15. *Renkou yanjiu* (Population research), no. 2 (1994): 27–28.

16. *Chengxiang jianshe* (Urban and rural construction), no. 4 (1994): 23.

17. *Jiefang ribao*, 16 June 1994, 1.

18. Land Administration Bureau, Zhangjiagang city, Jiangsu Province, *A Guide to Real Estate in Zhangjiagang City* (Zhangjaigang, Jiangsu: Zhangjiagang Shifu Publication, 1993); Guo Shuzhen and Ding Zhenyi, *Zhangjiagang Free Trade Zone* (Zhangjiagang, Jiangsu: Zhangjiagang Shifu Publications, 1993).

19. *Chengshi guihua* (City planning), no. 2 (1994): 40.

20. *Renmin ribao* (overseas edition), 19 December 1995, 1.

21. *Chengshi guihua* (City planning), no. 2 (1994): 40.

22. *Jiefang ribao*, 4 December 1994.

23. *Renmin ribao* (overseas edition), 19 December 1995, 1.

24. *Suzhou daxue xuebao* (Journal of Suzhou University), no. 2 (1993): 28.

25. *Renmin ribao* (overseas edition), 19 December 1995, 1.

26. *A Guide to Real Estate in Zhangjiagang City*; Guo Shuzhen and Ding Zhenyi, *Zhangjiagang Free Trade Zone*.

27. *Suzhou daxue xuebao* (Journal of Suzhou University), no. 2 (1993): 27–28; *Chengshi guihua* (City planning), no. 2 (1994): 40.

28. *Jiefang ribao*, 4 December 1994.

29. *Chengshi guihua* (City planning), no. 2 (1994): 40.

30. *China Daily*, 31 August 1994, 4.

31. Dai Junlian, *Zhongguo chengshi fazhan shi* (History of Chinese urban development) (Harbin: Heilongjiang People's Press, 1992), 8.

32. See chapters 7 and 8.
33. *Chengshi wenti*, (Urban problems), no. 4 (1994): 35.
34. *Baokan wenzhai*, 13 October 1994, 2.
35. Gu Shengzu and Zhu Nong, "Zhongguo chengzhen hua de fazhan yanjiu" (A study of the development of urbanization in China), *Zhongguo shehui kexue* (Social science in China), no. 5 (1993): 46.
36. Gu and Zhu, "Zhongguo," 54.
37. Tian Fang and Zhang Dongliang, *Zhongguo renkou qianyi xinduan* (New approach to the study of China's population) (Beijing: Zhishi Publishing House, 1989), 312.
38. Tian and Zhang, *Zhongguo*, 304.
39. *Shanghai Star*, 15 July 1994, 1.
40. Tian and Zhang, *Zhongguo*, 304.
41. *Cankao xiaoxi* (Reference news), 28 August 1994, 8.
42. *Chengshi guihua huikan*, (Journal of city planning), no. 1 (1994): 42.
43. *Chengshi guihua* (City planning), no. 3 (1993): 22.
44. *Cankao xiaoxi*, 12 June 1994, 8.
45. *Wenhui bao*, 14 March 1994, 1.
46. *Cankao xiaoxi*, 24 August 1994, 1.
47. *Wenhui bao*, 14 March 1994, 1
48. Yet some Chinese officials and scholars have continued to favor the growth of large cities at the expense of the development of small and medium-sized cities. See *Chengshi guihua* (City planning), no. 3 (1994): 22.

Chapter 10

1. *Shehuixue yanjiu* (Sociological research), no. 2 (1993): 17; *China Daily*, 12 November 1993, 6.
2. Audrey R. Topping, "Ecological Roulette: Damming the Yangtze," *Foreign Affairs* 74 (September/October 1995):133.
3. The dam itself is designed to withstand an earthquake that measures only 7.0 on the Richter scale. Dai Qing, ed., *Yangtze! Yangtze! Debate over the Three Gorges Project* (London: Probe International and Earthscan, 1994), 235, 258.
4. In the twentieth century alone flooding from the Yangtze River led to approximately 350,000 deaths. Frank Gray, "From Great Wall to Three Gorges" *Energy Economist*, (April 1992): 126.
5. *Gongdang wenti yanjiu* (Studies of Chinese Communist Party), (May 1993): 68–69.
6. Ibid., 69.
7. A Chinese official whom I met on the boat told me this story when our cruise boat was entering the Gezhou Dam area.
8. *Gongdang wenti yanjiu*, May 1993, 71.
9. *Ziran bianzhengfa zazhi* (Journal of dialectics of nature), no. 3 (1993): 41.

10. *China Daily*, 3 August 1994, 4.

11. *Shanghai Star*, 18 January 1994, 14.

12. *Shanghai Star*, 28 January 1994, 16.

13. *China Daily*, 12 November 1993, 6.

14. *Wenhui bao*, 26 November 1993, 5.

15. *Wenhui bao*, 14 January 1994, 5.

16. *China Daily*, 18 March 1994, 4.

17. *Christian Science Monitor*, 27 May 1992, 20.

18. *Shuili jingji* (Water conservancy and economy), no. 3 (1988): 50.

19. *New York Times*, 27 December 1994, 6. Quoted from David Welch, *China's Three Gorges Dam Project: Cost and Benefit Analysis* (Senior Thesis, Hamilton College, 1996), 34.

20. *China Daily*, 9 October 1993, 3.

21. *Wenhui bao*, 14 June 1994, 5.

22. *China Daily*, 30 October 1993, 1.

23. *Gongdang wenti yanjiu*, May 1993, 73–74.

24. *Ziran bianzhengfa zazhi*, 41–43.

25. Topping, "Ecological Roulette," 143; also see chapter 16.

26. Topping, "Ecological Roulette," 134.

27. Jung Chang, *Wild Swans: Three Daughters of China* (New York: Simon & Schuster, 1991).

28. *Ziran bianzhengfa zazhi*, 41.

Chapter 11

1. Ernest O. Hauser, *Shanghai: City for Sale* (New York: Harcourt, Brace and Company, 1940), 54–55.

2. Ibid., 53.

3. Ibid.

4. James Fallows, "Shanghai Surprise," *Atlantic Monthly*, July 1988, 76.

5. In 1993, three years after the establishment of Pudong, 1,334 foreign-funded enterprises, including 20 large multinational corporations, registered investment valued at $2,761 billion, 40 percent more than the domestic investment in the area. *China Daily*, 15 October 1993, 4.

6. James P. Sterba, "A Great Leap Where?" *Wall Street Journal*, 10 December 1993, R9.

7. *Report on the Morgan Stanley Tour of China* (Autumn 1993), 13.

8. *China Daily*, 24 February 1995, 9.

9. In his book, Ernest O. Hauser has recorded many stories about how local residents resisted colonists. For example, "the French felt the first broadside of Chinese hatred when they attempted to build a road through a cemetery." The burial grounds were attached to the joss house that migrants from Ningpo built. The migrants from Ningpo were too poor to ship the coffins back to their native

land. They did not allow the French to remove the coffins and disturb the peace of the dead. "A riot broke out, fires swept the French Concession, crowds were raging through the streets . . ." But after years of conflicts, the French eventually "laid their road right through the cemetery, killing 12 Chinamen who were trying to protect the spirits of their ancestors" (*Shanghai: City for Sale*, 84–85).

10. Andrew Browne, "Ugly Capitalism: Property Boom Sparks Shanghai Anger," Reuters News Service (Shanghai), 12 December 1994.

11. *Shanghai fangdi xinxi* (Shanghai real estate information), no. 5 and no. 6 (1994): 23.

12. Yu Tianbai, *Shanghai: Xingge ji mingyun* (Shanghai: Her character is her destiny) (Shanghai: Wenyi Press, 1992), 199.

13. *Shanghai fangdichan shichang 1994*, (Shanghai real estate market) (Shanghai: Zhongguo Tongji Chubanshe, 1995), 3, 25.

14. *Beijing Review*, 30 August–5 September 1993, 17.

15. Ibid.

16. Shann Davies, "Shanghai: Back in Business!" *Shanghai* 5, no. 2 (1995): 1.

17. *Wenhui bao*, 23 May 1995, 13.

18. Gao Ruxi and Yu Yihong, "Shanghai jingji: tingzhi yu zaiqifei, 1953–1993" (Shanghai economy, 1953–1993: Stagnation and take-off), *Ershiyi shiji* (The twenty-first century), no. 8 (1994): 155.

19. Henny Sender, "Eastern Promise: Hong Kong Developers Flock to Shanghai," *Far East Economic Review*, 17 September 1992, 72.

20. *Shanghai fangdichan shichang 1994*, (Shanghai real estate market) (Shanghai: Zhongguo Tongji Chubanshe, 1995), 9.

21. Tess Johnston and Deke Erh, *A Last Look: Western Architecture in Old Shanghai* (Hong Kong: Old China Hand Press, 1993), 53.

22. *Shanghai Star*, 9 December 1994, 1; 17 March 1995, 1.

23. *Jiefang ribao*, 6 May 1995, 1.

24. *Shanghai Star*, 22 April 1994, 2.

25. *Jiefang ribao*, 25 November 1993, 1; 6 May 1995, 1.

26. World Bank, *China: Urban Land Management: Options for an Emerging Economy* (Washington, D.C.: The World Bank, 1993).

27. David E. Dowall, "Establishing Urban Land Markets in the People's Republic of China," *Journal of the American Planning Association* 59 (spring 1993): 189.

28. Liu Junde, "Chuping Pudong kaifa yu Shanghai ji Changjiang sanjiaozhou quyu jingji fazhan" (A preliminary analysis of the Pudong development and the economic growth in Shanghai and the Yangtze Delta), in Yang Ruwan, ed., *Zhongguo chengshi quyu fazhan: zhanwang ersheyi shiji* (China's urban and regional development: Towards the twenty-first century) (Hong Kong: Research Institute of the Asian Pacific, The Chinese University of Hong Kong, 1993), 248.

29. Andrew Browne, "Shanghai Housing Protest Blocks: Golden Mile Road," Reuters News Service (Shanghai), 10 March 1995.

30. Henny Sender, "Stopping the Gold Rush," *Far Eastern Economic Review*, 12 August 1993, 70.

31. Andrew Browne, "Shanghai Housing Protest Blocks."

32. Andrew Browne, "Ugly Capitalism."

33. Ibid.

34. Tian Fang and Zhang Dongliang, *Zhongguo renkou qianyi xintan* (New approach to the study of China's population) (Beijing: Zhishi Publishing House, 1989), 304.

35. *Jiefang ribao*, 26 June 1992, 1.

36. *Jiefang ribao*, 15 June 1995, 5.

37. Henny Sender, "Stopping the Gold Rush," 70.

38. *Jiefang ribao*, 2 February 1994, 9.

39. *Xinmin wanbao*, 27 September 1993, 1.

40. *China Daily*, 24 February 1995, 9.

41. Johnston and Erh, *A Last Look*, 1.

42. Chen Qide, "German Buildings Recall City's Past," *Shanghai Star*, 18 April 1995, 16.

43. Quoted from *Cankao xiaoxi* (Reference news), 19 December 1993, 8.

44. Ibid.

45. Ibid.

46. As widely publicized in Shanghai by local newspapers, a Swiss biochemical company sold a large amount of banned medicine to the China market. *Wenzhai bao* (Newspaper digest), 28 November 1993, 3.

Chapter 12

1. *Jiangsu jiaotong yunshu* (Transportation in Jiangsu), no. 2 (1994): 10. In 1978, the average income of Sunan's Suzhou city was 151.8 yuan and the average income of Subei's Huaiyin city was 56.3 yuan. The difference was less than 100 yuan. But in 1987, the average income of Suzhou was 1,105 yuan while the average income of Huaiyin was 541 yuan. The difference increased to 564 yuan. Mu Guangzong, "Xiandai renkou zhuanbian de sunan moshi" (The Sunan model of population change at present), *Nongcun jingji yu shehui* (Rural economy and society), no. 2 (1993): 52.

2. *Qunzhong* (Masses), no. 4 (1993): 16–19.

3. In his study of the economic conditions in different regions on China's coast, Fei Xiaotong, a distinguished Chinese sociologist, wrote: "In 1984, I traveled from southern to northern Jiangsu Province. At first I assumed that the differences between the two areas were the result of different starting points in the process of development, but after research in Wenzhou City in 1986, I realized that each had taken a different path of development because of different conditions. . . . Later in 1988, during an investigation of Guangdong and Guangxi, the fact that local villages were quick to follow the Pearl River Delta model made me realize that my developmental concept was rather static—I had failed to take into account the fact that local conditions themselves can change." "The Course of

Development in China's Urban and Rural Areas," *Social Sciences in China* 15, (summer 1994): 74–81. Originally from *Zhongguo shehui kexue* (Social Sciences in China), no. 1, 1993.

4. *Jiangsu jiaotong yunshu* (Transportation in Jiangsu), no. 11 (1993): 11–12.

5. *Jiangsu qiye guanli* (Enterprise management in Jiangsu), no. 8 (1993): 40.

6. *Jiangsu jiaotong yunshu*, (Transportation in Jiangsu), no. 2 (1994): 10.

7. Gautam Kaji, "Challenges to the East Asian Environment," *Pacific Review* 7, no. 2 (1992): 205.

8. Vincent Benziger, "China's Rural Road System during the Reform Period," *China Economic Review* 4, no. 1 (1993): 3. The original data is from the Sichuan Provincial Traffic Bureau, *Sichuansheng nongcun jiaotongyunshu fazhan zhanlue* (Sichuan Province rural traffic transport development strategy) (Chengdu, Sichuan: Shifu Publications, 1994), 5.

9. Yan Wenbin, "Railway Construction Moves into Top Gear," *New China Quarterly*, no. 28 (May 1995): 36.

10. Gu Shengzu, *Feinonghua yu chengzhenhua yanjiu* (A study of nonagricultural development and urbanization) (Hangzhou: Zhejiang People's Press, 1991), 124.

11. Song Xiaoman, "Woguo tielu fazhan de xianzhuang yu celie" (Current situation and strategy of the development of China's railways), *Caijing Yanjiu* (Financial and economic research), no. 8 (1994): 38.

12. Zuang Jian, "Zhongguo disan chanye de fazhan yu wenti" (The status and problems of the development of China's tertiary industry), *Zhongguo disan chanye nianjian* (Almanac of China's tertiary industry, 1993), 969.

13. *Chengshi wenti* (Urban problems), no. 3 (1993): 47.

14. "Minister Huang Zhendong on China's Communications," *Economic Reporter*, no. 2 (1994): 12.

15. *Cankao xiaoxi* (Reference news) 10 April 1995, 8.

16. *Far Eastern Economic Review*, 10 November 1994, 56–58.

17. *Jingji yu guanli yanjiu* (Economics and management research), no. 5 (1993): 2.

18. Vincent Benziger, "China's Rural Road System during the Reform Period," *China Economic Review* 4, no. 1 (1993): 3.

19. Benziger, "China's Rural Road System," 1.

20. Song Xiaoman, Development of China's railways, 38.

21. Zhou Zongmin, "China All Out to Ease Economic Bottlenecks," *New China Quarterly*, no. 30 (December 1993): 9.

22. *China Daily*, 4 February 1995, 1.

23. Yan Wenbin, "Railway Construction Moves into Top Gear," *New China Quarterly*, no. 28 (May 1995): 36.

24. *Wall Street Journal*, 10 December 1993, R16.

25. Gu Shengzu, A study of nonagricultural development, 125.

26. *Far East Economic Review*, 10 November 1994, 56–58.

27. *China Daily*, 23 February 1995, 1.

28. *Far East Economic Review*, 10 November 1994, 56–58.

29. *Chengshi wenti* (Urban problems), no. 3 (1993): 48.

Chapter 13

1. *China Daily*, 16 November 1994, 4.

2. *Cankao xiaoxi* (Reference news), 16 September 1994, 8.

3. *Baokan wenzhai* (Newspaper and magazine digest), 9 May 1994, 2.

4. *China Daily*, 6 April 1995, 4.

5. Ibid.

6. *China Daily*, 6 April 1995, 4.

7. *Jingji gongzuo tongxun* (Economic work newsletter), 15 June 1994, 22.

8. *China Daily*, 14 June 1994, 4.

9. *China Daily*, 25 August 1994, 4.

10. *Cankao xiaoxi*, 16 September 1994, 8.

11. *Baokan wenzhai*, 24 March 1994, 1.

12. The total number of state employees in China is 110 million, of which one-third are employees engaged in "nonindustrial work"; 110 million state employees equals the total labor force of the United States. *Cankao xiaoxi*, 16 September 1994, 8; and 22 September 1994, 8.

13. Quoted in *Shanghai Star*, 4 March 1994, 2.

14. Shu Jian and Zu Yu, *Dangdai shunkouliu yu shehui lundian saomiao* (Current Chinese jingles and social issues) (Beijing: Zhongguo Dangan Publishers, 1994), 4.

15. Ibid., 3.

16. *Wenhui bao*, 17 December 1994, 1.

17. *Wenhui bao*, 13 July 1994, 1–2.

18. Richy Tung, "Zhongguo dalu guoyou qiye shichang hua zi yanjiu" (Market-oriented reform of state-owned enterprises," *Zhongguo dalu yanjiu* (Mainland China studies) 37, (November 1994): 19.

19. *Wenzhai zhoubao* (Readers' digest weekly), 20 February 1995, 1.

20. *Gongdang wenti yanjiu* (Studies of problems of the Chinese Communist Party) 12, no. 10 (1994): 39.

21. Chang Chen-pang, "The Resurgence of the Bourgeoisie in Mainland China," *Issues and Studies* 30, (May 1994): 43.

22. Chang, "The Resurgence," 43.

23. *China Daily*, 26 July 1994, 4; and *Wenhui bao*, 27 August 1994, 1.

24. *Cankao xiaoxi*, 7 October 1994, 8.

25. *Qiye guanli* (Enterprise management), 11 November 1994, 3.

26. *Cankao xiaoxi*, 7 October 1994, 8.

27. Dwight H. Perkins, "Why Is Reforming State Owned Enterprises So Difficult?" *China Economic Review* 4, no. 2 (1993): 149.

Chapter 14

1. Denny Roy, "Singapore, China, and the 'Soft Authoritarian' Challenge," *Asian Survey* 34 (March 1994): 231–242.

2. Lynn Pan, "Playing the Identity Card," *Far East Economic Review*, 9 February 1989, 32.

3. Michael Vatikiotis and Robert Delfs, "Cultural Divide," *Far East Economic Review*, 17 June 1993, 20.

4. *Xiandai lingdao* (Modern leadership), no. 1, (1994), 7. In a study conducted in the early 1990s, Huaxi hired 690 migrant workers in 1989; among them, 140 lived in neighboring villages or towns. The other 550 were from other provinces such as Sichuan, Guizhou, Hunan, Anhui, Henan, Shandong, Shanxi, and Xinjiang. Lu Xieyi, ed., *Gaige zhong de nongcun yu nongmin* (Countryside and peasants in the age of reform) (Beijing: Central Party School Press, 1992), 26.

5. Guo Jiong, *Huaxi, China: 1961–1993* (Jiangyin, Jiangsu: Huaxi Publishers, 1993), 3.

6. *Beijing Review*, 10–16 May 1993, 14.

7. *Nongcun dashijie* (Rural world), no. 9 (1993): 3.

8. *Yangzi wanbao* (Yangtze evening news), 23 December 1994, 1.

9. *Beijing Review*, 10–16 May 1993, 13.

10. *Zhongguo Jiangyin Huaxi jingdian jianjie* (Brief description of scenes in Huaxi in Jiangyin, China) (Jiangyin, Jiangsu: Huaxi Publishers, 1992), 7.

11. *Qunzhong* (Masses), no. 8 (1994): 5.

12. Ibid., 6.

13. *Sunan xiangzhen qiye* (Township and village enterprises of Southern Jiangsu), no. 3 (1994): 6.

14. Lu Yinchu and others, "Yige xiangdang fada de xiandai nongchun shequ" (A well-developed rural community), in Lu Xieyi, ed., *Gaige zhong de nongchun yu nongming*, 339.

15. *Jingji yu falü* (Economy and law), (June 1994), 68–69.

16. *Beijing Review*, 10–16 May 1993, 15.

17. *Qunzhong* (Masses), no. 8 (1994): 7.

18. Lu Yinchu and others, A well-developed rural community, 340.

19. *China Daily*, 1 July 1994, 4.

20. *Baokan wenzhai*, 14 July 1994, 1.

21. Guo Jiong, *Huaxi, China: 1961–1993*, 3.

22. *Yangzi wanbao* (Yangtze evening news), 23 December 1994, 1.

23. In the early 1990s, the industrial output remained over 99 percent of the total in Huaxi. *Beijing Review*, 10–16 May 1993, 14.

24. Ibid., 16.

25. *Jingji yu falü* (Economy and law), June 1994, 69.

26. *Jiangsu shen Jiangyin shi Huashizhen Huaxicun qingkuang huibao* (Report on Huaxi Village in Huashi Town, Jiangyin County of Jiangsu Province), May 1993, 21.

27. *Qunzhong* (Masses), no. 8 (1994): 7.

28. *Beijing Review*, 10–16 May 1993, 18.

29. Lynn Pan, "Playing the Identity Card," *Far East Economic Review*, 9 February 1989, 30.

30. Fareed Zakaria, "Culture Is Destiny: A Conversation with Lee Kuan Yew," *Foreign Affairs* 73 (March–April 1994): 125.

31. Jan Morris, "Singapore," *Encounter* 44, (January 1975): 34.

Chapter 15

1. Li Cheng and Lynn White, "The Thirteenth Central Committee of the Chinese Communist Party: From Mobilizers to Managers." *Asian Survey* 28 (April 1988): 379.

2. *Baokan wenzhai*, 9 December 1993, 1.

3. For the technocratic orientation in international affairs, see Qian Xuesen, "Scientific-Social Revolution and Reform," *Beijing Review*, 16 March 1987, 14–17; 23 March 1987, 21–23; ; and Li Cheng and Lynn White, "China's Technocratic Movement and the *World Economic Herald.*" *Modern China* 17 (July 1991): 342–388.

4. *Renmin ribao* (overseas edition), 28 October 1988, 1.

5. Cheng Li and David Bachman, "Localism, Elitism and Immobilism: Elite Formation and Social Change in Post-Mao China," *World Politics* 42 (October 1989): 73.

6. Cheng Li, "University Networks and the Rise of Qinghua Graduates in China's Leadership," *The Australian Journal of Chinese Affairs*, no. 32 (July 1994): 1–32.

7. For a case study of networks of Chinese civilian leadership, see Li, "University Networks," 1–32; for military elites, see Li Cheng and Lynn White, "The Army in the Succession to Deng Xiaoping: Familiar Fealties and Technocratic Trends." *Asian Survey* 33 (August 1993): 757–786.

8. *Economist*. 26 December 1992–8 January 1993, 20.

9. Samuel P. Huntington, *Political Order in Changing Societies.* (New Haven: Yale University Press, 1968).

10. Li Cheng and Lynn White, "Elite Transformation and Modern Change in Mainland China and Taiwan: Empirical Data and the Theory of Technocracy." *China Quarterly*, no. 121 (March 1990): 1–35.

11. *National Geographic* 185, no. 3, (March 1994): x.

12. *New York Times*, 7 September 1993, A10.

Chapter 16

1. Timothy Tung, "Changing China, A Personal Observation," *US-China Review*, (summer 1993): 13.

2. Geremie Barmé, a China expert from the Australian National University, is working on a book about Dai Qing. For his previous writing on Dai Qing, see "Using the Past to Save the Present: Dai Qing's Historiographical Dissent," *East Asian History*, no. 1 (June 1991): 141–181.

3. Dai Qing, "Wode jiandie shengya" (My spy career), in Dai Qing, *Wode sige fuqing* (My four fathers) (Hong Kong: Mingbao Publishing House, 1995), 93.

4. Li Cheng and Lynn T. White III, "China's Technocratic Movement and the World Economic Herald," *Modern China* 17, (July 1991): 342–388.

5. *Wenzhao bao*, 2 December 1993, 3.

6. *Cankao xiaoxi* (Reference news), 30 July 1994, 8.

7. *Baokan wenzhai*, 16 February 1995, 4.

8. Theodore Draper, "Intellectuals in Politics," *Encounter* 49 (December 1977): 60.

Chapter 17

1. Walter Laqueur, "The Moscow News, Tomorrow: Forecasting the Soviet-Russian Future," *Encounter* 74, (May 1990): 3.

2. James B. Rule, "Poland Today: Changes, Problems, Doubts," *Dissent* 37, (Fall 1990): 428.

3. Walter Laqueur, "The Moscow News," 3.

4. Nicholas D. Kristof, "China in the Year 2000," *New York Times Magazine*, 3 October 1993, 26–29.

5. For a detailed discussion, see Li Cheng and Lynn White, "The Army in the Succession to Deng Xiaoping: Familiar Fealties and Technocratic Trends." *Asian Survey* 33 (August 1993): 757–786.

6. Merle Goldman, *Sowing the Seeds of Democracy in China: Political Reform in the Deng Xiaoping Era* (Cambridge: Harvard University Press, 1994).

7. Jeffrey Sachs and Wing Thye Woo, "Structural Factors in the Economic Reforms of China, East Europe, and the Former Soviet Union," *Economic Policy* 9, (April 1994): 101–45.

8. Nicholas Kristof argued this in his concluding article on China in the fall of 1993. He noted that "in the 1990s the business of the party is business." *New York Times*, 6 September 1993, 5.

9. Andrew J. Nathan, "China's Path from Communism," *Journal of Democracy* 4 (April 1993): 42.

10. *Far Eastern Economic Review*, 2 March 1995, 15.

11. Michael Johnson and Yufan Hao, "China's Surge of Corruption," *Journal of Democracy* 6 (October 1995): 87.

12. Ibid., 86. The anticorruption campaign triggered about 12,000 major investigations in the first quarter of 1995 alone, resulting in 5,714 prosecutions. *Far Eastern Economic Review*, 1 June 1995, 16.

13. *Far Eastern Economic Review*, 12 August 1993, 13.

14. *Far Eastern Economic Review*, 2 March 1995, 16.

15. *Economist*, 6–12 May 1995, 36.

16. *Far Eastern Economic Review*, 27 April 1995, 15.

17. *New York Times*, 20 August 1995, E3.

18. Zhou Dongtao and Cui Quanhong, *Shizi lukov Shangde zhongguo* (China at the crossroads), (Lanzhou: Lanzhou University Press, 1992), 13.

19. David Shambaugh, "Growing Strong: China's Challenge to Asian Security," *Survival* 36 (summer 1994): 43–59.

20. Samuel P. Huntington, "The Clash of Civilizations?" *Foreign Affairs* 72 (summer 1993): 22–49.

21. *Cankao xiaoxi*, 11 December 1993, 4; 27 November 1993, 2.

22. The notion of *yin* and *yang* originated from the cosmology of ancient China and later became a philosophical way of thinking and an important means of analysis in Confucian culture. According to this philosophy, everything can be seen as a product of two interacting complementary elements, *yin* and *yang*. In other words, *yin* and *yang* represent two opposite but balancing aspects of nature or social reality. For example, *yin* represents feminine principles and gentle behavior while *yang* exhibits the masculine attitude and aggressive conduct.

23. Liu Binyan, "Civilization Grafting: No Culture Is an Island," *Foreign Affairs* 72 (September 1993): 19–21.

24. *Shijie ribao* (World journal), 9 July 1996, A12.

25. *Beijing zhichun* (Spring of Beijing), (February 1994): 22.

26. *Newsweek*, 1 April 1996, 31.

27. Ibid.

28. James A. Baker, III, "The United States and Other Great Asian Powers." Delivered to the Asia Society Conference, Rice University, Houston, 9 February 1996.

29. As Kenneth Lieberthal argues, "A secure and cohesive China will feel less need to build up its military and demonstrate its toughness, it will not confront the world with large refugee flows and internal warfare, and it will not invite external intervention because of political fragmentation." *Foreign Affairs* 74 (November–December 1995): 36.

30. Rabindranath Tagore, "East and West," in *Great Essays by Nobel Prize Winners*, Leo Hamalian and Edmond L. Volpe, eds., (New York: The Noonday Press, 1965): 155.

31. Sol M. Linowitz, *The Making of a Public Man: A Memoir* (Boston: Little, Brown and Company, 1985): 242.

Index

About the Author

Born and raised in Shanghai, Cheng Li left China in 1985 to pursue graduate study in the United States. He received his M.A. from the University of California at Berkeley and Ph.D. from Princeton University. He is now associate professor of government at Hamilton College. Li spent 1993 to 1995 in China as a fellow of the Institute of Current World Affairs.